CAMBRIDGE IBERIAN AND
LATIN AMERICAN STUDIES

GENERAL EDITOR

PROFESSOR P. E. RUSSELL, F.B.A.

EMERITUS PROFESSOR OF SPANISH STUDIES,

THE UNIVERSITY OF OXFORD

The fall of natural man
The American Indian and the origins of comparative ethnology

CAMBRIDGE IBERIAN AND LATIN AMERICAN STUDIES

*already published*

STEVEN BOLDY, *The novels of Julio Cortázar*
JUAN LÓPEZ-MORILLAS, *The Krausist movement and
ideological change in Spain, 1854–1874*
EVELYN S. PROCTER, *Curia and Cortes in León and Castile, 1072–1295*
A. C. DE C. M. SAUNDERS, *A social history of black slaves
and freedmen in Portugal, 1441–1555*
DIANE F. UREY, *Galdós and the irony of language*

*future titles will include*

ROBERT I. BURNS, *Muslims, Christians and Jews
in the crusader kingdom of Valencia*
JOHN EDWARDS, *Christian Córdoba*
MAURICE HEMINGWAY, *Emilia Pardo Bazán:
the making of a novelist*
JOHN LYON, *The theatre of Valle-Inclán*
LINDA MARTZ, *Poverty and welfare in Hapsburg Spain:
the example of Toledo*
JULIÁN OLIVARES, *The love poetry of Francisco de Quevedo:
an aesthetic and existential study*
FRANCISCO RICO, *The picaresque novel and the point of view*
HENRY W. SULLIVAN, *Caldéron in Germany*

# The fall of natural man

## The American Indian and
## the origins of comparative ethnology

ANTHONY PAGDEN

FELLOW, GIRTON COLLEGE, CAMBRIDGE

CAMBRIDGE UNIVERSITY PRESS

CAMBRIDGE

LONDON   NEW YORK   NEW ROCHELLE

MELBOURNE   SYDNEY

Published by the Press Syndicate of the University of Cambridge
The Pitt Building, Trumpington Street, Cambridge CB2 1RP
32 East 57th Street, New York, NY 10022, USA
296 Beaconsfield Parade, Middle Park, Melbourne 3206, Australia
© Cambridge University Press 1982

First published 1982

Printed in Great Britain by
Western Printing Services Ltd, Bristol

Library of Congress catalogue card number: 82–1137

*British Library Cataloguing in Publication Data*
Pagden, Anthony
The fall of natural man: the American Indian
and the origins of comparative ethnology.
– (Cambridge Iberian and Latin American studies)
1. Indians of Latin America
I. Title
980'.01    F2208
ISBN 0 521 22202 8

For Sylvia

...beaucoup de choses entreprises sur les ténèbres de l'esprit... et la terre livrée aux explications...

St-John Perse, *Anabasis*

# Contents

# Contents

# Acknowledgments

During the long years of its gestation this book has benefited, directly and indirectly, from the advice, encouragement and inspiration of various friends and colleagues. Hugh Trevor-Roper (Lord Dacre of Glanton) helped me to understand the wider context of the authors I had chosen to study and has been always unfailingly generous with his time. C. R. Boxer read through an earlier draft and, in addition to pointing out many details which I had missed, saved me from several errors of fact. John Elliott, in particular, read through various early versions of the entire work during the year which, thanks to his kindness, I was able to spend in Princeton, and did his best to impart some of his own clarity of mind to the final version. Charles Schmitt gave me the benefit of his unparalleled knowledge of Renaissance philosophy; and Rob Bartlett taught me most of what I now know about the medieval origins of my subject. Stephen R. L. Clark read a preliminary draft of what has subsequently become chapters 3 and 4 and compelled me to think again about Aristotle's psychology and its implications for the Spanish scholastics of the sixteenth century. My greatest single debt, however, and one which I have sustained for many years, is to Peter Russell, who has read through many early drafts of this book and whose acute criticism has given to it much of whatever form it might now possess. There have been moments, too, when without his friendship, encouragement and advice, the whole enterprise would certainly have been abandoned. None of these people, however, bears any responsibility for the uses to which I have put their advice.

Brian Hillyard and Jeremy Lawrence helped me with the transcriptions and interpretations of many of the Latin texts I have used. Nigel Griffin not only introduced me to the Jesuit archives in Rome and guided me through the tangled undergrowth of Jesuit historiography but has provided me over the years with countless references which I would never have discovered for myself. I have also learnt much from conversations at different times and in different places with John Barton, Nicholas Canny, Felipe Fernández Armesto, Valerie Fraser, Robert Hall, Geoffrey Hawthorn, Roger Highfield, Jacques Lafaye, Adriano Prosperi, Paco Rico, Alastair Saunders and D. P. Walker, all of which in often unforeseen ways have left their mark on my text. I also owe a debt of gratitude of another kind to two remarkable academic institutions, to the Warburg Institute (whose particular intellectual concern with the Renaissance use of classical texts will be apparent in the very subject of this book), where as Senior Research Fellow I did much of my research, and to the Institute for Advanced Study at Princeton, where, in an atmosphere of intellectual creativity few other communities can even aspire to, most of the book was written. I would also like to thank Mrs K. Saunders who typed and retyped numerous drafts with speed and accuracy – and great patience. I doubt, however, that it would ever have been written without the tolerant support and the confidence of my wife Sylvia to whom it is gratefully dedicated.

# Abbreviations

AGI Archivo General de Indias (Seville)
AGN Archivo General de la Nación (Mexico City)
ARSI Archivum Romanum Societatis Iesu (Rome)
BNF Biblioteca Nazionale (Florence)
BNM Biblioteca Nacional (Madrid)
BNP Bibliothèque Nationale (Paris)
BPM Biblioteca del Palacio (Madrid)
BUS Biblioteca Universitaria (Seville)
BV Biblioteca Vaticana (Rome)
*CDH* *Colección de documentos para la historia de la formación social de Hispanoamérica, 1493–1810*, ed. Richard Konetzke, Madrid, 1953–
*CDI* *Colección de documentos inéditos relativos al descubrimiento y colonización de las posesiones españoles en América y oceanía [sic], sacados, en su mayor parte, del Real Archivo de Indias*, ed. Joaquín F. Pacheco and Francisco de Cárdenas, Madrid, 1864–84. 42 vols.
*MB* *Monumenta brasiliae, Monumenta historica societatis Iesu. Monumenta peruana, Monumenta historica societatis Iesu.*
*MM* *Monumenta mexicana, Monumenta hitsorica societatis Iesu. Monumenta missionum societatis Iesu*, Rome, 1956– , 1–
*MP* *Monumenta peruana, Monumenta historica societatis Iesu. Monumenta missionum societatis Iesu*, Rome, 1956– , 1–
*PL* J. P. Migne, *Patrologia latina*, 221 vols., Paris, 1844–55
*PG* J. P. Migne, *Patrologia graeca*, 161 vols., Paris, 1857–66
RAH Real Academia de la Historia (Madrid)

The three parts of St Thomas Aquinas's *Summa theologiae* have been cited by part, quaestio and article number. The following abbreviations have been used:

Ia IIae   *Prima secundae*
IIa IIae   *Secunda secundae*

I have used the Leonine edition, *Sancti Thomae Aquinatis doctoris angelici opera omnia cum commentaris Thomae de Vio Caietani cura et studio fratrum eiusdem ordinis*, Rome, 1888–1906, vols. 4–12.

The works of Aristotle have been abbreviated as follows:

| | |
|---|---|
| *De gen. an.* | *De generatione animalium* |
| *De int.* | *De interpretatione* |
| *De mem.* | *De memoria* |
| *De mir. aus.* | *De mirabilibus auscultationibus* |
| *De part. an.* | *De partibus animalium* |
| *EE* | *Eudemian ethics* |
| *Hist. an.* | *Historia animalium* |
| *Meta.* | *Metaphysics* |
| *Meter.* | *Meteorologica* |
| *NE* | *Nicomachean ethics* |
| *Oec.* | *Oeconomica* |
| *Pol.* | *Politics* |
| *Prob.* | *Problemata* |
| *Rhet.* | *Rhetoric* |

# Introduction

I

Much of the ground covered in this book – though not, I hope, the path I have chosen to cross it by – will be familiar. In recent years there has been an ever-increasing number of studies on 'the impact of the new world on the old'. Most of these have focused their attention on the strategies used by Europeans to come to terms with the existence of a hitherto unknown continent whose inhabitants behaved in strange and often aberrant ways. Most also have chosen to imagine the observer crawling down some dark tunnel towards a light which, because of the inveterate slowness of the human intelligence, it will take him some two hundred years to reach. As his sight adjusts to the strangeness of the things about him, as the sheer presence of the newness of the new world presses in upon his mind, he becomes, little by little, more able to describe and to make some articulate sense of what he is assumed always to have been able to see.

It is a misleading image. Misleading because, in the first place, it is dependent upon a belief that changes in modes of perception are the consequence of a slow but inevitable recognition of the presence of a disjunction between fact and theory. The men of the sixteenth century, it is claimed, were too heavily laden with the baggage of Plinian ethnography and Aristotelian psychology to be able to give a proper account of the data before their eyes. Only when they were finally compelled, sometime at the beginning of the eighteenth century, to recognise that the theories with which they had been working could not be made to fit the facts before their eyes, were they able to come up with an adequate description of the American world. This interpretation supposes, of course, that our hypothetical observer's recognition that the reality 'out there' did not fully correspond to his perception of what it should be was an innate property of whatever it was that was out there. It is assumed in other words to be in the nature of facts that they will, sooner or later, press their claims to be taken at their face value; and when this happens any theory which does not fit them will invariably be discarded. But theories are nonetheless recognised to exercise a strong hold over the mind; and so it is thought that for nearly two hundred years men continued stubbornly to deny or misrepresent any fragment of the real world of America which threatened their preconceived social and anthropological notions about what *should* have been there. Their conceptual 'failure', to which the innumerable histories and ethnological reports of the period are thought to bear witness, lay simply in their unwillingness to face the true dimension of what stood before them.

Such an account relies upon a now discredited Cartesian belief in the fundamental innocence of the observer's eye. The act of seeing and the process by which what has been seen is classified and recorded are taken to be two separate and chronologically distinct mental operations. All men, the argument runs, possess the ability to see whatever passes before the retina; it is only *after* the mental image has made its initial impression, when the observer has to evaluate, classify and describe what he has seen, that his difficulties begin.

But observers in America, like observers of anything culturally unfamiliar for which there exist few readily available antecedents, had to be able to classify *before* they could properly see; and in order to classify in any meaningful sense they had no alternative but to appeal to a system which was already in use. It was indeed that system, not the innate structure of the world, that determined both what they actually believed to be the objective reality before them and the areas of it they selected for description.

The system itself is, of course, subject to frequent radical change. But such change does not generally come about as the consequence of a clash, however traumatic it might seem in retrospect, with a brute reality. It was perfectly possible, even for geographers, to persist in ignoring the very physical existence of America well into the mid-sixteenth century, just as it was possible for academic astronomers to modify the Ptolemaic image of the universe to fit some of Copernicus's conclusions while withholding recognition of the heliocentric principle itself. When such authoritative systems as Ptolemaic cosmography or Aristotelian psychology surrender to change they generally do so in response to the recognition of the need for some *internal* modification. If that need cannot be met then the whole system itself stands in danger of being discarded; but that, of course, can only occur once some new system has already come into being. It was not, for instance, what now appears to be its obvious failure to satisfy the facts of the case that led to the rejection of Aristotle's theory of natural slavery (discussed in chapters 3 and 4) as a possible explanation for the peculiarities of Amerindian social behaviour. There were those who persisted in believing, long after the theory had been abandoned by more reflective men, that the Indians had been equipped by nature (and hence by God) with inadequate brains and sturdy bodies to labour for the Europeans who, in their turn, were all of the delicate and refined physique suited only to intellectual contemplation and the business of government. The men whose writings I shall be discussing in this book rejected such an idea, not because they knew that the Indians were not strong and that most Europeans were neither delicate nor refined. They rejected it because they found it internally incoherent. Having rejected it they turned to other theories, also Aristotelian, also psychologically deterministic; but because those theories had to satisfy stringent demands of coherence, they also offered a denser and, from our point of view, more satisfactory account of the evidence.

The distance, then, between the kind of explanatory accounts of Indian behaviour current in the sixteenth century and those which had come into use by the beginning of the eighteenth must be measured in terms of historical changes which had little or nothing to do with the presence of the real world of America. Those two hundred years saw the decline of natural law theories and of Aristotelian and Thomist epistemologies, and the rise of truly experimental scientific methodologies which brought with them a belief in the primacy of experience and observation. Above all they witnessed the rise of a less deterministic view of the operations of the universe and of man's place within it.

But the observations in Joseph-François Lafitau's *Moeurs des sauvages amériquains comparées aux moeurs des premiers temps*, with which this book ends, are no less free from preselection and cultural bias than are those of Columbus and Peter Martyr with which it begins. The crucial differences between these writers are to be found, not in the fact that the one had achieved a greater power of recognition or greater intellectual honesty than the others, but rather in the very different kinds of goals they set out to achieve. Lafitau has often been praised by modern anthropologists for his notably 'modern' achievements, for being the first man to isolate and describe a kinship vocabulary or to pay serious attention to the importance of burial rites. But he was only able to do these things because his epistemologically very orthodox mind had been provided with the right set of questions, questions which were suggested, unlike those which occurred to his predecessors, by a concern with the social rather than the psychological sources of human behaviour. His descriptions of Indian society seem to us to be far closer to the truths of the Indian world – and in a sense, of course, they are – than those even of someone like the great Jesuit historian José de Acosta, only because his terms of reference are closer to our own than any available to equally perceptive, equally 'honest' men a century earlier. And, of course, if we step back from Lafitau's concern for precise ethnographical description, his modernism dissolves. For his perceptions are harnessed to an enterprise which is wholly alien to the modern mind: the attempt to demonstrate the truth of the Christian religion by the degree to which races which had had no knowledge of the Gospel unknowingly imitated the rituals and beliefs, the 'Symbolic Theology', of both Jew and Christian.

## 2

Many modern historians also seem to take it for granted that some accurate descriptive account of the seemingly obvious novelty of the American experience was what the early-modern observer had set out down his long tunnel to achieve. He kept on failing because his mind was cluttered with that assortment of prior assumptions and collective attitudes which are sometimes misleadingly referred to as 'prejudices'. But it is always assumed that he knew, whether by intuition or self-reflection, that there *was* a light at the eighteenth-century end of the tunnel.

The assumption is anachronistic. Very few of those who wrote about their experience of America did so in order to make sense of a new world. Even the great ethnological writings of Bernardino de Sahagún were composed with the simple intention of warning future missionaries of what they would have to contend with. Of course, there was also an undeclared purpose. Sahagún could never have written at such length, or in such detail, if he had not possessed a very real interest in Indian cultures. Similarly the works of José de Acosta, to which I have dedicated an entire chapter of this book, do far more than merely administer to the needs of the fledgling missionary adrift in an alien world – though it should never be forgotten that they served that purpose very well indeed. They are also an attempt to resolve what for the early-modern observer was the greatest ethnographical conundrum of all: what is the cause for the huge variation in the modes of human social organisation? But for all that, it is surely a mistake to regard as a

*failure* any enterprise which did not set out to achieve the aims ascribed
to it. It is a mistake, not only because it leads to improper judgments on
the success or failure of a writer's works, but because it prevents the
historian from asking what in fact the writer *himself* was trying to
achieve.

The sixteenth- and seventeenth-century observer also lived in a
society which believed firmly in the universality of most social norms
and in a high degree of cultural unity between the various races of man.
For such a person the kind of painstaking description, and the recognition of the 'otherness' of the 'other', which are the goal of the
modern ethnologist, would have been unthinkable. Michel Foucault is
probably right in claiming that at the beginning of the seventeenth
century men began, for the first time, to attempt to classify and describe
difference and discontinuity, that thought ceased 'to move in the
element of resemblance'. But this was only the thought of a very few.
Most men, and in particular theologians and historians (with whom
Foucault is, of course, largely unconcerned) went on searching in
human behaviour for 'the restrictive figures of similitude'.[1] And they
were still doing so at the beginning of the eighteenth century. None of
the writers whose works I have examined in this book was attempting,
consciously or unconsciously, to grope his way through an intellectual
miasma raised by the 'prejudices' of education, social background or
ideological commitment towards a more complete, more 'objective'
image of reality. Those prejudices constituted their world: to wish to
abandon them would have seemed foolish, dangerous, possibly heretical.
They were, furthermore, men who had few independent methodological
interests. With the exception of José de Acosta, they were not concerned
with the possibility of new modes of inquiry. The success indeed of the
enterprise to which they were committed depended to a very large
degree upon the certainty of the old modes. Their task, as they saw it,
was not to describe a remote 'otherness', but to arrive at an evaluation
of Indian behaviour which would eliminate that 'otherness' and by so
doing would bring these disturbing new men within the grasp of an
anthropology made authoritative by the fact that its sources ran back
to the Greeks.

Some very great and far-reaching changes in modes of perceiving
did, of course, take place during this period. These, however, were due
primarily to the presence within the wider intellectual community in
Europe of an increasing distrust of ancient science. The consequent
increase in the emphasis placed on experience and the development of

methods of inquiry which demanded a very high degree of evidential scrutiny gradually made their impact on ethnology as they had done on physics and astronomy. Any account of the changing interpretations of the Amerindian world must, therefore, if it is to possess any historical interest, attempt to interpret the texts, not in the light of some remote and anachronistic standard of objective accuracy, but in the context of contemporary epistemological concerns with the operations of what Acosta called 'the machine of the world'. This I have attempted to do.

## 3

Many of the works discussed in what follows had their origins in a particular, but as yet little understood, social and intellectual milieu: the lecture hall. For they were – or they started life as – university lectures and *relectiones*. Lectures were, of course, addressed to specific and familiar audiences whose knowledge, and the extent of whose probable understanding of what he was saying, was well known to the lecturer. All the lectures from our period, including very nearly the entire *oeuvre* of the Spanish theologian Francisco de Vitoria, survive only as detailed notes taken down by a pupil. Although in some cases these were carefully edited before printing, they still preserve much of the immediacy of the *aula* and are consequently often both elliptical and obscure. If we are to come at all close to what these texts may have meant to contemporaries, it is important to bear these facts in mind.

Chapter 4, for instance, is primarily an extended exegesis of Vitoria's famous *relectio De indis*. A *relectio* was a special lecture delivered on a topic and not, as was the case with other 'course' lectures, on a text. It was given at the end of the academic year and the topic chosen was supposed to be related to the text which the lecturer had been expounding in his student courses. But as this was always one of the three parts of Saint Thomas Aquinas's *Summa theologiae* or the *Sentences* of Peter Lombard, the lecturer was given a very free hand. Vitoria, like most of his colleagues and pupils, usually chose topics of some current moral or political concern, for example, the justice of the conquest of America, the limits of papal power, magic, and the English marriage, as well as more abstract themes such as homicide, charity and temperance. *Relectiones* were also attended by professors as well as students and were traditionally open to members of all faculties. The lecturer was thus addressing a large and very learned audience, and most *relectiones* were clearly aimed to impress the lecturer's peers, not his pupils. Certain remarks in Vitoria's own *relectiones* acquire a secondary meaning in the light of this information. His observation, for instance, at the very beginning of *De indis*, that the questions raised by the conquest of America were a subject for theologians, not jurists, was a specific – and pointed – claim for the primacy of theology in all moral issues, a tacit warning to his colleagues in the faculties of law not to attempt to handle matters in which they were 'not sufficiently versed to be able to act on their own'.[2]

The lecturer's audience would also have been thoroughly familiar with the texts he employed in his arguments. For the modern reader, not so familiar with the corpus of scholastic learning, utterances which rely heavily upon the reader's or the listener's ability to supply a reference may appear to be either baffling, obscure or, conversely, misleadingly straightforward. The density and the depth of much theological discourse in this period relied upon the presence within the lecturer's or the writer's text of a corpus of *auctoritates* or *loci communes* and on the arguments to which these in their turn referred. It is, for instance, crucial for an understanding of the ends to which the highly contentious theory of natural slavery was employed to know that this theory was based upon a widely accepted principle of faculty psychology and was expounded in a text – Aristotle's *Politics* – which, in Vitoria's day, was required reading on a course in moral philosophy which all theology students were expected to take.

Most previous discussion of the writings of Vitoria and his followers suffer not only from the general theoretical errors discussed above; they also seem to be labouring under the misapprehension that the analysis of texts which were written by men whose world was wholly unlike our own is essentially an unproblematical enterprise. The text is assumed to be merely what is there on the page. All but the minimum of contextual information is held to be irrelevant. What a sixteenth-century theologian might have understood by a word or phrase and what a modern historian might understand by the same word or phrase is assumed to be, in all significant respects, the same. This failure to perceive that words change their meaning and that issues of pressing intellectual concern for one generation may be of scant interest to the next, has led to much historically irrelevant and politically tendentious discussion by earlier scholars such as Angel Losada, Teodoro Andrés Marcos and Venancio Carro, over the 'rightness' or 'wrongness' of certain writers' arguments. To choose but one example: Carro's detailed and erudite study, *La teología y los teólogos–juristas españoles ante la conquista de América*, provides a far deeper analysis

7

of the concerns of the so-called 'School of Salamanca' than any previous work. But it is marred to the point of worthlessness by being, in great part, a defence of the 'justice' of the 'civilising' mission of the Spanish crown (and obliquely and in footnotes a defence also of the Axis), argued through the medium of sixteenth-century theology. The wholly anachronistic nature of this and so many other works like it may perhaps best be judged by Carro's truly remarkable concluding statement that 'the doctrines of the great theologian–jurists of Spain have not been surpassed. Today as yesterday, they should be our masters. Their triumph would be the triumph of Christ and the peace among nations.'[8]

The writings of Carro, Losada, Marcos and many other scholars of their generation were also closely identified with the ideological requirements – conservative Catholic and nationalistic – of the Franco regime. In the last decade or so, as that regime relaxed its hold on the intellectual life of the country, there began a renaissance in Spanish historiography. But the new historians have concerned themselves largely with the eighteenth and nineteenth centuries, the period which the Francoists preferred to ignore as the birth-time of liberalism, democracy and the final demise of Spain as a great power. As a result, the much-needed re-evaluation of the sixteenth century – always presented by the Caudillo's ideologues as the model for his new order – and with it of the intellectual significance of the discovery of America, is now long overdue.

Such a re-evaluation is beyond my present scope. In this book I have attempted only to re-examine a group of familiar texts in terms of their intellectual context and the wider programme to which their authors were committed, and to resurrect some of the hitherto ignored *loci communes* on which so much of their arguments relied. I have also tried to 'de-code' at least some of the commonplace assumptions and unstated attitudes on which the full meaning of any utterance must depend, and which sixteenth- and seventeenth-century writers shared with their readers but do not, any longer, share with us. To do this I have sometimes gone to out-of-the-way places – letters and petitions, Indian language grammar books and manuals on evangelisation – in the belief that these, as much as the better-known texts, will help to shed light into corners which have usually been either ignored or presumed to be both brightly lit and entirely empty.

Finally a word about the title of this book. The phrase 'natural man'

8

as it is usually understood, as it was understood by Rousseau, describes someone whose mind is unfettered by the moral and intellectual constraints of civil society. The Indian savage was, so some believed, capable of seeing the follies and the wickedness of our world more clearly than other men because he thought, and acted, according to natural reason alone. I have not used the phrase in that sense. For the men of the sixteenth and seventeenth centuries, with whom I am concerned, the image of the 'natural man' was somewhat different. Far from being the enlightened and enlightening child of nature he was merely someone who was compelled to live outside the human community. And all such society-less creatures, unless they were saints, were something less than human, for they had cut themselves off from the means which God had granted to every man that he might achieve his end, his *telos*. It is the fall of this image of nature's man that I have set out to describe.

Florence
August 1981

9

# I

# The problem of recognition

'The conquest of the Indies', wrote Father Pedro Alonso O'Crovley from the vantage point of 1774, 'filled all the vague diffusion of the imaginary spaces of man.'[1] Before 1492 those 'imaginary spaces' had been occupied largely by fantastic natural phenomena drawn from the imaginative literature of the late middle ages. Many of these, in particular the anthropological ones – the fauna and the satyrs, the pygmies, the cannibals and the Amazons – derived initially from a popular oral tradition and had then been recorded as fact by natural scientists and travel writers from Pliny to John de Mandeville. They constituted for many Europeans of the later middle ages a mental 'set', a cluster of images which were thought to constitute a real world of nature in the remoter areas of the world where, precisely because they were remote, the unusual and the fantastic were thought to be the norm. Like the natural scientists of O'Crovley's own day, who, though equipped with microscopes and telescopes still *saw* what contemporary science encouraged them to see – fully developed donkeys in donkey semen, for instance, or mermaids and little men talking to rocks[2] – the travellers of the sixteenth century went to America with precise ideas about what they could expect to find there. They went looking for wild men and giants, Amazons and pygmies.[3] They went in search of the Fountain of Eternal Youth, of cities paved with gold, of women whose bodies, like those of the Hyperboreans, never aged, of cannibals and of men who lived to be a hundred years or more.[4]

In conjunction with this world of imaginary places and fantastic beings, there also existed, in Black Africa, a real world of savage peoples and of unusual and unclassified flora and fauna. This world, too, was granted its share of fantastic creatures; but it was one which those who had seen it, men like the Venetian merchant Alvise da Ca' da Mosto, had made brave and often highly successful attempts to describe as an objective reality.

When Columbus sailed into the western Atlantic he drew, with no apparent sense of contradiction, on both these sources. He was, after all, widely, if also erratically, read in all the best geographical literature of the time.[5] He was also well acquainted with the Canary Islands, his last stopping post before he reached the Antilles; and he had had experience of the west coast of Africa, where the climate and the vegetation were not so very different from those of the Caribbean. His impression of the new world was therefore a mixture of fact and fantasy. He compared Indians to Africans and Canarians;[6] but he also spoke of the Amazons and of the man-eating Caribs who serviced them; and he took the trouble to record for his patrons that he had not discovered any monsters.[7] America as it emerges from the writings of Columbus and such later travellers as Vespucci and Antonio Pigafetta, who accompanied Magellan in 1519, was rarely seen as something new – indeed Columbus resolutely refused to believe until his dying day that it was new – but merely as an extension into a new geographical space of both the familiar and the fantastic dimensions of the Atlantic world as it was known through the writings of commentators both ancient and modern.

This assembly of the fantastic and the familiar amounted to a belief that the new could always be satisfactorily described by means of some simple and direct analogy with the old. It was a belief which could not last for very long. The early travellers to America recorded only hasty impressions and were content with simple comparisons. But those who went to settle in this new world had to come to closer grips with the intellectual problems it presented. The most immediate of these was the need for some system of classification, for without such a system, however rudimentary it might be – and greater familiarity demanded greater sophistication – no true description was possible.

The European observer in America, however, was not equipped with an adequate descriptive vocabulary for his task and was beset by an uncertainty about how to use his conceptual tools in an unfamiliar terrain. In the first instance he tended to describe things which looked alike as if they were, in fact, identical. For men like Gonzalo Fernández de Oviedo, chief overseer of the mines of Hispaniola and author of the earliest natural history of America, pumas *were* lions, jaguars tigers and so on.[8] Immediate perceptions of this kind relied upon an implicit and at first unchallenged belief in the interchangeability of types and the consistency of natural forms.[9] But it soon became obvious that this was not enough, that there were types that were not interchangeable and forms that were not consistent. As the Jesuit historian José de Acosta was later to remark, 'if we are to judge the species of animals by their properties, these are so varied that to wish to reduce them to the species known in Europe would be like calling the egg a chestnut'.[10]

When, finally, it became impossible to avoid the recognition of *difference*, the observer was tempted to abandon his task in despair. Some other methods, more direct than description and analogy, were required – something, indeed, which dispensed with language altogether. Alonso de Zuazo, a judge (*oidor*) of the island of Cuba, gave up trying to find words for the tropical flora to be seen in the great market in Mexico City because, he explained, 'you will not gain thereby any understanding of the quality of the fruit, for such things cannot be understood without the three senses of sight, smell and taste'.[11] Even Oviedo, though he was practised in exotic description, voiced much the same sense of helplessness before the indescribable, when he wrote of a remarkable tree he had seen in Hispaniola, 'it should rather be painted by the hand of Berruguete or another excellent painter like him, or by that of Leonardo da Vinci or Andrea Mantegna, famous painters whom I knew in Italy'.[12]

In the end, when description failed, the natural scientist could rely on drawing and, in the case of smaller objects, on samples. Confronted by the bewildering *varietas rerum* which the new world seemed to offer, men resorted to the museum and the cabinet. If language was not an adequate, or even a proper vehicle with which to describe the unfamiliar, then language would have to be replaced by some specimen of the unfamiliar itself. But despite these moments of doubt over the possibility of the enterprise, and the growing awareness that the flora and fauna of America might, in fact, belong to different species from those found in Europe, the observers of the American world made continual, and increasingly sophisticated, attempts to classify and describe what they recognised to be unfamiliar in what they saw. Both the botanists and the chroniclers of America (and they were frequently the same people) faced analogous difficulties: how to describe, and, more important, how to classify, what could be *seen*, with the vocabulary, and in the terms, of a system which had evolved piecemeal over centuries in quite a different environment and quite another culture.

The early natural historians of the Indies, by equating the lion with the puma, or by attempting to find a place for tobacco in the Dioscoridean system of classification,[13] inevitably attributed to the flora and fauna of the new world qualities which they did not possess. Errors at this level, however, were relatively easy to correct. The typology of plants, and even of animals, may easily be extended – witness the introduction into most European languages of such words as 'tomato', 'ocelot', 'avocado' and so on.[14] When it came to describing men, however, the problem grew far more complex. For describing objects does not commit the observer to more than the most superficial evaluation of what he has in front of him. Few men, after all, have any personal investment in tropical fruits or exotic trees; but when confronted by the actions of members of his own species every man's investment is very great. Classifying men is not, after all, like classifying plants. For when regarding his own species, the observer not only has to decide what he is seeing, he also has to find some place for it in his own world. This task is made all the more urgent, and the more difficult, if the observer is possessed, as all Europeans in the sixteenth century were, by a belief in the uniformity of human nature, a belief which required every race to conform, within certain broad limits, to the same 'natural' patterns of behaviour.

The methods of classifying men in use at the end of the fifteenth century depended on a number of general human attributes ranging from supposed physiological characteristics – the subject's size, the shape of his head, his humours and so on – to geographical location and astrological disposition.[15] But the most distinctive human characteristics were always behavioural ones. To decide what qualities any group of men possessed, the observer had inevitably to examine the society in which that group lived; and the things he looked for ranged from systems of belief and government, marriage rituals and laws of descent, to the means of subsistence, sumptuary norms and the ways in which food is prepared. From a description of such things – and they were, of course, always those which he considered integral to his own society – it became possible for the European observer to decide what kind of man he was dealing with.

But whenever he attempted to go beyond direct description, the would-be ethnologist was faced by severe semantic difficulties. For in sixteenth-century Europe, which had very little knowledge and still less understanding of the peoples beyond its borders, there were very few terms with which to classify men. What terms there were had also been used in so many different contexts that they had frequently come to acquire several, and sometimes conflicting, meanings.

In European eyes most non-Europeans, and nearly all non-Christians, including such 'advanced' peoples as the Turks, were classified as

13

'barbarians'. Since this word plays a crucial role in nearly every attempt to characterise the Amerindian and his culture, and because the meanings it was intended to convey vary so much with time and place, it will be useful to begin with a brief look at its history.

# 2

# The image of the barbarian

## I

The prime function of the term 'barbarian' and its cognates, 'barbarous', 'barbarity', etc., was to distinguish between those who were members of the observer's own society and those who were not. The observers themselves – those, that is, who applied these terms to others, since it was they who were faced with the task of classifying and describing something they felt to be alien to *them* – rarely troubled to attempt a self-definition. They assumed themselves to be all that the 'barbarian' was not; and the word 'barbarian' does have an antonym in the terms 'civil' or 'politic' (which are generally used as though they were synonymous) and their cognates. These terms derive, of course, from the words *civis* and *polis*, both of which, in their rather different ways, apply to cities – though the ways in which they apply are complex ones – and to man as a uniquely city-building, city-dwelling animal. The significance of this will become apparent later. For the moment, I wish to look not at the ways in which Europeans viewed themselves, though something of that will inevitably emerge from the discussion, but at how they classified and described non-Europeans, 'barbarians'. The terms of the particular discourse I am interested in derived in the first instance from Aristotle. Most of the writers I shall be discussing were self-declared Aristotelians and they understood the word 'barbarian' to mean what Aristotle and his commentators, in particular Saint Thomas Aquinas, understood it to mean.

'Barbarian', however, is an unstable term for it was applied to many different groups. The Berbers of North Africa,[1] the Turks, the Scythians, the peoples of 'Ethiopia', even the Irish and the Normans[2] were all described at one time or another as barbarians. Like all such categories of description, the word could readily be adapted to meet the user's particular needs. The one thing, however, which all usages had in common was the implication of inferiority. The Greeks of the seventh

15

and sixth centuries B.C. who coined the word employed it, it is true, simply to mean 'foreigner'; and they applied it to peoples such as the Egyptians, whom they respected.³ But by the fourth century, *barbaros* had become, and was forever to remain, a word which was used only of cultural or mental inferiors.

For the Hellenistic Greeks, the *barbaros* was merely a babbler, someone who could not speak Greek.⁴ But an inability to speak Greek was regarded not merely as a linguistic shortcoming, for a close association in the Greek mind between intelligible speech and reason made it possible to take the view that those who were devoid of *logos* in one sense might also be devoid of it in another. For most Greeks, and for all their cultural beneficiaries, the ability to use language, together with the ability to form civil societies (*poleis*) – since these were the clearest indications of man's powers of reason – were also the things that distinguished man from other animals. For only man possesses the reason required to communicate with his fellow creatures or, indeed, a tongue sufficiently broad, loose and soft to be able to form intelligible sounds (*De part. an.* 660 a 17–18).⁵ Barbarians, as we shall see, were considered to have failed significantly in respect of both these capacities. Non-Greek speakers, furthermore, lived, by definition, outside the Greek family of man, the *oikumene*, and thus had no share in the collective cultural values of the Hellenic community. The *oikumene* was, of course, a closed world, access to which was, in reality, only by accident of birth; but for the Greeks, for whom birth could never be a matter of accident, it was also a superior world, the only world, indeed, in which it was possible to be truly human.⁶

Since membership of any community must finally depend on recognition by that community,⁷ and if 'man' is to be taken as something more than a morphological category, the Greeks' failure to recognise the *barbaroi* amounted, in effect, to a denial of their humanity. For if only the Greeks have access to *logos*, those who are not Greeks must be rather less than fully human. The birds that watch over the temple on the island of Diomedia are able, thought Aristotle, to distinguish between Greeks and *barbaroi* (*De mir. aus.* 836 a 10–15) because no *barbaros* may have access to mysteries only Greeks can understand, and in which only Greeks may participate.

The Greeks were not, of course, alone in this feeling of isolation from the rest of the species. Most societies have, at one time or another, felt the need to distinguish between themselves and their neighbours in similarly radical terms.⁸ Many, indeed, seem to possess no word which can adequately render the concept 'man'. There exist, for them, only the name of their tribe and then another term, or terms, by which all those who do not belong to that tribe are known. When the Franciscan Alonso de Molina came to compile his Spanish–Nahuatl dictionary the only words he could find to stand for *hombre* were terms designating social groups: *tlacatl*, which (very roughly) means 'chieftain' or 'lord', and *maceualli*, the term by which all those who worked the land were known. For the rest he could only discover words which described particular types of men – holy-men, men-without-pity, men-experienced-in-war, men with big noses or large cheeks, men with six fingers or six toes. But no word to translate the expression *homo sapiens*.[9] For the Mexica, man, once he has left the group, ceased, in all important respects, to be 'man'. It is also, of course, a commonplace that to 'insiders', 'outsiders' frequently appear as, in some sense, members of another species, as humanoids, rather than human, or as supernatural beings. De-humanisation is, perhaps, the simplest method of dealing with all that is culturally unfamiliar.

To Europeans, the Amerindians and the Africans seemed to be, at worst, defective members of their own species. But the Arawak took the Spaniards to be sky-visitors, the Inca assumed them to be *viracocha*, a term which seems to have been applied to any supernatural being, and the Congolese imagined that the Portuguese, who carried large eyes painted on the prows of their caravels, were the spirits of the sea.[10] These 'primitive' reactions may be attributed not so much to fear of Spanish and Portuguese technology – by which neither the Indians nor the Africans seem to have been unduly impressed – but to the mere fact that the Europeans were outsiders, strangers – and very strange strangers at that.

Greek society, less restrained intellectually and geographically than the Arawak, the Inca or the Congolese, did not take quite such an extreme view. All Greeks, from Homer to Aristotle, were certain that man was, biologically at least, a single and unique genus.[11] The very great differences they saw to exist between the *barbaroi* and themselves had, then, to be judged under certain categories of value. For there are many degrees of humanity (*Pol.* 1252 a 1ff.). A man may sacrifice his right to be called a man by behaving in the cruel or savage ways that are characteristic of the *barbaroi* (*NE*, 1145 a 31) who, among other things, have a penchant for cutting off heads (*De part. an.* 673 a 25) and for eating the human foetus.

For the *barbaroi* are bestial because they act like beasts, because, for instance, like the Achaeans and the Heniochi, tribes of the Black Sea 'that have gone savage', they are said to 'delight in human flesh' (*Pol.* 1338 b 19 and *NE* 1148 b 19ff.). Cruelty and ferocity, the marks of unrestraint, were from the beginning the distinguishing features of a 'barbarous' nature. A man, after all, only becomes a real man (instead of a beast) by actualising what is potential within him, by learning through reason to control his animal nature. The process of becoming is a slow and uncertain one; and some men, the *barbaroi* among them, may ultimately fail to complete it. When this happens they will remain as children, devoid of a fully operational faculty of reason, 'and hardly different from an animal' (*Hist. an.* 688 b 1). This, it seems, is what became of the Thracians, who can only count in fours because, like infants, they cannot remember very far (*Prob.* 910 b 24–911 a 3).[12]

The teleological view of nature, to which all Greeks (and subsequently all Christians) subscribed, allowed for the existence of a scale of humanity going from the bestial at one end to the god-like at the other. On this scale the Greek, who alone had access to virtue, was the norm.[13] Though incapable perhaps, like all mortals, of becoming a true god (*Pol.* 1332 b 15f.), he was similarly unable to degenerate into a beast. The *barbaros*, on the other hand, lived somewhere at the lower end of the scale. Morphologically he was a man, but one who had no share in the life of happiness (*eudaimonia*) which is the highest end (*telos*) of all men (*NE*, 1095 a 17–22) and no knowledge of virtue (*Pol.* 1260 a 31ff.; cf. *NE*, 1142 b 34ff.).[14]

Greeks and barbarians may, therefore, be distinguished from one another by their behaviour. The *reason* why the Greek is civil and the non-Greek barbarous may, as we shall see, be explained in psychological terms. The difference first came about, however, as the result of an historical event – the creation of the city or *polis* (*Pol.* 1252 a 25ff.) – the full-dress political and moral community in which all civil beings – all *true* men – must live, if they are to be men at all.[15] In the eyes of the Greeks, they themselves were the first, and the only true, city-dwellers. All the other races of men remained literally 'outside', where they lived in loose-knit hordes like the earliest survivors of Deucalion's flood, without laws or any knowledge of arts and crafts, and consequently alien to any form of virtue, for virtue can only be practised within the *polis* (*Pol.* 1253 a 15ff.).[16]

When, later, the *barbaroi* did succeed in forming themselves into some kind of political group, they must have done so 'barbarously', for they have no natural rulers and live only in tyrannies, which are un-endurable to all rational men who are, by nature, free.[17]

The definition of the word 'barbarian' in terms that were primarily cultural rather than racial made its translation to the largely non-Greek speaking Christian world a relatively easy business. In the first place the criteria by which the barbarians were to be judged differed very little between the two cultures if only because the criteria for behaviour in the Christian world were largely derived from Greek models. The account of the prehistory of the human race (upon which much of the explanation of the structure of human society depended) to be found in book 3 of Plato's *Laws* was transmitted with only minor variations and some additions via Roman intermediaries, most notably Cicero, to Lactantius, Augustine and Isidore of Seville.[18] The Christian *congregatio fidelium*, the brotherhood of all men in Christ, was as convinced of its uniqueness and as concerned to avoid contamination through contact with the outside world as the *oikumene* had been.[19] Once again, those on the inside thought of themselves as almost another species from those on the outside.

The one significant difference – save for the obvious fact that the distinction between the 'us' and the 'them' in the Christian world was one primarily of belief rather than kin – between the *oikumene* and the *congregatio fidelium* was that whereas the *oikumene* had been an entirely closed world, Christendom was not. The Christian myth of a single progenitor of all mankind, and the Christian belief in the perfection of God's design for the natural world, made a belief in the unity of the genus *homo sapiens* as essential for anthropology and theology as it had been for Greek biology. The myth of the second coming, which played so large a role in the ideology of the Franciscan missionaries to America and later to China, was an obvious concomitant of this belief; for only when the spiritual and cultural world of man had, through conversion to Christianity, reached the same degree of perfection and unification as the biological world, would man finally be able to achieve his *telos* and earn release from his earthly labours.

It was, therefore, crucial that non-Christians should be granted access to the Christian community: and, indeed, cajoled or forced into entering it. Conversion to the Christian faith, however, meant far more than the acceptance of the truth of the Gospels. It demanded not only belief but also 'a radical change of life'.[20] For, in the words of Saint John, 'Except a man be born again, he cannot see the kingdom of God' (3,3). Baptism was literally a *rite de passage*, a means by which the convert was admitted to the only state where he might be able to fulfil his true humanity. Through baptism the neophyte entered, as Walter Ullmann has written, 'a "new life" which in ordinary language meant that he became subject to new norms of living, to a new style of life, to a new outlook and aim'.[21]

Christians were thus men set apart from all the category distinctions which had been employed in the pagan world. Eusebius of Caesarea felt called upon to persuade his readers that he and his kind were 'new men' for, he explained, 'we do not think like Greeks, nor live like the barbarians'.[22] It is, therefore, little wonder that by the time Gregory the Great came to use the word *barbarus* in the sixth century it had become synonymous with the term *paganus*,[23] a pagan, an unbeliever, a sense which it retained in the language of the curia until at least the late fifteenth century.[24]

But, again, the *barbari* were not merely men who did not, or would not, believe in Christ. They were men who, because of this, did not always act in accordance with true reason; for, as we shall see, although a non-Christian may possess the light of natural reason, a light that will allow him to 'see' his way without the aid of revelation, he will, unlike the Christian, easily be persuaded into sin by the conditions of the social environment in which he lives.

For the Christian, no less than for the Greek, the barbarian was a specific cultural type who could be characterised in terms of a number of antitheses to the supposed features of the civil community. Whereas the Christians lived in harmony and concord with each other – or at least in situations of carefully regulated violence – and ruled their lives according to an established code of law, the *barbari* spent all their days in ceaseless aggression and neither recognised nor observed any laws or rules of conduct whatsoever.

The true civil community was made possible through the persuasive power of language.[25] It was eloquence, not violence, that first coerced men to band together for their own protection, and it is the law that ensures that the community is able to survive. Barbarians have no access either to language or to laws. For Albertus Magnus (c. 1206–80), they were

those who do not observe laws and participation in the community ordained according to the principles of justice...For although the name *barbarus* is onomatopoeic, as Strabo says... nevertheless the man who does not observe the laws concerning the ordering of social participation is most certainly a *barbarus* since by this trait [such barbarians] incur many vices, confusing the interrelations (*communicationes*)[26] within society and destroying the principles of justice which operate in these interrelations.[27]

And, elsewhere, discussing the bestial/heroic opposition in book 7 of the *Ethics*, he went on to observe that

Bestial men, however, are rare, since it is a rare man who has no spark of humanity. It does, however, occur, and usually from two causes: physical handicap and deprivation, or from disease causing deprivation. For we call those who are not induced to be virtuous either by laws, by civility or by the regime of any kind of discipline 'barbarous'. Cicero, in the beginning of the *De inventione*, calls them 'wild men leading the life of animals with the wild beasts'...Or, in the same way, bestial men eat raw flesh and drink blood, and are delighted to drink and eat from human skulls.[28]

All the principal characteristics by which Albertus and his successors thought it possible to define the barbarian appear in these passages. For to all benefactors of the Greek notion of *politeia* it was man's relationship to man which alone guaranteed his humanity. For all true men must 'connect' with their fellows because men are, by their very nature, 'connecting' animals (*zōon koinōnikon*), just as they are city-building, social animals (*zōon politikon*). Man's relationship with his fellow creatures is strictly hierarchical, but it also involves at all levels a measure of the friendship that must inevitably spring from the fact that men, unlike all other animals, do possess the ability to communicate and that as members of a larger group they must all share a common purpose.[29]

The barbarian, on the other hand, was thought to live in a world where this all-important *communicatio* was ineffective, where men failed to recognise the force of the bonds which held them to the community, where the language of social exchange itself was devoid of meaning. In most respects the barbarian was another animal altogether. He was one of the *sylvestres homines*, the wild men of the literary imagination,[30] those creatures who were thought to live in the woods and the mountains far removed from the activities of rational men, which always took place on the open spaces and on the plains.

The cities where rational men lived were seen as outposts of order and reason in a world that was felt to be volatile and potentially hostile. Wild men were creatures who lurked in woodlands and mountain passes ready to seize upon the unwary traveller; and they were an ever-present threat to the civilisation of those who lived in the cities. These wild men and their companions – the pygmies and pilosi, the fauns and the satyrs – belonged to a clearly defined group, the *similitudines hominis*, a class of half-man/half-beast creatures.[31] As we shall see, the existence of a category of animal which possessed some, but not all, of the attributes of man created formidable problems. But it was not, even before the discovery of real 'primitives', unthinkable. For Christians, no less than for Greeks, the hierarchy of nature, the Great Chain of Being, was so constructed that the highest member of one species always approaches in form to the lowest of the next. Thus the higher primates were thought to have much in common with man; and man himself who, in Aquinas's words, is the 'horizon and boundary line of things corporeal and incorporeal',[32] has a body in common with the lower animals; but in his soul, he 'attains to the lowest member of the classes above bodies...which are at the bottom of the series of intellectual beings'.[33]

There might, therefore, be, in the interstices of these inter-locking categories – in what Aquinas called the 'connexio rerum', 'the wonderful linkage of beings'[34] – a place for a 'man' who is so close to the border with the beast, that he is no longer fully recognisable by other men as a member of the same species. Such 'men' would have basically animal minds capable of performing a limited number of human functions but be devoid of true reason, like the faun which was thought to have visited Saint Anthony the Hermit in the desert and to have asked him to pray for it.[35] Such creatures had for long been a part of the popular culture of most European peoples, and at times they even penetrated the scientific literature of the elite. The sixteenth-century physician, Paracelsus, created a world peopled with a huge variety of such beings; but even Albertus Magnus, who possessed a far greater sense of zoological probability than Paracelsus, cautiously suggested that both the wild men and the pygmies – in fact two species of anthropoid ape – not only resembled men in their outward appearance, but also had a share in man's *ratio*. 'These outward similarities', he wrote, 'also indicate an inner similarity, since these two animals command a degree of insight which is closer to reason than that possessed by other beasts.'[36]

Some later writers, most notably Paracelsus, another doctor, Andrea Cesalpino,[37] and the French Huguenot Isaac de la Peyrère[38] held that such humanoids as nymphs, satyrs, pygmies and wild men (a category which included the Amerindians) might be soulless men descended from another 'Adam' or created spontaneously from the earth. In Aristotle's classification of animals on which (or on some remote version of which) all these men relied, all creatures which were biologically perfect reproduced themselves. Those, however, which were classified as 'imperfect' – insects and some reptiles – were generated spontaneously from the earth or were the product of some fusion of rotting matter (*De gen. an.* 762 a 10ff.; *Meter.* 381 b 10). By suggesting that the Indians had originally been created in this manner Cesalpino, Paracelsus, Girolamo Cardano and even Giordano Bruno were, in effect, classifying them along with the insects. The belief in spontaneous generation (together with the second Adam theory) was generally held to be blasphemous and heretical as a dire threat to the unity and integrity of the human race. 'Nothing', wrote the Spanish Jesuit Martín del Río of Paracelsus, 'that this man has written is so false, so blasphemous, so alien to right reason.' For if men can be made out of the sod, then 'is not our own health in doubt and our own redemption?'[39] But despite fierce opposition, these theories enjoyed considerable popularity in the late seventeenth century as effective, if rather crude, explanations for the variety of human types.

The 'barbarians' whom Albertus classed with the wild men, clearly belong in the same general category of not-quite-men as these other *similitudines hominis.* And it was evidently with this idea in mind that observers such as the bishop of Santa Marta (Colombia) described the Indians as 'not men with rational souls but wild men of the woods, for which reason they could retain no Christian doctrine, nor virtue nor any kind of learning'.[40]

Albertus's work marks, of course, the reintroduction into Christian thought of Aristotelian anthropological categories. The term *barbarus* which, since the sixth century, had been used rather loosely to describe anyone 'out there' was now brought under closer scrutiny in the light of its use by Aristotle to classify a certain type of man. When Aquinas, to whom Albertus transmitted both his biology and his anthropology, came to make his own synthesis of Aristotelian and Christian thought, he was able to invest the word with a richer texture of meaning than it had enjoyed since the fourth century B.C. Aquinas not only probed deeper into the relationship between language and civility, he was also able to distinguish between a primary and secondary use of the word and to ask himself the question to which most commentators had hitherto paid little attention, namely under what condition does one race of men develop into 'civil' beings, while another remains, or becomes, 'barbarian'.

I shall examine Aquinas's treatment of the term *barbarus* in greater detail when I come to discuss the work of Las Casas, whose account of the Indian world owes so much to Aquinas's commentary on the

*Politics.* For the moment, however, we may assume that from the end of the twelfth century until the beginning of the sixteenth, the term *barbarus,* or whatever vernacular form it might take, had come to acquire two closely related meanings. As a term of classification it applied broadly to all non-Christian peoples, and more loosely might be used to describe any race, whatever its religious beliefs, which behaved in savage or 'uncivil' ways. In both cases the word implied that any creature so described was somehow an imperfect human being. Although the use of the term by Christians to describe other Christians is rare, it is not unknown. The Normans were often referred to as barbarians, and Las Casas described the Spanish colonists in America as 'barbari' because of their treatment of the Indians. By the fifteenth century, too, it had become common for Italians to refer to their Spanish and German invaders as 'barbarians'.[41] But most of these uses were either, as in the Italian case, deliberate learned archaisms serving a specific socio-political function, or were intended merely as abuse. By and large, for any serious purpose, 'barbarian' was a word reserved for those who neither subscribed to European religious views, nor lived their lives according to European social norms.

2

Although some of the earliest observers of the American world, like Oviedo, had an interest in botany and were thus deeply involved with the business of identification and classification, most of them made very little attempt to classify the Indians themselves. The Indians were certainly 'barbarians' and 'savages'; but these words were used loosely to imply only that they were neither Christians nor culturally very sophisticated. Those who took a more optimistic view of Indian life might be tempted, as the Milanese humanist Peter Martyr was, to speak of the Arawak in terms of the 'Golden Age...of their customs'.[42] But such portmanteau phrases could be used to accommodate a wide variety of conflicting behaviour. Martyr, for instance, seems to have been able to accept the idolatry of the Arawak, the fact that some of the Island Carib were said to be cannibals, that they fought wars with one another and that, although they wore no clothes, they wished to be instructed in the arts of medicine for all the world as if they were Egyptians or Persians,[43] and still refer, without fear of straining his readers' credulity, to their living in a 'Golden Age'.[44]

Oviedo, more concerned with recording what he saw and with making some kind of sense of it than with tantalising his readers with titbits of exotic information, chose to compare the Indians with a real rather than an imaginary race of people. The Indians, he thought, most clearly resembled the 'Ethiopians'[45] – the barbarian inhabitants of a vague geographical area that spread from the Atlas mountains to the Ganges – and Aristotle's favourite barbarians, the Thracians.[46] This method made possible the identification of certain types of behaviour – for instance, polygyny, polyandry and matrilineal descent.[47] It also placed the Indians quite firmly in the barbarian camp, although Oviedo himself offered no definition of the word. Categorising of this type was, of course, fairly common. Giovanni Pico della Mirandola, to mention but one well-known case, had classed the Amerindians together with the 'Ethiopians' and those legendary enemies of the Christian Church, the Scythians. He did this in order to make a point about the variety of human types; but his choice of races is no accident and the effect is to 'read off', so to speak, the unknown factors about Indian behaviour from the known ones about Scythians and 'Ethiopians'.[48] Oviedo uses the same method when he claims that, since both the Thracians and the Arawak practised polygyny, we should expect the Arawak to sacrifice all foreign visitors (it is very unlikely that they did; but the ill-treatment of visitors, which violated the laws of hospitality, was, in any case, held to be a characteristic of all barbarous peoples) because, according to Eusebius, the Thracians did this also.[49]

Such simple one-to-one identifications as these do not, however, take the reader very far; nor do they explain very much about the motives or the sources of Indian behaviour. But then, of course, they were not intended to do this. Whether they attempted to locate the Indian in some vague period of human prehistory, or to demonstrate by analogy that he belonged to the same genre as the familiar barbarians of the ancient world, these chroniclers were trying only to solve the immediate problem of what to look for in a world of bewildering and unrecognisable shapes.

The observer did not, after all, require much more unless he was also troubled by a philosophical cast of mind, which neither Martyr nor Oviedo really was. But very soon other men, men who were troubled by philosophical problems, were drawn into the business of classifying Indians. These men were all either university professors, or university-trained churchmen. Most of them were professional theologians and they took all knowledge for their province because, as one of the greatest of them, Francisco de Vitoria (c. 1492–1546), once observed, 'the office of the theologian is so wide that no argument, no dispute, nor any subject (*locus*) is alien to its profession'.[50] They, of course, were looking for answers to a rather different set of questions from those which seem to have troubled Oviedo. Questions such as, why did the Indians behave in such unstructured ways, instead of in the ways which nature should have taught them, as she has taught all other men? Why did Indian society not develop like European society? And, most crucial of all, how could the existence and the behaviour of the Indians be explained in terms of the system, part-sociological, part-psychological, which was known to control the behaviour of all the other peoples of the world?

It is clear that answers to such questions could be found in history. Broadly speaking, barbarians were thought of as men who had failed to progress. Their societies were primitive ones, their behaviour strikingly reminiscent of the descriptions of Plato, Aristotle and Cicero of the behaviour of the earliest men. Indians might, therefore, be described merely as 'backward'. But this explanation, though it had the merit of being both simple and obvious and, as we shall see, ultimately successful, begged a further question. Namely, why were they backward? Since all men were descended from one of the sons of Noah, and all were equipped with the same basic mental machinery, why had they not all learned to follow the same basic rules of behaviour, why had they not all, in the terms of the ancient metaphor, learned to read the same things in the 'book of the Creature', in the book of nature?[51] In the sixteenth century, fully persuasive answers to such questions were to be found, not in history but in faculty psychology. It was evident to all who encountered him that it was the Indian's mind, what the colonists referred to as his *ingenio* or *capacidad* – words of whose appropriateness they were aware, but of whose full significance they were almost certainly ignorant – that was ultimately at fault.

The very first 'model' used to *explain* the causes of Indian behaviour was consequently one based on psychology. This was Aristotle's theory of natural slavery.

# 3

## The theory of natural slavery

The suggestion that the Indians might be slaves *by nature* – a suggestion which claimed to answer questions concerning both their political and their legal status – was first advanced as a solution to a political dilemma: by what right had the crown of Castile occupied and enslaved the inhabitants of territories to which it could make no prior claims based on history? The men who were called in to resolve this dilemma were all either members of, or in some way associated with, the law or theology faculties of the universities, and for them questions about the nature of the Indians were but one part of a larger set of concerns about man's relationship with man and about his place in God's universe.

The university intellectuals' involvement in the debate over the justice of the Spanish occupation of the Antilles was the product of a long tradition. For centuries schoolmen in Spain, as elsewhere in Europe, had acted as unofficial advisors to the crown on intellectual and moral issues. During the reign of Charles V and Philip II the role of the universities in the affairs of state was greatly increased and some of the most gifted of the professors, men like Melchor Cano (1509–60) and Domingo de Soto (1494–1570), were removed from their lecture halls altogether to become councillors and diplomats or, more frequently, members of that elite corps of political-cum-spiritual advisors, the royal confessors. Consultation between the universities and the crown generally took the form of a *junta*,[1] an open debate between the representatives of the three branches of learning which had some claim to authority in moral issues – theology, civil law and canon law – watched over by select members of the religious orders and the royal councils. At the end of the meetings (which seem to have consisted of formal speeches, allowing for little or no interchange of ideas, though the form may have varied) each participant would provide the king or the Royal Council with a written 'opinion', a *testimonio* or *parecer*, or, if it were composed in Latin, a *dictamen*. What happened to these 'opinions' thereafter it is impossible to say. They vanished, in all probability unread, into the gaping maw of Spanish bureaucracy. And it would certainly be unwise to assume from the flurry of paper that these meetings produced, or the solemnity with which they were held, that they had much direct bearing on major policy decision. Their function was to legitimate, not to judge. If a *junta* challenged the royal will, it was usually ignored or silenced. 'Kings often think from hand to mouth', as Francisco de Vitoria observed in private, 'and their councils even more so.'[2] But, however ineffective they may have been in practice, the professors took their role as advisors seriously enough; and it was this role that was responsible for involving them directly in what Vitoria was later to call 'the affair of the Indies'.[3]

The judgments which these men passed may often have been intended (though not all of them were, as we shall see) to serve short-term political ends, to provide the crown with an ethical justification for a course of action to which, in most cases, it was already committed. But certain political ideas, particularly if they derived from what Suárez called 'the wider application of moral philosophy to the government and control of the political customs (*mores*) of the community',[4] cannot satisfactorily be abstracted from the concepts and norms on which the writers' anthropological and sociological worlds were built.

Any judgment on the *nature* of the Indians – and this ultimately was what the whole debate over the justice of the conquests turned on – had thus to have its origin in a scheme which offered an explanation for the structure of the whole world of nature and the behaviour of everything, animate or inanimate, within it. Any attempt to introduce a new element into that scheme could, if ill-conceived, threaten the whole. What the schoolmen were faced with was thus not simply the need to resolve a political conundrum, which would have meant answering questions posed in terms of the human law (*lex humana*); but, given that the only solution was, as Vitoria said later, a matter of divine law (*lex divina*),[5] they had also to resolve questions of a primarily ontological nature: who or what were these 'Indians' and what was their proper relationship to the peoples of Europe?

The first *junta* of 'civil lawyers (*letrados*), theologians and canonists' which met to discuss the legitimacy of the Spanish occupation was called by Ferdinand in 1504. Not surprisingly this meeting decided, 'in the presence and with the opinion of the archbishop of Seville [Diego de Deza] that the Indians should be given [to the Spaniards] and that this was in agreement with human and divine law'.[6] We do not know what prompted Ferdinand to call this *junta*, but it is unlikely, from what we know of his character, that the king's conscience moved him unaided. The heightened sense of religious piety which seems to have swept Spain after Isabel's death, and the fact that the queen had stated in her will that the Indians should be 'well and justly treated'[7] and compensated for any harm which the Spaniards had done to them, may have prompted Ferdinand to seek an authoritative legal ruling on their status with which to confound any future critic. Whatever his motive, one thing is clear: at this point the crown still held firmly to the belief that the bulls of donation granted to Ferdinand and Isabel in 1493 by Alexander VI conceded them the right not only to conquer but also to enslave the inhabitants of the Antilles.[8]

By the terms of these bulls the Catholic Monarchs had been granted sovereignty over all the new found lands in the Atlantic which had not already been occupied by some other Christian prince. The declared aim of the pope's concession, however, had not been to increase the might and wealth of Castile but to enable Ferdinand and Isabel to 'proceed with and complete that enterprise on which you have already embarked [namely] under the guidance of the orthodox faith to induce the peoples who live in such islands and lands [as you have discovered or are about to discover] to receive the Catholic religion, save that you never inflict upon them hardships or dangers'.[9]

The final phrase of this injunction would seem to preclude war being made upon the Indians for whatever purpose; and the whole text could be interpreted, and was by men like Bartolomé de Las Casas, merely as a charter for evangelisation, a charter whose validity was never challenged, in so far, that is, as it touched only on spiritual concerns.[10]

For the crown, however, it was the political message of the bulls that was crucial. And it seems probable that Ferdinand's reiterated claims to possess the right not only to occupy America in return for sending missionaries there, but also to enslave the Indians for his own purposes, derives from the terms of the bull *Eximie devotionis*. Like its successor *Dudum siquidem*, this bull was an attempt to avert the impending conflict between Spain and Portugal over their respective spheres of influence in the Atlantic. In order to maintain the balance of power between the two nations Alexander had conceded to Spain all 'the graces, privileges, exemptions, liberties, facilities and immunities'[11] formerly granted to the king of Portugal, a list which could not fail to cover the right, conceded by Nicholas V to Afonso V (in 1455), to reduce to perpetual slavery the inhabitants of all the African territories from Cape Bojador and Cape Nun, 'and...hence all southern coasts until their end'.[12] For if the Portuguese possessed the right to enslave all the pagans they encountered as 'the enemies of Christ', so too, it might be argued, did the Castilians.[13]

The pope's authority to grant such rights in the first place, however, rested on the two claims which Spanish jurists and theologians found hardest to accept: the claims that the papacy possessed temporal as well as spiritual authority and that it could exercise this authority over pagans as well as Christians.

It was ten years, however, before anyone was prompted to challenge the legitimacy of the papal decrees; and for those ten years the Castilian crown followed, undisturbed, in the wake of the Portuguese. The situation in America, however, was very different from that in Africa. Most Portuguese colonies were (with the exception of the island of Goa and later of Brazil), whatever their size and strength, 'factories' (*feitorias*), whose existence depended on the willingness of the local populations to tolerate their presence. The Africans whom the Portuguese enslaved were, for the most part, procured for them by other Africans; and the missionary presence, which might have served as a focus for protest against the slave trade was, because of the sheer physical difficulty of survival in West Africa, slight and dispirited. In America, on the other hand, the Spaniards had, even by 1500, seized entire islands, settled them with their own people, made determined efforts to change their ecology and turned the bulk of the population into an enslaved work force. Such behaviour towards a race whom Alexander VI – paraphrasing Columbus's own description – had described as 'a people who live pacifically and, it is said, walk about naked and eat no meat...and believe in a God of creation who is in Heaven, and seem to be capable of receiving the Catholic Faith and of being instructed in good customs',[14] could not go unremarked for long. For a while, however, the rulings of the *junta* of 1504 seem to have settled the conscience of the king, and we have no record of further protest for seven years. Then, in 1511, there occurred the most outspoken and 'scandalous' condemnation of the colonists and their behaviour ever uttered publicly in America. The story is now a famous one. On the Sunday before Christmas, a Dominican, Antonio de Montesinos, delivered a sermon to the Spanish population of Hispaniola denouncing them for their treatment of the Indians and warning them that if they did not mend their ways, they would 'no more be saved than the Moors or the Turks'.[15] Montesinos's attack, it should be noted, was aimed not at the legitimacy of the Spanish occupation as such but at the colonists' abuse of their position, at the 'cruel and horrible servitude' to which they had reduced the native population, and at their failure to provide the Indians with adequate religious and moral instruction.

Montesinos's targets were outraged by such a 'novel' doctrine and they wrote home in protest, rephrasing the Dominican's observations on their conduct as a challenge to royal authority, an attempt, as they put it, 'to deprive him [the king] of the lordship and the rents he has in these parts'.[16] Political instability within the colony and the persistent Spanish fear of an Indian uprising increased the concern of the metropolitan authorities. In March 1512, Alonso de Loaysa, the Dominican provincial, warned Montesinos in hysterical terms, 'you gave in your sermon occasion for all this to be lost; everything might have been disturbed, and, on account of your sermon, all of India might have rebelled so that neither you nor any other Christian would have been able to remain there'. To drive the point home he hinted that the 'novelties' dreamed up by Montesinos and his colleagues might have been suggested to them by the Devil. In such matters, he warned, simple friars should 'bend their minds' to the consensus of so many 'prelates of learning and conscience, and of our Holy Father'.[17]

Ferdinand himself, more concerned with the legal aspects of the situation, responded with an implicit reference to *Eximie devotionis* and the concessions he had received from it. Had not the friars heard, he asked, 'of the rights that we have in the islands. . .and the justification by which these Indians should not only serve us as they do now but may be held in even greater slavery'?[18]

Yet despite Ferdinand and Loaysa's confident tone the crown, or at least the Castilian crown, had never, in fact, been entirely certain about its right to enslave Indians. In 1495, for instance, Columbus had sent back to Spain a number of Indian captives which he had hoped to sell in the slave markets in Seville. Isabel, however, had intervened and stopped the sale: 'Because we wish to be informed by civil lawyers, canonists and theologians whether we may, with a good conscience, sell these Indians or not.'[19] We have no record of the verdict given by the queen's advisors but it cannot have been favourable, for one year later she ordered all the Indian slaves in Seville to be taken from their masters and sent back to their former homes.[20]

It would be wrong, however, to assume from this action that Isabel, or any of her contemporaries, entertained any doubts about the legitimacy of slavery as an institution. The enslavement of Muslims had been a feature of Christian Spanish society for centuries; and when during the fourteenth and fifteenth centuries this source of supply began to dry up, Spaniards began to import white slaves from the Balkans and the Black Sea, the principal source of the slave trade since the days of Polybius.[21] These slaves were taken in 'just war'. That is they were either pagans or, like the Greeks and the Russians, schismatics resisting the legitimate authority of the 'true Church'.

The status of such persons in their European host societies is difficult to assess. But, as they came from cultural backgrounds which shared some features in common with their master's own, it seems probable that they enjoyed a higher measure of respect within the family than either the Africans or the Indians were to do. Certainly the crown considered the possibility in 1512 of exporting white slave women to the Antilles where they would probably have become the wives of white Spanish settlers.[22] White slaves were always, one must assume (in the absence of any statistical information), relatively few in number, and most were probably employed in strictly domestic roles.

With the Portuguese incursions into Africa, however, a new source of labour became available. At the beginning of the fifteenth century the slave markets of Seville and Valencia were rapidly developed for the sale of Blacks[23] so that by the end of the century they had become among the largest in Europe. Even Isabel herself had, until 1479 when the Catholic Monarchs abandoned their claims to Guinea, taken a personal interest in the African slave trade.[24]

It was, however, the Portuguese, sometimes acting through Genoese middlemen, who supplied most of the produce for these markets. The Portuguese slave trade was, therefore, in the Castilian view, a foreign affair. It came in for very little local or international criticism until the mid-sixteenth century, when theologians such as Domingo de Soto and Martín de Ledesma, who had been involved in the debate over the justice of the Spanish conquests in America, turned their attention to the activities of the Portuguese in Africa.[25] Even then the protests against slavery were isolated and, for the most part, academic ones. The men who laboured hard in defence of the Indians often had little concern for the fate of Africans. The case of Las Casas, who at one time had advocated importing Blacks to ease the burden of the Indians, is well known;[26] but even Francisco de Vitoria, who by the tone of his correspondence seems to have been genuinely indignant at the Spanish colonists' treatment of the Indians, could find nothing wrong with the

Portuguese trade and concluded, as many did, that 'if they [the Africans] are treated humanely it is better for them to be slaves among Christians than free in their own lands, for it is the greatest good fortune to become a Christian'. The trade, he concluded, was legitimate so long as the slaves had, in fact, been taken 'in a just war'.[27]

The reason for the radical difference in Spanish opinion on slavery for Africans and slavery for Amerindians is not hard to find. It has nothing to do with the colour of the two races (the Spaniards noticed blackness more than they noticed redness, but at this early stage attached no great importance to the difference between them) or a difference in their social behaviour; it was merely a question of legal status *vis-à-vis* the Europeans. The slaves sold in Spain, be they black or white, came from regions where the Spanish crown had no political commitments. It was, therefore, possible for the Catholic Monarchs to disclaim any responsibility for the human merchandise being sold on their territory. It was not for them to ascertain whether in fact the slaves they purchased were, as their owners invariably claimed them to be, 'barbarians' in revolt against the authority of the Church. 'It is not necessary for us to examine', one jurist claimed, 'whether the captivity of a Negro is just or not, because the sale is presumed to be just unless there is evidence of injustice.'[28]

True there were some, like the Franciscan Bartolomé de Albornoz, who complained that insufficient trouble was taken to ascertain the status of a slave before he was seized.[29] But most Spaniards would have shared Vitoria's view on the matter. 'I do not see', he wrote to a fellow Dominican Bernardino de Vigué, 'why one should be so scrupulous over this matter, for the Portuguese are not obliged to discover the justice of the wars between barbarians. It is enough that a man be a slave in fact or in law, and I will buy him without a qualm (*llanamente*).'[30]

The Amerindians, however, were quite another matter, for they had, with very few exceptions, been pressed into service on islands which the Spanish crown claimed to hold in legitimate suzerainty and whose peoples it was committed to converting to Christianity without inflicting 'dangers or hardships upon them'. Making war on the Indians was, said Vitoria, like making war on the inhabitants of Seville.[31] For the Indians, unlike the Africans, were vassals of the crown of Castile, and the crown took such classifications seriously. Isabel, for instance, was insistent on this point. In 1501 she informed Nicolás de Ovando, the governor of Hispaniola, that 'we wish the Indians to be well treated as our subjects and our vassals';[32] and in the same year she ordered an inquiry into the slaving activities in Cumana of one Cristobál Guerra: 'for the above-mentioned [expeditions] were carried out against our command (*provisión*) and prohibition, for the aforesaid Indians are our subjects'.[33] Though none might question the right of the crown to *govern* the Indians there was, as Juan de Zumárraga, first bishop of Mexico City, later reminded Charles V, no law, 'neither divine, nor natural, nor positive, nor human, nor civil, whereby the natives of this land may, because of their condition, be made into slaves'.[34] But even in the absence of any such law, and in defiance of Isabel's edicts, the enslavement of Indians for local use and the local slave trade continued unabated. By the late 1520s it had even become the chief economic activity of the otherwise impoverished region of Nicaragua.[35]

Ferdinand, and later Charles V, more out of expediency than moral conviction, seem to have adopted a less uncompromising position with respect to slaving than Isabel had done. Frequent attempts, however, were made to restrict slaving activities to the colonies.[36] No Indians were officially imported into the Peninsula after 1501; although the record shows, as one might expect, that in fact Ferdinand's *cédulas* and the subsequent instructions issued by the Council of the Indies on these matters were consistently ignored. Indian slaves were still being con-fiscated from their masters and returned home as late as the 1540s.[37] There seems too, to have been a small colony of manumitted slaves living in or near Seville who refused to return home because, they claimed, they earned more in Spain in a week than they would in America in a year, 'and they had more security'.[38]

The object of Montesinos's protests, however, had been not the relatively small number of true Indian slaves, but the very large number of 'free' Indians living in virtual slavery under the *encomienda*. This institution, first introduced into Hispaniola by Columbus in 1499, provided the Indians with Spanish 'protection', religious instruction and a small wage in exchange for their labour. The principal function of the *encomienda* had been to supply the mines and farms of the islands with a free, or nearly free, work force. It was also the belief of the Spaniards, and in particular of the clergy, that the Indians would only become true Christians through daily contact with Christians.[39] To achieve both these ends it was thought necessary to herd the Indians together into new settlements close to the Spanish towns and to destroy their old homes. According to the Laws of Burgos of 1513 this last precaution was taken because the Indians would otherwise forsake 'the conversation and communication with the Christians and flee into the jungle', for they were inconstant in their Christianity, and 'their sole aim and pleasure in life is to have the freedom to do with themselves exactly as they pleased'.[40]

The dissolution of tribal unity[41] and of the group's sense of social cohesion which these moves created, together with crude attempts to impose such things as Christian marriage, with all that that implied (i.e. patrilocal residence and the education of the children by their fathers) on a people whose society had some matrilineal features and who may have practised matrilocal residence,[42] contributed, of course, to the dramatic decline of the native population of the Antilles after the Spanish occupation. The cultural and social demands of the *encomienda* may, indeed, have been directly responsible for some of the features of Indian life which the Europeans found most reprehensible; suicide, infanticide, induced abortions[43] and what the Spaniards generally referred to as the Indians' 'lack of charity', their willingness to abandon the sick or the old, even to mock the sufferings of the dying.[44] For similar cases were recorded on Franciscan mission stations in California in the eighteenth century,[45] and have been observed today among the Ik, an East African tribe displaced by the creation of a game reserve from their tribal homelands and their traditional means of subsistence.[46]

Predictably, Europeans attributed such features of Indian life to the Indians' nature. A few far-sighted missionaries, such as the Franciscan Pedro de Gante, were able to see the damaging effects which enforced acculturation had upon its victims. But they were very few indeed. Even Vasco de Quiroga's famous village-hospitals of Santa Fe, where Indians were to be given the opportunity to live decent independent lives out of the reach of the colonists, were organised into artificial 'families' composed of a single lineage through the male line. Quiroga's Indians, like Indians everywhere, were to live in emulation of their Christian rulers, in huts each housing a single nuclear family grouped around, not the log cabin and the dance floor, but the Church and the chapter house.[47]

Few, if any, of the great apologists for the Indians registered any serious protest against this dislocation of the Indians' tribal life. However humane their intentions may have been, men like Montesinos and Quiroga had come to America in order to convert, and conversion they knew meant replacing the old pagan customs, together with the pagan religion, by new Christian ones. Even Las Casas, like most of his

35

twentieth-century commentators, regarded the Laws of Burgos and similar edicts not as a death sentence on the Indian world, but as proof of the Spanish crown's 'kindly intentions' towards their new vassals.[48]

What both Montesinos and later Las Casas took such violent exception to was the sheer physical brutality of the colonists, their ingrained conviction that, as one of them put it, 'if you don't hit an Indian he can't make his limbs move',[49] and their failure to provide their Indian charges with the religious instruction they were supposed to. It was a constant problem for the clergy. The holders of *encomiendas* (*encomenderos*) were not very concerned with the spiritual welfare of their labour force. Most of them had come from a stratum of society where violence was endemic, and where religious beliefs frequently assumed highly unorthodox forms in which outbursts of frustration might easily express themselves by physical attacks on holy images.[50] Such people were hardly suited to play the role of 'civilisors'.[51] There were also, in many parts of the new world, insuperable practical problems in the way of any kind of forced acculturation. As the Laws of Burgos made clear, the Indians fled into the mountains if they were pressed too hard. And although the Church persisted in its attempts to compel the *encomenderos* to comply with their obligations, threatening them with excommunication, accusing them of heresy or denying them absolution,[52] its efforts seem to have had little real effect.

But although the *encomienda* failed dismally in practice to be the kind of quasi-contractual institution its defenders claimed it to be, although the colonists behaved as though 'their' Indians were merely slaves, to be sold or exchanged like any other form of merchandise, there was a distinction in law, if nowhere else, between the *encomienda* and true civil slavery. For the Indian who had been *encomendado* was technically a free man. True he could not exercise this freedom by walking away or by refusing to work for the Spaniards. But he did not *belong* to his master and could not, in law, be sold, or even exchanged for another Indian. These distinctions were doubtless no more obvious to him than they were to Las Casas, who referred to the *encomienda* as 'a mortal pestilence which consumed these peoples, [a device] invented by Satan and all his ministers and officials to drag the Spaniards down into Hell and all Spain to destruction'.[53]

But from the theoretical point of view the distinction was an important one because, as we shall see, the model of psychological dependence that emerged from the Spanish schoolmen's reading of the natural slave theory corresponded closely to the kind of contractualism that the *encomienda* was supposed to embody.

2

Montesinos's outburst, as we have seen, was about the *behaviour* of the colonists. He wished neither to challenge the authority of the king, nor even to protest at the existence of the *encomienda* system. But by shifting the emphasis of his arguments to suggest that he was, in fact, attacking the crown's *political* rights in the Antilles, the colonists, in their indignation, had effectively made it possible for potential critics of Ferdinand's policies to ask the fundamental questions: Did the crown in fact possess the right to colonise the Indies in the first place? What validity, if any, did the bulls of donation have as a political charter? And, even if it were conceded that the Spaniards did have a right to settle in America, what possible justification could they have for obliging the native population to do their manual work for them?

Behind questions such as these were ranged a number of disputes about the nature and the limits of the spiritual and temporal sovereignty of the emperor and the pope which had exercised the minds of jurists and theologians for more than two centuries. But few of the conclusions reached in previous debates seemed to be of much real use when it came to discussing the situation in America.

Alexander VI's bulls of donation granting to Ferdinand and Isabel sovereignty in the new world rested on the assumption that the pope possessed jurisdiction over the lands of pagans. In the formulation of Tommaso de Vio, Cardinal Cajetan, to which most of the jurists and theologians of this period refer, pagans may be divided into three broad categories.[54] In the first category are those who live outside the Church but on lands that had once formed part of the Roman empire, and thus came within the *dominium* of the Church; in the second are those who live anywhere in the world, but who are lawfully subject to a Christian prince; in the third are the true *infideles*, men who dwell in lands which are neither subject to legitimate Christian rule, nor had once been within the bounds of the Roman world. Those who belong to this final category are, obviously, subject to Christian rule neither *de iure* (as are those in the first category) nor *de facto* (as are those in the second). No-one could seriously claim – despite Oviedo's ingenious attempt to argue that they might be the remnants of a Visigothic diaspora[55] – that the Indians had ever been Christian vassals or incorporated into the empire. Thus neither the emperor nor the Church, whose temporal authority extended by historical right only over former imperial lands, could make any undisputed claim to hold temporal jurisdiction over them.

Furthermore, the pagans were traditionally divided into two broad groups according to the source of their paganism. In the one were all those who, in Aquinas's words, were 'invincibly ignorant', who had never, and through no obvious fault of their own, had the opportunity to hear the Gospel. In the other were the 'vincibly ignorant', men who, like the Jews and the Muslims, had heard the true Word and had refused to listen to it.[56] Most commentators were agreed – if we ignore the attempts to identify the Mexican deity Quetzalcoatl with the legendary Saint Thomas, prophet of Malabar[57] – that the Indians could have known nothing of Christ before the arrival of the Spaniards. They could not, therefore, convincingly be described as *inimicos Christi* and consequently in the opinion of many they retained their natural rights. Although there was no clear consensus as to the full extent of these, it was none the less plain that the traditional excuses offered by Christian princes for their territorial ambitions in non-Christian lands were, in the American case, insufficient.

Clearly some other argument, one that avoided the troubled area of the temporal authority of the pope, was needed. Just such an argument, as the crown's apologists were quick to realise, was available in a brief statement by John Mair, a Scottish theologian and historian who was at that time a member of the Collège de Montaigu at Paris, a university which had little tolerance for the universal ambitions of emperors and popes.[58] In a discussion on the legitimacy of Christian rule over pagans, in the forty-fourth *distinctio* of his commentary on the second of Peter Lombard's *Sentences*, Mair explained that:

These people [the inhabitants of the Antilles] live like beasts on either side of the equator; and beneath the poles there are wild men as Ptolemy says in his *Tetrabiblos*.[59] And this has now been demonstrated by experience, wherefore the first person to conquer them, justly rules over them because they are by nature slaves. As the Philosopher [Aristotle] says in the third and fourth chapters of the first book of the *Politics*, it is clear that some men are by nature slaves, others by nature free; and in some men it is determined that there is such a thing [i.e. a disposition to slavery] and that they should benefit from it. And it is just that one man should be a slave and another free, and it is fitting that one man should rule and another obey, for the quality of leadership is also inherent in the natural master. On this account the Philosopher says in the first chapter of the afore-mentioned book that this is the reason why the Greeks should be masters over the barbarians because, by nature, the barbarians and slaves are the same.[60]

There are two things to note about this statement. In the first place it uses a classical, pagan, authority in the context of a discussion usually limited to Christian sources. I shall return to this point later. In the second, it is clear that Mair regarded Aristotle's hypothesis not as an attempt to explain a real social condition in fourth-century Athens but as a classification, arrived at by deduction, of a particular kind of people whose existence had only now been proved by experience (*et etiam hoc experientia compertum est*). Ptolemy's environmentalism, a popular means of classifying peoples in the middle ages, offered further proof of both the validity of Aristotle's hypothesis and the accuracy of Mair's identification of the Indians as natural slaves.[61] The implication here is that the 'natural slaves' and the 'barbarians' (who are treated as one and the same class) constitute a category of creature which – like the wild men, the cannibals and the Amazons – had, before being discovered by the Spaniards, existed only in the 'imaginary spaces' of the European mind.

This text was immediately recognised by some Spaniards as offering a final solution to their problem. Mair had, in effect, established that the Christians' claims to sovereignty over certain pagans could be said to rest on the *nature* of the people being conquered, instead of on the supposed juridical rights of the conquerors. He thus avoided the inevitable and alarming deduction to be drawn from an application of those arguments – arguments which in other circumstances he had himself endorsed[62] – which denied to either pope or emperor the right to seize lands which they could make no claim to possess, in Cajetan's terms, by either *de facto* or *de iure* authority: namely that the Spaniards had no right whatsoever to be in America. And Mair had achieved this sleight-of-hand by drawing an argument from no less an authority than Aristotle, albeit from a text which had not been widely used in such theological-cum-juridical arguments as these. Mair's assertion also offered a possible solution to the problem of how, anthropologically, to classify the Indian. For, as will become clear when we discover just what kind of being a 'natural slave' is supposed to be, Aristotle's theory provided an explanation for devious or unusual behaviour which was couched in the familiar language of faculty psychology.

That it should have been Mair who first suggested that the Indians might be Aristotle's natural slaves is also significant, for it places the whole debate over the nature of the Indian in the context of an identifiable intellectual milieu. Mair's college, the Collège de Montaigu at Paris, had since its reform in the late fifteenth century by Erasmus's former master Jean Standonck, been the centre of a cautious 'humanising', if not exactly humanistic, approach to theological and philosophical learning.[63] Mair had himself studied under Standonck and had learned his Greek from Girolamo Aleandro.[64] His work, despite its verbosity and the 'barbarity' of its Latin, attempted to fuse classical learning, particularly ancient moral philosophy, with more traditional legal and theological studies. In a science such as theology or law, which operated within boundaries established by a fixed number of authoritative texts, the only certain method of change was to introduce a new text or group of texts into the existing corpus. This is effectively what Aquinas had done with such dramatic results in the thirteenth century; and it is what Mair and his colleagues, men such as Jacques Almain and the Fleming Peter Crockaert, were attempting to do in Paris in the late fifteenth century.

Mair's approach was, of course, nothing so innovative as Aquinas's had been. All he proposed was that theology should make greater use of moral philosophy, and consequently pay greater attention to ethical problems than it had done hitherto. To many, however, such a programme seemed if not unorthodox at least highly uncertain. For moral philosophy was, of course, dominated by the writings of pagans, and most theologians regarded the secular wisdom of the ancient world – the 'spoils of the Egyptians' – with some degree of suspicion, particularly when that wisdom pressed so closely on their own zealously guarded ethical concerns. Bartolomé de Las Casas, who, despite the radicalism of his political opinions *vis-à-vis* the Indians and the originality of much of his anthropology, was rigidly orthodox in his theological convictions, was only voicing a traditional unease about the use of pagan sources in theological discourse when he objected to the Franciscan bishop Juan de Quevedo's use of the natural slave theory that it was the work of 'a pagan now burning in hell whose principles should only be accepted in so far as they conform to our Christian religion'.[65]

Conscious of his somewhat exposed position, Mair was careful to point out that theology could never be at odds with 'true' philosophy.[66] These two methods of inquiry were, he believed, even necessary to one another and consequently the precepts of moral philosophy could be found to have direct analogies in the literature of revelation. Aristotle's view of ethics – for instance, his division of man's activities into a contemplative and an active life – had a parallel, and hence divine authority, in the biblical accounts of the lives of Rachel and Leah, Martha and Mary.[67] Only by drawing on *all* the sources of knowledge, human as well as divine, could theology hope to make the kind of discoveries which Vespucci had made in the natural world.[68]

### 3

Before we come to the methods by which the schoolmen and historians of the sixteenth century developed Mair's suggestion that the Indians might be natural slaves, it will be necessary to take a closer look at Aristotle's theory itself and at some of its implications.

The Greek world accepted, at least in theory, the existence of two distinct forms of slavery, the civil and the natural. Civil slavery was merely a social institution; and it was regarded as a normal, indeed as a necessary, part of every civil society. Without a dependent labour force the cities of the ancient world could not have been built, nor could their patrician classes have been maintained in the style which Aristotle (and Plato) described as 'the life of contemplation'. As an institution slavery was absorbed first by Roman society and then, with only a few mild protests from such men as Chrysostom,[69] into the Christian world. The term 'natural slavery' as defined by Aristotle, on the other hand, referred not to an institution but to a particular category of man. The theory of natural slavery was, in fact, the means to explain why it was morally right for one nation – in this case the Greeks – to enslave members of another. Although the theory found some support in the ancient world, it was never discussed at any length by a Christian author until its revival by Aquinas in the thirteenth century.

The civil slave was a man like any other who had, for reasons that have no bearing on his nature, been deprived of his civil liberties. Civil slavery was, as the Roman jurist Florentinus phrased it, 'an institution of the law of nations whereby someone is subject to another *contrary to nature*' (my italic).[70] The causes of this kind of slavery were, therefore, always accidental ones. Civil slaves were persons who had committed some illiberal act for which the punishment was slavery, or they were those who had been captured in a just war and had been spared their lives in exchange for their freedom.[71]

The origins of civil slavery were, for Christians at least, to be found in the imperfect spiritual condition of man. Before the fall there had been no servitude, no rule indeed of any kind. It was sin, and in particular the curse of Noah upon his son Ham,[72] which was the original cause of the creation of hierarchies within human society, though once these had come into being they took the same form as the hierarchies which already existed in the natural world, and became an intrinsic part of that world.

The origin of natural slavery, however, is to be found neither in the action of some purely human agent nor in the hand of God, but in the psychology of the slave himself and ultimately in the constitution of the universe.[73] It depends on the axiom, common to much Greek thought, that there exists in all complex forms a duality in which one element naturally dominates the other. 'In all things', wrote Aristotle, 'which form a composite whole and which are made up of parts, whether continuous or discrete, a distinction comes to light. Such a duality exists in living creatures but not in them alone; it originates in the constitution of the universe' (*Pol.* 1254 a 28ff.).

In man the ruling element is the intellect (*nous*) and the subordinate one the passions (*orexis*), for the intellect is the logical and the passions are the alogical part of man's bipartite soul (*psyche*). The passions are, by definition, unable to govern themselves; but the intellect of the fully grown male will, unless of course his mind has been impaired, be able to master this part of his whole character and direct it towards the good.[74] It is, indeed, man's ability to use reason in this way, together with his capacity for speech, which distinguishes him from all other animals.

Aristotle's natural slave is clearly a man (*Pol.* 1254 b 16, 1259 b 27–8), but he is a man whose intellect has, for some reason, failed to achieve proper mastery over his passions. Aristotle denies such creatures the power to deliberate but he does allow them some share in the faculty of reason. This, however, is only 'enough to apprehend but not to possess true reason' (*Pol.* 1254 b 20ff.). It was with this distinction in mind that the Spanish jurist Juan de Matienzo informed the readers of his *Gobierno del Perú* that the Indians were

participants in reason so as to sense it, but not to possess or follow it. In this they are no different from the animals (although animals do not even sense reason) for they are ruled by their passions. This may be clearly seen because for them there is no tomorrow and they are content that they have enough to eat and drink for a week, and when that is finished they search for [the provisions for] the next.[75]

For Aristotle such a failure to 'possess' reason would seem to mean that the natural slave, while incapable of formulating instructions for himself, is none the less capable of following them (cf. *Pol.* 1254 b 22);

42

he may be said perhaps to be capable of understanding (*sunesis*) but incapable of practical wisdom (*phronesis*), for 'practical wisdom issues commands...but understanding only judges' (*NE*, 1143 a 11ff.). *Phronesis*, as it is described in the *Nicomachean ethics*, is the supreme speculative faculty which allows a man to practise virtue. The natural slave, then, can have no share in virtue except with reference to another 'whole' person, his master (*Pol.* 1260 a 31ff.; cf. *NE*, 1142 b 20ff.), no share in the life of happiness (*eudaimonia*), which is the final good or end (*telos*) of all true men, nor any ability to participate in the civil community (*Pol.* 1280 a 33ff.), for 'slaves and animals do little for the common good, and for the most part live at random' (*Meta.* 1075 a 20–5). As man is a virtue-seeking – happiness-making – political animal, *zōon politikon*, whose end can only be achieved within the context of the community (*koinōnia*), the slave who is excluded, *by nature*, from all these activities would appear to have been stripped of his humanity altogether. But as we have seen, Aristotle is insistent that he *is* a man. Incapable, however, of deliberate choice (*prohairesis*)[76] or moral action, his position in the hierarchy of nature is at the bestial end of the human scale, since he differs from the beast only in his ability to apprehend reason (*Pol.* 1254 b 23); and his role in the household would seem to be similar to that of the domestic animal (*Pol.* 1254 b 16–17). He is condemned to a life of perpetual servitude, his obligations are indistinguishable from those of the beast of service (*Pol.* 1254 b 20ff.) and his acquisition may be likened to hunting (*Pol.* 1255 b 34ff.; cf. 1333 b 38).

The function of the natural slave is clearly, therefore, to *be* a slave. In his wild state the natural slave is incapable of fulfilling his proper function. While free he is only half a man, for not only does his master do his thinking for him (*Pol.* 1252 a 31) but he is himself almost literally a 'living but separate part of his master's frame' (*Pol.* 1254 a 8) who shares all his master's interests (*Pol.* 1278 b 33). Once the natural slave has been caught his condition must improve, just as the condition of the wild animal is said to improve once it has been domesticated (*Pol.* 1254 b 10). By sharing his life with true men, the slave may himself become more man-like, if only by imitation, for although he may not be able to perform rational acts unaided, he is susceptible to reasoned admonition (*NE*, 1120 b 34). It was, in short, in the interests of both the master and the slave that the slave should be deprived of a freedom which was 'unnatural' and thus – since it permitted him to continue in the ignorance of his savage ways – harmful to him.

The natural slave is not, however, the only psychologically defective

43

creature in Aristotle's human hierarchy. For occupying similar positions are both the woman and the child. Like the natural slave both are, in a sense, incomplete men. Women, who are in any case little more than defective males (*De gen. an.* 737 a 28), possess the capacity to reason, but they lack authority (*akuron*). The child also possesses a deliberative capacity but his is only partly formed, for the alogical soul is prior in generation to the logical (*Pol.* 1324 b 21–2).

Like slaves, neither women nor children can participate directly in the life of happiness nor take an independent part in the life of any civil society, though, of course, they may achieve both these things by reference to their husbands or their fathers. The male child, however, is unlike either the slave or the woman in that one day he will become a fully grown man. He should be ruled, therefore, not despotically as are slaves and women, but 'by virtue of both the love and respect due to age' (*Pol.* 1259 b 12). As he grows he will perfect his faculties through training and habituation (*ethismos*). His mind, unlike that of the slave, and even perhaps of the woman, may be permanently improved through learning or, to put it in other Aristotelian terms, the potential in the child will be actualised in the man.[77]

Comparisons between Indians and women, though they found expression in such simple-minded legal equations as Philip II's decree 'that in every case, two Indians or three women presented as witnesses are worth one Spanish man',[78] were not, for obvious reasons, much exploited by later commentators. But Aristotle's belief in the importance of training in the development of the faculty of reason with its implication that men are, to some extent, the creatures of the environment in which they have been reared, was, as we shall see in a later chapter, to prove a useful device in subsequent attempts to explain the behaviour of the American Indians.

Having reached a definition of the natural slave and intimated something about his relationship to the other members of the human household – the master, the woman and the child – Aristotle was left with the problem of deciding how the psychological peculiarities of the slave manifest themselves in practice. How is the mere observer able to distinguish a natural slave from a free man, for souls are not, after all, things that one can see? (Cf. *Pol.* 1254 b 38.)

Aristotle offered three possible solutions to this problem. Ideally the natural slave should always be equipped with a powerful body capable of performing the labours nature has assigned to him. He should always be a slouching beast of great physical strength, while the natural master, in keeping with his superior powers of reason, should be both delicate and well-proportioned. 'Nature would like to distinguish between the bodies of free men and slaves', wrote Aristotle, 'making the one strong for servile labour, the other upright and although useless for service, useful for the political life in the arts of both peace and war' (*Pol.* 1254 b 27ff.).

This means of identifying the natural slave is, however, evidently unsatisfactory. Inferior men, be they European peasants, Scythians, Negroes or Indians, are not always and everywhere strong, nor are their natural rulers always and everywhere delicate and refined. Indeed, as Aristotle admitted, 'the opposite frequently happens – that some have the souls and others the bodies of free men' (*Pol.* 1254 b 30ff.). The body is no real mirror of the soul and although nature may have intended it to be so, she has been unable to fulfil her purpose (*ibid.*).

Yet for all the seeming contradictions inherent in a belief in the existence of such a parallel between physiology and psychology, the idea that a man's intellectual faculties should, in some measure, be reflected in his physical appearance exercised a tremendous hold over the European imagination. It had the authority of a popular pseudo-Aristotelian work, the *Physionomica*, and it seemed to offer a direct correspondence between what can and what cannot be seen (*Pol.* 1254 b 38). Cripples and hunchbacks were 'unnatural' with, in the popular imagination at least, minds as disturbed as their bodies were warped. The intelligent and the virtuous, on the other hand, were thought to be well-proportioned, healthy and frequently beautiful.

The suggestion that the physique of the American Indians provided the necessary proof that they were natural slaves was not one that could be either corroborated or refuted with any satisfaction. Every observer tended to form his opinion on the appearance of the Indians and most of the descriptions we have of it are contradictory.[79] But despite their evident inability to withstand the white man's demands for their labour or to resist the white man's diseases, the suggestion that the Indians might be physically equipped for a life of slavery was taken very seriously. Las Casas, for instance, as part of his complex attempt to prove, by the use of empirical evidence, that the Indians were no more natural slaves than any other race of men, went to some length to demonstrate that the natural beauty of the Indian body argued for a high level of natural intelligence. 'The native peoples of these Indies are', he wrote, '...by reason of the good composition of their bodily parts, the harmony (*convivencia*) and proportion of their exterior sense organs, the beauty of their faces or gestures and their whole *vultu*, the shape of their heads, their manners and movements, etc., naturally of good reason and good understanding.'[80] While as late as 1600, when the whole question of natural slavery had ceased to be of much interest to the learned public in Spain, an anonymous 'expert' on Indian affairs seriously expected Philip III to believe that

The Indians can be said to be slaves of the Spaniards...in accordance with the doctrine of Aristotle's *Politics*, that those who need to be ruled and governed by others may be called their slaves...And for this reason Nature specially proportioned their bodies, so that they should have the strength for personal service. The Spaniards, on the other hand, are delicately proportioned, and were made prudent and clever, so that they should be able to lead a political and civil life (*tratar la policia y urbanidad*).[81]

But if physical determinism was an ideal which nature had ultimately failed to attain (*Pol.* 1255 b 30), there might instead exist, Aristotle thought, some principle of genetic transmission whereby natural slaves are always born of natural slaves (*Pol.* 1255 a 30). Such a principle would confirm, once again, the essential harmony of nature by conforming to the biological rule which required all creatures of a certain type always to produce offspring of that same type, and in their own form. Natural slaves should, therefore, produce natural slaves, just as dogs should always give birth to dogs (*De gen. an.* 715 b 1ff.).[82] Such a belief in the hereditary transmission of psychological characteristics presented, however, even greater difficulties to later commentators than the notion of physical determinism had done. For in the absence of any obvious species distinction between men and slaves, it would first be necessary to establish that the slave's mother (in Roman law slave status was transmitted through the female line)[83] had also been born a slave. The result of any such inquiry would inevitably be an infinite regress. Perhaps for this reason, I have found only one instance of its use in the subsequent discussions over the nature of the American Indians. This is the statement by the canonist Diego de Covarrubias (1512–77) that 'all women are natural slaves in relation to their husbands. Also, the slaves who are born of slave women are natural slaves, for they are born natural slaves',[84] which may after all, be little more than a confusion with the Roman law principle that the offspring of slave women are the property of that woman's owner.

In the light of the evident deficiencies of these first two attempts to find precise means by which to single out the natural slave from the rest of humanity, Aristotle suggested a far broader, far simpler distinction; a distinction, furthermore, which not only fulfilled the biological need of every type to reproduce itself by the same type, but also offered a psychological-cum-biological explanation for the superiority of Greeks over all the other races of men, namely 'the assumption that *barbaroi* and slaves are by nature one'. 'Among the *barbaroi* no distinction is made between women and slaves because there is no natural ruler among them: they are a community of slaves male and female. This is why the poets say that it is meet that the Greeks should rule over the barbarians, the assumption being that barbarians and slaves are by nature one' (*Pol.* 1252 b 5ff.). 'Wherefore Hellenes do not like to call Hellenes slaves but confine the term to barbarians. Yet in using this language they really mean the natural slave of whom we spoke first' (*Pol.* 1255 a 29ff.).

It was only this identification of the natural slave with the barbarian that made the theory of natural slavery of any use in the discussion over the nature of the American Indian. For the fact that the Indian was, in some sense, a 'barbarian', that his culture and the societies in which he lived were insufficient, inferior to those of the white men, seemed evident to all those who encountered him. It was thus a simple matter for those in search of explanations for patterns of behaviour which they regarded as deviant to classify the Indians as men whose minds were unequipped to deal with the complex business of living 'rational' lives. The Indian in the wild was like a dog in the wild; he was failing to fulfil his allotted place in the world, a place which made of him, in Aquinas's words, 'almost an animated instrument of service'.[85]

It is also easy to see how attractive Aristotle's theory, in whole or in part, was to those who could find no place in their picture of the world for cultural forms like those of the Amerindians which were so different from their own as to defy the very premises on which human behaviour was thought to be based. The Indians were clearly 'barbarians', and 'barbarians', said Fr. Tomás de Mercado, placing Aristotle's theory in a nutshell, 'are never moved by reason, but only by passion'.[86]

The first time that Aristotle's theory was employed in Spain was in 1512. In that year, Ferdinand, evidently in response to continuing pressure from the Dominican order – an order to which he claimed, probably with some truth, to be particularly devoted[87] – summoned another *junta* to meet at Burgos and decide on the legitimacy of the conquest and the employment of native labour.[88]

Unfortunately only two of the opinions (the *testimonios* or *pareceres*) presented at this meeting, those of Bernardo de Mesa, later bishop of Cuba, and a certain *licenciado* (bachelor of arts) called Gil Gregorio, seem to have survived.[89] Both of these, however, rested their arguments for the subjugation of the Indians on the claim that the Amerindian peoples were obviously barbarians and thus the natural slaves described by Aristotle in the *Politics*, 'where it appears', said Gregorio, 'that through the barbarity and wicked disposition of the people of the Antilles they may, and should, be governed as slaves'.[90] Tyranny is the appropriate mode of government for the Indians because 'slaves and barbarians...are those who are lacking in judgment and understanding as are these Indians who, it is said, are like talking animals'.[91]

In further support of this contention Gregorio cited the second chapter of the third book of Thomas Aquinas's *De regimine principum* (in fact the work of Thomas's pupil Ptolemy of Lucca).[92] The passage he actually quoted is merely a reaffirmation of the familiar Aristotelian principle, that since tyranny is the only government known to barbarians and since it is also a rule over slaves, it follows that barbarians are, by nature, to be ruled as slaves.[93] But there is more to Gregorio's argument than that. His readers, or listeners, would have been sufficiently familiar with such a much-used text as *De regimine* to have been able to supply the context of Gregorio's quotation. And the context gives far greater resonance to his utterance. For Ptolemy of Lucca links Aristotle's observation about the natural government of slaves analogously to a law of the physical world, namely the famous statement in the *Physics* (258 b 10–259 a 20) that as all material bodies in the universe are in motion, each one must be moved by another that is more powerful than itself, the entire universe being set in motion by a Prime Mover who alone is unmoved. Now since there exists a harmony between the various parts of the natural order, it follows that what is true in the world of physical matter must also be true in the invisible world of the spirit. Thus men with weak minds must be 'moved' by those with strong ones, just as a stick when thrown, to use Aristotle's own example, must have an arm to throw it. The Indians, who are 'idle, vicious and without charity',[94] exist only incompletely until they have been mastered; for they are the moved and the Spaniards, their natural masters, are the movers. Their freedom is thus a violation of the natural order and, consequently, it is 'harmful to them'.[95]

For Gregorio movement in the physical world and the 'movement' between men within the social order were governed by the same immutable laws. This, of course, is a commonplace of sixteenth-century thought, and we shall encounter it again when we come to consider more fully the position of the Indian under the law of nature. But it is worth stressing at this point because it makes plain the fact that the theory of natural slavery was seen as part of a wide network of beliefs, not only about the structure and function of the human mind, but also about the organising principles of the universe itself, of which man is only one small part.

Because the relationship between Indians and Spaniards is thus determined by a natural, universal, not a human law, the kind of slavery that Gregorio had in mind for the Indians was not one that would have made of them mere chattels, 'that may be bought or sold, for no-one possesses them in this manner'; but what he referred to as a 'qualified slavery'. Gregorio says nothing about the details of this; but we may assume, in view of the fact that he *is* defending the rights of the colonists, that it would correspond to the status of Indians under the *encomienda*, an institution which had always been conceived as, in some sense, contractual. In exchange for their labour – hard work was, in any case, a part of the civilising process – the Indians would learn through Spanish example to live 'like men'. 'It is beneficial for them', Gregorio concluded, 'to serve their lord without any payment or reward...for total liberty is harmful to them.'[96]

Mesa's approach to the question was similar to Gregorio's, but rather more explicit about the possible sources of the Indians' barbarous and slave-like disposition. The Indians were, he claimed, clearly not slaves in the common legal sense of the word for they are the vassals and subjects of the queen, and vassals possessed political rights independent of those of their master. Although the queen might legitimately impose upon them 'such services as were within the limits of those performed by vassals', the Indians could not be bought or sold like merchandise.[97] Mesa's concern at this point is to legitimate an existing situation, not to consider whether or not that situation is, of itself, a just one, justice having been conferred upon it by those (the Catholic Monarchs) in whose name it was created in the first place. Any legitimate explanation for the *de facto* servitude of the Indians had, therefore, to be sought outside the framework of a conventional legal argument.

And he says [reported Las Casas] that he could see no reason for their slavery except the natural, which was their lack of understanding and mental capacity, and their lack of perseverance in following the faith and observing good customs; for that is natural servitude according to the Philosopher. Or, he says, perhaps they are slaves by nature because of the nature of the land; because there are some lands where the configuration of the stars makes slaves of the inhabitants, and they could not be ruled if there were not some measure of slavery practised there, as in France where the people of Normandy, which is a part of the Dauphinage, have always been ruled like slaves.[98]

But the critics – alas, we do not know to whom he is referring – of the opinion that there are some races who are slaves *by nature* had pointed out, he went on,

that the incapacity we attribute to the Indians contradicts the bounty of the Creator, for it is certain that when a cause produces its effect so that it is unable to achieve its end, then there is some fault in the cause; and thus there must be some fault with God for having made men without sufficient capacity to receive the faith and to save themselves.[99]

Mesa recognised the validity of this argument and claimed that all he had really intended to say was that there was in the Indians 'so little disposition or training (*habituación*) that a great labour is necessary before they can be brought to the faith and to the practice of good customs'.[100]

Mesa's statements, in this cryptic version of Las Casas, are, as we shall see, not in themselves very original. But they do state the case, and in terms of the same basic principles to be used by many later writers on the subject of the nature of the Amerindian: climatic and geographical determinism, the crucial recognition that any suggestion that Indians might be an inferior species threatened an essential belief in the perfection of the creation, and, most enduring of all, the emphasis on the Aristotelian theory of habituation (*ethismos*) as a key factor in determining a man's behaviour.

### 4

The outcome of the Burgos *juntas* evidently failed to satisfy the crown, for that same year Ferdinand asked two of its members, the civilian lawyer Juan López de Palacios Rubios and the canonist Matías de Paz, to draw up separate, and more detailed, opinions of their own.[101]

The treatises that Matías de Paz and Palacios Rubios wrote for Ferdinand are the first full-length legal and ethical considerations of the justice of the conquest to have survived.[102] Of the two, Palacios Rubios's 'Libellus de insulanis oceanis' is, from our point of view, by far the more interesting. To Paz the problem was one of the justice of war and its consequences, of the secular authority of the pope and of the sovereign rights of pagans. Palacios Rubios considered these matters, too, but he came upon his task from a different direction. Like Mair, Gregorio and Mesa, he assumed that the answer to the question of whether or not the Indians might legitimately be conquered and enslaved lay in the *nature* of the Indians themselves, and he consequently dedicated the whole of the first part of his work to a discussion of the theory of natural slavery and its implications.

Palacios Rubios was an ardent regalist. He was the author of a gloss on the Laws of Toro, a spirited defence of Ferdinand's 'Holy War' against the kingdom of Navarre,[103] a commentary on Aristotle's *Politics*, and perhaps also of a now lost *Tratado esforzando los indios a la fe católica*.[104] He was also the creator of the famous – or infamous – *Requerimiento*, that curious declaration of the Indians' obligations to submit to Spanish rule and be converted to the Christian faith, which all the *conquistadores* carried with them and were required to read out loud to the Indians before attacking them.[105]

Despite the fact that 'De insulanis' was evidently written as an apology for the royal cause, it is somewhat more speculative than its brief required and even mildly sympathetic to the plight of the Indians. For this it won qualified praise from Las Casas, who urged that it should be 'printed and carried to the Indies...and it should be known that those Indians are men and free and must be treated as such'.[106]

Both Gil Gregorio and Mesa had merely stated that the Indians were barbarians and hence natural slaves. Palacios Rubios, on the other hand, began his 'Libellus' with a brief account of the evidence for this barbarism based, so he claimed, on 'reliable reports'.[107] Whatever these reports may have been, they were couched, or interpreted by Palacios Rubios, in terms of a number of traditional 'primitivist' *topoi*. At first sight, he claimed, the Indians appeared to be 'rational, gentle and peaceful men, capable of understanding our faith'.[108] They owned no property, and farmed in common what few lands they had under cultivation. They also lived by fishing and each man shared his day's catch out among his fellows. In this way they had no reason to be either greedy or avaricious. Although, in common with all men, they fought wars from time to time, they never took their enemies prisoner which, to Palacios Rubios, indicated that civil slavery was unknown in America, from which it may be inferred that the primitive law (*ius primaevum*) which granted to man his freedom and independence had not changed, but on the contrary endured[109] – an observation applauded by Las Casas. Like all such peoples who lived, or seemed to live, in an age of innocence – what Aquinas, with a clear sense of its historical reality, had described as the 'age of the natural law'[110] – the Indians dwelt in peace with the world of nature. 'They loved the birds and the domestic animals', wrote Palacios Rubios, 'as if they were children and they would not eat them, for that would have been as though they devoured their own offspring.'[111]

This jumble of real ethnography and fantasy offered the reader a familiar picture of a 'primitivist' – what Lovejoy and Boas would call a 'soft primitivist'[112] – world. Men do not seek for gain; having no technology, no real agriculture and no economy, they depend on the benevolence of nature for their survival. They do not eat the food that is proper to civilised and complex societies (i.e. meat), for vegetarianism is another feature of the 'age of the natural law'[113] where also, as in Eden, the wolf will lie down with the lamb.

The willingness to create this kind of social image and the conclusions to be drawn from it varied with the observer's own personal preoccupations. To some such as Columbus, his head filled with the imaginings of Aeneas Sylvius and Joachim of Fiore, and to the neo-Platonists such as Peter Martyr, the Indians may have seemed a docile, if rather stupid, *tabula rasa*, waiting patiently for the imprint of the Christian faith. To others, such as the Sceptics from Pico to Montaigne, they appeared to have retained many of the virtues which civilised man had lost. The very difference between their customs and the customs of Christians seemed to demonstrate that the law of nature was truly invisible to man and that no certain knowledge was possible without revelation.

To Palacios Rubios, however, the simplicity of Indian society appeared somewhat differently. He was an Aristotelian, a jurist, a man with no inclination to question the norms by which his own society lived, nor the premises on which his knowledge of the world was based. He had no reason to believe that the 'state of innocence' had survived among the Indians of the Antilles. The primitivist virtues of these people were, he knew, only on the surface. Not far beneath the seeming harmony of Indian life he found those unnatural and disruptive customs which are the mark of all 'barbarian' peoples.

All Indians, for instance, lived together in one hut which meant, of course, that they failed to preserve the proper physical distance between persons of different social status, the distance between husband and wife, between parents and children.[114] The Indians, furthermore, wore no clothes, which increased intimacy and encouraged promiscuity; and the men took several wives. Their nakedness, communal life and ignorance of true marriage made the women generous with their favours. 'They give themselves', Palacios Rubios recorded, 'readily, considering it shameful to deny themselves.'[115] As a consequence of such 'liberality' descent in Indian society was through the female line, because, he thought, only the women were in a position to identify the offspring. This conclusion, like Oviedo's assumption that the same descent system was the consequence of a 'natural' taboo against incest, is an obvious attempt to make sense of a matrilineal and possibly even matrilocal society in terms of European sexual ethics.[116]

Underlying Palacios Rubios's critique of Amerindian sexual life was the tacit assumption, made by all Europeans at the time, and for centuries to come, that the origins of civil society were to be found in the family and, furthermore, in a family whose natural ruler was the father. Any community where, because there was no marriage, there was no proper family structure, and where women ruled over such loose unions as did exist (in the crucial sense that they were responsible for the education of the children), was not only guilty of sanctioning un-natural practices, it was no community at all but a mere horde.[117]

This horde had no true religion either. Some Indians, claimed Palacios Rubios, in a last bid to preserve the early optimistic belief in the American *tabula rasa*, may have 'observed the precepts of the natural law and, naturally, illuminated by a certain light of reason, have venerated and paid homage to a single God'.[118] But they were few: most Indians were either simple idolaters or mere hedonists.

These broad observations were, for Palacios Rubios, sufficient to establish the fact of the Indians' barbarism. Though they may not be as savage as the Turks, who are 'almost like animals devoid of reason',[119] the life-style of the Indians would seem nevertheless to indicate that they were mentally incapacitated. Though they live in a state of in-vincible ignorance,[120] had they been a more worthwhile race God would surely have taken pity on them before now and have sent them missionaries, as he sent Saint Peter to Cornelius, Saint Paul to the Corinthians and Saint Augustine to the English.[121] What then can be the status of such a clearly mediocre race?

The second section of 'De insulanis' sets out to answer this question in the light of the now familiar premise that the world is divided into natural rulers and 'those who are born to serve'.[122]

Certain conclusions follow from this. In the first place there are different kinds of rule. Just as there is an established social hierarchy,[123] whose presence is recognised by all men because it has a counterpart both in the natural and in the supernatural worlds (for even the

Kingdom of Heaven has a political structure),[124] and in which a man's place is, or at least should be, a reflection of the quality of his mind, so, too, there is hierarchy of command. The quality of the rule (*arche*), Aristotle had said, reflects the quality of the thing being ruled (*Pol.* 1254 a 25). A man does not use his donkey as he uses his wife or his children; and it is 'better' to command a man than it is to command a woman, better to command a woman than a child and so on. In Palacios Rubios's world a man was to be judged not only by the number but also by the kind of creatures he was able to control. A king, for instance, was known by the company he kept. Faced with a naked chieftain in Africa, the Venetian Alvise da Ca' da Mosto had recognised him for what he was, not, as he pointed out, because the African had any obvious wealth or even, indeed, a set of clothes, but because 'the ceremony [with which he was attended] and his following of men (*seguito de zente*)' was suitable only for a true monarch.[125]

Each creature, too, has a special function in the community as a whole and each one is allotted a particular task according to his, or her – though Palacios Rubios does not actually use the word – disposition (*diathesis*). Thus, as nature never fails to provide for what is necessary in life[126] there must be those fit only for a life of banausic labour since without anyone to draw its water and hew its wood no society can survive.

The Indians who, on the evidence of their social behaviour, would appear to belong at the very bottom of the social hierarchy, are 'so inept and foolish that they do not know how to rule themselves'. They may thus, 'broadly speaking, be called slaves as those who are almost born to be slaves'.[127]

But only 'broadly speaking' and only 'almost'. Palacios Rubios is very careful how he equates the Indian with the natural slave. As we have seen, Aristotle made it clear that the natural slave's relationship with his master was, in part at least, contractual, for both parties shared the same interests. The cause of the natural slave's servitude also derives from the slave's own disposition, which is something outside the merely human law that actually binds him to his master. We are thus faced with the paradox which is present but never stated directly by Gil Gregorio, that natural slaves, though slaves, are also free men: 'liberi et ingenui'.[128]

This paradox was to be repeated again and again. At one level it is, of course, quite a simple one to resolve and merely depends on how we interpret the word 'free' and its cognates. The slave is not 'free' in the

54

sense that he is able to depart his master's service, because left to his own devices he would only harm himself. Most sixteenth-century males would have said much the same thing about their wives and children and the learned among them could have cited Aristotle in evidence of the truth – both biological and psychological – of their convictions.[129]

But there is another level of discussion, a level at which it becomes possible to ask why the natural slave should have half a mind in the first place. For the paradox that allows a man to be at once both a slave and a free man can only be resolved by reference to the fact that the slave belongs to a different category of *man* from his master, whereas the civil slave, although he too is condemned to a life of drudgery, belongs to the same category. Barbarians, Aristotle had said, could only be noble and be free in their own lands where barbarism was the norm, 'thus implying that there are two sorts of nobility and freedom, the one absolute, the other relative' (*Pol.* 1255 a 35). The same is true of the Indians. Although, as one ecclesiastical official charged with the task of assessing the Indians' capacity for becoming 'civilised' beings phrased it, 'they do not at present have sufficient capacity or understanding (*saber*) to conduct themselves according to our manner and polity (*manera y policia*)...they do have enough understanding, and a little more, to live according to their ancient ways (*por su manera antigua*)',[130] the assumption being, of course, that these ways were no longer valid ones.

In his own world, then, the Indian was a free and independent being; but he lost his authority over his own affairs, and in some sense his humanity too, once he had been brought into contact with civilised men. Once, that is, a society had come into being which included both natural slaves *and* natural masters, the slave had to begin to fulfil his function as a slave; but he retained, as Domingo de Soto was later to note, his status as a free agent.[131]

Arguments such as these may seem highly casuistical to the modern reader, and seemed no less so to Las Casas, who scribbled angrily in the margin of Palacios Rubios's manuscript against the passage where the Indians are described as being slaves but 'liberi et ingenui', 'False testimony, a contrived argument for tyranny'.[132] But, casuistical or not, they betray an obvious unease with anything so deterministic as Aristotle's theory which, if strictly applied, would, of course, have denied the Indian the capacity for self-improvement. For although no man is born perfect all true men are born with an innate potential for perfection.[133] The natural slave, on the other hand, comes into this world an incomplete being, and cannot hope to achieve perfection in his own right. If the Indians were natural slaves they would, in effect, be prevented – as Mesa had intimated – from fulfilling themselves as men and thus prevented from achieving salvation through conversion to Christianity.

The paradox which makes of the Indian both a slave and a free agent was also an attempt to save the phenomenon of the harmony of the natural world, which demanded that, within certain well-defined limits, all men must behave alike or resign their claims to being men. It also sought to preserve the perfection of God's creation which required that all men, if they are to be called real men, should have real minds. The power of the human mind may, of course, vary, but not the type. This last point had, as we have seen, been touched on by Bernardo de Mesa. In the years that followed the Burgos *junta*, as the 'affairs of the Indies' grew ever more complex, it was to become the crucial issue in any discussion on the nature of the Indian.

# 4

## From nature's slaves to nature's children

### I

Some of Aristotle's psychology might strike us today as, at best, implausible; and many modern commentators have had understandable difficulties in imagining a creature who is somehow 'sharing' a faculty of the mind without being in possession of it.[1] The Spanish schoolmen I shall be considering in this chapter were to have similar problems with this aspect of Aristotle's hypothesis; but the supposition that the Indian was a creature whose slavery was intrinsic to his whole being seemed, at least on first examination, to offer a much-needed explanation of the *nature* of the Indian which made of him a recognisable, even a useful part of God's creation. The efforts of Mair, Gregorio, Mesa and Palacios Rubios to find a place for the Indian in the Aristotelian universe did not, however, go very far; and with the composition of 'De insulanis' in 1513 they seem for a while to have ceased altogether. The impassioned encounters between the 'pro' and the 'anti' Indian factions which took place in Salamanca in 1518, in Barcelona in 1519 and in La Coruña in 1520 seem, so far as one can tell from the fragmentary evidence, to have been restricted to legal squabbles and disputes over the proper methods of evangelisation.[2] These meetings were bitter but they were also inconclusive. Even the most widely reported of them – the clash between Juan de Quevedo, bishop of Darién and Bartolomé de Las Casas in 1519 – resulted, through each man's wilful misreading of Aristotle or through Quevedo's failure, in the words of Las Casas, 'to penetrate to the marrow of his [Aristotle's] theory', in little more than metaphorical abuse.[3]

In the late 1520s, however, the situation began to change. As more and more information was made available, the inhabitants of the Indies, their flora and fauna, together with the political consequences and possible injustices of the conquests of the new lands, became a subject of increasing public interest. The famous *Cartas de relación* of Hernán

57

Cortés appeared in several editions and five languages between 1522 and 1525. Gonzalo Fernández de Oviedo's *Sumario de la natural historia de las Indias* was first printed in 1526, offering the curious reader a mixture of botany, zoology and ethnography. Peter Martyr's *De orbe novo*, the first complete 'history' of the new world for the learned public, was issued in 1530. In 1534 Francisco Jerez's *Verdadera relación de la conquista del Perú* was printed in Spanish, German and French; and a year later the first part of Oviedo's *Historia general y natural de las Indias* appeared in Seville, a work which was to provide most of the members of the 'anti' Indian faction with their ammunition for years to come.[4]

Between 1522 and 1535 all the major texts (with the exception of López de Gómara's *Historia general de las Indias*, which did not appear until 1552) that were to be cited as empirical evidence in the ensuing debates over the nature of the Indians had been printed. Though few in number and modest in scope compared with the works that were written at the end of the century – works, for instance, such as Antonio de Herrera's massive *Decades* (1601–15) and Juan de Torquemada's *Monarchía indiana* (1615) – they nevertheless offered the European reader a diverse, not to say conflicting, picture of the American world from the baroque splendours of Montezuma's 'court' to the squalor of the agave huts of Hispaniola.

The main reason for this increased interest in the American Indian and his world is obvious enough. In 1513, when Palacios Rubios wrote his 'Libellus', the Spaniards occupied only a handful of islands in the Caribbean – Hispaniola, Cuba, Jamaica and Puerto Rico – and some scattered locations on the mainland.

The peoples who inhabited these places, the Circum-Caribbean tribes as they are known, lived, for the most part, in loose-knit communities with no real leaders, no technology, no personal property and frequently no clothes. The Europeans who encountered them found it very difficult to take seriously as human beings creatures whose social presence and personal appearance was so strikingly unfamiliar. By 1532, however, the great Amerindian 'empires' of Mexico and Peru had both been discovered. The conquests of Hernán Cortés in 1519–22 and of Francisco Pizarro in 1531–2 revealed to Europeans, for the first time, the existence of highly developed native American cultures. Though the societies of the Mexica and the Inca were in many respects neolithic ones and far removed in reality from the oriental fantasies portrayed in Cortés's *Segunda carta de relación*, they belonged, nevertheless, to a very different, and in European eyes far superior, world to the primitives of the Caribbean. The Mexica and the Inca 'empires' were recognisable polities. They were ruled by a 'nobility' and had, or seemed to have, an economy with markets, a merchant class and even a means of exchange. Their citizens fought organised wars against their neighbours, collected revenues from their dependencies and possessed a structured and ritualistic, if also bloody and idolatrous, form of religion.

None of these things was quite as Spanish observers imagined it to be: but whatever unsuspected forms of barbarism lay hidden beneath the surface, here, at least, were communities which were evidently the work of true men and therefore, perhaps, even worthy of close and detailed examination. There are no 'histories' of the Circum-Caribbean tribes. Works such as Jean de Léry's *Histoire d'un voyage fait en la terre du Brésil* (1578) and André Thevet's *Histoire de deux voyages* though they offer abundant ethnographical information on the Brazilian tribes provide little suggestion of the density or the continuity of Amerindian culture.[5] To write a history of a people required not only some evidence of an historical past, of which the Arawak had but little; it also demanded of the historian that he consider the people he was describing as living in societies which, typologically at least, were comparable to his own. The attitudes of most European observers of the Caribbean tribes, however, are summed up in the observation of Cosimo Brunetti, a wandering Florentine merchant of the seventeenth century, that a people 'without any form of government, deprived of any light of religion or of any form of commerce cannot be the material for much speculation'.[6]

The very size of the Spanish empire after 1532, the huge number of Indians now officially vassals of the Castilian crown, also made the possible illegality of the Spanish conquests more obvious than it had once been. With a far greater number of Indians to abuse and greater prizes to be won, the colonists' excesses grew. And with them grew the indignation of the missionaries and the doubts in the minds of many thinking men, sensitive to the possible rights of non-European peoples, that all this might not have been well done. Sooner or later, the long and bitter debates that had been going on *in camera* since 1513 were bound to appear in the open.

2

There was also another and very different reason for the new wave of intellectual speculation on the nature and the status of the Amerindian which began in the mid-1530s. The years around 1520–30 mark the beginning of a major change in direction in the intellectual life of Spain. For these were the early years of a new movement in theology, logic and the law, whose creators have come to be known as the 'School of Salamanca'.[7] The members of this 'School' from the generation of the Dominicans Francisco de Vitoria (c. 1492–1546), Domingo de Soto (1494–1560) and Melchor Cano (1509–60) to that of the Jesuits Francisco Suárez (1548–1617) and Luis de Molina (1535–1600) were to influence, and in many areas substantially restructure, the theological thinking of Catholic Europe. Their learning was immense and their interests, which ranged from economic theory to the laws of motion, from eschatology to the law of contract, practically unlimited. But it was in theology, jurisprudence and moral philosophy that their achievements were the most far reaching.

The members of this 'School', who often displayed a clear sense of their identity as a group, were united in having either been trained in Salamanca, or having spent most of their working life there. Most of them were united, too, in being Dominicans and in having at some stage in their career passed through the house of San Gregorio at Valladolid. The 'School' also had a single master, for all its members had been either pupils, or pupils of pupils, of Francisco de Vitoria. 'In so far as we are learned, prudent and elegant', wrote Melchor Cano of his generation, 'we are so because we follow this outstanding man, whose work is an admirable model for every one of those things, and we emulate his precepts and his examples.'[8]

Vitoria, who occupied the Prime chair of theology at Salamanca from 1529 until his death in 1546, had studied at the Collège de Saint Jacques at Paris between 1507 and 1522. There he had read logic under such pupils of John Mair as Juan de Celaya and Juan de Fenario and theology with the Fleming Peter Crockaert, who seems to have been responsible for instructing him in the theology of Thomas Aquinas, whose powerful influence was to determine both the scope and the method of all his later work.[9]

When Vitoria returned to Spain in 1523 he came with a wide knowledge of the 'new' theology of the Paris schools; and it was the injection of this into the moribund body of the theology faculties of Salamanca, and later of Alcalá and Coimbra, which gave the 'School of Salamanca' both its creative energy and its intellectual cohesion.

Although Vitoria was far from being the 'humanist' that many historians have attempted to make of him (he regarded Lefèvre d'Etaples as a 'heretic'[10] and looked upon Erasmus, whose works he helped to have condemned in 1527, as a dangerous jumped-up grammarian[11]), he acknowledged, as Mair had done before him, the urgent need to extend the scope of theological inquiry. This was to be achieved through a greater emphasis on moral philosophy and by turning away from narrowly theological problems to the ethical concerns which troubled the everyday lives of men.

The School of Salamanca was also a 'school' in the sense that all its members shared the same preoccupation with the need to describe and explain the natural world, and man's place within it, in the same rationalistic terms as Aquinas himself had used in the *Summa contra gentiles*. The truth of the Gospels and the Decalogue, the primacy of the normative behaviour of Christians and the rightness of the political and social institutions of Europe had all to be defended, without recourse to arguments from revelation, as the inescapable conclusions of the rational mind drawing upon certain self-evident first principles.

In practice this meant that their principal task, as they saw it, was to provide an exegesis of the law of nature – the *ius naturae*. For Saint Thomas the law of nature was the efficient cause which underpinned man's relationship with the world about him and governed every practice in human society. It alone could provide the basis for ethical judgments in those areas where no previous rulings exist, just as it offered a rational explanation for all existing ruling, from the sweeping injunctions of the Decalogue to mere sumptuary regulations.

The law of nature is not, however, a codified body of precepts ('there has never been a doctor of natural law', Cano once observed, 'each man is obliged to teach the truth [for himself]')[12] but a system of ethics, a theory in part epistemological, in part sociological, about the mechanisms which permit men to make moral decisions. In its simplest form it consists of a number of 'clear and simple ideas',[13] the *prima praecepta* implanted by God at the creation *in cordibus hominum*,[14] to enable man to encompass his end *qua* man. It is a form of illumination granted to *all* true men, whether they be pagans or Christians, an instrument of cognition which allows man to 'see' the world as it is, to distinguish between good and evil and to act accordingly. It is thus, in a very real sense, a part of his being (*ens*)[15] as a living creature, and it could plausibly be argued that any creature which did not manifest an awareness of it was not a man. For such is the constitution of the human mind that man, unlike all other animals, 'knows' by 'natural reason' what the natural law forbids.[16]

By a process known to the scholastics as 'synderesis'[17] (an approximation to Aristotle's practical syllogism) these *prima praecepta* are translated into secondary precepts which provide the base for all those codes by which men regulate their social behaviour. The greater the number of stages that are interposed between the original cognitive act and the codification of the law, the greater the possible source of error, and consequently the lesser the coercive force, of the final command. But all human laws and norms, if they are just ones, have a discernible origin in some *primum praeceptum* of the law of nature. This applies not only to such obvious laws, as those against killing, theft or adultery, but also to simple customary behaviour: the way a man eats, the modes of address he uses with other members of his group, the clothes he wears and so on.[18] Every aspect of human behaviour can thus be judged natural or unnatural – and since the discovery of secondary principles depends on deduction, also rational or irrational – by abstraction from some highly general first principle.

The most commonly used example of the 'fit' between the first and the second precepts of the *ius naturae* is provided by the commandment 'do unto others as you would have others do unto you'.[19] For as man is by nature a social animal every rule of human conduct, no matter how trivial it might seem, could ultimately be drawn from this premise. It may take the form of a divine commandment but its force is self-evident and it would still be true even if God had not uttered it, or even if God, *per impossibile*, did not exist.[20]

As man is a part of a creation which is both perfect and harmonious, it follows that the laws which control his social world may be observed in the same way, and with the same degree of accuracy, as the behaviour of objects in the material world. For if we assume that all the observed regularities in nature, whether they apply to man or to inanimate matter, are equally decreed by God, there can be no substantive difference between a law which, for instance, forbids the eating of human flesh and a law which decrees that all apples when dropped shall fall. No difference, of course, save one: man, unlike the apple, possesses a will. Only he may choose to defy the law of nature.[21]

The method used for discovering the first principles of the natural law as it applies to man depends, in the first instance, upon a consensus, this being the efficient cause of the whole social body since a consensus derives from the collective *moral* action of its members.[22] Thus, if I, and all my fellow citizens, feel compelled to behave in a certain manner, that manner must be a natural one and consequently any form of behaviour which is contrary to it must be unnatural. Even the veracity of things outside the social order and about which we can acquire no certain knowledge – e.g. whether or not the world is eternal – may similarly be demonstrated by this 'common persuasion'.[23] Anyone who believed that the world might be otherwise arranged than the way the majority of men saw it, was, for the scholastics, either a madman or a jester. The suggestion – to give a specific example – that the education of children is not the natural duty of the father (as opposed to the mother) is simple lunacy; anyone rash enough to propose such a notion could, in the nature of things, only do so as a joke: 'Non serio sed joco diceret', as Vitoria told his students.[24] In most cases (though, as we shall see, not all) the opinion of the majority is nothing short of certain knowledge.

This conviction also derived from a basic premise of the natural law: namely that if what the whole society of men, or even the largest part of it, considers to be true is, in fact, not so, then God must be at fault for it is he who first implanted in man's mind the clear and simple principles by means of which he is able to reach his understanding of the world: 'Our intellect is from God', said Vitoria, 'and if it were to have a natural inclination towards error or falsehood then this would have to be attributed to God.'[25] Any such hypothesis is evidently untenable, therefore 'knowledge is that thing on which all men are in agreement'.[26]

Aquinas's 'ontological divinised natural law'[27] had the effect of liberating the humanity of man from any Christological base. For the Thomists *all* men, whether Christian or not, were human. The notion of *humanitas*, a category which bestowed upon man what Walter Ullmann has called 'a fully autonomous, self-sufficient and independent character',[28] covered both the Christian *homo renatus* and the non-Christian *homo naturalis*. The presence of the natural law in all men meant in effect that there must exist a community of all men.

For Aquinas and his followers the biological and psychological unity of man was taken to be a fact. All men, Aquinas had said, are, so to speak, part of a single body, the harmony of their movements resembling that of the spheres.[29] And if they are unified through their minds, their cultural and social activities must also be as one. 'All men', concluded Jean Bodin in what by the mid-sixteenth century had become a commonplace, 'surprisingly work together in a world state as if it were one and the same city state.'[30]

In a world where all men are thought of as citizens of the same global *polis*, 'man' becomes a term which can only be defined as a set of behavioural norms. For the Thomists man was, quite literally, what man does. Such a conceptual scheme as this, if it is to preserve its integrity, cannot give much room to scepticism or relativism, or permit its adherents much freedom in their definition of categories. Although a wide variety of local customs was accepted as a part of the natural *varietas rerum*, these had all to be contained within certain well-defined boundaries. For the natural law was, to quote Clifford Geertz on another, and not unrelated way of describing the world, 'the conviction that the values one holds are grounded in the structure of reality, that between the way one ought to live and the way things really are there is an unbreakable inner connection'.[31]

If the American Indians were men as Europeans were, then their presence was an obvious challenge to such a view, because their un-structured, often aberrant behaviour was obviously no mere local variant of some well-known pattern. In many respects it was simply 'unnatural'. And a man who, regularly and with no sense of being at fault, acted against nature, could make no unassailable claim to being fully human.

3

The theory of natural law determined the course of the Salamanca theologians' analysis of the 'problem' of the American Indian. It had, of course, been alluded to before, by Gil Gregorio, Bernardo de Mesa and Palacios Rubios, but it was never so sophisticated nor wielded with such confidence as it was in the hands of Vitoria and his successors. The Salamanca School's particular contributions to what Vitoria called 'the affairs of the Indies' were also, unlike those of previous commentators, unsolicited by the crown. Their opinions were expressed, not in the limiting context of a *junta*, but in a series of university lectures. The level of discussion was thus higher than that of most of what we have encountered hitherto and directed at a problem which was thought to require an explanation and a solution rather than a simple legal ruling. Any interpretation of the writings of Vitoria and his successors which views them as either mere scholastic attempts to legitimate the expansionist policies of the crown or – more unsatisfactory still – as a pious and humane bid to challenge Spanish claims to sovereignty in the Indies, is all too likely to miss the main thrust of their arguments. For Vitoria was a theologian, a point on which he was insistent, and theology, unlike the law, is primarily demonstrative rather than deliberative.[32] There is no *conclusion* to Vitoria's *relectio De indis*, beyond the pragmatic observation that in the absence of any just title for the conquest, the whole intellectual inquiry would have to be dropped, because the Spaniards could never in fact abandon the Indies as this would bring 'great detriment to the Spanish princes and is thus unacceptable to us'.[33] For Vitoria the situation in America possessed a self-evident reality, and because of this it had to be explicable in terms of one or other of the precepts of the natural law. Thus the Indian 'problem' became, at base, the problem of the nature of the relations between the different groups of men within, as Vitoria termed it, 'the republic of all the world (*respublica totius orbis*)'.[34]

4

Questions about the nature of the Amerindian and his society and the possibility that the Spanish conquests might have been unjust were first voiced by Vitoria in his lecture course on the *Secunda secundae* for 1526–9, where he discussed the possibility that the anthropophagy of the Indians of the Antilles might have provided the Spaniards with a legitimate reason for enslaving them, but concluded that it had not.[35] In 1534, evidently angered by news of the massacre at Cajamarca and the subsequent imprisonment and execution of the Inca Atahualpa, he wrote to Miguel de Arcos, the Dominican provincial of Andalusia, 'As regards the question of Peru...nothing that comes my way has caused me greater embarrassment than the corruption of benefices and the affairs of the Indies (*cosas de Indias*) which freeze the very blood in my veins.'[36] And, he went on, not even the offer of the see of Toledo, if he had had an ambition for such things (which he clearly had not), could have tempted him to declare that the *perulanos* were innocent of acts of injustice.

In 1537 Vitoria also delivered his *relectio* 'De temperantia' ('On temperance'),[37] a work primarily concerned with dietary norms, which returned, albeit only briefly, to the subject of cannibalism. We also know that at the suggestion of Juan de Zumárraga, bishop of Mexico City, he was chosen by Charles V to find a dozen members of his order 'of good life and example' for the Dominican mission in Mexico, and that in 1539 he was asked by the crown to assess the orthodoxy of 'certain doubtful passages which have arisen concerning the instruction and confession of the natives'.[38]

That same year he delivered his most extended and, so far as we know, his final statement on the subject in the *relectio De indis*, a work which, although it did not appear in print until 1557, eleven years after its author's death, circulated widely in manuscript before that date both inside and outside the university of Salamanca and had a lasting impact on every subsequent discussion of *las cosas de Indias*.[39]

*De indis* set out to find a solution to a problem – what, if any, were the just titles for the conquest of America? – which, Vitoria professed to think, most Spaniards either no longer thought about or had abandoned as insoluble in the light of that famous Aristotelian maxim, 'if one were always deliberating, one would keep on doing so until infinity' (*NE*, 1113 a 3).[40] Furthermore the undoubted charity and justice of both the Catholic Monarchs and Charles V were surely proof enough that 'these matters had been conducted with a clear conscience'.[41] Yet for all that, there were, Vitoria informed his audience, sufficient doubts over the issues in question to warrant their re-examination. So much had been heard, of 'so many massacres, of so many innocent men despoiled and robbed of their possessions, that there is ample reason to question whether all this had been justly done'.[42] The whole issue was, after all, a complex one and clearly could not be resolved by a single ruling. 'The matter of the barbarians. . .is neither so evidently unjust that one may not question whether it is just, nor so obviously just that one may not wonder whether it might be unjust – but seems rather to partake of both justice and injustice (*sed in utram partem videtur habere speciem*).'[43]

Still more important than these uncertainties is the fact that the civil lawyers who had previously addressed themselves to the problem were ill-equipped to deal with it adequately. 'For as those barbarians are not, as I will explain, subject under human justice, their condition cannot be considered under human law, but only under divine law in which the jurists are not sufficiently versed to be able to act on their own.'[44]

The Spaniards' rights to conquer and settle Indian territories, which had always seemed to be a *legal* question, was, in fact, Vitoria was now maintaining, a theological one, for only the theologians were equipped to discuss the divine law. Thus since theology is concerned with essentials not accidents and since its prime business is the analysis and explanation of things about whose reality there can be no doubt (*re certa*),[45] it was perfectly legitimate for the theologian to reopen the Indian question.

By asserting that 'the affairs of the Indies' were a matter for the theologian Vitoria was also, of course, asserting that the issues under examination turned on something more fundamental than the territorial

rights of pagans or the validity of Alexander VI's bulls of donation –
something which, in effect, came very close to being the nature of the
Indian *qua* man and his proper place in the natural world. For the *lex*
(or *ius*) *divina* is the creative *ratio* of God himself, and was conceived by
the Salamanca theologians as a set of norms or *regulae* used by God at
the creation, as an architect – the simile is Soto's – might use a set of
drawings.[46] The natural law is the mediator between this level of divine
intelligence and the rational soul of man.[47] To speak, therefore, of
something belonging to divine law is to imply that that thing is intrinsic
to the whole structure of the creation. If the Indian question was to be
considered as a part of divine law then it became, by definition, a
matter touching on the very nature of man (anthropology) and the
metaphysics of the social order.

Having thus prepared his audience, Vitoria went on to examine first
the titles of conquest which he considered to be unjust and then those
which he held to be just. His treatment of the question of natural
slavery, on which I shall concentrate in what follows, is divided between
both these sections for reasons which will eventually become clear.

## 5

There are, Vitoria began, only four possible reasons for denying that
the Indians had possessed true *dominium* over their affairs before the
arrival of the Christians and might thus legitimately be deprived of
their natural rights. These are, 'either because they are sinners or
because they are infidels; either because they are foolish (*amentes*) or
because they are irrational beings (*irrationales*)'.[48] The first of these
categories implies the assumption of an old heresy, which Vitoria
associates with Wycliff and Hus, that all true *dominium* must be
founded on grace.[49] The second may be discarded as inapplicable since
the Indians were clearly in a state of invincible ignorance before the
arrival of the Spaniards. That leaves categories three and four, both of
which depend on Aristotle's hypothesis that 'there are those who are by
nature slaves, that is those for whom it is better to serve than to rule.
They are those who do not possess sufficient reason even to rule themselves, but only to interpret the orders of their masters and whose
strength lies in their bodies rather than in their minds.'[50] If such
creatures do exist in large numbers – and Vitoria is not committed to
the supposition that they do – then they must be 'these barbarians who
do truly seem to be very little different from brute animals and who are
incapable of ruling [themselves]'.[51] But such a hypothesis raises deeper

problems. Animals and other *irrationales* 'belong' to men absolutely as members of an inferior species, which is why they may be hunted 'even for pleasure'.[52] The fact that these beast-machines are alive is immaterial since the only part of any living body to possess a transcendent quality is the rational soul; and this, of course, is unique to man. But it was clear to Vitoria from the reports he had received from America – and someone in his position was doubtless in receipt of detailed information from Dominican missionaries in the field – that the Indians were not simply *irrationales* or some other species of beast-men. As he had written to Arcos five years earlier, 'If the Indians were not men, but monkeys, they would be incapable of injury.'[53] They would also be Spanish property since animals have no territorial rights, and the whole matter would be a simple question of human law. But any common-sense observation would be enough to demonstrate that 'these are men (*sunt illi homines*)'.[54]

Nor are the Indians simpletons (*amentes*), the mentally subnormal who are rational only in a limited mechanical sense. For simpletons, like cripples and other deformed creatures, are an aberration of nature – *malum naturale* in Soto's phrase[55] – if only in the sense that being crippled is contrary to the natural way of walking, and being a simpleton is contrary to man's natural way of reasoning. But the Indians, Vitoria concluded, clearly do have the use of reason, *pro suo modo*. They possess, that is, 'a certain rational order (*ordo*) in their affairs', an *ordo* which is similar to that observed by other men and which finds expression in the following things: 'they have properly organised cities, a recognisable form of marriage, magistrates, rulers, laws, industry (*opificia*), commerce, all of which require the use of reason. *Item*, they have a form of religion.'[56]

Vitoria was addressing a learned audience skilled in supplying the references, explicit and implicit, on which the substance, and in many cases the coherence, of the lecturer's discourse relied. They would have known that, in the first place, this simple list is a modified version of the one provided by Aristotle in *Pol.* 1328 b 5ff., and, in the second, that each item on it can be linked to one or another theoretical assumption about the necessary conditions for the true civil society. For they are *topoi*, commonplaces, *argumentorum sedes*, in Quintillian's memorable phrase,[57] and to Vitoria's audience they would have been instantly recognisable as the pieces of a complete picture of the social order as God had intended it to be.

First, and most obviously, there was the city. This was not merely a place, though physical structure, even physical location, contributed to the definition (no-one would call a cluster of mud huts a city); it was for Vitoria, as it had been for Aristotle, a metonym for the entire human community, the largest, most perfect unit of society, the only place where the practice of virtue and the pursuit of happiness, which are man's purpose, his *telos*, are at all possible.[58] 'It comes into being', said Aristotle, 'for the sake of bare existence, but when it comes into being it is for the good life' (*Pol.* 1252 b 29ff.). Man is born for citizenship, he is *phusei politikon* (*NE*, 1097 b 7–11) and life in an organised community is not, for him, a simple preference or even a mere means of protection in a world where he is often physically weaker than his potential enemies;[59] it is a response to a psychological law of motion which 'drives' him to form communities.[60] Outside the city there is scope neither for that *hominium consortia* on which all friendship (the highest of the purely human virtues) is based,[61] nor the possibility of acquiring true knowledge of the world since, as we have seen, knowledge depends on a consensus and this can only be achieved when men live in close and structured proximity with one another.[62]

This was the gist of the classical view of the constitution of the city, the view, as Soto phrased it, of the 'secular philosopher'.[63] Once, however, the inhabitants of the city become Christians, the *polis* is transformed into a spiritual community with a quasi-mystical presence.[64]

Vitoria, in common with most neo-Aristotelians, thought of the city and the 'social body' itself – what we might call the state – as coterminous.[65] A human group becomes a *civis* once it begins to live an organised political life. But although this form of association exists independent of any physical reality – exists, and has always existed as a *regula* in the mind of God – it nevertheless has a distinctly human history. Men have not always lived in cities, and some men, the 'barbarians' among them, still do not do so. Like the living organism which they resemble, civil communities also have a cycle of growth and decay, and any attempt to explain the history of this cycle traditionally began with an account of the patterns of behaviour natural to man in his pre-social condition.

Men have always, it was believed, lived monogamous lives by nature.[66] Even at their most primitive they created families and cared for the welfare and the education of their children. Necessity, their own physical inability to cope single-handed with the exigencies of a hostile environment, first drove them together for protection into wandering bands.[67] Later, these bands grouped themselves together into larger aggregates and from the merger of these the true *polis* was created. The force which first persuaded men to take the crucial step from band to phratry was eloquence, the power of language. The most frequently cited account of this comes from Cicero's *De inventione* (1.2.2):

Men were scattered in the fields and hidden in sylvan retreats when he [the first orator] assembled and gathered them in accordance with a plan; he introduced them to every useful and honourable occupation, though they cried out against it at first because of its novelty, and when through reason and eloquence they had listened with greater attention, he transformed them from wild savages into a kind of gentle folk.

The emphasis placed on the role of language in the formation of the human community was a commonplace of much Greek and later Roman thought. Its significance lies in the fact that speech and the perception of right and wrong are treated as relative precepts (*Pol.* 1253 a 14–17), which are unique to man in relation to all other animals (*De anima*, 414 b 18–19) whose natures extend only so far as the appreciation (*aisthesis*) of pleasure and pain. Not only was the concept of 'barbarism' in origin a linguistic one but, as we shall see, the evaluation of Indian languages played a crucial role in assessing the status of their users.

All true human societies, in addition to their ability to act together in *consortium*, possess an inherent political structure, similar in form to the political order of the Kingdom of Heaven. This originated with the hierarchical arrangement of the family: father, mother, and finally children; and it is capable of generating for itself an irresistible force for order, what Vitoria called the 'vix ordinatrix'.[68] For just as the human body would not be able to survive if all its members were of equal importance and uncoordinated, so the city, which is similarly organic, could not hope to survive intact, or to function as a community, if all its members were of equal status. Thus although the political body is in essence a *corpus mysticorum* as a physical reality, as a body of men living in a specific place and observing specific laws which require both promulgation and enforcement, it was the creation of a single human individual. This individual was usually identified by Christians as Nimrod.[69]

The city, therefore, is the natural mode of habitation for men. Those who choose to live outside it or, like Timon,[70] to leave it of their own free will, are either beasts or the Christian equivalent of Aristotle's heroes – angels.[71] Long before the Spaniards encountered the Indians, failure to build cities had been seen as incontrovertible proof of barbarism. 'They viewed the treasures of the city with no ambition', said Gerald of Wales of the ancient Irish, 'and refused the right and responsibilities of civil life. Hence they did not abandon the life of the woods and pastures which they had led up to then.'[72]

It was with precisely the same set of standards in mind that the Italian polymath Giovanni Botero, in his history of man's city-building career, later approached the Brazilian Indians. The causes of their barbarism (which was evident in, among other things, their apparent inability to learn Latin), could be found, he said, in their 'inhospitable dwellings' and scattered way of life, their failure, in short, to build for themselves the cities that would convert them into civil beings.[73]

The belief that the city was a necessary condition of the civilised life – which in origin at least was by definition a life spent in cities – had thus a powerful theoretical base. But it was also rooted in experience. For medieval and early-modern Europe had inherited from the late Roman world, the world of Saint Augustine (for whom both the human and the celestial realms had been conceived of as cities), a strongly urban character. This the Spaniards did their best to export to the new world, setting up *ciudades* and *villa*s to mark the progress of their conquests. These 'cities' frequently rose and fell in a week, but their importance lay in the fact that they were, in a sense, deemed to exist even when they possessed no physical presence and thus to represent the king and emperor and with them the forward march of Spanish civilisation.

With such presuppositions constantly in their minds, whether consciously or unconsciously, it is no wonder that for Europeans the great 'cities' of the Mexica and the Inca, which Cortés compared to Seville and Cordoba,[74] Toribio de Motolinía to Jerusalem and Babylon,[75] and Garcilaso de la Vega to Rome,[76] were the object of such attention. Clearly any race which could build such places – and it was obvious to most they *had* been built by Indians[77] – could not be the barbarians Aristotle had classified as natural slaves.[78]

The other signs of civility which Vitoria attributes to the Indians follow inevitably from this supposed ability to create cities. The family was, of course, regarded as the basis for every social group,[79] as every civil society was created from an aggregation of progressively larger units of which the family was the first, and the city the last stage in the continuum. 'Magistrates, rulers and laws' were vital to the existence of any city. Without such things the all-embracing *vix ordinatrix* would have no obvious means of expression, and there would be no channel through which the institutions of the community as a whole, its collective understanding of the law of nature, could be translated and promulgated as commands. For, as Vitoria said, citing an Aristotelian commonplace (*Pol.* 1280 b 35ff.), 'the end of the city is peace and the laws that are necessary for the good life'.[80] Laws clearly exist for the purpose of making men into good citizens. 'Thus', wrote Soto, echoing another familiar axiom, 'the effect of the law is to make men mindful and diligent (*studiosus et probos*).'[81]

So, too, with rulers. Society is, by nature, hierarchical, as the Aristotelians never tired of saying, and the advanced Indian communities had, on the surface at least, achieved an ordered society ruled from above by an elected monarch who was rigidly separated from the mass of the people, and attended with the ceremony Europeans recognised as the mark of kingship. Descriptions of the Mexica and the Inca from those who had been exposed to the ancient Indian world, if only at the very moment of its collapse, dwell on Indian ceremonial, Indian ritual and the power with which the Indian 'lords' ruled over their peoples.[82] The plebeians respected the nobles, the young respected the old, claimed Juan de Palafox y Mendoza, bishop of Puebla, in his curious little treatise on Indian virtues, 'their courtesy is very great, because they are very observant in the ceremonies by which they revere and venerate their superiors'.[83]

The military capabilities and what the Spaniards frequently saw – when they were not attempting to prove that they were tyrannical usurpers – as the civilising mission of the Inca 'emperors' were similarly regarded with respect, sometimes even with awe. They had, concluded Hernando de Santillán, 'forms of government so good that they might be praised or even imitated'.[84]

The ability to build cities, the existence of families, the rule by an elite, the presence of laws and of a judiciary to enforce them, all these were obviously essential for the creation of a civil community. The remaining items on Vitoria's list, industry, commerce and religion, are a rather different measure of Indian capacity.

They are all evidence of the power of man's speculative intellect, the instrument which allows him alone among God's creatures to exploit the potential in the natural world.[85] Industry and commerce are both 'mechanical arts', things created (*techne*), whose purpose is to adapt the environment to meet man's very special needs. It was a common assumption, implicit for instance in Aristotle's much-quoted hierarchy of the means of subsistence (*Pol.* 1256 a 30ff.), that the more gifted, the more hard-working a man was, the more splendid would be the material culture in which he lived. On the basis of this simple thesis it became possible to construct an entire hierarchy of occupations, building materials, clothes, types of food and so on. Stone, for instance, was more 'noble' than wood and wood more noble than mud. The Indians who could construct stone buildings were evidently more advanced than those who lived in adobe huts. It was, wrote Las Casas, 'no small indication of their sagacity (*prudencia*) and good order (*buena policía*)' that these peoples were able to build 'domed buildings and quasi-pyramids...and buildings on hills and mountains'.[86] But even if built of stone these edifices might still be only primitive adaptations of a natural material. Man's gift for creation must be observed as much in architectural *inventio* as in the simple skills of stone masonry. José de Acosta tells how, when a group of Indians observed the Spaniards building a bridge on arches over the river Jauja in Peru, they were awestruck and declared 'truly we must serve these men for they do indeed seem to be children of the sun'.[87] The story must surely be apocryphal but it sums up well enough the European attitude towards technology. More even than the canon and the swords such things as the ability to throw arched bridges across a river demonstrated the superior knowledge of the more advanced civilisations.

For most Europeans, the measure of civilisation could be found, too, not only in the dynamics of the arch, but also in mere complexity.[88] The more complex a man's way of life the more civilised he became. The inversion of this image of man as an essentially complex – and complexity-seeking – organism was to be found, of course, in the so-called 'Golden Age' or 'age of the natural law'.[89] In these quasi-mythical periods men had depended for their survival, as did all other animal species, merely on what nature produced. Whether a man in the state of nature was judged a fortunate being whose simplicity all civil men should try to emulate as best they could within the constrictions of their artificial world, or, in Hobbes's famous description, one whose life could only be 'solitary, nasty, brutish and short',[90] the myth of 'natural man' provided an archetypal image of what uncultured human nature was like.

For Vitoria, however, natural man had perished long ago. He had been cut off by an historical event of cataclysmic proportions: the Flood. After the Flood men had had to exploit their intellectual resources which, in the age of the natural law, they had had no reason to do. There was now no going back nor even any lingering behind.

To use Vitoria's own classifiers, the 'age of the natural law' had been an age of vegetarians, the modern age was an age of cooked-meat eaters.[91] Those Indians who appeared to live in primitivist conditions did so not because they lived in some alternative world but because they had failed to understand this world as it really is. The inevitable result was that they spent their lives not in the blessed state of natural man, but in the miserable existence on the edge of starvation that the ancient historians had ascribed to the earliest civil men.[92]

Post-diliuvial man was a city-dweller, a social creature by natural inclination and dependent for survival upon his ability to make his environment work for him. But the resources of nature are potential rather than actual.[93] Man's unique qualities, his brain, his upright stance, his remarkable hands which can be 'talon, hoof and horn at will' (*De part. an.* 687 a 1) and his ability to communicate discoveries and to record their existence for later generations make him alone capable of exploiting this potential. Animals merely forage on the surface of the planet. Men build on it, dig into it and finally transform it.

The means to this end are tools, crafts, arts, all the varied mechanical activities contained in the word *opificia*. These are the means by which men are able to 'fill up' the deficiencies of nature (*Pol.* 1337 a 2). For nature provides only the materials out of which man creates culture which is *his* unique environment. Man's *scientia*, what Pierre Charron later called 'the controller of nature, of the world, of the world of God',[94] completes and makes perfect what nature has begun (*Physics*, 199 a 5–20).[95]

But each one of the arts had, of course, to be discovered and discovery depended on the power to ratiocinate correctly.

God endowed our understanding [wrote Soto] with the light of [first] principles so that with them we might discover the results and conclusions (*proles et opiniones*) of the several types of sciences, and the diverse arts that there are in stone, in wood, in wool and in other materials which are useful to us, so that we might clothe, protect, feed and amuse ourselves.[96]

Men who failed to benefit by these resources had evidently failed in so far as their speculative intellect was concerned, and failed, too, in some sense, as men, for man is, above all, a discovering and inventive creature. It is precisely his ability to build bridges, weave cloth and forge steel, which makes him a microcosm poised half-way between the natural and the supernatural worlds.

European observers of the technically less sophisticated Indian tribes looked with contempt upon the Indian's inability to exploit his natural habitat. The Portuguese Jesuit Manuel da Nóbrega wrote from Bahia in 1579, surprised at the mystery of God's design in having given 'such a good land for so long to such an uncultivated (*inculta*) people, who know so little, for they have no god and will believe anything they are told'.[97] For Nóbrega such 'primitive' tribes who had failed to benefit from the natural wealth of their environment – even their inability to exploit their (largely imaginary) gold reserves, might be held against them[98] – were evidently so far removed from any understanding of the world of nature that they could not even perceive the necessity for some kind of religious worship, a point to which I shall return.

Indians such as these could hardly be distinguished from the beasts of the jungle. But the Indian groups to whom Vitoria is clearly referring, the Mexica and the Inca, had achieved a higher level of material culture; and there are abundant records of the Spaniards' awareness of this fact. Take for instance the description written by the Franciscan Jacobo de Testera in 1533 as proof of the innate *capacidad* of the Mexican Indians. Though jumbled and unsystematic it is none the less one of the most comprehensive lists of the requirements for the civil life ever compiled.

How can they be incapable, [he wrote,] with such magnificent buildings, with such skill in making intricate things by hand, [with] silversmiths, painters, merchants, tribute collectors; [with] the art of adjudication and [the means] to distribute *per capita* men and services, [with] a gentility of speech, courtesy and style, [the ability] to exaggerate things [i.e. a gift for hyperbole?] to persuade and attract [others] with their services; [with] disputes, feast-days, pleasures, expenses, solemn occasions, marriages, entails (*mayorazgos*), succession rights both *ex testamento* and *ab intestato*, an elective kingship, the punishment of crimes and excesses, [the custom] of going out to receive distinguished persons when they arrive in their villages, feelings of sadness, the ability to weep (*usque ad lacrimas*) and to express gratitude when good manners require it. Finally they are very capable of being trained in the life of ethics, politics and economics [i.e. in the three parts of moral philosophy][99]

Broken down into five main groups of ideas this list reads as follows: (i) The Indians possess developed imitative and speculative skills; they are, in other words, as gifted as any race, in both the mechanical and the liberal arts. Few people who had had prolonged contact with them would have questioned the truth of this observation. 'He who taught men science', wrote the Franciscan Toribio de Motolinía, 'also provided and gave these people great ingenuity and ability.'[100] Not only, he went on, were the Indians able to imitate artefacts, they could sing European music, read and write Latin and paint European pictures. (ii) The Indians are able to communicate – in the widest possible sense – with their fellow men both through trade and through properly modulated linguistic expressions ('gentility of speech, courtesy and style', etc.). (iii) Their social world is articulated in a formal manner ('disputes, feast-days, pleasures, expenses, solemn occasions, marriages') and is (iv) controlled by the same means as the civil communities in Europe, that is, by kings and their legal officers. Finally (v) the Indians possess an awareness of the need to manipulate their 'social space'. The custom of going out to receive a visitor and the existence of regulations governing the precise distance appropriate to men of differing status were common to both Christian and Muslim societies and were consequently regarded as natural to all social men.

These features of the Indian world, these obvious parallels between Indian and European society, indicated to men like Testera that whatever the causes of his past actions, the Indian was fully capable, if properly schooled, of learning to live 'like other men'. Indian groups such as the Mexica and the Inca who were skilled in *opificia* also practised the next item on Vitoria's list, commerce. Exchange and trade, which Cicero and Seneca had classed together with walled cities as man's greatest achievements,[101] possessed for Vitoria and his contemporaries, as they had done for the ancients, more than a simple economic function. For the exchange of goods (*commutatio*) was conceived as a further dimension of the civil association between men. The realities of sixteenth-century economic practice were far removed from the earlier notion of commerce as an extension of gift exchange, so far removed indeed that it was impossible for the missionaries to understand the social importance of the Indian chieftains' lavish and destructive feasts.[102] They interpreted these assertions of power and status merely as evidence of the individual wantonness and failure to appreciate the value of material goods.[103] But for Vitoria (to whom every activity possessed a larger frame of meaning) no less than for Aristotle, all forms of transactions were civil activities functioning, as Edouard Weill has phrased it, 'within the framework of the community'.[104] The *polis* itself depended on proportional reciprocity,[105] as Aristotle himself made clear (*NE*, 1133 a 3–5), which is why the Spanish scholastics were so insistent that it was natural for a man to honour any form of economic transaction and to charge for his goods only the just price. Thus there was a sense in which peoples like the Chichimeca who lived in unstructured groups with no means of exchange, no communication (*conversación*)[106] with other groups – as well as no identifiable social organisation and no material culture – could not be considered a society (*societas*) at all.

Trade between peoples was also a means of establishing what Vitoria called the 'vitae communicatione',[107] the channels along which knowledge – the human consensus – was transmitted from one group to another. The right to keep these channels open was a right of the natural law,[108] partly because human communities can only exist by exchanging the things of which they have a surplus for the things they need; partly because, at a deeper level still, trade is a part of the communication between men, the *consortium hominum*[109] which is the necessary cause of the highest of human virtues, friendship. One of the just titles for conquering the Indians might be, Vitoria thought, that by refusing to 'receive' the Spaniards the Indians were attempting to close these natural lines of communication.[110] By so doing they had revealed the full extent of their barbarism, a point on which Vitoria cited Aeneas's surprise at finding himself refused a landing for his storm-tossed ships by the barbarous Italians.[111] To this he added, in a passage which must have seemed ironic even to his listeners, that as the command 'love thy neighbour' had the force of the natural law, it placed upon the Christian the obligation to love the barbarians. By denying the Christian access to their lands without good reason, the Indians were refusing to be loved and hence violating the law of nature, for of course no man may love another without knowing him.[112]

But even if their attempts to refuse the Spaniards access to their lands could be construed as a sign of barbarism (and at least one of Vitoria's pupils, Diego de Covarrubias, thought the idea an absurd one),[113] it was evident that the Indians – the Mexica and the Inca at least – did trade among themselves. They possessed markets of considerable size which, as Spanish observers duly noted, were organised according to strict rules of law.[114] They even had a class of merchants whose puzzling behaviour and curious rituals men like Sahagún and Motolinía described at considerable length.[115] Clearly these peoples, at least, knew how to exploit those channels of communication which God had provided so that men might improve their environment and their understanding of each other.

Last on Vitoria's list, and most vital of all the requirements for civility, was religion. Sixteenth-century men, no less than modern anthropologists, knew that the structure of a man's beliefs, and the cosmologies and theologies on which these rested, were an integral part of his social world. 'Religion' belonged, as its presence in Vitoria's list makes plain, to the world of invention, since the understanding of truths about God was as much a part of the understanding of the natural world as was the discovery of fire or the plough. It was, indeed, the highest possible manifestation of man's creative reason, since only religion offers access to the deeper mysteries of the universe. 'Religion', observed Louis Le Roy, 'is more natural to men than all his other arts and inventions.'[116] And, as we shall see when we come to consider the work of Acosta, religion – even the false religions of the pagans – like all the other arts displays varying degrees of perfection. Religious observances and social practice were thus observed to be intermeshed and inseparable. 'For the point of religion', wrote André Thevet in 1555 at the beginning of his account of the Tupinamba of Brazil, 'is the first of all, and it is the point at which all peoples begin their government.'[117]

The Franciscans, who sought to dismantle Indian society in order to get at its idolatrous practices, knew what they were doing.[118] The Jesuits, whose approach I shall be discussing in a later chapter, have our admiration for their tolerance and sympathy towards Indian culture. But their attempt to separate the sacred and profane in a society where no such division existed was, from the missionaries' point of view, a disaster.

And just as the social order was assessed by Europeans in terms of the degrees of complexity which it displayed, so too was religion. 'The greater the labour and the difficulty [the worship of the gods] involved', wrote Las Casas in characteristically tortured prose, 'the greater the zeal and religious piety and the reverence for the gods, and thus the more noble their [the Indians'] conception and estimation of them; and consequently this argued for greater judgment and power of reasoning (discurso de razón) in them.'[119]

The kind of tabula rasa Columbus had attributed to the Arawak might, as he had observed, have made their conversion easier.[120] The fact that they recognised (or so he thought) a 'god in heaven' meant that they had at least some understanding of the natural law. But their very simplicity in this, as in other matters, did not say very much for their intellectual capabilities. The religious practices of the Indians of Central and South America, on the other hand, though they might be satanic in inspiration and foul in practice, possessed, none the less, an identifiable structure. The Mexica and the Inca had all the things that Christians understood by the word 'Church': a cult, places of worship and a priesthood – an organisation, that is, which was empowered to mediate between man and God and which played a directive role in the life of the community.[121] In all this the Indians were demonstrating – as Las Casas was later to emphasise – a cultural sophistication in compliance with those Aristotelian requirements for civility which demanded 'care of religion, which is commonly called worship, and a priesthood' (*Pol.* 1328 a 13ff.).[122]

The very size of Indian religious structures,[123] the devotion of the Indian priests, which the friars constantly held up to their brethren as an example they could well do to follow,[124] the presence of 'vestal virgins' and of 'monasteries' which demanded the most strict adherence to a rule of sobriety and sexual abstinence[125] – all of these things were proof that, although the Indians may have wandered very far from the truth, they knew at least what form the truth should take.[126]

## 6

With such a list of attributes before them, Vitoria's audience might be justified in assuming that the Indians lived in a society which fulfilled all the basic requirements for a civil way of life. If this were the case, then on the empirical evidence alone they were not 'barbarians' in Aristotle's sense of the word and hence could not be deprived of their rights and property on the grounds that their culture was one created by men incapable of deliberate choice.

But, of course, the mere presence of social forms says nothing about their quality. And although Vitoria's list may provide sufficient evidence for believing that the Indians were clearly not *irrationales*, nor simpletons (*amentes*), he had not thereby excluded the possibility that they might belong to some third category as yet unspecified.

To be truly civilised men had not only to live an ordered life in cities; they had also to live by laws and customs that derived from the law of nature. Indian society, however, was an obviously ramshackle affair whose members, Diego de Covarrubias later observed, did not even live such integral lives as the Turks who, though Christians often spoke of them as if they were little more than animals, in fact ruled their states in every respect like civilised men, save, of course, for their refusal to observe the laws of Christ.[127]

In the second part of *De indis*, therefore, the part that deals with the supposedly *just* titles for conquest, Vitoria raised the question of whether the Indians, though not natural slaves, might yet be 'so little removed from the foolish (*amentes*) that they are not able to constitute nor administer a legitimate republic in civil or human terms'.[128] This is the seventeenth and final title of the *relectio* which (as we have it) thus begins and ends with the theory of natural slavery, the only heading used by Vitoria which bears directly upon the *nature* of the Indians.

Vitoria is now, of course, offering the *contra* arguments and it was thus not on the positive features of the Indian world that he focused his attention but on the negative ones, not on what Indian societies possessed but on what they did not.

Though doubtful about the full force of his own proposition – 'I do not dare affirm this position', he declared by way of a caveat, 'but neither do I deny it' – Vitoria pointed out in its favour that 'The Indians have neither laws nor magistrates that are adequate (*convenientes*); nor are they capable of governing the household (*rem familiarem*) satis-factorily.'[129]

These, of course, were significant failures. Domestic management was the basis of every other form of government (*Pol.* 1252 b 12ff.); and if the Indians were found wanting on this level, it is little wonder that they were unable to build a satisfactory society. But the laws which the Indians had created and the judiciary they had trained to administer them were to Vitoria's mind 'unsatisfactory', not because they derived from a weak domestic base but because they so obviously failed to perform the function that all true laws must perform. This, of course, was to make those who observed them into good citizens and hence into virtuous men, for virtues, like arts, are acquired by exercising them (*NE* 1103 a 26ff.). Any code which fails to achieve this end is, by definition, a violation of the law of nature and would thus appear to be the work of an unsound mind.[130]

Vitoria's contention that Indian laws were inadequate in this sense hardly required illumination in view of the discussion earlier in the *relectio* of those twin horrors of many Amerindian societies on which most sympathetic views of Indian culture finally came to grief: canni-balism and human sacrifice.[131] The cannibalism, real or supposed, of the American Indians, is so fundamental a part of the European assess-ment of their nature – and, indeed, of the nature of so many other 'barbarian' peoples – that it is worth looking at in some detail.

7

The European interest in man-eating amounts almost to an obsession. Anthropophagi, as they were called before the discovery of America, have played their role in the description of non-European cultures ever since the first Greeks ventured out into the western Mediterranean. Polyphemus and the Laestrygones, who fed off Odysseus's crew (and whom Peter Martyr identified with the unfortunate Arawak),[132] the Achaeans and the Heniochi, who lived on the shores of the Black Sea, the Massagetae and the Padeans (in fact the Birhors) of India, the famed anthropophagi of Pliny, even the ancient Irish and the 'Scots', whose behaviour St Jerome recounted in careful detail – all these races, to name only a few, were thought to possess an insatiable craving for human flesh.[133] All, of course, were in one sense or another outsiders to those who described them; all lived far beyond the limits of the inhabitable world. And so, too, of course, did the Indians.

Classical accounts of man-eating were popularised by Christian encyclopaedists such as St Isidore of Seville and Tertullian[134] and extended to include other races (Tartars, Thracians, Mongols), so that by the end of the fifteenth century the anthropophagi had become a regular part of the topography of exotic lands. When Columbus entered unknown water in 1492 he inevitably made inquiries into the existence of such peoples, just as he asked after the Amazons and the giants which Pierre d'Ailly had led him to believe he would find in the southern latitudes.[135]

On 4 November he was told by a group of obliging Arawak that on an island to the south there lived a race called the 'Caribs' – hence the term cannibalism – 'who eat men'.[136] In addition to a passion for human flesh the Caribs were also, Columbus learnt from his informants (with whom, however, he had no common language), the men who, once a year, 'had intercourse with the women of Matinino...where there is no man'.[137] Columbus had thus successfully located both the anthropophagi and the Amazons. Only the giants still eluded him; but later explorers unfamiliar with mammoth bones would make good his failure.[138]

Accusations of cannibalism contributed to the de-humanisation of the outsider, for men who ate other men were never thought to be quite human. In the minds of many who claimed to have encountered them they were neither culturally, nor indeed physically, like others of their species. Columbus was surprised to find that the Caribs had not been deformed by their foul diet.[139] The English settlers in the short-lived Sagadahoc colony in New England were convinced that their supposedly cannibal neighbours were equipped with a special set of canine teeth three inches long[140] and the Arab merchants of the Sudan described the Azande – the most famous of the African cannibals – as having dog-faces, dog-teeth and dog-tails.[141] The association with dogs as symbols of unselective eating habits is a commonplace.[142] Columbus, for instance, claimed that his Arawak informant described the Caribs as having 'dogs' noses',[143] although the Indian could never have seen a dog.

Man-eating was not only thought to be a cause of physical transformations in the consumer, it was also believed to create an insatiable craving for human flesh. Once hooked on the meat of his own kind, the cannibal would be satisfied by no other. This belief, like so many other aspects of the cannibal myth, occurs in a number of cultures – in Azande accounts of man-eating, for instance, and in Iroquois creation myths[144] – so we may assume it to be the result of inference rather than observation.

Nearly all supposedly eye-witness accounts of Amerindian cannibal rituals follow closely an established pattern. The link with human sacrifice, the propitiatory rites to placate the gods, the orgiastic wine-sodden 'mingling of males with females', the total collapse of an in any case fragile social order so that the proper distinction between the social categories male/female, young/old, kin/non-kin dissolves in a tumble of bodies 'devoid of any sentiment of modesty' and finally in the frenzied consumption of the sacrificial victim, all, or most, of these – details of Livy's account of the Bacchanalia[145] – may be found, *mutatis mutandis*, in most European accounts of Indian cannibal festivities. Not surprisingly they also appear in many pagan accounts of the Christians' 'Thystean feast'. In this travesty of the Eucharist the celebrants were said to venerate the head of a donkey or the genitals of the presiding priest, to slaughter and eat the body of a child and finally to copulate with one another in a darkened room regardless of age, sex or consanguinity. The Christians in their turn went on to accuse witches and many kinds of doctrinal deviants – Paulicias, Bogomiles, Waldesians and most persistently the Jews – of similar acts of cannibalism, animal worship and sexual aberration.[146] The associations in all these fantastical accounts are clearly set out. The 'outsider', whatever the cause of his foreignness, is marked down, not only as a man-eater, but also as one who is willing to violate both the incest taboo and the traditional lines of social demarcation.

Such denunciations are both ancient and widespread, and they are not restricted to Europe. The Arawak who told Columbus that their neighbours were cannibals were defiling a dangerous enemy; so, too, were the Mani of the Gambia,[147] who believed that the Portuguese took so many men away from their coasts each year in order to eat them. Many Africans today still believe, literally as well as metaphorically, that the white men have come to their lands in order to eat their flesh and suck their blood.[148] Accusations of cannibalism have always gone both ways.

The most famous of the Amerindian cannibals were, of course, the Mexica, whose spectacular bouts of human sacrifice were assumed to have been followed by orgiastic feasts on the flesh of the victims. But there were many others. The nomadic Xixime and Chichimeca of northern Mexico, the Guarani of Paraguay and the Maya of the Yucatán were all, at one time or another, accused of being cannibals.[149] So, too, were the Tupinamba of Brazil, who, thanks to the lurid account of a German castaway called Hans Standen,[150] earned themselves a fearsome reputation as frenzied man-eaters, prepared, as one Spaniard put it, to 'eat their victims down to the last fingernail'.[151] The Jesuit Manuel da Nóbrega, who lived among them for many years and even wrote a treatise denouncing cannibalism[152] (although he never once pretended to have witnessed the gruesome meals he described), claimed that the Tupinamba's whole existence depended on two things: the possession of women and the killing of their enemies. 'And these', he wrote, 'they inherited from the first and the second man and learnt from him who lived at the beginning of the world when all was homicide.' Because of their closeness to the unrestrained violence of the animal world of Cain, the Tupi, claimed Nóbrega, ate not only men, 'but also fleas and lice and every form of filth'.[153] The link between sexual excess and cannibalism in these claims is a commonplace; so, too, is the association between the eating of human flesh and the eating of filth. Both, as we shall see, form part of a comprehensive evaluation of the significance of the man-eating act.

But why did Indians and other barbarians eat men? It is very likely that, except for survival cannibalism and acts of extreme revenge, the Amerindians at least did not. From the perspective of four hundred years it is easy enough to explain away accusations of cannibalism by 'primitive' peoples as a device to make conquest and exploitation morally legitimate.[154] But everyone in the sixteenth century, even men like Las Casas,[155] seems to have believed these stories of Indian cannibalism. And for them some immediate explanation of the motives behind such anti-social behaviour was urgently required. Two related theories were offered. The first was the supposedly universal human desire for revenge. Eating one's enemies as the ultimate expression of hostility was not an unfamiliar occurrence even in Europe. Galeazzo Maria Sforza had been torn to pieces in Milan in 1476 and his dismembered limbs eaten by a furious crowd.[156] During the Wars of Religion in France worse acts were perpetuated on Catholics by Protestants and on Protestants by Catholics than, as Montaigne observed, any Tupinamba ever visited on his enemies.[157] Parts of butchered Huguenots had been sold publicly in Paris and Lyon in 1572; and in a bizarre act of ritual murder the miraculously preserved body of Saint Fulcran at Lodève was said to have been shot full of holes and eaten at a solemn feast by local Protestants.[158]

The list could be further extended. But as Cornelius de Pauw noted later, the eating of the remains of the Maréchal d'Ancre in 1617 and of the body of Johan de Witt in 1672 did not mean that either Frenchmen in the reign of Louis XIII or seventeenth-century Dutchmen were habitual cannibals.[159] Such acts were not, in Europe, a part of daily life. The revenge killings of tribes like the Tupinamba were, however, assumed to be a significant, indeed a central, feature of their culture. So integral indeed was cannibalism believed to be to their social world that one Jesuit, fearful for the consequences of a too rapid exposure to European norms, argued that 'they should not be dragged too hastily from a practice in which they place their greatest happiness'.[160]

The second motive was the cannibal's supposed need, in the absence of any native livestock, to make good a protein deficiency. Human flesh was merely food. The protein argument (which still appeals to Professor Marvin Harris)[161] conjured up in the sixteenth-century mind the image of human butchers' shops among the Arawak and the Maya, even among the supposedly Christian 'Ethiopians'.[162] Sober-minded royal officials like Tomás López Mendel were fully convinced that the Mexica and the Maya cut up and weighed the limbs of their victims for all the word as if they were 'sheep or pigs or some other animal, because it is meat which they desire and they eat it with pleasure'.[163] And in 1534 the Castilian crown urged Cortés to step up the importation of cattle into Mexico, 'so that they [the Indians] may have meat to eat and with which to support themselves'.[164]

In discussing cannibalism, and particularly the cannibalism of the Indians, Vitoria was dealing with an aspect of 'barbarism' with which his audience would have been entirely familiar. But the problem he faced was not why Indians eat men, but why was it considered to be against the natural law for them to do so? Only the answer to this question would reveal something about the mind of the man-eaters:

and it was their minds with which Vitoria was concerned. 'Eating human flesh', he told his listeners, 'is abominable to all nations which live civilised and not inhuman lives.'[165] The force of this observation could be established by a glance at the historical record. All those peoples – the Laestrygones, the Issidones, the Massagetae – who are known man-eaters have been cited by 'the historians and poets' of the past as evidence of their 'ferocity and inhumanity'. Even among pagans man-eating was held to be abhorrent and, as we have seen, the eating of embryos and 'what is said of Phalaris' (*NE*, 1148 b 19ff.) are signs of bestiality common among the 'barbarians'.[166] The first condition for declaring cannibalism to be 'against nature' had thus been satisfied by an appeal to consensus. If all men 'have held this custom to be a vile one this is because it is so according to natural law'.[167]

But this is clearly not, in itself, sufficient, for it failed to answer the prime question: why have past generations been so insistent in their condemnation of this act and, perhaps more important for the whole attempt to evaluate the sources of Indian behaviour, why have so many 'barbarian' races failed to respond to the demands of the natural law at this particular point?

An answer to the first question is simple enough: cannibalism involves homicide which, since it both violates the sixth commandment and poses a threat to the community as a whole, is clearly against the natural law. Cannibalism also denies the victim his natural right to be buried where he chooses. For Christians, for whom the day of judgment involves the resurrection of the body (albeit in another form), what becomes of the corpse and the ritual which attends its disposal are of crucial importance. Acts of revenge which involve cutting up and scattering – or eating – pieces of a dead man, judicial burning and so on, all reflect, in their different ways, an ambiguous, and always disconcerting, preoccupation with physical presence of the body in a religion which insists – both theologically and sacramentally – on the transcendence of the soul.[168]

But despite the Christian concern with burial and the sanctity of the human body these are only the *a posteriori* reasons why cannibalism is unnatural. The central reason why civilised men do not eat each other operates at a deeper level.

For Vitoria cannibalism was, above all else, a failure to distinguish what is fitting as food from what is not. Cannibals were guilty not only of evidently anti-social acts: in eating their fellow men they were committing a simple, but radical, category mistake.[169] God created the natural world for the sole use of man, for man is the most perfect of living beings and the universe is, of course, so constructed that 'the imperfect creature falls to the use of the perfect, as material does to form or plants do to animals'.[170] Man himself, who stands on the boundary between the material and the spiritual worlds, is God's 'creature', for only God (and the Heavenly Host) are more perfect than he. Men, therefore, can 'belong' to no other being but God. Certain men may be subject to other men in such a way that they have no freedom of their own whatsoever; but although slaves, they still do not 'belong' to their masters as do the members of the sub-human stages in the scale of being.[171] And because they do not belong to them they may not be eaten by them. The social order, which determines men's relationship to each other, is natural and therefore modelled on the natural hierarchy; but it does not, because of that, condition the ontological associations between human beings. Men remain men even when they are slaves.

When eating one another cannibals were not only committing the sin of ferocity (*peccatum ferocitas*)[172] by breaking the law of nature which forbade the killing of innocent men; they were also violating the hierarchical divisions of the creation. For in the nature of things, no man may possess another so absolutely that he may make use of him as a foodstuff. 'Man', Vitoria concluded, 'is clearly not a food for man.'[173]

By thus failing to perceive that for all living creatures, foodstuffs are confined to organisms which live on levels lower than that of the consumer, the cannibals were clearly behaving in an unhuman and hence unnatural way. Like the two sexual crimes – sodomy and bestiality – of which the Indians were also accused (a point to which I shall return), their cannibalism demonstrated that they could not clearly distinguish between the rigid and self-defining categories into which the natural world was divided. The Indian could not see that other human beings were not, for him, a natural food any more than he could see that animals or creatures of the same sex were not his natural mates.[174]

Cannibalism, sodomy and bestiality all offended man's rational nature. But they were also an abuse at a lower level, for man is, as Soto said, a creature of three worlds, a living thing among living things, an animal among animals and finally, uniquely, a man.[175] By committing acts which, so it was supposed, even the brute beasts did not commit, the Indians were violating the natural order both as men *and* as animals.[176] Indeed only acts such as these might, in the opinion of some of Vitoria's successors, be grounds for describing the Indians as *irrationales*.[177]

The Indians had also demonstrated in another related way their simple though drastic failure to interpret the natural world correctly. Dietary norms, like sexual ones, were a precise measure of a man's power of reason, his ability to conduct himself like a man. At the end of the *quaestio* of *De indis* which we have been discussing Vitoria concluded that 'the same arguments may be applied to these barbarians as to simpletons (*amentes*) because they cannot govern themselves any better than they, and because *their food is no better in quality nor better prepared than that of the wild beasts*' (my italic).[178] For the Indians not only ate men, who were too high in the scale of being to be food, they also ate creatures which were too low.[179] The Indian willingness, as one Jesuit complained of the Xixime of northern Mexico, 'to eat from dawn until dusk. . . without a qualm, rats, snakes, locusts and worms'[180] was a sure sign of their barbarism because by such unselective consumption the Indian revealed, once again, his inability to recognise the divisions between species in the natural world and the proper purpose of each one. Worse still, locusts, worms, fleas and spiders are not only uncooked and improper by virtue of the places where they live; they also belong to the 'lower' species of animals which, in Aristotle's taxonomy, are spontaneously generated (*Hist. an.* 539 b 5–10). Such creatures are an inversion of the world of the higher animals, for when the 'lower' types copulate the law which requires each species to produce something of its own kind is reversed; 'when these copulate a product results which is never the same as the parents' (*Hist. an.* 539 a 22). That men, who were so unselective in their food consumption as to fail to perceive this crucial division in the natural world, were equally prepared to eat their own kind was hardly surprising.[181] Some Indians, according to one man who claimed to have observed them closely, were so indiscriminating that they were willing to slide down the whole length of the natural food chain from men to roots. 'Their bellies', wrote Dr Juan de Cárdenas of the Chichimeca, supposedly the most 'barbarian' of Indian tribes, 'are a sepulchre of human flesh, and this is their principal sustenance and delight. When they lack this food they eat the raw meat of other animals, not caring whether they be snakes, frogs or lizards; and from this they leap to eating roots and certain wild plants.'[182]

The readiness with which the Indians consumed unclean food was also an indication of their failure to respond to the presence of pollution.

Instead of expelling foul substances, the Indians ingested them. Even the more civilised tribes 'eat the fleas from each others' heads'.[183] It was hardly surprising, therefore, that, according to Cárdenas, the wild Chichimeca defecated in public and, 'like beasts, performed in front of one another their carnal acts'.

Unsavoury eating habits were, of course, nothing new. The eating of unclean food had for long been a feature of the barbarians' way of life. Mongols were said to eat dogs, wolves, foxes and mice;[184] the Anglo-Saxons ate their horses[185] and the Troglodytes 'nourished themselves on serpents'.[186]

It is clearly unnatural for men to eat mice and dogs. But there is a further sense in which any diet based on foods other than cooked meat is not unnatural but certainly inappropriate, for cooked meat is the proper fare of those people who live what Vitoria in *De temperantia* called a 'refined and complex way of life'.[187] Primitive men, those who live in the 'age of the natural law', eat only 'what the earth produces', a category of food which, since it exists on a level of the natural scale lower than the animal, is only appropriate for those who live 'a simple life'.[188] Such a life was proper – there is even some reason to believe that it may have been a blessed one – before the Flood, but it is no longer so. Hence Vitoria's rejection of Aquinas's suggestion that vegetarianism may still be man's 'natural' dietary state.[189]

The general drift of Vitoria's argument is that the quality of the thing being eaten reflects the quality of the eater. Thus it is 'better' to eat a cow than a cabbage for precisely the same reason that, as we have seen, it is better to command a woman than a donkey. The better a man is, the better and the more complex will be the things over which he has authority, the food he eats, the house he lives in and so on. The Indians who eat frogs and forage for roots are little different from the brute animals with which they have to compete for their sustenance.

The food of civilised man had therefore to be not only natural but also appropriate to his status. To achieve this it had to be both the right kind of food and correctly prepared. The preparation of food possesses great social significance for most, if not all, cultures. But the Christian case is a special one, since the preparation of a 'food' lies at the very heart of the Christian mystery. At the most elementary level transubstantiation was a miracle which involved the transformation of one kind of food – a wafer – into another – the flesh of Christ himself. Christian theologians were, therefore, very sensitive to the possible spiritual implications that could be attached to the preparation of foods and sensitive, too, about handling the host even before transubstantiation.[190] The link between the divine cult and everyday eating was difficult to define and potentially dangerous, but it was explicit none the less. 'The preparation of the things used in the divine cult', said Vitoria, 'is in some way related to food and drink',[191] which is why only certain kinds of bread are fit to use in the mass. Barley, for instance, is unsuitable for transmutation into the body of Christ, for barley 'is not a food of men but of beasts'.[192]

A clear distinction between prepared and unprepared food had, therefore, a central place in any Christian, and in particular any Christian theologian's, assessment of cultural behaviour. In the Mass the 'preparation' is a ritual one; but in everyday life it consists of cooking.[193] The consumption of raw things – especially of raw living things – was, like nudity, a sign of technological inadequacy, of the barbarian's inability to modify significantly his environment. Perhaps because of this it was thought to be the closest a man could come to the eating of human flesh. For Aristotle, at least, the Achaeans and the Heniochi, who 'eat raw meat and human flesh' (*NE*, 1148 b 22–3), the two acts would seem to have been analogous in kind and identical in significance.

But eating raw things was also, in some sense, 'unnatural'[194] because it indicated a failure to understand that food, like everything else in nature, exists *in potentia* and must suffer change before it becomes actual and hence, in this case, edible. Only milk, observed Las Casas citing Albertus Magnus, may be taken raw, presumably because all men begin their lives by living off it.[195]

In their different ways both cannibalism and the consumption of any food that 'is no better in quality nor better prepared than that of wild beasts' provided evidence of the inability of the Indians and other such barbarians to see the world as it really is: on the one hand, a biological hierarchy, teleological, and in a constant state of 'coming to be and passing away', and on the other, a place where in order to survive and to fulfil the end for which God had intended him, man had to exploit to the full both his moral and his intellectual resources.

Human sacrifice presented similar problems of interpretation to cannibalism. The sacrifice and the eating of men were thought to be closely associated;[196] but here the problem of explanation was complicated rather than resolved by reference to nature's hierarchy. For there is an obvious sense in which we should all sacrifice to God what we hold most dear, and that clearly is human life.[197] Christ, after all, sacrificed himself on the cross.[198]

Las Casas's attempts to portray the sacrifices of the Mexica as little more than misguided piety[199] won few adherents, but they could never be condemned as blasphemous. Furthermore they had biblical support in the stories of Abraham and Jephthah the Gileadite (Judges 11.30–40). Abraham, of course, was prevented from slaying Isaac and Jephthah may have been, as Vitoria claimed, 'foolish in making the promise and impious in carrying it out',[200] but no-one could accuse either man of behaving, or intending to behave, 'unnaturally'. Human sacrifice, indeed, posed a problem which frequently arose in any discussion on the natural law: when two opposing courses of action both seem to be natural, how do we know which one to choose? In this case, thought Vitoria, the choice was clear. The preservation of the distinction between the various levels in the scale of being was more binding than the demand that man should offer up to God all that he most valued. God, argued Vitoria, had provided animals for sacrifice; though by definition lower than men they were far more pleasing as objects of sacrifice, precisely because the Creator had no wish to see the destruction of *his* creations. Human lives 'belong' only to God, and it is in no man's power to destroy what is not his, even in the pursuit of a higher good.[201]

Human sacrifice may not, Vitoria conceded, be unnatural – for the urge to pay proper homage to God, even if that God is not the true one, is undeniably strong – but its practice by the Indians indicated once again that they possessed only a blurred vision of reality, that on crucial matters they had failed to interpret correctly the *prima praecepta* of the law of nature.

8

Crimes such as human sacrifice and cannibalism, especially since they were sanctioned by the laws of the community, were a clear indication that the Indians' mental world was in significant respects a seriously defective one. Further evidence of this was provided by their culture which, said Vitoria in *De indis*, lacked 'all the arts and letters, both the liberal and the mechanical, a diligent system of agriculture (*agricultura diligenti*) or artisans and many other things necessary for human life'.[202]

Here again those who had gathered to hear him were being provided with a highly resonant list of cultural determinants. They describe a hierarchy of occupations beginning with the highest and ending with the lowest. I shall reverse the order and move up from agriculture to the liberal arts.

Every level of civility which men may achieve in the organisation of the community has a corresponding level of cultural, or technological, achievement. The clearest measure of this (apart from language, which I shall come to later) is the means by which the society acquires its food supply. 'It is the distribution of land', wrote Montesquieu, 'which is responsible for the increase in the civil code. Among nations where there is no such distribution there are very few civil laws.'[203] It was an ancient belief. The complete dependence of early man on 'what the earth produced' prevented him from forming civil associations. The hunters and the gatherers merely foraged on the surface of the planet. So, too, in a sense, did Aristotle's 'lazy pastoralists' who followed them. Only agriculture can make a man civilised, not only because agriculture is natural to man (*Oec.* 1343 a 25ff.), but because only the agriculturalist tamed the earth; only he converted nature's potential into actuality. All Indian tribes had some form of agriculture; but the single crop culture and the crude use of a planting stick which struck many observers as being in Vitoria's terms not 'diligent' was evidence of only the barest knowledge of how to cultivate the soil.

So too with the mechanical arts. The ability to make things, in particular the tools men require to tame their natural environment, was a further distinction between civilised man and the barbarian. The Mexica and the Inca did, of course, possess considerable artistic and mechanical skills, of which neither Vitoria nor his audience could have been unaware. In the first part of *De indis*, as we have seen, Vitoria himself cited the Indians' *opificia*, as evidence of their rationality. But here, as with Indian laws, magistrates and agriculture, it is the quality of the work that counts, not the simple fact that it exists. The feather-work and the gold which so impressed Dürer and Cosimo de' Medici,[204] were regarded by most Europeans as little more than exotic novelties. What the Indians so obviously lacked in their neolithic world – though Vitoria does not himself say so – was iron. As John Locke was later to observe, the distance that separated his world from that of the Indian could be measured in terms of the 'discovery of one natural body'.[205] For it was the ability to mine and smelt the hard metals that had made the weapons and the machines of European culture possible. Without access to such metals the Indians were permanently thwarted in any natural inclination they might have to progress.

Iron was for many the only 'true' metal. Nicolás Monardes, a natural scientist with long experience of the Americas, rejected the supposed merits of gold and silver as merely founded on 'opinion'. For none of those substances did anything. Iron, on the other hand was the only 'true' metal precisely because it is so crucial in the practice of the arts: 'Without it', he concluded, 'we would not be able to live nor would men be able to exercise their arts and professions.'[206] The Spaniards who described the great stone buildings of the Inca and the Maya may have marvelled at how much had been achieved without the use of iron tools.[207] But it was also recognised that, in the end, these achievements did not add up to an adequate material culture.

The Indians' *opificia* was thus in at least one basic respect inadequate, and without the proper means for the creation of a material culture Indian society had never developed the artisan class whose presence was, as Aristotle had made clear (*Pol.* 1328 b 5ff.), essential for any civil community. It was this class, too, which was doubtless responsible for the creation of those unspecified things that are 'necessary for human life'.

The existence of a stable food supply, the presence of tools and a labouring class capable of using them in the creation of the goods that make life endurable – these are the essentials of any civilised environment. Once this environment has been established it is up to the gifted few to develop what Soto referred to as 'amusement' (*oblectamentum*),[208] the whole life of the mind which is captured by the phrase 'liberal arts'. As Vitoria knew, the 'life according to the intellect is the best and most pleasant' (*NE*, 1178 a 5–6). Only very few men are, of course, capable of reaching this condition; but any society in which such activities are totally unknown must indeed be a 'barbaric' one. The arts, and in particular the use of letters, which in effect meant the ability to record and hence to analyse the world of experience, were an integral part of that much-vaunted modern notion of the *dignitas hominum*. Juan Maldonado, addressing the arts faculty of the university of Burgos in 1545, told his listeners that the Indians provided the proof that men who lived without laws or letters were entirely deprived of their humanity (*humanitatem penitus exuerant*).[209] They went in ignorance of the true nature of the world 'not because they lacked reason, but because they lacked culture, not because they lacked the will to learn or a ready mind, but because they had neither tutors nor teachers'.[210]

Reason, and from reason the ability to create and use language: these were two things which had raised man from barbarism to civility.

To live without letters, Maldonado concluded, employing a well-worn Ciceronian *topos*, was virtually equivalent to not being a man: *humanitatem...renunciare.*[211]

The absence among the Amerindian tribes of 'arts and letters' was, for Vitoria, no less than for Maldonado, proof that, like the wild beasts, Indians lived only in order to go on living. They had yet to arrive at that stage in man's development where they would be able to create for themselves a second world, in which the members of the quasi-mystical body politic are endowed with the ability to work in harmony with one another for the purpose of a higher good.

## 9

Vitoria's two brief surveys of Amerindian culture provided two apparently contradictory pictures of the Indian mind. In part this is because they belong to separate sections of the *De indis* whose arguments proceed from different premises. But only in part, for the 'advanced' Indian cultures did offer a genuine challenge to the classifying habits of the sixteenth-century scholastic. On the one hand such Indians evidently led a way of life which could only be that of rational beings. Gil Gregorio's description of Indians as 'talking animals' and García de Loaysa's belief that they were soulless parrots in human guise might just fit the Arawak;[212] but they clearly did not fit the Mexica, the Inca and the ancestors of the Maya, peoples who had demonstrated their ability to create for themselves a recognisable, if rather primitive, culture. On the other hand it was precisely these peoples, evidently capable in so many respects of interpreting the law of nature as God had intended, who were so shocking in their violation of it. If they were *irrationales* or *amentes*, what could account for their cities, their civil and religious administration and so on? If they were rational men, how could one explain their cannibalism, the human sacrifices, their primitive agricultural techniques and the imitative nature of their 'arts'?

For Vitoria the answer to these questions could be found, once again, in the formal structure of the universe. Like all matter man contains within himself both potentiality and actuality. The Indians, Vitoria had noted in the first part of *De indis*, do not 'err in those matters which are obvious to others'.[213] The mistakes they made were, for the most part, limited to areas which are not immediately obvious, which require, in fact, a degree of trained intellectual perception before they can be 'seen'. Such things would be, for instance, the liberal, and at least some of the mechanical, arts, things which do not, in other words, exist obviously in nature. Of course, truly civilised men have learnt to acquire knowledge in these areas; but the fact that the Indians have not is an indication not that they are irrational but that their rationality is still *in potentia*. 'God and nature', said Vitoria, 'have not failed them in what is necessary for the great majority of the species. Most important for man is reason and the *potentia* that fails *in actu* is useless (*frustra*).'[214]

The utterance is gnomic and may have been garbled in transmission, but the conclusions to be drawn from it are inescapable. If the Indian was, as Vitoria had made clear, fully able to perform some rational acts but *psychologically* incapable of performing others, then his mind must, of necessity, have been frozen in a state of becoming; and any man in this condition would be useless *as a man*. It is, however, inconceivable that any such creatures could exist in a world where, as Vitoria's pupil Domingo de Cuevas explained, echoing Aristotle's much-repeated axiom, *nihil facit frustra*,[215] 'God and nature never create anything that is useless.'[216]

In a sense Vitoria had exposed – though this was clearly not his intention – the major contradiction in Aristotle's original hypothesis. For if the natural slave is incapable, as Aristotle says he is, of participating in a state of happiness (*eudaimonia*), then he must also be incapable of achieving his proper end (*telos*) as a man. If nature never creates anything which is, of itself, incapable of accomplishing its ends – for such a thing would be useless – then the natural slave cannot be a man. By the same argument, the Indian who has demonstrated so many man-like attributes cannot be a natural slave.

By stressing the belief that once reason is present *in potentia* it cannot, however long the process might take, fail to achieve actuality, Vitoria was making much the same point as Bernardo de Mesa had made twenty-six years earlier: if we attempt to apply the category 'natural slave' to any creature we have reason to believe is in fact a man, then the conception of the essential harmony of God's universe is at risk. For in order to be a man in the first place, the Indian must be *in possession* of a faculty of reason and that faculty must be capable of achieving a full state of actuality through moral education.[217]

To attempt to avoid the consequences of Aristotle's argument, as Palacios Rubios had done, by implying that the Indian was neither quite a man nor entirely a natural slave, would now, in the terms established by Vitoria (the need for all natural things to accomplish their ends), be merely to obscure the categories under discussion.

Categories, in particular anthropological ones, must, as Vitoria knew, be decided by criteria that are 'fixed, static and almost indivisible'. Biological and psychological species-distinctions have to be, if they are to be anything at all, as clearly defined as numbers. Add or subtract a unit and you have different number.[218] The same is true of the human brain, which is not a substance that will admit of degrees (*Meta.* 1043 b 33).

Vitoria's implicit insistence that no *man* can be potentially human without being actually so was crucial both for him and for his successors because it touched on the principal factor in their interpretation of the law of nature, its essentiality. For the Thomists the properties of things were not, as they were for the nominalists, wholly dependent on the will of God; but instead an essential part of them. Heat, to use Vitoria's own example, is the essence of fire.[219] It is what distinguishes it from the other elements, and fire would continue to be hot even if there were no God. God could, of course, create a substance that was like fire in all respects save for the fact that it did not burn. But we would be mistaken if we took this to be the *same* substance as fire, for so significant a change in the property of a thing places it in another category. The stuff that did not burn Shadrach, Meshach and Abed-nego in the furnace was not cold fire but a unique element created by God for one special purpose.

Obviously some of the properties of things are more essential to them than others. In mathematics the 'fit' is said to be exact. A triangle is nothing more nor less than a figure with three sides. But in more complex cases a thing may, in fact, contain accidental properties, or attributes which do not substantially affect its essence.[220] The essential property of man is, of course, reason. It is even possible that men may be found in other forms (*Meta.* 1044 a 9–11).[221] Indeed, reasoned Vitoria, God might create a creature which had no eyes, no ears, no legs and lived in the dark, but we should still have to call it a man if it displayed evidence of possessing a rational mind.[222]

Indians, like the limbless, senseless creatures of Vitoria's imagination, differ in many of their properties from other men, but this does not deny them their essential humanity. For a man to be both human *and* incapable of deliberation – for a man to fulfil Aristotle's conditions for natural slavery – he would, in effect, have to live in another world, in a world where the necessary conditions for human life are other than those which we know in this world. Melchor Cano was getting at much the same thing when in a lecture on the *Secunda secundae* delivered some seven years after *De indis*, he said that if the Indians had been natural slaves 'God would have provided some other solution.'[223] But theologians are notoriously uncomfortable with counterfactual questions and Melchor Cano summarily dismissed this one. There is simply no way for the paltry human brain to know what kind of 'other worlds' God could create (or perhaps has already created) if he so chose; but for the Thomists one thing was certain: whatever they might be like they must observe the same laws of probability that apply in this one. Anything else is beyond the realm of possibility and, as Cano informed his audience, 'the arguments of moral philosophy should not be concerned with things that are impossible'. The Indians do not, nor could they, belong to some unimaginable world in which categories were established by wholly unfamiliar criteria. They were men 'and their customs were ordinary ones'.[224]

True natural slaves may yet, of course, exist, along with the wild men, pilosi, satyrs and the like – for the varieties of which nature is capable are infinite – but they will not be, as the Indians are, creatures capable of civilised behaviour, however crude or inchoate that behaviour might be.

I understand [wrote the jurist Diego de Covarrubias in 1547] that his [Aristotle's] words refer to men created by nature to wander aimlessly through the forests, without laws or any form of government, men who are born to serve others as the beasts and wild animals are. But I doubt that the Indians are among these, for on the evidence of those who have travelled among them and have known their institutions and their savagery, one thing is certain, and obvious, that they live in cities, in towns and villages, that they appoint kings whom they obey and institute many other things besides – which proves that they have a knowledge of the mechanical and the moral arts and a knowledge of the things of the world and are provided with reason.[225]

Covarrubias was making much the same general observation about the psychological implications of Indian culture as Vitoria had. Because Indians have, or seem to have, demonstrated by their social organisation that they have access to a knowledge of reality (*res*), they can only belong to the genus *homo sapiens*. The true natural slave, on the other hand, is a frightening marginal creature which could be hunted down like a wild animal, for its very existence was a threat to human nature.[226] But as José de la Peña (1513–64), a long time companion of Las Casas, and Vespers professor of theology at Salamanca, observed, 'no such race (*natio*) has ever been discovered'.[227] The generation to which Peña belonged, that of the theologians who had been the pupils of the pupils of Vitoria, Soto, Domingo Báñez, Martín de Ledesma and finally Suárez, were all of the same opinion.[228] Like one of Aristotle's modern commentators, the School of Salamanca could, in the end, only make the theory of natural slavery logically and morally acceptable by denying the very existence of the creature it was intended to describe.[229]

## 10

Vitoria had clearly demonstrated that the theory of natural slavery could not be used to explain the Indians' frequently 'unnatural' behaviour. But that behaviour still remained to be explained, and explained in a way which offered no threat to the conviction that all true men must be perfectable creatures and that every cause should, in Bernardo de Mesa's words, 'produce its end'. Vitoria's solution to this problem was the obvious one: nothing, he argued, is inherently wrong with the composition of the Indian mind, it is the influences to which it has been subjected that are at fault. 'I believe', he said, 'that if they seem so insensate and foolish (*insensati et habetes*) this comes, for the most part, from their poor and barbarous education.'

In this they were very like the labouring poor of Europe. 'Even among our own people', Vitoria went on, 'we can see many peasants who are little different from brute animals.'[230]

The analogy was an obvious and instructive one. To all educated town-dwelling men the peasantry seemed close in condition, if not in kind, to the animals among which they worked. Like the Indians they were deprived of any real understanding of the world about them. What Voltaire later mockingly described as 'les prétendus sauvages d'Amérique' were in no way inferior to those savages one met every day in the countryside, 'living in huts with their mates and a few animals, ceaselessly exposed to all intemperance of the seasons'.[231] The European peasantry, 'speaking a jargon which no-one in the towns understands, having few ideas and consequently few expressions', had no obvious share in the civil life and were thought to be still less capable of what one observer called 'the superior exercises of the soul'[232] than even the artisan class, precisely because that class, however low it might be, was, none the less a 'people of the city'.[233]

Peasants, like Indians, were thought to be proverbially stupid and thus easily overcome by their passions. Few men could, if pressed, have denied that peasants possessed a fully developed faculty of reason like all other men. But what was abundantly clear to the civilised man was that this faculty was rarely given the opportunity to exercise itself. The observed similarities between peasants and Indians worked, also, both ways. The word 'Indies' soon became a term to describe any environment in which men lived in ignorance of the Christian faith and of the proper modes of human life. Jesuit missionaries spoke constantly of 'these Indies' of Asturias, of Calabria and Sicily, of the Abruzzi, regions where, they claimed, the country people lived like 'savages', polygynous and apparently polytheistic.[234] Little wonder, too, that the word 'Indian' should have rapidly been extended to all men, regardless of their race, who deviated from the orthodox faith – even to such otherwise civilised beings as the Dutch.[235]

Vitoria's simple comparison was echoed by nearly everyone who came into contact with the Indians.[236] The theologian Alonso de la Veracruz, for instance, who had spent many years in Mexico City, pointed out to those who claimed that the Indian was an inferior species of man, that their life-style, like that of Spanish farmers, was due to the fact that they did not live in a true *politia*. Once brought together into political assemblies and housed in cities, their innate ability to govern themselves as human beings became immediately apparent.[237] The minds of men were, in other words, determined almost wholly by the environment in which they lived.

But the peasant who lived 'with the beasts' beyond the city walls was also, like all the masses of the labouring poor, a necessary part of God's design for human society. For, said Soto, using once again Aristotle's body/soul dichotomy, God had created the rich to govern and the poor to labour, 'And this was the wisdom and the providence of God, that there should be rich men who, like the soul, should be able to sustain and rule the poor, and poor men who, like the body, should serve the rich by working the land and performing the other tasks that are necessary for the republic.'[238]

The implications of this statement are clear enough. In an ideal world the elite of any society should be composed of its ablest members, while those over whom they rule provide the banausic labour required by all well-ordered civil communities. The social status and obligations of the poor are very similar to those of the natural slave, with the one fundamental distinction: the poor man is not *innately* inferior to his master; though less gifted, less intelligent, he is none the less capable of observing the *prima praecepta* of the natural law and, with assistance from his masters, even of making the transition to the *secunda praecepta*; he is capable, therefore, of acquiring knowledge and virtue and, in short, of achieving his end *qua* human being. For Vitoria and his successors, the Indian, like the poor peasant, was a man, an inferior sort of man perhaps, but a *homo sapiens*, none the less. As Paul III had asserted in forthright terms in the bull *Sublimus Deus* of 1537, the

98

Indian was perfectly qualified for admission to the *congregatio fidelium* and thus to the possibility of eternal salvation.[239]

There was also a further, and for our purpose more far-reaching, theoretical dimension to Vitoria's analogies. For by insisting that it was education that was responsible for the Indian's behaviour, Vitoria had effectively liberated him from a timeless void of semi-rationality and set him into an historical space where he would be subject to the same laws of intellectual change, progress and decline as other men are, be they Christian or non-Christian, European or non-European.

II

By 'education' Vitoria meant not the simple schooling given to the child – though that too played a part in the formation of the mind – but what Aristotle called habituation (*ethismos*; *NE*, 1103 a 23–6), the training of the 'speculative intellect'[240] to the point where it is able, accurately and without assistance, to deduce the *secunda praecepta* of the law of nature. As we have seen already, the first principles of the law of nature are God-created, exist out of time and are implanted in man at birth (although they will not become visible to him until he has reached a certain age). But the deduction of the *secunda praecepta*, from which all the norms and the promulgated laws of the community derive, depend on the operation of the human intellect, and as this is necessarily an imperfect instrument, it is possible, even for wise men, to arrive at false *praecepta*. Christians, who are guided by revelation, rarely go astray except when they allow themselves to be drawn aside into sin by the machinations of Satan. 'Barbarians' and other pagans, who have no such guidance, do so frequently. Thus the Augustinian chronicler Diego Durán noted that although some Christians may be as dim-witted (*toscos*) as the Indians they will nevertheless be provided with the guidance they require because their minds are rooted in faith. Indians, on the other hand, forced to depend on human intuition (*la fe humana*) are unable to interpret the world correctly and consequently will believe anything they are told. To prove his point Durán cited the many cases of syncretism in post-conquest Indian religious observance. The Indians, he said, were ignorant of the law 'which is fundamental and total, that [no man] may believe in God who worships another god; and this is general to all men and all the races of the world'.[241] The point of this example was to show that, by failing to distinguish clearly between a set of beliefs that were true and another that were false, the partially Christianised Indian was demonstrating, in effect, an inability to

99

perceive what was right and what wrong. Worse still, by conflating the two, he revealed that he was unable even to recognise that right and wrong were different and diametrically opposed things.[242]

'Barbarians' and pagans generally, though they may be guided in many things by the light of natural wisdom, frequently, like Durán's Indians, fail to interpret the law of nature correctly. This, however, is not necessarily because they are, as those like Cardinal García Loaysa would have us believe, men without true minds and hence incapable of syllogising accurately; it is because the natural law, though generally considered to be immutable, is none the less frequently obscured. 'It is possible', commented Soto, 'that there are some barbarians who are so perverse in their customs and so blinded by error that they do not consider what the natural law prohibits to be a sin.'[243] The kind of error to which Soto is referring may occur not only with those precepts which are remote from first principles – such as officious lying and simple fornication – but also with others which are close (such, presumably, as cannibalism) and thus more easily known. 'There are', Soto went on, 'men in the new world (according to reliable information) who permit nefarious crimes against nature and do not hold them to be a sin; for which reason it is possible for governments and peoples who set up laws against nature to exist.'[244] The existence of such groups poses a problem, however. If the consensus is an accurate instrument of cognition, how can it be possible for large groups of men to act against reason? In other words, why and how could the natural law become so deeply obscured? The most persuasive answer lay, as Soto had already suggested, in the coercive force of custom. For men, no less than Lycurgus's dogs,[245] were creatures of the environment in which they were reared. The customs which controlled the unthinking moments of their everyday lives were impressed upon them from above and made acceptable to them by habituation. So deeply ingrained were they thought to be that Vitoria calculated that it would require six hundred years before a custom which, for historical reasons, had ceased to be binding, finally fell out of use.[246] 'The influence of customs (consuetudines) and training', wrote Jean Bodin summing up Aristotle's teaching on the matter, 'is so great in natural and human affairs that generally they develop into habits (mores) and take on the force of nature.' Custom was, indeed, for man a 'second nature'.[247]

The laws and customs of true civil societies, as we have seen, are intended to make their members into good citizens and hence into virtuous men. If the laws and customs of the community are, on the other hand, 'unnatural' ones, the men who observe them will be made wicked rather than good, and will very soon become incapable of following the dictates of reason. Thus the natural law may itself be eroded by habitual action so that 'as regards its secondary precepts and commands it may sometimes be erased from the minds of men'.[248]

This, of course, raises a further question: how is it possible for rational creatures to devise unnatural laws by which to live? The answer is to be found in the ultimately social and human origin of normative practices. Laws and customs are, as we have seen, built up by deduction from the first principles of the law of nature. But before they can become binding all laws, and some customs, have to be promulgated. Promulgation is an historical act dependent on the authority of one man or group of men, the 'ancient legislators' of the race; and not all such men, as Soto warned, had acted in accordance with the natural law.[249] Once promulgation has taken place, however, these ancient observances acquired such enormous authority that it became difficult, if not impossible, for the members of the community to *see* them for what they were without the assistance of some outsider. For false conscience will bind a man as strongly as true. The impulse to follow a 'bad' ruler – if he has some claim to legitimate authority – is as strong as the impulse to follow a 'good' one.[250]

Customs were social dictates and however foolish they might have seemed to an outsider, the insider rarely, if ever, saw any need to question them. When a French traveller asked the Indians about the purpose of the couvade ('une coutume assez particulière') the only answer he received from 'un sauvage de bon sens' was 'because it makes the women more docile and it was introduced long ago'.[251] In other words, they had never seen any reason to wonder why they were practising what was an age-old custom. Modern anthropologists are accustomed to such responses, but to the sixteenth- and seventeenth-century traveller they merely confirmed the view that natural reason is rarely, if ever, capable of overcoming the force of custom. Even when reason asserted itself sufficiently to indicate that something was amiss, it was never strong enough to persuade man to take the drastic step of abandoning age-old practices. The Franciscan Juan de Torquemada noted that some Indians performed rituals 'in secret and hidden places, in high and mountainous regions surrounded by trees and shrubs'. They did this, he believed, because they were rational enough to sense that they should be ashamed of what they were doing and 'wished that no-one should witness their foolish acts'.[252] But before the Christians had arrived they had neither the courage nor the guidance necessary to change them.

Tradition, therefore, and the respect due to one's ancestors, were thought to have a hold over men's minds which, in circumstances where there was no divine guidance, might lead men to act consistently in defiance of the natural law. For, as Las Casas pointed out, a child reared among 'Saracens' could never hope to come to a knowledge of the articles of the Christian faith – and hence to a true understanding of life – 'by the ordinary route...by virtue of the infused habits'. Only by training, by living continuously among Christians, 'by forming an acquired habit', would such a child be led to the truth.[253]

Such a view of the origin of the law and of the role of normative practices in the structure of the community was deeply sympathetic to the strongly conservative character of sixteenth-century political thought in Spain. The laws of the Indians may have been wicked ones, but in defending their right to observe them the Indians were demonstrating a commendable loyalty to their traditions. Even men like Palacios Rubios conceded that Indians had the right to defend their old laws until such times as the folly of them had been made clear.[254]

In the light of such beliefs the missionaries saw their task as primarily one of instruction. The Indians were not Jews or Muslims who had to be forced to accept a religion which their own beliefs held in contempt. They were merely ignorant misguided people who would soon see the light of reason once the baggage of their old way of life had been swept away. Once, that is, the effect of what Soto called the 'humana impedimenta',[255] which had for centuries prevented the Indians from correctly deducing the *secunda praecepta* of the law of nature from the *prima*, was finally lifted, they would be able to see for themselves the rational principles upon which every form of knowledge must rely. For it was clear to most Europeans that the Indians lacked a proper understanding of reality[256] – what is frequently referred to as 'things', *res* – of the formal object of knowledge. They lacked, that is, any *scientia*, because science is precisely the ability to draw conclusions from stated premises and to infer covering laws from such conclusions.[257] For the Thomists this ability springs from a single mental habit[258] which the Indians, because of the peculiar circumstances in which their culture had developed, had lost, and which it was now the task of the Europeans to return to them. They must, as missionaries like Pablo de Arriaga insisted, be educated first in the liberal arts and then in the sciences, including theology.[259] It was, after all, a commonplace, reiterated by Las Casas, by Acosta and by those like them who had some faith in the natural abilities of the Indian mind, that a knowledge of divine things could only be reached once some understanding of the things in the sensible world had been acquired. Even Moses, wrote Acosta, 'who taught us the principles of divine eloquence', could only do so after 'he had trained his unformed mind in all the things of the Egyptians' (i.e. the natural sciences).[260] Only through training his mind to the point where he would be able to interpret correctly the real world of nature in which he lived, would the Indian ever acquire an understanding of the mysteries of the Christian faith.

The method [Las Casas told would-be missionaries] used to lead men to a knowledge of the religion and Christian faith is, or ought to be, similar to that used to lead men to a knowledge of science. The natural method to lead men to [an understanding of] science is by persuading the intellect and [thus] enticing, moving or exciting the will.[261]

The Christian faith was not, as the Jesuit Ludovico Bertonio advised, 'against reason', despite the obvious complexity of its theology. Faith itself is acquired through baptism but the necessary understanding of 'the matters of the mysteries' of that faith will only come through a careful training of the rational mind.[262]

But in the view of many – in particular after it had become clear that the Indians still continued to practise their old religions in secret – this cleansing of the Indian mind through an education in European *scientia* might reveal not only theological truths but also hitherto undreamt of powers with which to harm the Christian Church. The missionary trod a narrow and a dangerous path. Even his questions in the confessional might 'open their eyes to malice'[263] and reveal things which should best be kept hidden.

Most of the more sympathetic observers, however, rejected this notion that an educated Indian would be more of a danger to the delicate fabric of the Christian world in America than an ignorant one. But all recognised that the process of education would, at best, be a slow one. Nearly a century after Vitoria delivered *De indis*, the Franciscan Juan de Silva explained in the same Aristotelian terms as Vitoria had employed that the Indians were still incapable of understanding either the natural world or the moral order, incapable, as he put it, of distinguishing 'between the right and wrong or between a thistle and a lettuce'.[264] Indians had to be taught all that other men knew by intuition; they even had to be taught, in Silva's opinion, that they *were* 'rational men who have a sensitive, rational and immortal soul'.[265]

For Vitoria and those like Silva who followed in his intellectual train, the relationship between the Indian and his master could only be construed as paternalistic. The Indian's mind was as complete as that of his master; but because it had remained so long in the darkness of infidelity and under the sway of a brutal and diabolic religion, its rational faculties were still immature.

## 12

What Vitoria provided in *De indis* was an argument to refute those 'persons whom', in the words of Bernardino de Minaya, 'the common people regarded as wise men' and who held firmly to a belief that 'the American Indians were not true men, but a third species of animal between man and monkey created by God for the better service of man'. And he had done this by shifting the direction of his argument from one path of Aristotelian faculty psychology to another.[266] For the obvious deduction to be drawn from all that has been said is that the Indian is no 'third species' but some variety of fully grown child whose rational faculties are complete but still potential rather than actual. Indians have to be trained to perceive what other men perceive without effort, to accept what other men regard as axiomatic without prior reflection. Children, as we have seen, were regarded by Aristotle as little more than animals so long as their reason remained in a state of becoming.[267] They were not free agents, they had, as Vitoria observed, no access to the natural law, and they shared the same social status as the slave. 'While the heir is a child', said Vitoria quoting Saint Paul, 'he does not differ from the slave.'[268] So, too, with the Indian. Like the children of other races he will one day grow into a free and independent citizen of a true *polis*. Until that time arrives, however, he must, for his own benefit, remain in just tutelage under the king of Spain, his status now slave-like, but not slavish. The Indian is, said Soto, echoing the reflections of Palacios Rubios, both a slave and a free man whose condition, as Domingo Báñez was later to describe it, implied a 'wide and general acceptance' of a relationship between him and his master which demanded love and trust from both parties.[269]

*De indis* effectively destroyed the credibility of the theory of natural slavery as a means to explain the deviant behaviour of the Indian. After Vitoria's analysis it was clear to all his followers that as a model, as a paradigm, it had failed dismally to satisfy the evidence it was intended to explain. Henceforth the Indian would cease to be any form of 'natural man' – however that ambiguous phrase might be interpreted. He was now, whatever his shortcomings, like all other men, a being whose actions could only be adequately explained in terms of his culture. This 'barbarian', by definition an 'outsider', had now been brought 'in'; 'in', it is true, at the lowest possible social and human levels: socially as a peasant, a brutish creature living outside the discrete web of affiliations, patterns of behaviour, modes of speech and of expression, which made up the life of the civil man; psychologically as a child, that unreflective, passion-dominated, half-reasoning being. But 'in' none the less.

By moving the source of the Indian's inferiority to the European upwards, so to speak, from the first to the secondary precepts of the natural law, and by altering the analogy used to define the Indian's relationship to his master, Vitoria and his successors were effectively claiming, as the great seventeenth-century natural law theorists – Puffendorf in particular – were to do, that any man who is capable of knowing, even in retrospect, that something is in his own interest may be said to have consented to it, even where there is no question of his having exercised any freedom of choice.[270] Such inescapable contractualism fitted conveniently with the claims made by most of the Salamanca School, from Vitoria to Suárez, that although the ultimate power of the state depends on a contract between the people and their rulers, the conditions of that pact are not the consequence of a free agreement, but have been determined beforehand by the natural law.[271]

Although all human communities have historical origins, the social order is, for man, a predetermined condition and existed in the mind of God even before it was enacted on earth. Once, therefore, the original contract between men had been made it was thought of as having a timeless existence and as being unaffected by local social change. Power always rested with the people but only, to use Suárez's terms, *in fieri* not *in conservari*.[272] The socially inferior had no choice over how or by whom they were governed. But government was still conducted with their consent. They had, to complete their part of the social contract, to enter it willingly, just as the Indian had to accept his subjugation willingly. The 'barbarism' of the Indian thus conferred on the Spaniards political *dominium* but only so long as it was exercised in the Indians', and not in the Spaniards', favour. So long, indeed, as the Indians remained as children the Spaniards had a duty to take charge of them (*accipere curam illorum*). Consider, Vitoria told his audience, the case of a region in which all the adults have perished leaving 'only the children and the adolescents who had some use of reason but were still in the years of childhood and puberty. It seems evident that the princes could take them into their care and rule them so long as they remained in that state.'[273] It might even be argued that Spanish rule was not so much a right as a precept of charity, a notion, however, which Melchor Cano later rejected on the grounds that no act of charity could ever involve coercion.[274]

The effect of Vitoria's arguments was to render the natural slave theory unacceptable while still retaining the original framework of Aristotle's psychology. The suggestion that the Indian was a natural child was not, in itself, a novel one. It echoed the unreflective opinions of countless colonists and missionaries who had come face to face with real Indians.[275] It is even, in a sense, a natural reaction for anyone faced with peoples who seemed to behave in curious and senseless ways and who, since they were unaccustomed to having to explain their behaviour, could rarely give an adequate account of why they acted in the way they did. But Vitoria's hypothesis, because it was grounded in a theory about the way in which *all* men come to understand the law of nature, provided a reasoned explanation for an assumption others had reached intuitively. By couching his argument in terms of Aristotle's bipartite psychology he had explained just what it meant to be a child, and by doing so he had opened the way to an historical and evolutionary account of the Amerindian world, something from which, as we shall see, other men pursuing other intellectual objectives, but indebted, none the less, to Vitoria's achievements – men such as Las Casas and Acosta – were ultimately to benefit.

13

*De indis* was not, from the political point of view, an obviously radical document. But in its rejection of all the more traditional arguments for conquest in favour of a series of precepts derived from natural law, it was unusual enough to frighten one colonist into the belief that the professors were about to argue their emperor out of his empire.[276] It also angered the emperor himself who responded with a sharp rebuke to the prior of San Esteban (the Dominican house to which Vitoria belonged) for having allowed his charges to 'discuss and treat in their sermons and *relectiones* the right that we have in the Indies, Islands and Tierra Firme of the Ocean Sea...for to discuss such matters without our knowledge and without first informing us is most prejudicial and scandalous'.[277]

All public discussion of the subject was henceforth prohibited and all papers already in circulation were ordered to be confiscated. In the years that followed the delivery of *De indis*, however, this, like so many such edicts, had little or no effect. On the Indian question, at least, the School of Salamanca presented a united front. In 1540, for instance, Bartolomé de Carranza, the ill-fated cardinal archbishop of Toledo, delivered a *relectio* at San Gregorio de Valladolid on the 'affairs of the Indies'. In his lecture course on the *Summa* for the following year he discussed the subject again, and at some length, under the uncompromising title 'Ratione fidei potest Caesar debellare et tenere Indos novi orbis'.[278] His conclusion was the same as Vitoria's, and it was expressed in a language which was even more 'prejudicial and scandalous'. The king of Spain was the tutor to the Indians – a position which had, after all, been conferred, or imposed, upon him by Alexander VI – and 'when [the Indians] no longer require any tutor the king of Spain ought to leave them in their first and proper liberty'.[279]

At about the same time Melchor Cano delivered a *relectio* from which I have already quoted, 'De dominio indorum', the general thrust of whose argument is identical with Vitoria's, going so far as to repeat, almost verbatim, Vitoria's analogy between the Indians and the hypothetical land of abandoned children and adolescents.[280] The same work, or a fragment of it, found its way into Cano's first lecture course at Salamanca as Prime professor of theology in 1546. One year later Diego de Covarrubias discussed the Indian problem at some length in a series of lectures on the rules (*regulae*) of law given to the law faculty at Salamanca with the title 'De iustitia belli adversus indos'.[281]

If we add to these lectures the observations on the Indian question, which appear in works that began their life as *relectiones* or lecture notes, by Soto, Báñez, Ledesma, Domingo de Cuevas and others, it will become clear that in the years which followed the delivery of *De indis* the justice of the Spanish conquests and the nature of the American Indian formed a staple part of any discussion on the nature and origin of human societies or on the rule of law. It will also be clear that Vitoria's pupils followed faithfully his approach to these subjects and that they regarded his opinions as something of an orthodoxy.

Within the limits of the academy the work of Vitoria and his successors was evidently regarded as conclusive. But the debate over the nature and status of the Indian was also being conducted in other, less ordered places than the halls of the great universities.

Ever since the fifteen-twenties the Council of the Indies had listened to a flood of conflicting opinions on the mental status of the Indians and on the proper and just way to govern them. In 1542, in an attempt to bring some order into the affair, the crown had promulgated the famous New Laws which finally abolished the *encomienda*. Three years later, however, the emperor was obliged to repeal many of them in the face of a fierce rearguard action by the *encomenderos* and the practical impossibility of enforcing highly unpopular legislation on the other side of the world.

During these years, too, the missionaries' struggle to secure humane treatment for the Indians erupted into open warfare when Las Casas and his followers began to refuse absolution to *encomenderos* who had not made restitution to the Indians they had wronged.[282] These battles involved the universities at several points. The professors, in particular Domingo de Soto and Melchor Cano, were in close contact with the court. Both the theology faculties of the universities and the missionary enterprises were at this date dominated by Dominicans, just as, in the latter part of the century, they were both to be taken over by the Jesuits. Finally, there was the presence of Las Casas, the constant agitator. Between 1547 and 1551 Las Casas spent a considerable amount of time at San Gregorio de Valladolid where, if the accusations of his enemies are anything to go by, he occupied himself in persuading his fellow religious of the justice of his personal crusade against the 'impious bandits' who had devastated the Indies and left them 'by the death of thousands of peoples almost like a desert'.[283] His influence upon certain members of the School of Salamanca, most obviously the theologian Juan de la Peña, is evident from the texts. But it is also probable that he helped to keep the realities of the situation in America in the minds of even such men as Soto, who clearly found his interminable rhetoric wearisome and unconvincing.[284]

The loudest, and for our purposes most decisive, contact between the Salamanca theologians and the polemicists from the non-academic world took place at the famous debate in Valladolid in 1550–1 between Las Casas himself and the Cordoban humanist, Juan Ginés de Sepúlveda. One of the results of this contest, which I shall examine in the following chapter, was to demonstrate to a later generation of writers the ways in which the anthropology of the Salamanca theologists, their insistence on the role of habituation in the formation of human communities, might be used to explain some of the real facts about Indian societies.

# 5

## The rhetorician and the theologians:
## Juan Ginés de Sepúlveda and his dialogue,
### *Democrates secundus*

In 1548 three of Vitoria's best pupils, Melchor Cano, Bartolomé de Carranza and Diego de Covarrubias were called in to examine a work by the emperor's chaplain and official chronicler, Juan Ginés de Sepúlveda. Called *Democrates secundus sive de justis causis belli apud Indos*, it was, as we shall shortly see, the most virulent and uncompromising argument for the inferiority of the American Indian ever written.[1]

Sepúlveda, however, came from another intellectual world than Cano and his colleagues. Although educated initially in Spain, he had spent much of his adult life in Italy. There he had studied, or so he claimed, under Pietro Pomponazzi while attending the Spanish college at Bologna.[2] He had been patronised by Alberto Pio, prince of Carpi, whom he had publicly defended against Erasmus; and he had been a friend of, among others, Paulo Giovio and Aldus Manutius. Sepúlveda was a skilful, if not distinguished, translator of Aristotle and the author of several works on history and politics, and even on theology and the law.[3] But, despite his association with the wider intellectual world of Italian Aristotelianism, his mind seems to have remained rigidly orthodox and highly chauvinistic. Uncertain even about the dangers of his own love of classical learning, Sepúlveda was far from being the enlightened humanist many of his historians have tried to make him.[4] In his own way he was, in Marcel Bataillon's words, typical of those responsible for preparing the ground for 'the dogmatic restoration of Trent'.[5]

*Democrates secundus*, which is both chauvinistic and dogmatic, was probably composed in 1544 at the suggestion of Fernando de Valdés, the cardinal archbishop of Seville and president of the Council of

Castile. Sepúlveda submitted the work, as was customary, to the royal censors and it received the *nihil obstat* from Francisco de Vitoria's brother Diego and a civil lawyer named Alvaro Moscoso. At this stage, however, 'certain persons from the Council of the Indies' intervened and, afraid no doubt that the book's inflammatory tone might create political unrest in the Indies, recommended that it should not be printed.[6]

*Democrates secundus* was then passed to the universities of Alcalá and Salamanca for judgment. Although one of the judges, Diego de Covarrubias, clearly had some admiration for both Sepúlveda and his work and even went so far as to allude to *Democrates secundus* in his lectures for 1547–8,[7] both universities condemned the book. Sepúlveda himself, however, claimed later that this did not reflect the view of the university but had been the work of a few 'corruptors', an unnamed group, the prestige and learning of whose members was such that it had managed to suborn all the other judges.[8] And behind the machinations of this group he perceived, probably rightly, the hand of Las Casas. In July 1550 he wrote to Antoine Perrenot de Granvelle, bishop of Arras and at that time Charles V's chief minister at Augsburg, that his book

has been approved by all those learned men who read it without passion, before the bishop of Chiapa [Las Casas] took it upon himself to weave the web he wove in Salamanca and Alcalá with his intrigues, and with the help of others who were disturbed by the fact that I had declared the truth against what they had advised and written.[9]

Unfortunately none of the depositions which the judges must have written on this occasion has survived, so we have no means of knowing whether Sepúlveda's version of the events has any truth in it. It seems, however, at least probable, given the widespread support which *Democrates secundus* received from members of the religious orders, royal officials and even from the non-Vitorian contingent (jurists such as Moscoso, for instance) within the universities, that Sepúlveda's principal opponents, the 'others' to whom he referred in his letter to Granvelle, were indeed the theologians.[10] Certainly in an acrimonious correspondence with Melchor Cano which followed the condemnation of *Democrates secundus*, Sepúlveda accused the theologian of being his harshest critic and the principal architect of his defeat.[11] Cano's reply is also instructive. It was not the fact that Sepúlveda had written a morally offensive book that troubled him, it was Sepúlveda's challenge to the authority of Vitoria, and to Vitoria's method of inquiry. Cano wrote simply, 'as the celebrated doctor Fray Francisco de Vitoria, who is worthy of every respect, has written at length on this matter and in opposition to your views, we could do little else than reject your opinion, there being arguments against it that were not to be despised'.[12]

In the absence of any deposition, however, it is impossible to know on what, if any, precise grounds the theologians based their rejection, since clearly the fact that Sepúlveda had not heeded the opinions of Vitoria would hardly have been sufficient reason to refuse the work a licence. Here again we only have Sepúlveda's word for what happened. The chief objection to *Democrates secundus*, the 'certain doctrine' to which Alcalá referred in their final report, was, he said, the 'causa de belli barbarica' and, more explicitly, the 'dogma derived from the first book of Aristotle's politics' (a clear reference to the theory of natural slavery). And this he exclaimed, was beyond dispute since it not only originated with Aristotle, but was also in accordance with natural law.[13] That is all; and, as Sepúlveda's reading of Aristotle turns out in the end to be not so very far from Vitoria's own, it is difficult to see what all the fuss was about.

*Democrates secundus* clearly, however, did arouse a great deal of unease among its readers; and it has continued to do so. I would suggest that the very allusiveness of Cano's criticisms, and of Sepúlveda's own attempts to 'refute' the objections of the Salamanca doctors, makes it plain that the problem lay not in what Sepúlveda 'said', but in how he chose to say it. For if *Democrates secundus* had, indeed, said no more than what Sepúlveda later claimed it to say, and what, if one reduces it to simple propositions, it does say, namely that the Indians should be subject to the Spaniards for the good of their souls and made to work for their salvation,[14] there should have been no objection from the theologians. But *Democrates secundus* 'says', and its author clearly intended it to say, a great deal more than any simple exegesis of its basic arguments can reveal.

Sepúlveda's dialogue is clearly not, as one of its modern commentators has taken it to be, 'an inquiry' into something so remote from Sepúlveda's intellectual world as 'the precise position occupied by the Indian as an individual entity within the universal brotherhood of man'.[15] For it does not, nor was it intended to, observe the recognised linguistic conventions for such an enterprise. *Democrates secundus* was the work of a man who, despite his claims to be learned in every branch of knowledge – philosophy, rhetoric, the law and even theology[16] – was best known for his literary achievements. Sepúlveda was a humanist, and a humanist, in the view of the Salamanca theologians, with the presumption, shared by many of his kind, to dabble in subjects which he was not adequately trained to understand. His dialogue, though it dealt with matters which Vitoria and his successors had judged to be theological in nature, was explicitly a work of literature, an exercise in the persuasive art of eloquence. But the judges from the universities, who had been asked to assess only the doctrines it contained, had read it as though it were a treatise in moral theology. *Democrates secundus* had failed at Salamanca and Alcalá to win approval because it had failed to secure what J. L. Austin called 'uptake'[17] from a group of readers who had no knowledge, or who pretended ignorance, of the complex set of intentions of its author. For if Sepúlveda's work is read as theology its tone is hysterical, its judgments – as the judges of Alcalá and Salamanca declared – 'unsound' and its methods of argument, which shift constantly from one mode of speech to another, improperly formulated.

Sepúlveda himself was acutely aware of the marked difference between the linguistic context in which he had intended his work to be read and the one in which he knew his judges would read it. This is evident not only from his own indignant observations on the manner in which his words had been interpreted but also, and more tellingly so, from the methods of argument used in the *Apologia* for *Democrates secundus* which, in an attempt to confound his critics, he published in Rome in 1550.[18] This text is described as a résumé 'in the scholastic manner'[19] of the original dialogue; and its purpose was precisely to undo the damage done by the fact that Melchor Cano and his colleagues had failed to grasp Sepúlveda's linguistic intentions, 'because they are not accustomed to reading books of a *literary* nature' (my italic).[20] This it set out to do by demonstrating that the same conclusions as those reached in the dialogue could also be arrived at by conventional scholastic methods and by using traditional scholastic sources. The *Apologia* thus reduces what the principal speaker in the dialogue, Democrates himself, has to say to a set of simple propositions. Sepúlveda's main rhetorical device in the dialogue, Aristotle's theory of natural slavery (to which I shall return), is omitted and in its place we find the Augustinian argument, with which few of the Salamanca theologians could have taken issue, that slavery is a punishment for sin. This Sepúlveda maintained could be applied to the Indians because of their crimes against nature.[21] The *Apologia* also makes use of a rather loose interpretation of Aquinas's observations on natural slavery in his commentary on the *Politics*. This text, too, provided Sepúlveda with an endorsement from an impeccable *theological* source for the otherwise highly dubious proposition which underpins much of the argument in the dialogue that the cultural 'barbarian' is subject to the 'civilised' man *by nature*.[22]

Sepúlveda was conscious throughout his struggle with the doctors of the universities that not only was his work being read in such a way as to falsify its true meaning but also that in offering his opinions of the subjects raised in *Democrates secundus* – subjects which the theologians believed that they alone were fully competent to discuss – he was crossing a perilous and near-invisible boundary line between what Peter Winch has labelled one 'coherent universe of discourse'[23] and another. The theologians of Salamanca were zealous guardians of the integrity of their discipline. No-one who had not undergone the necessary training and who was not practised in the methods used in theological inquiry could be allowed to offer an opinion unchallenged, in particular an opinion on so delicate an issue as the status and nature of the Indian. Sepúlveda, like Erasmus before him, was an academic outsider, an interloper, a rhetorician; and to make matters worse he had chosen to argue his case on the basis of what Melchor Cano described as the 'authority of the philosophers who followed natural reason'. Such sources required, the theologians insisted, careful evaluation both by 'natural human reason', and, more crucially, in the light of the teaching of the fathers of the Church.[24] While Sepúlveda was doubtless capable of performing the first kind of examination, his weakness, in Cano's eyes, as a theologian made it unlikely that he would be able to perform the second.

A gift for 'philosophy', and in particular the kind of humanistic exegesis which Sepúlveda practised, could, he knew, be all too easily dismissed by the theologians as mere literary dilettantism. The doctors of the universities, Sepúlveda complained to his friend Martín de Oliván, who praised him for his literary skills and secular learning did so only to throw doubts upon his abilities as a theologian.[25] This sense of frustration at having been misread and then excluded from an intellectual club to which he felt his work entitled him to belong, is also evident from his letter to Granvelle. 'They', he complained of his judges, 'seek to diminish the authority of my book by saying that I have studied more in languages than in theology.'[26] His complaint was certainly not unfounded. Melchor Cano's brief correspondence with Sepúlveda is full of languid insinuation that rhetoricians would do well not to meddle in theological issues; and in *De locis theologicis*, while graciously conceding that Sepúlveda was not wholly ignorant (*abhorrens*) of theology, Cano described him as one 'distinguished in the art of eloquence' (i.e. rhetoric) and went on to show how this had led him (in *Democrates secundus*) to misuse his sources.[27]

*Democrates secundus* was certainly intended to be read as a work of literature. It is a skilful exercise in political rhetoric on behalf of the Castilian crown's Indian 'wars'. It is also a contribution – as its setting, the name of its protagonist and its title all make plain[28] – to another debate only circumstantially related to the nature or the status of the American Indians, a debate between those who, like Sepúlveda, saw virtue in military glory and those, most notably Erasmus and Vives, who regarded war as an evil which it was every Christian's duty to avoid.[29] *Democrates secundus* is, in fact, the final work in a trilogy which began in 1529 with Sepúlveda's *exhortio* to Charles V to mount another crusade against the Turk. None of the works in this trilogy – neither *Ad Carolum ut bellum suscipiat in Turcas*, nor *Democrates primus*, nor *Democrates secundus* – was intended either to inspire or to explain or to legitimate, as the utterances of the theologians were: their purpose was to persuade.

The main thrust of Sepúlveda's argument for a 'just war' being made against the Indians is carried by Aristotle's theory of natural slavery. Sepúlveda seems to have chosen this in part, at least, because at the time of writing he appears to have regarded it, supported as it was, or seemed to be, by both John Mair and Palacios Rubios, as uncontroversial. Although later, in his letter to Granvelle (written after his work had been rejected by Salamanca and Alcalá), he attacked Vitoria and his successors as the political enemies of the crown's policies in America,[30] there is no suggestion in *Democrates secundus* itself that he had read or knew anything substantial about the arguments set out in Vitoria's *De indis*. But it was not only its apparent orthodoxy and its origins in a text by the most authoritative of the ancient philosophers that gave the theory of natural slavery its appeal. It also suited Sepúlveda's purpose in another and perhaps more significant way, for in its use of simple polarities it was, as we shall see, particularly well adapted to the highly popular rhetorical trope which provides the organisational structure for much of *Democrates secundus*.

The principal speaker in the dialogue, Democrates himself, is a rigidly orthodox Christian and a Spanish chauvinist, using the language of a Roman moralist, skilled in transforming the complex arguments of ancient philosophers into easily comprehensible maxims, of transmuting axioms into metaphors.

The work is built up by means of a device known to sixteenth-century rhetoricians as *antitheta* – the contrast of opposites which, in Augustine's words, 'provide the most attractive figures in literary composition'.[31] Thus Sepúlveda's dialogue begins with the meeting of two speakers, the imperial mouthpiece Democrates and the mildly Lutheran Leopoldo, both obviously rational, even reasonable men, but one of whom is clearly right in his views, the other clearly wrong. Then there are, as Democrates explains, two systems of knowledge capable of defining the behaviour of men: the law and what he calls 'philosophy'.[32] Though not in themselves antithetical, they may yet yield antithetical definitions of key words. The word *servus*, for instance, has a different meaning in each system. For the jurist the slave is merely a war captive (and is referred to by Sepúlveda as *mancipium*);[33] for the 'philosopher' he is a creature who displays 'an innate weakness of mind and inhuman and barbarous customs'.[34] For each type of *servus* there is also a particular type of rule. The former is merely servile. The latter, however, says Democrates, borrowing a term used by Plautus to describe the relationship between the highest and the lowest levels of the domestic hierarchy, is 'herile'.[35] Needless to say, Democrates regards the American Indian as a 'natural' slave who possesses some rights – similar to those of 'free' domestic servants (*ministri*)[36] – but no freedom of personal action.

Finally Democrates offers two separate sets of psychological metaphors which legitimate these types of rule. Sepúlveda, conflating the Platonic, tripartite division of the soul with what W. W. Fortenbaugh has called Aristotle's 'political–ethical psychology',[37] manages to contrast the rule of the mind (*mens*) over the body, which is 'herile', with the rule of the soul (*anima*) over the passions, which are servile.[38] The former implies a degree of friendship (the body being principally a passive sensation – transmitting entity) in accordance with Aristotle's own characterisation of the relationship between the natural slave and his master, for 'where the relationship between the slave and his master is natural, they are friends' (*Pol.* 1255 b 12).[39] The latter, on the other hand, is proper only to the *mancipium*, the civil slave (for the passions are active and rebellious entities); it is a relationship in which tyranny is the proper rule, for here the relationship between master and slave rests merely on law and force. If we were to place these sets of opposites into two columns they would look like this:

| 1 | 2 |
|---|---|
| The law | Philosophy |
| The civil slave (*mancipium*) | The natural slave (*servus*) |
| The soul/passion dichotomy | The mind/body dichotomy |
| Servile rule | Herile rule |

Towards the end of the work, where Democrates is no longer arguing with Leopoldo (nor Sepúlveda with his readers) but merely explaining to an acquiescent auditor how things are, the Indians are granted a certain power of self-improvement. 'Thus with the passage of time, *when they have become more human*[40] and when our rule has confirmed in them good customs and the Christian religion, they may be treated with greater freedom and liberty.' (My italic.)[41]

Ideologically, there is no inconsistency between this observation and Democrates's earlier attempts to define the Indian as a natural slave. Sepúlveda was a good enough Aristotelian to know that all creatures, even wild animals, may learn through imitation; and the natural slave, who is capable of understanding (*sunesis*), will become more man-like in the company of men, much as a dog does. Indians, we must assume, are capable of receiving instruction in menial skills and this may even be said to constitute their slavish *epistēmē* (*Pol.* 1255 b 22–3) which had been taught to slaves at Syracuse for a fee (*Pol.* 1255 b 23–5).[42] But no matter how long they live or how skilful they become, Indians will never be like other men, full citizens of a true republic. They may not, as Democrates concedes, *be* monkeys or bears, but their mental faculties are still only mechanical ones much like those of bees and spiders.[43]

None of these suppositions (not even Sepúlveda's doctrinally suspicious attempts to reintroduce the notion that the real difference between men and the *similitudines hominis* is one between Christian and pagan) was so very new nor particularly offensive to a sixteenth-century learned public, which, as we have seen, viewed its own labouring classes in very much the same light. What *was* new – and offensive – was the rhetorical mode Sepúlveda used to present the evidence for his contention that the Indians belonged to the category 'natural slave', because, as he phrased it, they are 'barbarous and inhuman peoples abhorring all civil life, customs and virtue'.[44] This is demonstrated in a number of linked passages where the contrast between the Indians and other men (Spaniards in particular) is worked into a mounting crescendo or, to use the technical term, *climax*.

After a lengthy preamble on the nature of the just war and the legitimacy of the pursuit of 'solid glory', Leopoldo is asked to compare the Spaniards with the Indians, 'who in prudence, wisdom (*ingenium*), every virtue and humanity are as inferior to the Spaniards as children are to adults, women are to men, the savage and ferocious [man] to the gentle, the grossly intemperate to the continent and temperate and finally, I shall say, almost as monkeys are to men'.[45]

This is followed by a eulogy on the virtues, nobility and piety of the Spaniards, in particular of those Spaniards who helped sack Rome in 1527 but who, before dying, attempted to repay their victims with the goods they had robbed from them. 'Compare the gifts of magnanimity, temperance, humanity and religion of these men', continues Democrates, 'with those *homunculi* [i.e. the Indians] in whom hardly a vestige of humanity remains.'[46]

After this outburst there follows a conventional list of Indian defects: their lack of any culture or civil organisation, their cannibalism and so on. As evidence of the weakness and instability of such a society Democrates recites the history of the fall of Mexico, contrasting a noble, valiant Cortés with a timorous, cowardly Montezuma, whose people by their iniquitous desertion of their natural leader demonstrated clearly their indifference to the good of the commonweal. The Mexicans, 'who are said to be the most prudent and brave'[47] (and also 'the most human')[48] of the Indian peoples, are to be at once both derided for their cowardice and condemned for their ferocity, which can only compare with that of the Scythians. 'Is this not proof', concludes Democrates triumphantly, 'that they are slaves by nature?'[49] Like all true barbarians, the Indians are creatures of extremes, denied all access to virtue, which can only be found in the mean. Such a people, whose religion is an inversion of true piety, are truly 'like pigs with their eyes fixed always on the ground'.[50] 'Now that they have received our law', Democrates concludes, 'our rule, our laws and customs, and have been imbued by the Christian religion', their condition is as different from their previous one, 'as the human men (*humani*) are to the barbarians, as those with sight are to the blind, as savages are to the gentle, as the pious are to the impious and, I say once again, almost as men are to beasts.'[51]

The acerbity of this language – the use of images of inversion, commonly reserved for witches and other deviants, and of such descriptive terms as *homunculus*, which suggests not only stunted growth but, since *homunculi* were things created by magic, also unnatural biological origins, the persistent reference to animal symbolism, monkeys, pigs and beasts in general – was intended to create an image of a half-man creature whose world was the very reverse of the 'human' world of those who by their 'magnanimity, temperance, humanity and religion'[52] were the Indians' natural masters. Sepúlveda may have meant to 'say' only that Spanish rule should help to raise the Indians from the pitiful state in which they found themselves to the level of true Christians. He probably did, but the effect of his rhetoric was to thrust the Indian back again among the *similitudines hominis*. It is, perhaps, then little wonder that Sepúlveda's vituperative dialogue should have seemed to the university theologians, as it seemed to the Greek scholar Juan Páez de Castro, the work of a man *non sani capitis*.[53]

# 6

## A programme for comparative ethnology
## (1) Bartolomé de Las Casas

I

The interest of *Democrates secundus*, for my present purposes, lies less in what it is than in the effect it had. For Sepúlveda's dogged insistence that his book should be printed aroused the indignation of the ageing Las Casas. The struggle that followed was ultimately to result in a serious attempt to negotiate for the Indian a definitive and unassailable position in the human community as a 'civil' and 'human' being.

Although it is evident, if only from the series of events which led to the great debates between Sepúlveda and Las Casas in Valladolid in 1550–1, that Las Casas's anger had been fired by Sepúlveda's work, it is also apparent that he was never given access to *Democrates secundus* itself despite his request to the crown that Sepúlveda be obliged to send him a copy.[1] From some of his later attacks on Sepúlveda, it seems possible that he had some knowledge of its contents, possibly from Cano or Soto; but what he actually read, and what his refutation of Sepúlveda is based on, was a vernacular version of an *Apologia* of 1550.[2] This work, as we have seen, reduced the arguments of *Democrates secundus* to three basic propositions: that the Indians are culturally inferior to the Spaniards and require 'tuition'; that their 'unnatural' crimes deprive them of their rights of *dominium*; and that the bulls of donation are a valid charter for the Spanish conquests.

For Las Casas, the first and the second of these propositions were anathema because they presupposed an anthropology in which cultural forms were accepted as being indicative of innate dispositions. The attempts to refute this basic claim are contained in a massive rambling work entitled *Argumentum apologiae...adversus Genesium Sepulvedam theologicum cordubensem*, a version of which was read at the famous debate between Las Casas and Sepúlveda which took place in Valladolid in August or September of 1550, under the aegis of, *inter alia*, Melchor Cano, Domingo de Soto and Bartolomé de Carranza.[3]

119

It is, however, as we shall see, far more than a mere refutation of either Sepúlveda's *Apologia* or *Democrates secundus* or even, as Soto drily observed, 'everything that the doctor had ever written'.[4]

In reply to the *Argumentum*, Sepúlveda, who had not been present during Las Casas's reading, composed twelve objections to his theses. Some of these reiterate points made originally in *Democrates secundus* (but omitted from the *Apologia*). None, however, offers any new light on Sepúlveda's anthropological or psychological opinions. Las Casas countered with twelve objections to the replies. These consisted largely of a restatement of his earlier arguments, though occasionally – as with his claims for an evolutionist interpretation of history – they employed ideas also used later in his massive essay in Amerindian ethnology, the *Apologética historia*. The text of the dispute, together with a summary of Las Casas's *Argumentum apologiae*, was printed at the instigation of Las Casas in 1552, without a licence and to Sepúlveda's annoyance, with the title, *Aquí se contiene una disputa o controversia entre el obispo fray Bartolomé de las Casas y el doctor Ginés de Sepúlveda.*[5]

Las Casas's attempts to find a satisfactory classification of the Amerindian peoples and a convincing, but non-deterministic, causal explanation for their behaviour, is developed in all three of these works. The mention of the *Apologética historia* in the context of the Valladolid debate, however, requires some comment, since the possible influence of the debate and of Sepúlveda's writings on its composition has been the subject of lengthy disagreement.[6]

The tone, the method and the very length of the *Apologética historia* make it clear that the work was intended for a larger audience than the judges at Valladolid. It also seems evident, on internal evidence, that, as the Mexican scholar Edmundo O'Gorman has argued, the bulk of the text was completed after 1551 and could therefore have played no direct part in the sessions at Valladolid. In the *Argumentum apologiae*, however, Las Casas refers at several points, as both Angel Losada and Lewis Hanke have observed, to a 'second part' of his defence of the Indians which had been composed in the vernacular and which contained all the necessary empirical evidence to confound Sepúlveda.[7]

On the basis of internal evidence collected by O'Gorman and the scrupulous avoidance of any reference to Sepúlveda or the Valladolid debates, it seems likely that the text of the *Apologética historia* was indeed written after 1551 and that it was an attempt to present Las Casas's arguments to a wider audience unfamiliar with the terms of their author's struggle with Sepúlveda. There may well have existed an earlier version which was more directly allied to Las Casas's efforts to demonstrate on empirical grounds the falsehoods of Sepúlveda's claims that the Indians were 'barbarians'. But if so this has not survived.

What has been ignored is the fact that the sole surviving manuscript of the *Argumentum* is clearly *not* the deposition presented by Las Casas at Valladolid. There are sufficient similarities between this text and Domingo de Soto's summary to make it plain that the former is a version of the latter; but it is also clear from the introductory letter by Bartolomé de la Vega[8] that the text of the *Argumentum apologiae* we have today has been rewritten for publication. The manuscript – which is unfoliated – has also been divided into gatherings of sixteen folios each lettered from A to I, which might suggest that it had, in fact, been copied from a printed edition. It also contains references to such things as Sepúlveda's contempt for the 'mechanical arts'[9] of the Indians which since they are not mentioned in Sepúlveda's *Apologia* but do appear in his 'objections' could only have been added after the debate.

Both the *Argumentum apologiae* and the *Apologética historia* were, then, intended to be *read*, and read by a public larger than the judges at the debate. Although the *Argumentum* would be largely unintelligible without a knowledge of the issues at stake in that encounter, there are extensive parallels between the two texts which make it possible to read the first section of the *Argumentum apologiae* (a discussion of the uses of the term 'barbarian') as a theoretical statement which informs the entire structure of the *Apologética historia*, a possibility made the more plausible by the fact that a shortened vernacular version of this appears as an epilogue to the surviving manuscript of *Apologética historia*.[10]

The *Apologética historia* is firstly an attempt to demonstrate, on the basis of a huge body of empirical and historical data, that the pre-conquest Indian communities fulfilled all of Aristotle's requirements for a true civil society, and secondly to explain in a way which made no appeal to Aristotelian bipartite psychology why Amerindian culture differed sometimes radically from European norms.

It is, in many respects, a truly 'original' work. The ancient historians who attempted to chronicle remote or 'barbarian' societies – Herodotus, Xenophon, Apollonius of Rhodes or Diodorus Siculus, all of whom are invoked from time to time by Las Casas – had seen their task as primarily descriptive. Certainly none of them had had any desire to *prove*, as Las Casas had, that beneath the glaring cultural differences between the races of men there existed the same set of social and moral imperatives. Since Las Casas's purpose was to demonstrate a fundamental similarity between widely separated cultural groups, the *Apologética historia* is in effect an expansive piece of comparative ethnology, the first, so far as I am aware, to be written in a European language. And it begins, not as most Christian histories had done with an account of the origins of mankind since Adam, but, for reasons which I shall discuss later, with a full description of the physical environment in which the Indian had to live. This blend of natural 'history' is not, of course, remarkable in itself. But in other histories of America, such as Oviedo's, which had modelled themselves on Pliny, ethnography forms only a part of a general encyclopaedia of the new world. In Las Casas's work, however, the account of the American biosphere and of the physical condition of American man provides the basis for the ethnography. But both the *Apologética historia* and the *Argumentum apologiae* were also part of an explicitly polemical programme. The difficulties which both texts present to the modern reader, and would doubtless have presented to a contemporary one – the mis-quotation and mis-citation, the overlay of different kinds of argument, the sudden shifts in emphasis, the reliance on argument by association and so on – derive not only from the author's mode of presentation but also from the fact that they were written (and one of them at least was intended to be read) as part of a debate over the status – human, social and legal – of the American Indians which had reached a crisis in the 1550s.

The historical method Las Casas employs in the *Apologética historia* consists primarily of juxtaposing short essays on aspects of ancient or 'primitive' cultures (such as those of the Celts or the Iberians) with the comparable aspects of Amerindian ones, the reader being left to 'read off' the similarities, or dissimilarities, for himself. The interest of the work from our point of view lies less, however, in the content of these essays than in the theoretical propositions and assumptions which underpin the whole enterprise.

These have their source in the Aristotelian–Thomist conceptual scheme used by the Salamanca theologians. But Las Casas makes it work in a different way. In all the other writings I have discussed, the Indian and his social and mental world have been subsumed into a wider account of the sources of human behaviour, or the explanation (and legitimation) of a particular political event. In Las Casas's work the reading of Aristotle and Thomas, wildly inaccurate though it sometimes is, determines the very structure of the observations. Instead of encountering a short list of attributes as in Vitoria's *De indis*, the reader of the *Apologética historia* is exposed to a detailed description of a wide variety of cultural forms, drawn from a vast range of ancient and modern authors (some 370 different sources are cited) and Las Casas's own long personal experience. The result of all this does not, of course, provide the modern reader with a convincing picture of the ancient Indian world. But that, after all, was not the purpose of the work. What it, and the first part of the *Argumentum apologiae*, do offer is a demonstration that the world of America could be explained by means of a familiar conceptual scheme, once, and only once, the terms of classification being used in that scheme had been adequately defined. The terms Las Casas set out to examine were, of course, those employed in Aristotle's definition of the 'barbarian' as a natural slave. It was, as Las Casas knew, crucial when engaged in the uncertain task of extending an authority-based system to include new areas of knowledge – and he was more conscious of the newness and the unfamiliarity of the American world than any of his professiorial colleagues[11] – to 'interpret' the categories and the principles employed in that system.

Las Casas took Aristotle's theory of natural slavery quite literally. If natural slaves, who are psychologically imperfect creatures, are to be identified simply with all those peoples who are called 'barbarians', then the Indians, who *are*, in some sense, barbarians, must also be natural slaves. Like Vitoria, Las Casas could see that there was an error in this piece of reasoning; and his understanding of the nature of that error was, as we shall see, very similar to Vitoria's own. But Las Casas was also unhappy about the assumption that Aristotle's hypothesis was of a piece. He insisted that there *was* an interpretation of the passages in the *Politics* relating to slavery and barbarism which could be made to explain the nature of the American Indian. Such an interpretation assumed, however, that the *Politics* in fact contains a description of two separate cultural types, to both of which Aristotle had given the name 'barbarian'. With this reading of his sources Las Casas succeeded in dismantling Aristotle's thesis and constructing from the pieces a picture of the relationship between 'barbarians' and civil men which had the effect of discarding not only the biological elements in Aristotle's theory but also its principal psychological base.

Las Casas was not, of course, the first to realise that a generalised use of the term 'barbarian' to designate everyone who is not a member of the observer's own group was unsatisfactory. Even before Aristotle had devised his psychological classification of the 'outsider', Plato had voiced the obvious objection to such a simple division of all the races of the world into 'them' and 'us'. The Eleatic Stranger – an outsider looking in on the Hellenic sense of uniqueness – complained that 'In this country they separate the Hellenic races from all the rest as one, and to all the other races, which are countless in number and have no relation in blood or language to one another, they give the single name 'barbarian'; then because of this single name they think it a single species' (*Statesman*, 262d).

Sixteenth-century observers who had some experience of the Amerindian world, Las Casas among them, came to similar conclusions. A category which failed to distinguish between tribes as unlike in cultural behaviour and technological achievements as the Inca and the Chichimeca suffered from the same faults as any which could effectively be made to accommodate *all* the properties of a thing: it would ultimately fail, in Acosta's famous metaphor, to distinguish between a chestnut and an egg.

The trouble with a term like 'barbarian' is, of course, that it is both a classification and an evaluation. It does not derive from the need to categorise something 'out there', as botanical and zoological terms do, but, as we have seen, merely serves to express a sense of the difference felt by one cultural group when confronted with another of which it has had no prior experience. By the sixteenth century, if not long before, the word had become a *topos* carrying a wide range of explicit and implicit meanings, the number of which are apparent from the definition provided by the seventeenth-century lexicographer Sebastián de Covarrubias: 'We call barbarians those who are ignorant of letters, those who have bad customs and who act badly, those who are wicked and will refuse to communicate with other men of reason (*que no admiten la comunicación de los demás hombres de razón*) and live without [reason] and finally all those who are without pity and cruel.'[12] When with the discovery of America this ill-controlled term was put to use as a precise social category, some confusion and a great deal of concern over definitions were bound to result.

For although barbarism was evidently a cultural condition, the term was, as we have seen, frequently used simply to describe non-Christians. Unless, therefore, he was of the opinion that all non-Christians were culturally deficient, a position which in view of the Christian debt to the ancient world it was hard to maintain, the user of such a word was faced with the necessity of saying more, sometimes much more, than he intended.

This was apparent to contemporaries. Cortés, for instance, wondered how it was that a people such as the Mexica could create a sophisticated material culture, 'considering that they are barbarians and so far from the knowledge of God and cut off from all civilised nations'.[13] But the questions should, as Las Casas's contemporary, Alonso de Zorita, realised, never have been posed in such terms, for if they *could* create such a culture it was illogical to suppose that they were 'barbarians'.

The problem, in Zorita's opinion, derived precisely from the ambiguities inherent in the terms Cortés was using. All peoples, he observed, tended to describe as 'barbarian' those who did not possess the one thing which *they* held to be essential to 'civilisation' (in Cortés's case, this would be Christianity and contact with Europe, which he assumed to be the natural source of all culture, as it was of all human life) and to disregard all other cultural achievements. Thus the Psalmist had referred to the Egyptians, one of the wisest peoples in the ancient world, as 'barbarians', 'because they were idolaters'. The Egyptian Hermes Trismegistus had also used the word of all the races which he saw as 'outsiders', whom he defined as 'those who did not practise the ceremonies of Egypt'. The Greeks and the Romans called everyone who spoke neither Greek nor Latin barbarians; and now all Christians called all non-Christians barbarians.[14]

Las Casas was even more acutely aware of this problem of classification than Zorita. The application of models from the remote past, unhistorically and uncritically, to present situations was not, he insisted, a very reliable means of coming to grips with a body of empirical data. The traditional categories were, of course, still the valid ones; but before they could be used to describe American Indians, they had to be examined and adapted to meet changed circumstances.

The natural slave theory could, of course, have been deduced from Aristotle's psychology even if Aristotle himself had never formulated it; but the formulation might nevertheless still be a misleading one. Aristotle was, after all, a Greek who, as Melchor Cano observed, had believed that 'all the other nations [of the world] were barbarians',[15] and his distinction between barbarians and civil men might, Juan de la Peña warned, have originated in nothing more than a wish to flatter Alexander.[16] Like Las Casas's own earlier objections to the use of a pagan source in the context of a Christian philosophy, this remark is a comment on the *status* of Aristotle's ideas. Peña's warning derives from an historical awareness of the possible intention behind Aristotle's particular 'speech act', the awareness that at this point the Philosopher was not, in fact, speaking as a philosopher but as a royal advisor – a distinction of which both Peña and Las Casas would have been very much aware. In such circumstances, the Christian commentator must proceed with caution and, in Diego de Covarrubias's words, not merely 'use' but also 'interpret' Aristotle.[17] Las Casas set out to do this in the most orthodox manner possible – by reading the *Politics* primarily through Aquinas's commentary on that work.

2

The term 'barbarian', Las Casas maintained, could be understood to refer to a number of different cultural types. Following, so he says in the *Argumentum apologiae*, Aristotle in books 1 and 3 of the *Politics* and book 7 of the *Ethics*, 'and Thomas Aquinas and other doctors', he divided 'barbarians' into four separate groups.[18] The first of these depends on a different set of premises from all the others, and is in fact a separate category. It has no cultural base as the other three do and applies not to races but to individuals. It includes all men everywhere who, momentarily and under special circumstances, have lost control of themselves, whose minds have been overwhelmed by their passions.[19] The courtiers who attended Theodoric and treated Boethius so cruelly, the tyrant Nicanor who wished to fight the Israelites on the Sabbath and the Milanese mob who, according to Gregory the Great, rioted 'impelled by barbarous ferocity' following the appointment of an unpopular bishop are all given as examples.[20] In each case the established order has been overthrown, but in no way that is amenable to reasoned analysis. This sort of barbarian may be found anyway even in the 'finest polities'. He is simply 'any cruel, inhuman, wild and merciless man acting against human reason'.[21] As a category this also includes the Spaniards in America who, in the 'cruel acts they have carried out against those peoples [the Indians] have exceeded all the barbarians' and anyone, in short, whose behaviour is marred by the sin of *ferocitas*.[22]

The terms used for the second and third of Las Casas's types, the crucial ones for his classification of the American Indian, rely on the traditional Thomist distinction between precepts which are clear in relation to themselves, and those which are only so in relation to something *outside* themselves; things that is which are true *simpliciter* and those which are so only *secundum quid*. This distinction, and the analogous belief in the existence of primary and secondary causes, that certain things are the way they are in essence while others are so only through accident (*per accidens*), was Las Casas's principal device for explaining the Indian's social and ontological status.

Las Casas's second type of barbarian is described in the first instance in terms of language. Language confers power upon its users. Adam, in naming all the objects in creation, acquired control over them, a control, furthermore, which is unique to man and superior to the partial control exercised by other species over their environment. With the confusion of tongues after Babel the full force of the authority conferred by the primitive adamic language was diffused. But language still remained the prime instrument both of dominance and of understanding. It was also, as we have seen, the necessary condition for the creation of the civil community. By allowing primitive men to agree among themselves it had conferred on man the initial means of transforming his original defensive unions into civil communities. This view of the evolution of human society was a commonplace in European political thought from Diodorus Siculus and Vitruvius to Rousseau and Condillac. Rousseau, indeed, ascribed such a fundamental role to language in the creation of society that he seems to have been unable to decide whether language was a social institution or society merely a linguistic artefact.[23]

A similar indecision hovers over the observations of Aquinas. Men demonstrate their rationality by gathering together into societies and by conversing with one another, first through language, later through ritual behaviour, through trade and exchange, through, that is, the whole gamut of activities subsumed into the term *communicationes*. In the simplest of terms civil beings were those who could 'converse' adequately. Barbarians, who are non-social men, were those who could not. But Aristotle's theory of language (adumbrated in very different circumstances from his observations on barbarians), and with certain qualifications Aquinas's also, was conventional.[24] Language, it was supposed, had, like all else in the universe, evolved through a number of different stages. It had begun with a natural cry much as an animal makes, and had then coalesced into the specific and unique forms we call words. Finally these words were given meaning as a result of an agreement among those wishing to engage in speech to employ the same word when referring to the same thing. Language is therefore not only, in an important sense, the medium through which civil societies are created, it is also only possible when there exists a social environment in which to operate. Outside society there can be no true language just as a gathering of men which does not possess a common tongue could not be called a society. Men outside society might perhaps grow up, as von Helmont the younger had supposed, speaking Hebrew since that was the language of God.[25] But the chances were that they would not be able to speak at all. In an ideal world, of course, there would be, as there had once been, only one universal language. Babel had made this impossible; but if complete verbal harmony was unobtainable each individual culture should still be united in its linguistic habits. All Christians who not only profess the same faith but are also one 'in commerce and culture', argued Juan Luis Vives, should share a common tongue.[26] It was, furthermore, not a matter of indifference *which* language was selected, for certain languages – Hebrew, Greek and Latin in particular – were evidently superior to others. Latin, in Vives's opinion because it possessed a musical softness and the proper words for expressing the Christian doctrine, was the best candidate for the Christian universal language. Even the candidature of Latin, however, was proposed not because it was, in any way, believed to correspond to the original *ursprach* revealed by God to the first man, but because of the 'variety and the wealth of words' it possessed,[27] and these (despite Vives's Platonic view of the origin of languages) were not the result of any inherent properties but had evolved because it had been refined for so long by so many men of letters. If language in the post-lapsarian world was thought to create power, it was still man who created language. Language was therefore a clear expression of a people's culture. 'Le langage symbolize ordinairement nos moeurs' observed La Popelinière.[28] And all the communities of men, however unsophisticated their *moeurs* might be, had some crude form of linguistic tool to hand; they could communicate – even if nothing more – with their fellows. A simple linguistic definition of barbarism could, therefore, at best be only a relative one. On this Aquinas reminded his readers of Saint Paul's famous warning, 'If then I know not the meaning of the voice, I shall be to him that speaketh a barbarian, and he that speaketh will be a barbarian unto me' (1 Corinthians, 14.11).[29]

But in an attempt to preserve Aristotle's linguistic distinction between 'barbarians' and other men, Aquinas differentiated between a primary and a secondary use of the term. The word 'barbarian', he supposed, evidently connotes 'foreignness' and 'strangeness'. If a man is said to be a stranger to another man (that is if he is a member of another culture), then his barbarism is purely relative (*quod aliquem*). He belongs, of course, with 'the other' but is human none the less. If, on the other hand, a man is a stranger to the human race as a whole, then his barbarism is clearly primary, and absolute (*simpliciter*).[30] This 'barbarism' is, then, precisely the feature which distinguishes him from the rest of mankind: 'all those who do not know their own speech', wrote

Aquinas, 'the speech that they use between one another, may be called barbarians in relation to themselves'.[31] At first this may seem a rather puzzling observation since clearly no-one can fail to *know* his own speech or to understand the words he is using for otherwise he would, in Aquinas's own understanding of the origin and function of language, not be speaking at all.

But the passage does not seem to have troubled Las Casas (or indeed any of his contemporaries) who understood it to mean two things: in the first place there is a state of barbarism where men of the same culture fail to understand each other. For as language is conventional in origin it is always possible, if something causes the normal channels of communication to fail, that different groups of people, or even different individuals, will come to understand different things by the same words. Such people live in what J. G. A. Pocock has called 'the linguistic equivalent of a Hobbesian state of nature', believing that words can be made to mean what they wish them to mean.[32] Since, in order to achieve this sort of linguistic mastery, the prime question becomes, as it was for Humpty Dumpty, 'who is to be master?' it is no surprise that linguistic anarchy should be associated with social anarchy. Thus, said Las Casas, during the revolt of the Comuneros in Castile in 1520, men became 'barbarians' and 'strangers to reason' because 'their furious impulses and fearful opinions' had effectively destroyed their linguistic unity. They therefore 'failed to understand each other because of the diversity of their language'.[33] In a world in revolt, where all social communication has broken down, the linguistic ties between men – the most vital because they are both the earliest and the most compelling – vanish also. The rebel, like the true barbarian, is a destroyer of social unity, of *consortium*, and thus a babbler who is barely human at all, for 'barbarism' implies, said Las Casas, 'a strangeness, an exorbitance, a novelty which disrupts the nature and the common reason of men'.[34]

There is, however, a further, and ultimately more instructive, dimension to the linguistic distinction between 'barbarians' and civilised men. This involves a shift from the spoken to the written word. In Las Casas's world, all knowledge (*scientia*) was textually dependent. It was therefore obvious to construe the distinction between the knowledge-less 'barbarians' and civil men as a distinction between peoples who have a written script and peoples who have not. The ability to create a system of writing, and the access to the power and knowledge that such a system conferred, was the ultimate token of the superiority of the 'civil' man over the 'barbarian', who lived always as a slave to those with greater wisdom than himself. It was, Sepúlveda had claimed in 1529, in recognition of the liberating power of letters that the Ottoman sultans had forbidden their people any knowledge of the liberal arts.[35]

For Aquinas and his sixteenth-century readers the written language belonged essentially to a different category from the spoken one, the difference being represented in most cases by the difference between the vernacular tongues and Latin.[36] 'The second class of barbarians', wrote Las Casas, 'are those who lack a literary language (*qui literali sermone carent*) which corresponds to their maternal idiomatic language, as is Latin to us, *and thus do not know how to express what they think.*' (My italic.)[37]

Only through the proper modes of speech can thought – by which, of course, he meant scientific thought – be expressed. Written speech, what Aquinas called the *locutio litteralis*, is, in a real sense, a different language from the vernacular or common tongue (*vulgare idioma*).[38] The view that there existed two categories of language, of discourse – one which merely achieved the cohesion between men necessary for the survival of a community, and the other which was a vehicle for the understanding of and power to control nature – was a common and enduring one. Mersenne, for instance, in the mid-seventeenth century, made a similar observation with regard to what he saw as the foolish contemporary belief that all knowledge of nature could be acquired, as the Indians were thought to have acquired it, through direct observation. For knowledge, science, precisely does *not* consist of untutored empirical observations. We all have to learn to interpret what we see and this can only be achieved through the use of books. The illiterate Indians, in Mersenne's view, were like European peasants: though they may be intelligent by nature their lack of learning leads them to make ridiculous observations even about those things, such as the stars and the elements, with which they are most familiar.[39]

Without the kind of knowledge which is passed down from generation to generation and is increased and perfected in the process, the community will have to rediscover, every generation or so, the cultural knowledge it requires to improve itself. Without a script no community could hope to create what Louis Le Roy called 'les choses les plus utiles au monde', things such as 'laws, the sentences of judges, wills, contracts, public treaties and other things necessary for the understanding of human life'.[40]

For Sepúlveda it was a certain indication of Indian barbarism that they possessed no script, 'nor preserve monuments of their past deeds [but live] in obscure memory of certain deeds consigned to some pictures. They lack all written laws and [thus] have barbarous customs and institutions.'[41]

In a passage which was often cited in this context Aquinas had described how Bede had first translated the liberal arts into English in order to lift his countrymen out of barbarity. Although one might perhaps argue that English, a vernacular tongue with no literature, was hardly the proper medium for knowledge, it was still better than the 'barbar' which, according to Gregory the Great, had hitherto been the Britains' normal mode of discourse.[42]

The *locutio litteralis* not only makes *scientia* possible, it also provides, as Sepúlveda's identification of a lack of writing with 'barbarous customs and institutions' makes plain, the means by which the laws of the community are codified. Without a written language it is impossible to legislate or to establish precedent; and without legislation – without, that is, the promulgation of the *lex humana* – men are forced to rely for guidance in their daily lives entirely upon custom. And because customs, as we have seen, exist not as a code but as a part of each man's moral education, they are not subject to reasoned examination and, as the case of the Indians seemed for Soto to have proved, may cut men off from the natural law.

Aquinas's barbarian *secundum quid* might, therefore, be described as any man who lives in a community without the benefit of training in letters and is thus denied access to knowledge and also to natural justice (*ius*). The distinction in Aquinas's commentary on the *Politics* between a secondary and a primary sense of the linguistic dimensions of the term 'barbarian' compelled Las Casas to search for a corresponding division in Aristotle's own account of the *social* characteristics of barbarism. And he found it in the slightly different accounts of slavery provided in books 1 and 3 of the *Politics*.

Thus [he wrote], from what has been said and demonstrated, it is clear that the Philosopher makes a manifest distinction between the aforementioned classes of barbarians; for those to which he refers in the first book of the *Politics*...are barbarians *simpliciter* in the proper and strict sense of the word [that is they are natural slaves]...In the third book of the *Politics*, however, he refers to another class of 'barbarians' and affirms that they have a legitimate, just and natural government (*principatus*) although they lack the art and exercise of letters.[43]

What Las Casas is referring to here is Aristotle's second type of monarchy which occurs in Asia and is supported willingly since the

Asiatic peoples are barbarians 'by nature' and hence 'are more servile in their customs than the Greeks'.[44] The rule of the kings in Las Casas's reading is thus not truly tyrannical, since the Asiatics voluntarily accept such a leadership, but is 'legitimate and paternal [in origin].[45] It is, said Las Casas, employing a word which, as we have seen, Sepúlveda had used to describe the ideal of *Spanish* rule over Indians, a 'herile' one.

What Las Casas is claiming here, and what he spelt out at greater length in the *Apologética historia*, is that the governments of pre-conquest Indian society, although tyrannical in form, were none the less legitimate ones, because the Mexica and the Inca chieftains ruled 'according to custom and the law'. They guided their peoples 'like elder relatives and the fathers of families' which, since the family is the origin of the state, 'was an argument and manifest demonstration that their regime and government were most natural, as the rule over fathers is over their sons'.[46] Such forms of government may be classified as 'barbarous' if only because they are indubitably primitive, but barbarous *secundum quid*.

## 3

Las Casas's third category of barbarian is the barbarian *simpliciter*. 'Taking this term in its proper or strict sense', he wrote, '[it applies] to those men who, through impious or perverse understanding (*impio et pessimo ingenio*), or on account of the miserable regions they inhabit, are savage, ferocious, slow-witted (*stolidi*) and alien to all reason.'[47] Such peoples are not governed by laws, nor have they any understanding of justice. They neither practise friendship nor live in communities (*respublicae*) and cities 'constituted in a politic fashion'. They do not have proper marriage rites, nor human commerce, for they neither buy, nor sell, nor give, nor take from one another; instead they lead scattered lives in woods and mountains alone except for their women, 'as not only tamed but also wild animals do'.[48] They must, therefore, be compelled to live 'more like men', or at least be prevented from harming those who do.

These 'barbarians', Las Casas went on, are the creatures whom Homer characterised as 'clanless, lawless and homeless' who, since they do not live in cities and know nothing of friendship, are a constant threat to peaceable men, for 'one by nature unsocial is also a lover of war' (*Pol.* 1253 a 7–8). In short, they are the natural slaves described in the book 1 of the *Politics* (as opposed to those described in book 3).

They were probably the original inhabitants of the ancient province of 'Barbaria' (a general term for the North African littoral) and the origin of their unwillingness to follow the path taken by all rational men is simply that 'they lack reason and the morale (*morum*) appropriate to men, and those things which are admitted among all men by custom (*consuetudine*)'.[49] That is, they lack both the capacity to create cultural forms and an ethical context for their behaviour.

The significance of the components of this description requires no explanation. Though greater in number and more erratic in arrangement, they are, none the less, basically the same as Vitoria's. Such creatures exist at the far end of the heroic–bestial continuum, 'low in the scale of humanity' (*Pol.* 1253 a 1ff), and their number must, thought Las Casas, be very small, just as 'those whom we call heroes or demi-gods are rare'.[50] The argument for the scarcity of such creatures is once again an assertion of the unity, harmony and ultimate perfectability of God's creation.

Nature is the medium through which God works in the world, and, said Las Casas, quoting one of Aristotle's now familiar dicta, 'Things which are the result of nature are all those of which the cause is in themselves and regular; for they turn out always, or generally, in the same way' (*Rhet.* 1369 a 13).[51] Thus it is only very rarely that 'natural causes fail to produce the effects which are congruent with their nature (*naturae suae congruentes*)'.[52] The true barbarian must, therefore, be a great rarity, as rare indeed as men born lame or blind or the monstrous creatures Saint Augustine and others had recorded in Africa, who have only one eye or 'the soles of their feet upwards'.[53] For, as we have seen, every species, except those lower animals which generate spontaneously, must reproduce itself in its own form. All beings in nature, and man in particular, are self-sustaining and self-perpetuating. The genus *homo sapiens* is characterised not by its mere physical structure but by its capacity to understand first principles, and hence to create a rational and social environment in which to live. If the barbarians are 'imperfect and perverse (*pessimi*)' as men, then they must be anomalies, 'sins of nature and monsters of rational nature'.[54] The intellectual error and false opinion of which these 'barbarians' are consistently guilty are – if we accept (as Las Casas did) an absolute parity between the mind (or intellective soul) and the body – the equivalent of physical deformities. Such 'men' have no apparent place in a perfect creation, except, perhaps, as Augustine believed, to provide evidence of the range of God's creative *ratio*.[55]

To imagine, then, an entire continent filled with this type of barbarian would be to accept that nature is, to a very large degree, capable of imperfection; and such an hypothesis is, as we have seen, on at least two occasions, impossible. 'Those men', wrote Aquinas, 'who have sufficient knowledge (*scientia*) to govern their lives are in the majority; and very few are those who lack such knowledge, who are called imbeciles (*moriones*) and idiots.'[56] Had, indeed, the reverse been true, had so vast a number of 'men' as the Indians been created 'deprived of the light of reason' and thus incapable, by their very nature, of 'knowing, invoking and loving God', then God's intention would have failed *in actu*. For the Christian, such a proposition is literally unthinkable.[57]

### 4

The fourth category of barbarian merely describes all those who are not Christians. 'Every race (*gens*), no matter how politic', wrote Las Casas, 'every man, no matter how great a philosopher he may be, is exposed to the greatest barbarities, to the most obnoxious vices, if he is not imbued with the mysteries of Christian philosophy.'[58] Even Romans, 'famous and praised in their day for their political virtues', were guilty of heinous crimes against nature, particularly in their games, their theatre, their Bacchic and Priapic rites. These aspects of ancient life are, as Las Casas demonstrated in the *Apologética historia*, similar in their form, in their unbridled excesses and in their ultimate purpose to certain Indian rites. In religious observances and communal play, in those moments when the community acts together, the greatest demand is placed on the consensus and it becomes very difficult for man's natural reason to assert itself. Even among Christians, Las Casas noted, in such outlandish places as Bohemia, the urge to indulge in 'unnatural' rituals may get the better of the rational mind, as the case of the Adam and Eveites had made plain.[59] Outside the *communitas fidelium* no truly politic society can exist. Las Casas, like his arch-enemy Sepúlveda, was willing to concede not only the primacy of the social norms of the Christian world but also the highly dubious proposition that no state which is not founded on grace is a complete one.[60] The city is an association of men for the pursuit of happiness. It can be created only by Christians, since happiness – or what he calls 'speculative happiness' – which is 'the soul's perfection and last end',[61] is possible in terms only of Christian salvation, because it requires 'a contemplation of spiritual and abstract substances'. No man, therefore, who does not have access to the knowledge of such substances can be truly 'happy'. But Las

Casas, unlike Sepúlveda, also maintained that all pagan communities could, through the practice of civil virtue and the creation of settled communities, achieve a state of 'active happiness' in many respects adequate to the needs of most men and a fitting preparation for the coming of the Gospel. Indians and other 'barbarians' may possess the capacity to acquire a knowledge of the three parts of moral philosophy, that is, ethics, politics and – in the original sense of the science of domestic management – economics, whose ultimate purpose is to enable men to live in peaceful cooperation with one another. But no non-Christian is able to invest this life with some ultimate spiritual purpose.[62]

The key to this discussion lies in Las Casas's somewhat loose use of the term 'city' (ciudad). A Christian city is, as we have seen, a quasi-mystical union of men, a means to a state of perfection. The Indians, however, as pagans, can only create what Domingo de Soto had called the city of the philosopher, that is the secular human community. This, of course, possesses the power to civilise;[63] and since it is as much a construct of the rational mind as a simple response to necessity (which is how Sepúlveda had characterised Indian cities),[64] it is the most obvious means by which pagans may be brought close to the Christian ideal. Cities play a large role in the Apologética historia; ten chapters are dedicated to a lengthy description of those built by the Mexica and the Inca. But although these descriptions of Tencochtitlán and Cuzco were written to demonstrate the civic capacity of their builders,[65] Las Casas's definition of a 'city' is simply a number of groups (barrios) of families or kin-groups (linajes) who build houses together.[66] It is of no consequence whether these houses are built of stone, straw or wood, for a city is composed of citizens necessarily grouped, according to the requirements in the Politics, into six social classes: workmen, artisans, warriors, rich men, priests, judges and rulers.[67] Much of the Apologética historia is dedicated to proving that all Indian communities, even those of the most primitive inhabitants of Florida, are divided according to this rule and thus possess the full potential for civility.

5

Of the four categories of barbarians described in the Argumentum apologiae only two concern Las Casas's attempt to classify the American Indian. All Indians are, for the purposes of definition, non-Christians, and many may also be 'wild and merciless men acting against reason'. But as cultural groups Indian tribes – and this includes both the settled communities such as the Mexica and the Inca as well as the nomadic peoples of Florida[68] – belong to the second category of barbarians. They, or at least the majority of them, live 'in a politic and social' manner, and they have 'great cities, kings, judges and laws all within an organisation in which commerce is practised'.[69] They have, too, magnificent temples which are set apart and built in high places, in keeping with Aristotle's dictates for the construction of an *agora*. Their law also forbids, as Aristotle said it should, any farmer, artisan or merchant – anyone, that is, concerned with the means of production – from entering the temple precinct.[70] Had the Indians not been fully rational beings it is inconceivable that they would have been able to create such a polity in the first place, much less maintain it for any length of time.

Indian communities may, Las Casas conceded, lack the ability to write or the systems of knowledge that are possessed by other civil beings, but they are skilled in the mechanical arts. In *Democrates secundus* Sepúlveda had derided the Indians' *artificia* as being merely the product of a mimetic faculty, 'for we can see how certain small animals, such as bees and spiders, can make things which no human mind could devise'. All that these abilities demonstrated in the Indian case, claimed Democrates, was what no sane man had ever doubted; that the Indians 'are not bears or monkeys, wholly lacking in reason'.[71]

For Las Casas, however, mechanical arts, while evidently lesser activities than the liberal arts, are no different in kind. Both are a 'habit of the operative intellect',[72] which is to say that they require the use of deliberation, the faculty which natural slaves (and the third class of barbarians) lack.

Indians, furthermore, were very quick to learn from the Europeans the things which were missing from their world. Once an Indian had been introduced to European cultural forms he immediately recognised their obvious superiority over his own. On this point, which was to be reiterated by Acosta, Las Casas, turning one of Sepúlveda's sources against him, quoted Paulo Giovio's description of the Indians' intellectual progress under European guidance. 'They abandoned the hieroglyphs with which they used to write the annals of their kings, decorating them with various pictures for posterity, and instead they now learn with pleasure and admiration our means of writing.'[73]

Las Casas's insistence that the Indians' ability to assimilate European culture in this manner was proof of innate intellectual capacity was a commonplace among the missionaries. If the Indians responded well to training, it would seem only logical to attribute their previous unnatural behaviour to the circumstances in which they had been reared. The conclusions which the Salamanca theologians had reached by induction, men like Las Casas claimed to have deduced from empirical evidence alone. 'Thirty years spent among them' was, claimed Las Casas, sufficient, in the face of no matter how many 'vain lies' from such historians as Oviedo,[74] to demonstrate that the Indian, like all other men, was in full possession of a rational soul.

6

If 'barbarism' of the type manifest in Indian societies is relative, *secundum quid*, it must have some causes which are subject to observation and description. What leads one group of men, supposing that all true men have the will to act in their own best interest, to choose the higher forms of human behaviour and another to cling to the habits of the beast? Aquinas provided Las Casas with two answers to this question. They are (a) the influence of the physical environment, the *climata*, 'either on account of the intemperate zone that has fallen to their lot, so that from the very character of the region they are forced to be exceedingly dull-witted', or (b) an explanation we have already seen employed by Vitoria, the impact on the human mind of an adherence to perverse customs, 'as a result of which it happens that men are made irrational and almost bestial'.[75]

Behind both these assumptions lie long histories of reflection upon the factors which were thought to determine man's behaviour. The theory of climate, or the 'milieu-theory' as it is sometimes called, had, since the days of Hippocrates, seemed to offer a certain guide to why some races develop customs which are so very different from others.[76] Its attraction lay in its supposed dependence on observable phenomena – geographical location, climate and terrain – and in the fact that it was, as all successful scientific, or pseudo-scientific theories must be, at once both conceptually very simple and an assertion of the unity of the natural world.[77]

The milieu-theory maintained that all men's actions, their psychological make-up and sometimes even their physique are determined by the climate and terrain in which they live and by the conjunction of the stars under which their habitat happens lie. As the alogical soul is prior in generation to the logical and is formed by habituation as it grows, so the conditions in which a man finds himself must have some influence on the way in which his mind develops. Both Aristotle and

Aquinas – on both of whom Las Casas based his long defence of the American *climata* in the *Apologética historia* – were certain that there was no way in which the environment could change a man's disposition (*diathesis*).[78] No man could become wise or brave who was born to be foolish and cowardly. But his bravery and his cowardice, his wisdom and his folly could be diminished or increased according to the environment in which he was compelled to live. For as sensation is held to be a wholly physical activity, the body may influence the mind *secundum quid*.[79] Bodily sensations are the vehicle for communication between the 'real' outside and the intellectual 'inside', 'And this', wrote Las Casas, 'is the reason why we see some men who appear to be more subtle and ingenious than others, and more gifted with the natural virtues of the soul, for the soul is not informed in a like manner in every body, although it always remains the same according to its species.'[80]

The theory behind this had a clear biological base, at least as regards the influence of climate and terrain. The organs of the body respond adversely to external conditions. Thus human beings have 'a natural tendency which counteracts the effect of locality and climate' (*Prob.* 910 a 37ff.). The body is controlled by its humours and those races, such as the Scythians, who live in cold climates were said to have 'hot' humours which made them impetuous and 'very like the drunken' (*Prob.* 910 a 30). They were brave and impulsive perhaps but also cruel and stupid. So, too, according to Jean Bodin, were the races of the south, which explained, so he thought, the savagery of the Brazilians.[81]

The milieu- theory could, as Las Casas pointed out, if reduced to fine enough details, explain the difference between groups living only short distances apart, for 'no two points on earth have the same properties, no matter how close they are'.[82] The proof of this was to be found in the fact that if we uproot a plant, transplant it 'with all its roots and the earth on them' but ten paces and then replant it, 'it will become stained and droop until little by little it acquires the property of the other earth to which it was transplanted. . . and then it will revive'.[83]

The notion that successful transplantation involved the acquisition by the plant of intrinsic properties in the soil was, given the evidence, a perfectly logical one. Men, of course, were more complex organisms than plants, but the law of uniformity demanded a relationship between the organism and its environment which was typologically the same. As Leibnitz was later to observe, pondering the attempts by 'a certain traveller' to create a taxonomy of human races, all mankind must be of the same species, but 'they have been changed by different climates just as we see that animals and plants change their nature, in becoming better or degenerating'.[84]

All men, of course, have been granted the power of self-determination, the means to improve their speculative faculties through training. But even if all men are assumed to be in possession of the same basic mental equipment, certain environments would tend to favour its development while others might hinder or retard it.

The trouble with the milieu-theory, however, was that in order to account for the very large number of divergencies from type that any one people is likely to display, a large number of variables had to be added to the base hypothesis. These, together with the need to accommodate the interaction between climate, terrain and astrological disposition, meant that wholly contradictory interpretations were possible on the basis of the same set of evidence. Even Jean Bodin's subtle and very complex attempt to explain national histories in climatic terms, though much admired, failed to find any adherents.

Las Casas accepted the premises of the milieu-theory largely, one suspects, because they could be made to suit his case. The Indians, or at least the Indians of the Caribbean and Central America, with whom he was mainly concerned in the first part of the *Apologética historia*, lived in a climatic zone which ancient authors had considered propitious; and the terrain of Hispaniola, the only location he was able to describe in any detail,[85] was clearly an ideal place for the human mind to develop. The *Apologética historia*, therefore, begins with an elaborate demonstration, parading (like all the other 'proofs' in the book) as a piece of objective scientific reasoning, of the existence of the six necessary and the four accidental conditions for Indian rationality and their potential for civility. Las Casas's account of the Indian environment extends, in fact, to a description of the whole physical environment of the Indian mind, from the soil to the senses, from the stars to the state of each man's heart and liver. 'For', he said, 'if God wishes to infuse a perfect soul that possesses all the natural virtues, then he begins with the body.'[86] The *Apologética historia* claimed to offer the reader (prepared to stumble through its clotted prose) what no other history had done before – a complete account of the Amerindian world which combined description with causal explanation. The result of this elaborate inquiry had, of course, been established from the beginning. It was to show that 'all these Indian peoples are, without taking them away from their natural state...well disposed and well proportioned to receive noble souls'.[87]

If the conditions in which the Indians live are propitious to the human intellect, then Indian barbarism comes down, once again, to a question of cultural variables, to, in Aquinas's phrase, 'the long exposure to perverse customs'. These customs were, generally, considered to have been the creation of early legislators. But for Las Casas, who was keen to demonstrate that Indian rulers were not the kind of tyrants such a theory supposed them to be, the possibility that some cultural phenomenon unique to the Indians might be responsible for 'unnatural' behaviour was not an appealing one. Instead he sought a common ground on which the present customs of Indian societies could be equated with the practices of other races – Greeks, Romans, Babylonians – who were accepted to be, despite certain anomalies in their behaviour, civilised peoples. This, since it required comparisons between races which were separated not only in space but also in time, necessarily involved him in a theory of cultural evolution.

For Las Casas the cause of the Indians' 'barbarism' was to be found in the classical account of human prehistory. In the *Apologética historia* this is taken from Cicero's now familiar version in *De inventione*. In the beginning all mankind lived an itinerant life, without any form of civil organisation 'or any knowledge of God'. At some point a single man arose who, 'knowing the dignity of the material before him and the excellence and the virtue of the souls of men', persuaded them through the force of his rhetoric, 'to live together and gather themselves into societies'.[88] The passage from Cicero, which Las Casas is paraphrasing here, had been intended to demonstrate the force of language in the creation of the first human communities. By using it to explain the essential cultural similarity of all men, Las Casas was, as his subsequent discussion of the origin of the arts makes clear, committed to the view that the moving force in human progress is *sapientia*, the knowledge of things (*res*) to which, as we have seen, language alone can provide access.

For Las Casas, as for Cicero, the universe was 'a single joint community of gods and men'.[89] 'All the races of the world are men', wrote Las Casas in a passage which has now become famous, 'and the definition of all men, and of each of them, is only one and that is reason.'

This does not, of course, mean that men are not divided from one another by behaviour, but only that, in Las Casas's words, 'all the lineages of men are one',[90] and alike as regards their relationship with the natural world. Within the human, as against the divine order, the distinction between types was not psychological, but cultural. It was a familiar Stoic argument, but one whose full implication had never before been explored in the context of the anthropology of the American Indian. The cultural forms which men create change over time and as they do so they increase in complexity and in quality. All nations begin as groups of individuals living in unsocial hordes. The ability to create civil societies out of these hordes exists equally in all men, but not all men are able to exploit it equally. In time, however, Indians and all other 'barbarians' will become 'civilised' beings, just as the Europeans climbed up from barbarous beginnings via the civilisations of Greece and Rome until finally they reached the condition of the Christian *homo renatus*.

The Germans described by Tacitus, the Latins whose culture was now almost too complex, too civilised for Las Casas's taste – 'the most curious, superfluous and delectable to sensuality'[91] – had all once been barbarians. So too had the Greeks before Lysanias brought culture to them. Even the Spaniards could not have been much different when they arrived on the Meseta; and, said Las Casas, barely eight hundred years ago the Flemings were still living in caves.[92]

Las Casas viewed significant change in history as essentially charismatic. Traditions and the institutions which sustained them – the collective consensus of the human community – progressed steadily by a slow process of internal refinement. But the radical changes which alone carried men out of one 'age' of creation and into the next could only be achieved by figures with charismatic and sacred powers, the 'ancient legislators' and culture heroes of the race, those whom the pagans had venerated as gods and of whose deeds the garbled myths of antiquity preserved a faded symbolic record.

The kind of historical account with which Las Casas was concerned in the *Apologética historia* was one in which time was constructed in what J. G. A. Pocock has called 'the terms of moments of creation rather than moments of transmission'.[93] Each creative epoch in the human past is thus conceived as a single unit of time in a history which is lacking in any precise temporal indicators. Neither Las Casas nor his (primarily classical) sources ever state *when* speech or agriculture were invented or when iron was discovered. Even the creation of the city, although attributed to an historical figure, has no place in any chronology, real or symbolic. As each 'moment of creation' is achieved, the epoch changes and the community passes into a new historical phase, thus moving inexorably towards true civility and the final stage of all, when the greatest of the sacred creators, who alone can provide access to the full understanding of the world – Christ himself – will bring this universal process to a close.

Las Casas's actual account of the flow of human prehistory follows the traditional classical pattern. The earliest men were wild, unsocial and ignorant. Like the autochthonous inhabitants of Latium described by Virgil, they lived in caves and mountains – both places unfit for human habitation – and mingled with the fauns and nymphs, the *similitudines hominis* whom they so closely resembled.[94] At this stage the human mind was as unreceptive as wood and dense as stone. The mythologisers of the ancient world in their attempt to offer a symbolic account of the human past had, therefore, described the first men as being literally born from trees, or springing up from the stones which Deucalion and Pyrrha had been instructed by the oracle of Themis to throw behind them as they walked.

Men remained in this obdurate condition until a single individual arose among them, or came to them from outside, to bring the 'excellence and virtue', the knowledge and understanding of their human status and of their relationship with the natural world. These 'inventors' of culture transformed the primitive horde into a social body. The next stage was religion, for, as Las Casas observed, 'once men have been persuaded to live in communities, it is not difficult to lead them to knowledge of God and the exercise of religion'.[95]

Culture itself, which follows these two 'arts' – that is government and religion – is also the work of a single individual or sometimes a group of individuals. Saturn, for instance, said Las Casas (citing Macrobius in what was a popular account of the origins of European culture),[96] brought to the Latins not only the principles of social organisation, which are laws, marriage rituals and a knowledge of the city, he also introduced them to 'moral teaching', that is the knowledge of how to conduct their affairs, and he taught them the basic 'arts' which are, of course, agriculture and the preparation and cooking of food.[97] And what Saturn brought to the Latins, Solon and Lycurgus brought to the Greeks, King Arthur to the English and, some thought, Quetzalcoatl to the Indians.[98]

For Las Casas, no less than for Vitoria, culture is primarily the medium through which men learn to exploit the God-given potential in nature. Once this initial culture-acquiring stage of human development has been reached, the social order of each race begins to grow in complexity, until finally it reaches the level of civility immediately prior to the final step forward. This step is, of course, conversion to Christianity and through conversion the acquisition of true *scientia*, the access to a fully evolved cultural world. Thus the Roman empire preceded the coming of Christ himself and the 'empires' of the Mexica and the Inca preceded the coming of the Spaniards. To Las Casas, as for the other historians who adopted similar interpretations of world history – José de Acosta and Garcilaso de la Vega[99] – this view seemed not only in keeping with ancient and Christian historiography, it also promised an explanation of both the cultural distance between the Indians and the peoples of Europe and that between the different Indian tribes. Finally it provided a justification for the conquest which suited the millenarian ambitions of the missionaries: if the 'advanced' Indian groups had reached the limit of their evolutionary potential as pagans, then the evangelisation of the Amerindian peoples could be interpreted as historically inevitable.

Las Casas's thesis claimed that all men. whatever their condition, have a place in an historical scale which is the same for all peoples. Those who are near the bottom of the scale are simply younger than those further up it, for all men have the same set of sense perceptions which are activated by the same set of objects in the physical world,[100] and the necessary culture heroes must inevitably arise among all the peoples of the earth. But the information which men receive through their senses has to be interpreted. Just as the child is taught by his elders to understand the physical and moral world in which he is to live, so too entire races of men may be taught by those who have reached a higher level of civility than they.

For Las Casas the wisest peoples on the earth are literally the oldest. The peoples of Arcadia, for instance, who were, according to Theodosius, so old that the poets believed them to have been born before the creation of the sun and the moon,[101] were the savage ancestors of the ancient Athenians, the earliest of the civilised peoples of Europe. The Indians, whose societies still retained features long since abandoned by more civilised peoples, and whose social forms were evidently inchoate, were culturally a still 'young' race because they had come to their settlement areas late, or found themselves in areas where settlement was either not possible or not convenient.[102]

Las Casas's hypothesis is 'proved' by the telling case of human sacrifice. In *Democrates secundus*, Sepúlveda had claimed that such sacrifices represented a diabolic category mistake, a substitution of a living organism, the heart, for a metaphysical entity, 'the pious and sane minds of men'. Instead of metaphorically 'sacrificing' the latter, the Indian literally immolates the former.[103] For Las Casas, however (who was clearly aware of Sepúlveda's argument), the mistake involved is not the over-literal interpretation of 'the letter that kills', but what he called borrowing, a familiar Aristotelian term, a 'probable' error, an error, that is, which had been adopted by 'the general consensus of all the peoples known in the Indies'.[104] The origin of all behaviour is, at least in part, voluntarist, and, as Las Casas told Sepúlveda at Valladolid, 'the lesser peoples and the plebeians cannot go and ask the wise men of other nations if the way in which their betters act or legislate is probable in accordance with right reason',[105] for no peoples are in a position to leave their communities and seek advice from outsiders on the status of their normative behaviour. The Indians, like all pagans, had no means of criticising their culture from within. Human sacrifice also derives, as I mentioned earlier, from the natural impulse of all men to sacrifice to their gods what they hold most dear, just as the idolatry which accompanies it springs from the natural desire to reverence one's deities in some tangible form. The Indians' sacrifices reveal a genuine devotion to their gods, for 'mistaken conscience bids and obliges in the same manner as true conscience'; and Cicero had rightly deemed the French degenerate for not defending their gods against the Romans.[106]

Since both Aquinas and the Salamanca theologians had accepted the possibility that for a man in a state of invincible ignorance human sacrifice might in fact be a legitimate form of devotion, Las Casas was able, with evident polemical intent, to invert the normal order of praise and blame. The more devout the people, he claimed, the closer they came to understanding the complexities of true religion and thus the greater the number of their sacrifices. The French, he said, came first, followed by the Spartans, followed by the Carthaginians and so on. Not even the Spaniards 'seem to have been left behind, for they sacrificed men by the hundreds together'.[107]

All the races of the world had passed through this transitional stage on their progress towards a more metaphysical understanding of the relationship between gods and men. The fact that all the other races described had abandoned these practices in the remote past is further indication that the difference between the Indians and the now civilised Christian peoples of France and Spain is not one of kind, but merely a measure of the space between nations at separate stages of a natural, and ineluctable, process of historical evolution.

Both the *Apologia* and the *Apologética historia* derived their initial inspiration from a very specific set of political circumstances.

*Democrates secundus* and Sepúlveda's *Apologia* may not have been very original works as far as their arguments were concerned. But they represented the most forceful, most articulate and, for many, the most persuasive expression of a widely held image of the Indian's nature and the status of his intellectual and cultural world. Las Casas set out to correct that image and the supposition, both explicit and implicit, on which it was based, through the use of the empirical data which, he claimed, his enemies had either ignored or wilfully misrepresented. The *Apologética historia*, in particular, owes both its novel form – not to be repeated until the early eighteenth century – and its principal hypothesis to the fact that it was the first large-scale attempt to apply the categories of sixteenth-century Aristotelian anthropology to a substantial body of empirical data.

# 7

# A programme for comparative ethnology
## (2) José de Acosta

### I

Bartolomé de Las Casas's *Apologética historia* was the first detailed
comparative analysis of Amerindian culture. But both it and the
*Argumentum apologiae* remained unpublished during their author's
lifetime. Although the *Apologética historia* was used as a source by the
Franciscan chroniclers Gerónimo de Mendieta and Juan de Torquemada[1] and was doubtless read by many others, it exercised no significant
influence upon Las Casas's contemporaries. The work which did, the
work which for the latter part of the sixteenth and for most of the
seventeenth century dominated speculations on the Amerindians and
their culture, was José de Acosta's *Historia natural y moral de las
Indias*. This and Acosta's treatise on evangelisation, *De procuranda
indorum salute*, have much in common with the *Apologética historia*
and the *Argumentum apologiae*, for *De procuranda* provides the
theoretical framework for the *Historia* much as the *Argumentum
apologiae* did for the *Apologética historia*. But although Acosta was
certainly aware of the Valladolid debate and could perhaps have had
access to *Aquí se contiene una disputa*,[2] there is no evidence that he had
read or even knew of the existence of Las Casas's two other works.

Both Las Casas and Acosta, however, came from very similar intellectual backgrounds and had very similar intellectual concerns. Both
men had spent long periods in the Indies and both insisted on the
primacy of empirical knowledge as the basis for any inquiry into the
structure of 'barbarian' societies. Both men had also, in one way or
another, been greatly influenced by the theological ideas of the
'Salamanca School'. As a consequence both grounded their anthropological theories on a belief in the essential sameness of all human
minds, on man's innate susceptibility to moral training and on the
necessity for an essentially historical explanation of cultural differences.
Acosta's work, however, is not polemical, served a different purpose and
is structured in quite a different way from that of Las Casas.

Acosta was also linked to Las Casas and to the School of Salamanca in another way. Vitoria, Soto, Carranza, Cano and their contemporaries and immediate successors were, like Las Casas, Dominicans. They shared the intellectual ambitions of their order: the creation of a moral *ordo* based on Aquinas's singular merger of ancient philosophy and Christian theology, which would afford a greater understanding of man's essential *humanitas*. The Dominicans' successors in this programme, however, were the Jesuits. It was they who, by the end of the century, had not only seized effective control of the theology faculties of the great Spanish universities, but, in the writings of men like Luis de Molina and Francisco Suárez, had also begun to extend and systematise the new Thomism first introduced into Spain by Francisco de Vitoria. José de Acosta was a Jesuit and, like many of his order, his mind had been formed by the writings of Vitoria and his successors. His vision of the Indian, however, was conditioned by his experience – he was one of the founders of the first 'reduction' (an Indian village outside secular control) at Juli on Lake Titicaca in 1578[3] – of attempting to put into action a policy which laid heavy emphasis on the need to understand the inner workings of the Indian world.

2

José de Acosta was born in Medina del Campo in 1540.[4] In 1552 he was admitted to the Society and between 1559 and 1567 he studied theology at the Jesuit college at Alcalá de Henares. He was a gifted student, writing school plays – a common Jesuit practice – while only fifteen and debating publicly on philosophical themes 'with such brilliance and facility that the doctors who heard him were loud in his praise'.[5] He was ascribed to the province of Toledo in 1562 and ordained the following year. In 1567 he began teaching theology in Ocaña and then, in 1569, moved to Plasencia where he remained until his departure for Peru in 1571. Acosta was never a very active missionary. His health was poor and he seems to have been subject to long fits of depression.[6] His gifts were clearly intellectual and administrative rather than pastoral and he spent much of his time at the college in Lima teaching theology. It was his pedagogical experiences – though he never once refers to them – which must have determined his subsequent views on Indian rationality and the desirability of instructing the Indians in theology as a means of persuading them of the truth of the Christian faith.

In 1573, however, he set out on the first of three long and difficult journeys into the interior of Peru which took him to Cuzco, Arrequipa, La Paz, Potosí and as far south as Chuquisaca. He returned the following year for the trial by the Inquisition of a Dominican Francisco de la Cruz and was appointed to the office of assessor (*calificador*).

The case of Francisco de la Cruz, who claimed to have received communications directly from God through the medium of a mestiza, one María Pizarro, who believed herself to be an angel,[7] greatly disturbed the ecclesiastical authorities. Cruz had a large following, some of whom, such as Luis López, had been close companions of Acosta. His vision of a new Church – which included marriage for the priesthood and polygyny for the laity – seemed to many not only to raise, once again, the spectre of the *alumbrados*, it also threatened the fragile relations between the Church and the colonists and the crown. For Cruz not only taught that his new world Church was to replace the old and corrupt Church in Europe, he also advocated that the Indians, who were to be the instruments of the coming apocalypse, should be kept in perpetual *encomienda*. This support for an institution which both the crown and the Church regarded as a threat to their authority was, needless to say, warmly welcomed by the colonists themselves. Cruz's heresy was thus not only doctrinally unsound, and spectacularly so; it was also politically highly explosive. After a lengthy and very public trial, the Dominican was condemned and together with a number of his accomplices duly burned at the stake in 1578.[8]

In 1576, while Cruz's trial was still in progress, Acosta had been appointed provincial of Peru. In 1582 the Third Lima Council opened with Acosta serving as resident theologian, in which capacity he wrote the Spanish text of three catechisms, probably drafted the final decrees of the Council and had a hand in the composition of a confessional[9] and various sermons.

In 1586, after what appears to have been a period of severe heart trouble (although Acosta himself claimed that the cause of his illness was moral rather than physical), he set out for home. He went first to Mexico, however, where he remained for a year, during which period he collected the material for the Mexican chapters of his *Historia*. He finally reached Spain in 1587 and spent the remainder of his life engaged, not always creditably, in ecclesiastical politics. He died as rector of the Jesuit college of Salamanca in 1600.

3

Acosta was the author of several printed works, as well as numerous sermons and *litterae annuae*, the yearly reports which all Jesuit missions sent back to Europe,[10] but the most influential of his writings were the *Historia natural y moral de las Indias* and *De procuranda indorum salute*. This last work, which was written in Lima in 1577, first appeared in 1588 in Seville and was reprinted in Salamanca the following year and once again in 1595. It also appeared for the first time outside Spain in Cologne in 1596. All of these editions were prefaced by the original Latin text (with the title *De natura novi orbis*) of what later became the first two books of the *Historia*, dealing with the location of America, its *climata* and the origin of the Amerindians. It is clear that the book was originally meant to be read as a piece. *De natura novi orbis* provided the novice missionary with some idea of the physical and human environment in which he was to apply the lessons taught in *De procuranda*. Acosta later separated the two works and developed the *Historia* into a complete analysis of the Amerindian world. But it remained both in its narrower purpose and in its formal structure closely linked to *De procuranda*.

Acosta's *Historia* is in many ways a remarkable book. It was both a more thoughtful and a more thorough account of the Indian world than anything then available. Its novelty, of which Acosta was justly proud, is apparent even from the title. The idea of a 'moral history', a history, that is, of *mores* – of customs – was an unusual one in the sixteenth century. No one, as Acosta was at pains to point out, had ever attempted to write a true 'history' of the Indians,[11] though there had been many accounts of the origin and growth of the Spanish colonies which included a (usually cursory) glance at the indigenes. He was even somewhat apprehensive about how his work would be received. Reading a history of 'barbarians' was, he feared, likely to be regarded in much the same light as reading romances of chivalry.[12] But for Acosta the Indian world was not, like the world of Amadís, Palmerín or Don Belianís, a dangerous fantasy whose irreality might endanger the sanity of those foolish enough to read about it. It was, however barbaric, still a real world and, he assured his potential readers, there was much to be gained from studying it, for 'no matter how low the subject may be, the wise man will derive from it wisdom; and from the basest and the smallest of little animals it is possible to extract the highest reflection and very beneficial philosophy'.[13] Acosta was appealing to one of the most widely employed devices in European historiography: the use of an 'imaginary world', or of a real but remote one, the properties and internal relations of which are used to impute causes in the real world. Polybius, for instance, explained his understanding of the purpose of historical writing in terms which, if we allow for the very great difference in their material, are not unlike Acosta's own:

The mere statement of a fact may interest us [he wrote], but is of no benefit to us; but when we add the cause of it, the study of history becomes fruitful. For it is the mental transference of similar circumstances to our own times that gives us the means of forming presentiments of what is about to happen and enables us at certain times to take precautions and at others by reproducing further conditions to face with more confidence the difficulties that menace us.[14]

Acosta was not, of course, concerned with the possibilities of accurate prediction and only in a very restricted degree with the need to avoid past errors. But he did believe – and the *Historia* was written to demonstrate the truth of his case – that the history of the 'real' but remote Indian world could illuminate the historical process itself and that by studying such a seemingly alien society his European readers might come to understand something about the natural behaviour of all human communities including their own. 'And because', he wrote, 'these nations are so different from our European ones, it is even more pleasant to learn about their earliest origins, their behaviour and the history of their prosperous and adverse fortunes.'[15]

His predecessors in America who had attempted to obliterate all memory of the Indian past had been consumed, Acosta maintained, 'by an ignorant zeal which, without knowing or wishing to know the truth, asserts without evidence that everything about the Indians is the work of superstition'.[16] Correctly interpreted, the Indian past which the ignorant friars had assumed to be an hallucination of the Devil could be made to yield invaluable information both about the world in which the missionary had always to negotiate for his faith with those who were sceptical or 'of poor understanding' or downright stubborn, and about the ways in which all men unfortunate enough to be cut off from the light of God's true Word interpret the world in which they live. America, Acosta believed – and many of those who read his books shared his belief – was a laboratory for studying non-Christian man, and the lessons learnt therein might be applied elsewhere, in India and China, in 'Ethiopia', even in the mountains of Calabria and Granada.

The *Historia* is divided into two parts. The first deals with the material world, the 'works of nature in America', the second with anthropology, with what Acosta significantly called 'the things of the free will',[17] a phrase used to describe the normative behaviour, patterns of belief and past history of the American man. The concept of a work which sought to provide a description of both the natural and the human world was not, of course, itself very novel. Both Pliny and Herodotus, whose works offer closer parallels with Acosta's than any 'history' of a European people does, had aimed at a similar kind of 'total history'; and the similarities were not lost on contemporaries such as Acosta's French translator, Robert Regnault, who called him 'the Herodotus and the Pliny of this newly discovered world'.[18] Acosta, too, saw himself as heir to the great naturalists of the ancient world. 'If these natural things of the Indies', he wrote, 'were written out fully and with the degree of speculation which such remarkable things require, I do not doubt that it would be possible to write a work to compare with those of Pliny, Theophrastus and Aristotle.'

He denied, however, any ambition to rise to such heights. He would, he claimed, merely be content to note down 'a few natural things which I saw and thought about while I was in the Indies, or which I heard from reliable people, and which I believe are not widely known in Europe'.[19]

But despite this piece of rhetorical modesty, this *captatio benevolentiae*, it is clear that the *Historia* was intended to break new 'philosophical' ground; and it offered a clear, self-conscious programme for all future historians of the Indies. For the *Historia* was not only descriptive, it was also analytical; and thus, like the works of the ancient philosophers, it offered, on however reduced a scale, a universal account of its subject. Not only was the work 'in part philosophy and in part history',[20] but since it also provided an account of 'things' which are 'the marks not of men but of the creator', it was, said its author, also 'excellent theology'. In his introductory chapter to book 3 (the first of the five to be written independently of *De natura novi orbis*) Acosta leads his readers through a summary of his work which, he says, begins with history and then proceeds through an account of the 'natural causes of effects' to consider the overall structure of nature itself.[21] The *Historia* was, in short, meant to be read as a complete system of knowledge about the new world of America.

Acosta's most obvious predecessor was, of course, Oviedo (whom, however, he never once mentions). But despite the superficial similarities between the work of the two men – duly noted by Humboldt, who hailed them as the first true natural scientists of America[22] – Acosta owed very little to Oviedo. Oviedo's *Historia*, although it contains a wealth of detailed ethnographical observation among the fantastic account of 'unnatural' Indian practices, possesses very little structure;[23] and, beyond a few rudimentary comparisons with ancient barbarians, such as the Scythians, it offers no analysis of the material it collects. Acosta's *Historia*, on the other hand, sets out, as his own comparison with Theophrastus and Aristotle makes clear, to classify and to explain.

'Until now', he wrote, 'I have not seen a work which attempts to lay down (*declarar*) the causes and the reasons for so many novelties and strange things in nature.'[24] The *Historia* was meant to make good this omission, to provide causal explanations for what Acosta described to the Infanta Clara Eugenia as the diversity of 'the works which the Most High God has created in the machine of the world'.[25] For this reason alone it had, he believed, 'some claim to being called new'.

Acosta's self-conscious 'novelty' is apparent not only in what he attempted to do, but also in the methods he employed. Throughout the *Historia*, and to a lesser degree in *De procuranda*, there is a persistent emphasis on the demonstrative value of experience. Contemporary accounts of the Indies, Acosta believed, had so often proved to be inadequate or simply wrong because they had relied too heavily on imprecise data of the kind employed by those previous historians of America who had had no real experience of the Indians, 'either because they did not know their language or because they made no effort to learn about their past'.[26] Methodologically, too, both natural history and ethnology had, he believed, been too tightly constrained by the teachings of the ancients whose science was, as he put it, 'short and thin' not only in 'divine things' but also in human affairs.[27] The real, tangible experiences of the new world, its vegetation and mineralogy, its fauna, its climate and its geography had all revealed how false some of the assumptions made on the basis of ancient hypotheses had been.

Such observation on the failure of ancient theory to explain adequately all the facts of the new world would not have been unfamiliar to Acosta's readers. The challenge to received opinions offered by the geographical discoveries in the study of natural philosophy had long been accepted and geographical discovery had also become a common metaphor for discovery in other areas, including theology.

Acosta's proposal, however, was to exploit this insight in a comprehensive study of the entire American world including its inhabitants. For although novelty in nature was often readily apparent, 'novelty' as it concerned the behaviour of men had been almost invisible to previous commentators except as mere aberration. Acosta was, himself, a close observer of nature both animate and inanimate. The *Historia* not only contains the first noteworthy description of such things as altitude sickness and an account of the distillation of mercury as applied to the bonifaction of silver[28] but also, as we shall see, the first systematic attempt to distinguish between the various Indian cultures in the new world. With a keen eye and an acute sense for the differences between natural forms in the new world and the old, Acosta was highly sensitive to the possible errors in the uncritical use of ancient science in a world of which the ancients had had no experience. On finding himself cold at midday with the sun directly overhead – an impossible situation according to ancient meteorology – he 'laughed and made fun of Aristotle and his philosophy'.[29]

But his mockery of the 'ancients' should not be taken to mean that Acosta was a 'modern'.[30] He was deeply concerned with such things as the possible date of the end of the world – on which he wrote a lengthy treatise – which would have been wholly alien to the thinking of the Enlightenment. He might scoff at the conclusions of Aristotelian meteorology but his mental world, the conceptual cast of his mind, remained, none the less, firmly Aristotelian. His thinking was the thinking of the Jesuit school where he learned his philosophy and theology, and these had been dominated by the Thomism and the Aristotelianism of Vitoria and his successors.

It was, thus, not Aristotle's general method that Acosta attempted to challenge, much less Aristotle's accounts of the covering laws of nature; it was the uncritical way those laws had been applied to the phenomena in America. The declared purpose of the *Historia* was to 'first state the truth as certain experience has revealed it to us and then attempt (although this will be an arduous business) to provide the proper conclusions according to good philosophy'.[31] It was not the propositions in, for instance, the *Physics* that are under attack here, for these belonged to the realm of 'good philosophy', but the observations in the *Meteorologica*.

Acosta's insistence on the primacy of experience over received opinion amounts only to a recognition of the need for all the premises of philosophical inquiry, when these are to be extended to new areas of knowledge, to be carefully examined in the light of whatever empirical data are to hand. For since in any given situation there may exist a variety of different explanations, all of which may *appear* to satisfy the basic criteria for truth, the only means of knowing which hypothesis to select must be personal experience. Similarly, when, as in the case of Augustine's denial of the possible existence of human life in the 'Antipodes', on the grounds that all the races of men must be descended from Adam,[32] the premises of a seemingly impossible hypothesis are known to be absolutely true, experience will be the only means we have to demonstrate the falseness of the conclusions which have been drawn from them. And once we have learned some new truth by experience – in this case that there *are* men living beneath the tropics – then it is 'natural' to look for some alternative cause which satisfies all the facts of the case.[33]

For Acosta, Augustine's failure consisted not in the belief that all men are descended from Adam, because that was a matter of faith. It lay in the false assumption that there could be no possible geographical connection between Europe and the 'Antipodes', and consequently that if men lived on the far side of the globe they must somehow be *sui generis*.

A further plea for a critical evaluation of the necessary criteria for explanation informs his statement in *De procuranda* that missionaries should attempt to understand the Indians on their own terms and not by means of simple comparison with other races.[34] By this he did not mean to imply that all forms of human behaviour were equally valid and should be assessed by independent standards. He meant that an attempt to *understand*, or even to describe, an alien culture without some grasp of what sort of thing was being examined would inevitably lead to the use of absurd and inappropriate analogies. For, like Las Casas, like perhaps all those who had had prolonged contact with the Indians, Acosta was highly sensitive to the fact that America was another world from Europe, a world which only those who had lived in it could fully understand. Barchilón, the principal speaker in the Franciscan Pedro de Quiroga's dialogue *Libro intitulado coloquios de la verdad*, issues what must have been a typical warning to his friend Justino who has only recently arrived from Spain: 'have no dealings with the things of this land until you understand them', he cautions, 'because they are strange affairs and a strange language, which only experience will reveal to you'.[35]

The information received in Europe from the new lands was never very reliable and usually succeeded in conveying a false image even if the individual details were largely true. In most cases the reader was, in Acosta's opinion, simply unequipped with the conceptual tools with which to interpret correctly what he read. In quite another context, Acosta, in his treatise on the end of the world, *De temporibus novissimis*, wrote of his own first exposure to the realities of America:

Does this not happen every day when we go on a journey by land or sea or change our environment? For, indeed, in my case the things of the Indies seemed after I had had personal experience of them to be both the same as I had heard and not the same. Indeed I found them the same in that those who told me about them had not actually lied to me about them; but nevertheless I judged them to be different and very unlike what I had first thought. For this reason I found that my way of thinking about them was different.[36]

Facts no longer spoke for themselves; and in the *Historia*, since he was writing about things which were then past, he was particularly concerned with this crucial problem of how to understand what he had been told. Lactantius, he observed, had argued that the notion that there might be men in the Antipodes was absurd because as the world was round such men would have to be living upside down, in a world where trees grow down rather than up, and rain and snow 'fall' up rather than down.[37] The fallacy of this sort of argument, according to Acosta, lies in the fact that the human imagination is capable of perceiving connections between things where common sense dictates that none exists. Imagination is clearly essential to every form of scientific inquiry,[38] because very few areas of knowledge are open to direct empirical observation. We cannot, for instance, *know* that the world is suspended in space without imagining it since it is clearly impossible (or at least it was for Acosta) to secure any empirical evidence on the matter. Only the fact that in this case the 'picture' which our imagination presents to our intellect does not conflict with 'reason' will afford us any certainty that our intuitions are accurate. But if we 'let go' of our sense of what is plausible, we are, like Lactantius, likely to find ourselves believing in some very implausible things, for imagination is 'for the most part false' (*De anima* 427 b 25ff.). Lactantius's mistake was a conceptual one. His imagination presented to his rational mind an image of the world as a house, 'whose foundations are in the ground and whose roof is in the air'. Had Lactantius been more critical of his intuition he would have seen that since the antecedent of his counterfactual assumption was evidently false the consequence was bound to be false also.

In addition to its natural tendency to play tricks on us, our imagination is also, like our powers of observation, constricted by both time and space.[39] Any attempt, therefore, to project our understanding by imagination alone beyond those areas of experience over which we have no control will inevitably lead to error. An example of this, Acosta claimed, was to be found in man's persistent tendency to ask counter-factual questions. Although we know that the universe was created in a particular time and as a particular place, we none the less persist in attempting to imagine times before time and a place before the creation. 'Our reason', he wrote, 'clearly shows us that there was no time before there was movement, whose medium is time, nor was there any place before the creation of the universe which encompasses every place.'[40]

Any assessment of the Indians must, if we apply the lessons to be learnt from this epistemological digression, be based upon the kind of controlled imaginative exercise which will show, Acosta believed, that, for instance, although the world is round, we can no more fall off it than the stars and the planets can fall out of the universe on their daily journey westwards.[41] In the simplest terms we should not attempt to compare like with unlike. Those, for instance, who have tried to prove that the Indians were Jewish in origin have behaved very much as Lactantius. The apparent similarities between the supposed natural characteristics of the two races – their mendacity, ceremoniousness, deceitfulness and timidity – had led to a widely held belief that the Indians were the ten lost tribes described in the Book of Esdras. But a thorough examination of the cultural features of the two races revealed, to Acosta's satisfaction, the fallacy of this assumption and indeed of any identification made on the basis of characteristics which, whether they are real or (in this case) imputed, are not verifiable of themselves and may be subject to cultural change. It is precisely the culture of a people, their 'language and antiquities', their normative behaviour, and in the case of the Jews, 'their lineage, their law, their ceremonies, their Messiah and finally all their judaism', which mark them off from other races. The Indians, who have none of these things, who do not practise circumcision and have no alphabet (the Jews were, of course, thought of as the creators of the first alphabet) and who are far from being monotheistic cannot plausibly be associated with any Jewish race.[42]

It was Acosta's recognition of the uniqueness of cultural traits and their consequent importance for the classification and description of peoples, and the clarity with which he tied his observations of these traits to his 'philosophy', which made the *Historia* so enormously popular. Of all the vast literature on the Indies during this period Acosta's *Historia* was perhaps the only work which contemporaries recognised as having broken new ground.

4

Both the *Historia* and *De procuranda* had, however, another less detached purpose than either scientific investigation of a remote culture or the instruction of missionaries. Like Las Casas's voluminous writings, Acosta's two works were aimed at quashing the 'common and ignorant contempt in which the Indians are held by Europeans who think that these peoples have none of the qualities of rational men'.[43] Such attitudes of contempt towards the Indians had led to a fatal inability on the part of the Europeans to understand the peoples they were trying to convert not only to their system of beliefs but also to their way of life. Acosta recognised – and it was a recognition that many missionaries had had impressed upon them by often bitter experience – that true conversion depended upon communication and that communication could only be established once the missionary had come to know something of the density of the native cultures. For it was evidently impossible to say anything without a language; and a language is clearly more than an assembly of lexical and syntactical skills; it is a knowledge of what it is meaningful to say in any given context. Acosta's colleague in Brazil, Manuel da Nóbrega,[44] had complained in 1588 of the Tupinamba:

If they had a king it would be possible to convert them or if they worshipped something. But as they do not even know what it is to believe or to worship, they cannot understand the preaching of the Gospel; for preaching is based on being made to believe in and adore God and to serve him. And as these people worship nothing, nor believe in anything, nothing that is said to them means anything.[45]

Like Nóbrega, Acosta knew that it would be no good talking to Indians about 'churches', 'monasteries' and 'priests' if the potential convert had no experience of such things. In order for these 'objects' to be presented to the Indian they had to be explained in accordance with his degree of understanding. America was, Acosta knew, a place of wide cultural diversity, and before the fledgling missionary could carry out his task it would first be necessary for him to possess some understanding of the culture to which each group of his potential converts belonged. Methods of instruction, even modes of address, if they were to have the desired effect, had to be determined by the cultural background of the audience. It was no good talking to a nomadic culture-less being such as a Chichimeca in the same terms used to address an Inca or a Mexica.

The missionaries were very conscious of the high degree of misinformation which could be conveyed to the Indians in the course of religious instruction. As the authorities listened to stories of crucified children, of sacred bundles buried under the altars of churches, of the substitution of the names of Indian deities for those of the saints,[46] it became clear that most Indians had woefully failed to grasp the true significance of the Christian message. Ignorance of Indian languages and of the full meaning of certain Indian words meant, in the words of the Franciscan Maturino Gilberti (himself guilty of some curious behaviour in the quest for greater communication), 'that instead of being preached the truth they [the misisonaries] would be preaching error and falsehood'.[47] His fears were fully justified. Pablo José de Arriaga explained how incompetent preachers learning sermons in Quechua by rote, frequently garbled their words 'saying in the credo *Pucllachacuita* which means "the jesting or merriment of the saints" rather than *hucllachacuininta* which means "gathering of the saints" '.[48] It was no easy task to convey in an alien language a message which was itself alien to the culture which that language articulated. 'It is no small work', wrote one exhausted Augustinian, 'inquiring and discovering in a foreign tongue the property of the terms.'[49] In order to achieve this end the missionary had first to know all that was possible about the peoples among whom he was working. Both *De procuranda* and the *Historia* were intended to offer this much-needed guidance 'to those who have to deal with them [the Indians], for an understanding of their affairs will *encourage them to believe in ours*' (my italic).[50]

## 5

Like Las Casas, Acosta recognised that a correct understanding of the possible meanings inherent in the term 'barbarian' was crucial to such an enterprise. In general Acosta's opinion of the Indian mind was low, certainly far lower than that of Las Casas, and he believed that Indians were, in some sense, servile by disposition.[51] This fact had been demonstrated by experience, for 'if they are not obliged through fear and compelled by force like children, they will not obey'.[52] Some of the wildest of them, like the Chichemeca and the Otomí, who, as we shall see, played an important role in Acosta's account of cultural variation, may even, he thought, possess a mixed nature, part-man, part-beast, so that they seem to be indeed 'monsters of men'.[53] For there are, he reflected, peoples whose 'thought is so rebellious and sunk in evil' that it would be as difficult to change their ways as it would be to persuade an 'Ethiopian' to change his colour, or the leopard his spots.[54] Such creatures, he concluded, are perhaps the slaves of whom Chrysostom spoke as 'petulant' by nature and difficult to control.[55]

But all these reflections should not be taken too literally. In the first place they occur at the beginning of De procuranda, a work which is both organised along traditional scholastic lines (and thus presents both the pro and the contra of any argument), and which begins with an explicit denial of the possibility, or desirability, of providing a wholly coherent description of any complex reality, 'for whoever would be prudent will easily understand that a single thing cannot always be treated in an identical manner, and that this is not [the consequence] of the dictates of passion or caprice, but [the consequence] of following the demands of truth'.[56] The quotation from Chrysostom is also, in effect, a refutation of the theory of natural slavery. For not only was Chrysostom an opponent of slavery on the grounds that it conflicted with the Christian's understanding of the natural relationship between men, but he concluded the passage quoted by Acosta with the observation that the slave's brutish behaviour is not, indeed, to be attributed to the state of his mind, but to his contact with a slavish environment and to neglect by his master.[57]

However deep in darkness the Indians – and it is clear that this applies to all Indians – may now appear to be, there can be no doubt that their hour of light will come.[58] No man is born without sufficient grace for salvation, neither is any human being, however lowly, incapable of reason, and through the use of reason, of achieving perfection.[59]

The whole movement of Acosta's discussion both of the psychological disposition of the Indian and of the justice of the Spanish conquest derives from Vitoria's relectio De indis. Like Vitoria, he held that the only possible legitimation for the conquest lay in the natural right of all men to communicate with each other, and in the Christian's right, under divine law, to be allowed to preach the Gospel to the heathen.[60] Unlike Vitoria, however, he rejected the view that wars may be made against Indians in defence of the innocent;[61] and he does seem to have believed that the peoples he classified as belonging to the third type of 'barbarians' could be forcibly 'civilised' – at least in order that they might be converted.

Acosta's observations on the nature and cause of Indian servility are also made explicitly in the same context as Vitoria's had been, that is the theory of natural slavery. His remarks begin with a veiled reference to the debate over this theory ('leaving aside the partiality of the various groups which like a fog obscures the truth') and end with an explicit one to the condemnation, by Salamanca and Alcalá, of *Democrates secundus*.[62]

Acosta's own discussion of the subject is also, as he says, dependent on the works of Vitoria, Soto, Covarrubias and the Franciscan theologian Antonio de Cordóba, men 'whose opinion has, for some time now, triumphed over all others in the celebrated universities of Salamanca and Alcalá'. Like these authorities, Acosta concluded that natural slaves did not exist, and that slavish behaviour was, for the most part, the product of habituation. 'The incapacity of their minds', he wrote, 'the ferocity of their customs, does not derive from natural inclination or from the effect of climate, so much as from a prolonged education and customs like those of beast. I have long been persuaded that this was so, and I am now certain.'[63]

In further support of this conviction, he cited Aristotle's discussion of *akrasia* (incontinence) in book 7 of the *Nicomachean ethics*.[64] Aristotle offers three possible explanations for akratic behaviour: it arises either from some damage to the biological system of the individual, or from some natural perversity, or from the impact of custom on the mind. For Acosta, as for Vitoria, only the last of these hypotheses provided a satisfactory account of Indian social practices. Acosta knew, as he claimed, by experience, that Indians were neither mad nor incapable of deliberation; even the most brutish of them had some measure of *scientia*. They knew full well, as an Indian of Potosí had once told him, 'that this shirt of ours is white and the coat you wear is black, and which priest comes in search of our souls and which in search of our silver'.[65]

Every human mind, he maintained, following a traditional Aristotelian argument, acts in accordance with 'the forms it carries within itself';[66] and those forms were, in effect, the patterns of social expectation impressed by the community upon the growing child. Most Indians clearly possessed enough natural reason to be able to distinguish black from white and a bad priest from a good one; but beyond such simple cognitive acts they relied wholly upon the customs which their ancestors taught them. They could, however, like all reasonable beings be made to perceive the truth of the Christian 'law'. In the end they would come to laugh at the now self-evident folly of their ancient ways.[67] For these 'have so little basis (*fundamento*) in themselves that they are things to be laughed and mocked at'. Once the Indians have been made to 'see' the truth, they will, Acosta assured the future users of his *Confesionario*, 'submit to the truth as a thief surprised in his crime is caught'.[68]

But instruction, he knew, would not be an easy business. For customs possess, as we have seen, a directive force which is denied to 'natural reason' when the power to perceive the *prima praecepta* of the natural law has already been obscured and the mind, in Soto's phrase, 'made brutish'. 'In all nature', wrote Acosta, 'a motion which is directed towards some end is always the most prolonged and unswerving. Thus it is impossible for a stone to roll uphill, it is difficult to tame wild animals and hard indeed to persuade a man of little intellectual power to abandon his customs.'[69] But in refusing to abandon their perverse customs, Indians were, in fact, only behaving in a manner common to the unschooled masses of any society. Echoing Vitoria once again, Acosta pointed to the case of the Castilian peasant. 'We may see', he wrote, 'even in our own Spain, that men born in villages, if they remain among their own kind, persevere in their inept and gross customs; but if they are taken to schools, or to the court, or to famous cities, they are remarkable for their ingenuity and ability, and are overtaken by no-one.'[70]

Even the 'Ethiopians' (by which he meant all black Africans), who were generally held to be the most barbarous of peoples because they were commonly believed to 'live without laws and sell their own children',[71] could, if they were taken from their environment and reared 'in a palace' become, in all but the colour of their skins, just like other men.[72] Man is what he is taught to be and all those who behave like beasts do so only because they have been reared like beasts. As we have seen, this analogy between Indians and the European peasantry was widely used. Acosta's own insistence on the similarity between the two groups certainly did much to popularise the view of the American tribes as an entire 'nation of peasants'. It also convinced his fellow Jesuits in European rural areas that they should adopt similar teaching methods to those being used in America. Acosta's classification of 'barbarians' could be, in effect, applied as readily to the European 'rudes' as it had to the American Indians.[73]

The effects of such observations were, once again, to exclude the possibility that the Indian might belong to a category of half-men and to bring all barbarians 'in' to the world of the civilised man at the lowest possible social level. And if the Indian's patterns of behaviour were thought of as similar to those of a European peasant, so Acosta, like Vitoria, saw the Indian's psychological condition as similar to that of the child.[74] 'Barbarism' is said to be learnt; but the mental disposition which leads to a willingness to follow such customs is evidently 'puerile'.[75] 'The Indians', Acosta warned their future instructors, 'are more timid and more like children [than other peoples] and if they become afraid they will harbour secret hatreds.'[76]

The Indians do, therefore, possess a psychological disposition to act as children. But this, as we shall see, is only because the cultural world in which they live is, by comparison with Europe, a 'new' and hence a childish one.

The existence, furthermore, of certain groups of men whose cultural status was so low that they came close to being natural slaves was essential to Acosta's view of Indian culture. But before we look at this category of man it will be necessary first to make some preliminary remarks about Acosta's interpretation of the term 'barbarian'.

All Indians were obviously men and equally obviously they were, in some sense, to be classified as barbarians. But experience had taught Acosta, as it had taught Zorita and Las Casas, that to use the same term to describe all the 'Indians' 'that in our day have been discovered by the Spaniards and the Portuguese'[77] would only result in false analogy. 'The nations [of America]', he wrote in the preface to De procuranda, 'are very varied and diverse and very different from one another as much in climate, environment and dress as in intelligence and customs...It is a vulgar error to assume that the Indians are a single field or city, and because they are all called by the same name to ascribe to them a single nature and mind.'[78] Acosta the natural historian was well aware that to understand and to classify men one had to treat their cultural differences with as much care as one would the differences between separate species of plants.

## 6

Acosta was also aware, as Las Casas had been, that, however defined, the term 'barbarian' ultimately described the levels of communication that were possible between different groups of people. The more sophisticated the means of communication, both linguistic and social, at its command, the more civilised the group. In De procuranda, therefore, Acosta began his classification of the different types of 'barbarians' with language. The barbarians of the world could, he thought, be divided into three categories. In the first are those 'who are not much estranged from right reason and the customs of the human species'.[79] They possess at least the form of all those things which we have come to associate with 'civil' beings: stable republics, civil laws, fortified cities and rulers. But, 'what is more important, [they have] the use and the knowledge of letters, for wherever there are books and written monuments people are more humane [*humaniores*] and more politic'.[80] The Chinese, whose writings Acosta had seen in Mexico,[81] are such a race; and so too, perhaps, are the Japanese and the inhabitants of certain parts of India. Although such peoples are truly barbarous and in many respects defy the natural law, they are to be converted in a way analogous to that used by the Apostles to convert the Greeks and the Romans. For since there exist obvious channels of communication between such barbarians and Christians, their conversion can be effected merely by demonstrating to them where they have gone wrong in their understanding of nature. This belief in the ready availability of the Christian message was a common one among the Jesuits. Culture was, of course, held to be inseparable from the religious beliefs which informed it. And so once the Christian's superior knowledge of the world and his superior technology had been demonstrated to the barbarians, they would, it was thought, readily agree to accept his superior religion. The suggestion of Mateo Ricci, one of the early missionaries in China, that the Chinese emperor would be converted by the gift of a clock, may now seem naive, but the principal supposition which underlay it was not far removed from Acosta's own.[82] When, it was assumed, the emperor had seen how the Europeans were able to measure time with such accuracy and simplicity, he would also come to accept their interpretation of the universe and their account of the God, the great clock-maker, who had created it.[83]

The second category of barbarians lacks both a system of writing and, thus, all philosophical or 'civil' wisdom, though such peoples still possess the forms of social organisation common to civilised men and 'some solemn form of religious cult'.[84] The Mexica and the Inca who do, as Acosta was to explain at greater length in the *Historia*, possess ingenious approximations to a written script, belong to this category, and therefore constitute an immediately preliterate phase in the evolution of society. They form 'empires' and they 'live in villages and settlements and do not wander about like beasts'.[85] The transition to Christian forms both of worship and of behaviour should be effected through all the means of communication possible, and these include not only the language of words but also the language of symbols. The indigenous rites, customs and ceremonies, Acosta believed, could not, should not, be obliterated. Instead they should be translated into other rites. customs and ceremonies, the pagan being substituted by the Christian.[86] He believed also in preserving as much as possible of the ancient Indian social fabric, what he described as their 'fueros', so long as these did not conflict with Christian practice.[87] It was, he warned, not wise when dealing with such 'higher' barbarians 'to attempt to make them Spaniards in all things because apart from being very difficult it will cause the downfall of everything and do great harm to their government and republic'.[88] But the new Christian Indian world could only function within the framework of the 'higher' social order provided by the European political community. Communication could only occur within the limits imposed by the more powerful and, in Acosta's view, culturally superior, authority.

Finally, at the bottom of the human scale there are the 'savages who are close to beasts and in whom there is hardly any human feeling'.[89] These would seem to lack all communication with their fellow men. They are nomadic and live outside all known forms of civil organisation. Sometimes, too, like the Caribs, they are man-eaters and walk about naked, thus clearly demonstrating their lack of both *scientia* and *opificia* for there is, as we have seen, nothing so ignorant as a cannibal nor anyone so unskilled as the man who cannot even make himself a set of clothes. The number of these creatures is legion. They are the Chuncos, the Chiriguanes, the Moxos, the Yscayingos, all the peoples of Brazil and the inhabitants of Florida. Such peoples have to be driven out of the jungle and into settlements and there be instructed in the ways of true men like children before they can be converted. They would appear to be similar to Aristotle's natural slaves. But although Acosta, like Las Casas, believed that a form of tyranny is the proper mode of government for barbarians, and that there are some people who are so far beyond the pale of civilised society that they do not behave like men at all, he rejected the suggestion that such things might have an innate cause. In his discussion of slavery Aristotle had, in Acosta's view, made an unwarranted analogy between the 'natural' inferiority of women and children to adult males on the one hand, and the distinction between the *barbaroi* and the Greeks on the other. The natural slave theory, he suspected, had been prompted by Hellenic xenophobia and came 'not from philosophical reason, but from popular opinion'.

Acosta's argument, like that of Las Casas and Juan de la Peña, constitutes an attack upon the status of a single theory within a text which he was otherwise prepared to accept as authoritative. Since Aristotle had evidently created the natural slave theory in order to please Alexander, he was, at this point, 'adulating rather than philosophising'.[90] His words, therefore, have no authority, and the whole theory may legitimately be extracted intact from the body of the *Politics*, without doing damage to the main points of Aristotle's definition of the 'barbarian'.

Acosta's third class of barbarian, therefore, although it retains all the outward features of the natural slave, is no 'third species' between man and animal. However wild such creatures may be, they are still as men perfectable creatures capable of salvation. That this is indeed how contemporaries read Acosta is clear from the remarks of the jurist Juan de Solórzano Pereyra. Commenting on this category of barbarian, he observed that Acosta had not been describing wild men 'who have nothing of men' and would indeed have been slaves by nature, but 'true men born of Adam' who, although they live in caves and woods, go naked, lack all communication with their fellow men and are thus 'similar to the brute beasts',[91] may, with assistance and a better institutional existence in which to learn to practise virtue, come finally to perfection. Despite the 'vain opinion of some', he concluded all men may *learn* reason, for all human beings are capable of understanding rational speech, no matter how brutish they may be, and through language may come to acquire the customs of civilised men.[92]

## 7

This grouping of barbarians into three distinct types separated from each other by their cultural habits is repeated, with a rather different configuration and less theoretical emphasis, in the *Historia*.

There, however, Acosta began his description with the forms of Indian government. 'For it is a known thing that barbarians demonstrate their barbarism most in their government and mode of command.'[93] In the first category there will still be the Asiatic barbarians who, like the Chinese, could be said to 'exceed all other peoples in the preservation of their laws, ceremonies and politic government'.[94] But in the *Historia* these are conceived only as a highly developed version of the kind of society which exists among the 'monarchies' of Mexico and

Peru. Such barbarians live in cities, in ordered societies under a rule of law. They began their existence, like the Tepaneca, the ancestors (in Acosta's account) of the Mexica, as elective monarchies whose kings 'ruled like a consul or *dux*'.[95] Later, however, their rule became 'pure and tyrannical', for as barbarian societies lack a social contract, a barbarian ruler is unable to perceive that his superiority over his people derives not from any innate quality of his own but from his responsibility for the welfare of the community as a whole. It is the office that makes the man. Those who ignore this fact, like the 'kings' of Mexico and Peru, who disguise themselves as gods and treat all other men as beasts, create tyrannies.

But for Acosta, as indeed for Las Casas, this kind of tyranny where the ruler was chosen by the people, not imposed by an outsider, was the highest form of civil association to which the non-Christian could aspire. Tyrannies of the kind that Aristotle had ascribed to the Persians might be imperfect from the point of view of the 'civilised' man; but as they were more complex and thus a superior form of society to any other in the barbarian world, they would sweep all lesser forms before them. Pedro Mexía de Ovando, a royal official in Mexico in the 1630s who had clearly absorbed the message of Acosta's *Historia*, noted that the success of the Mexica provided evidence of the comforting truth that a government with proper laws, legitimate and firm rulers, clear and natural customs, will inevitably triumph over a society which is institutionally and culturally weak, even when it is militarily less powerful.[96]

Beneath groups such as these came tribes which possessed a far looser political structure. In *De procuranda* Acosta had classified them – in particular the Araucana and the Tucapel of Chile – together with the 'monarchical' Mexica and Inca. In the *Historia*, however, they exist in a category by themselves. They are described as living in settlements but not in cities and as being ruled not by 'kings' but 'by the advice of many in councils'. In times of war they elected a chieftain 'whom the whole nation or province obeys'.[97] This description applies to some form of 'segmentary system',[98] where political power is subsumed into the kin structure of the group, and it was likened by Acosta to the voluntary feudatories, the *behetrías* or *señoríos libres* of Castile. Landa described such political organisations among the Maya;[99] and it is probably true that, in a general sense, as Acosta said, 'the greatest part of the new world is governed in this manner, where there are no established kingdoms nor republics, nor princes, nor kings'.[100]

Finally there is the third class of barbarian. As in *De procuranda*, these are said to lack any form of *consortium*. They dwell outside the human community, shunning the natural settlement areas on the plains, and living instead 'among the rocks and the most barren places in the mountains'.[101] They survive by hunting, or by eating unclean food, 'snakes, lizards, rats, locusts and worms'.[102] They have no true family structure, and (and this is important for reasons that will be clear later) they are nomadic.

In reality this last group was largely the creation of the European imagination. Many of the tribes which Acosta ascribes in both the *Historia* and *De procuranda* to this category – the Otomí, the Chichimeca, the Chiriguanes, the peoples of Brazil – were probably segmentary groups. A reading of some of the reports by Acosta's colleagues is sufficient to demonstrate that much.[103] Acosta himself did not, of course, invent this category. Its existence is inferred from the presence of the other two classes of barbarians. Races who, as one observer phrased it, 'live alone like animals or birds of prey and do not [even] come together to protect themselves or to find their food'[104] are simply the lowest type of man imaginable, society-less, virtually speechless and so persistently nomadic that their women are forced to give birth while on the move.[105]

But although Acosta was only appropriating a familiar type, its existence was essential to the coherence of his classification of barbarians. For he, like Las Casas, was willing to accept that all the races of men had once been such primitive culture-less beings. Certainly the evidence of Saint Bernard and of Bede had convinced him that the Irish and the English had once lived similar lives.[106] If even they had now risen to acceptable levels of civility, then there was every reason to suppose that the Indian might also. All the races of men had at some stage in their history passed through each of these three levels of barbarism before becoming fully civilised human beings. Since, in this post-lapsarian world, true civility can only be achieved through final conversion to Christianity, one day all the races of the world must be gathered into the fold of the Church. And when that day comes, of course, the millennium will begin. Acosta, like Las Casas, like the great historian of the Inca world Garcilaso de la Vega, believed that the highest stage of barbarism, represented in America by the Mexica and the Inca, had served to prepare the way for the coming of the faith, just as the empires of the ancient world had prepared the way for the coming of Christ himself.

Acosta's own commitment to a providentialist interpretation of human history is apparent not only in *De procuranda* and the *Historia* but also in *De temporibus novissimis* which appeared in Rome in the same year as the *Historia* and was probably written during the same period. *De temporibus* is an attempt to resolve a problem of much contemporary concern: the possibility or – in Acosta's view – impossibility of determining the date of the end of the world. Its arguments display the same concern with method and the same insistence on empirical data to be found in his other writings. It is not, for all that, a very original work; but its existence alone reflects its author's concern with the logic of the historical process, with the relations between the human and the divine time scales and, above all, with the nature and purpose of human evolution.[107]

## 8

Each stage in the evolution of the barbarians' social order is accompanied by a comparable stage in the manner of their religious observance. Religion is an integral part of every social activity as much for the idolatrous pagan as for the Christian. 'Neither in war nor in peace,' wrote Acosta, 'nor in rest nor at labour, neither in the public nor in the private life, nothing are they [the Indians] capable of doing unless it is first preceded by the superstitious cult of their idols.'[108]

All barbarians are, of course, by definition pagans, but paganism took many forms, all of which were regarded as, in the ancient sense of the word, an 'art'. And all of them could thus, like any other human activity, be graded for civility and located on the historical scale.

In the *Historia* Acosta divides paganism ('idolatry') into three distinct categories which, it should be noted, correspond to the three major links in the hierarchy of the natural world. In the first category is the worship of natural phenomena – stones, streams, mountains, etc. – in the second, the worship of animals and in the third, the worship of anthropomorphic idols.

Man's religious consciousness is said to begin as simple superstition. Although the distinctions are rarely precise, Acosta, like many of his contemporaries when speaking of the Indians, revived the ancient dichotomy between the idea of a religion, which was an organised controlled activity, and superstition, which was an unfocused and disordered one. In Roman eyes *superstitio* had been characterised by such things as an excessive belief in omens and magic; superstition was the 'religion' of the lower orders and the word was also used to describe imported foreign cults such as Druidism and Christianity, which were believed to lay great emphasis on secret and frenzied rites. *Religio*, on the other hand, was the official state religion, the forms of worship followed by the patrician class whose rites were public and orderly.[109] Both types, of course, reflect accurately the social order of those who practise them. Thus in Acosta's opinion the Mexica and the Inca who lived in recognisable communities had a 'religion' – however bloody and unnatural its rites. But those peoples whose social life was in disarray, those who, as Jean de Léry said of the Tupinamba, were wholly ignorant of the things of this world,[110] having no means of measuring the passage of time, nor any explanation either of the origins of the world or of the existence of a life beyond this one, could not possibly imagine a deity either celestial or terrestrial. All they were capable of worshipping – for all men possess a natural instinct for veneration – are the objects they see before them. In such a world every man has his own god; like the inhabitants of Mandeville's island of Chana, they worship whatever they so please, most being content with 'the first thing they meet in the morning'.[111]

Superstition bred off social and intellectual disorder because it was conceived as the belief that the natural world was composed of separate autonomous parts, each of which possessed its own power over human destiny. It had for long been considered a distinguishing mark of the barbarian and of all those who, like certain heretics, had lapsed into inarticulate forms of religion. 'They have many superstitions', wrote one churchman of the Maya, 'which seem to resemble those of the sect of the *alumbrados*.'[112] Like magic, such superstition was, as Edward Tylor phrased it in the late nineteenth century, characteristic of 'the lowest known stages of civilisation, of the lowest races who have not partaken largely of the education of the world'.[113] Acosta would have agreed with him; for the significant fact about superstition is that it is based on a category mistake which is only possible for people who lack true *scientia*, who have indeed 'not partaken largely of the education of the world'. Those Indian tribes, like the inhabitants of 'Barbaria' whom Gregory the Great had chastised for worshipping stone and wood 'like insensate animals',[114] had confused the creature with the creator. By so doing they had, in Saint Paul's words, 'changed the truth of God into a lie' (Romans 1.25).

Acosta, like most of the missionaries in America, failed to understand what a man who pays homage to a carved image or a piece of stone is *doing*. For him, as for all Christians generally, every form of worship had, by its very nature, to be directed towards a creator–deity. If the

Indians worshipped rocks and stones they did so because, in some inexplicable way, they had been persuaded that those things had an independent creative power of their own. It therefore only required a persuasive demonstration of the category error on which such beliefs were founded to eradicate them. For the Franciscan Diego de Valadés it would have been sufficient to point out to Indians who worshipped animals that as animals are evidently unworthy creatures, lower in the natural scale even than man, they must, of necessity, have been created by some higher being. So, too, with wooden images. Since these must clearly have been manufactured by men, they could not possibly be themselves creators.[115] For the Christian all of the things the Indians worshipped were simply inappropriate as god-material, for true gods had to be remote, abstract and intellectual beings. But even when the Indians did seem to worship such beings the same method of instruction was recommended, only in this case, since a man's readiness to venerate an abstract entity already indicated a high level of religious intelligence, the hoped-for result would be easier to obtain. Acosta described how 'an intelligent captain who was a good Christian' had converted a sun-worshipping Indian chieftain.

He asked the chieftain and principal lord to give him a swift-footed Indian to deliver a letter. The chieftain did so and the captain asked him, 'Tell me who is the lord and chieftain, the Indian who carries that letter or you who sends it.' The chieftain replied, 'I am in no doubt because that man does only what I tell him to do.' 'The same relationship', replied the captain, 'exists between the sun we see and the Creator of all.'[116]

Once the Indian had had explained to him in terms he could understand, terms which appealed to his own experience of reality, the true relationship between the things in nature, he could see immediately the falseness of a religion which implied an inversion of that relationship.

All forms of superstition, whether they consist of the simple adoration of stones, rocks and trees or of the more sophisticated adoration of natural forces whose power over the lives of men is evident enough, are based on the kind of fundamental category mistake which Acosta's chieftain had made in confusing the sun with 'He who moves it'. But *superstitio* also lacks the structure and above all the necessary ritual expression, the cult (*cultus*) which is the essence of a true *religio*. Religious beliefs which possess no means of expression are proper only for those peoples without any real communication with each other, because religion is, of course, a form of discourse, an essential part of the natural *consortium* between men. Giovanni Botero, whose classification of 'savagery' (*fierezza*) in his *Relationi universali* follows closely that of Acosta in *De procuranda*, described the superstition of the Brazilians and the Chichimeca as being 'without foundation or probability of any kind, closer to dreams than reasoned human discourse'.[117] Such inarticulate and unstructured religious forms clearly belonged to the primitive pre-social and almost pre-linguistic phase of man's development. For these are the peoples, Botero says elsewhere, 'who do not display in their behaviour (*operationi loro*) any other discourse save that which is necessary for survival'.[118] Which is why, thought Acosta, they could only be converted through the ample use of ritual, for ritual is, of course, another mode of speech, but one that requires less rational understanding than language does.[119]

Once men have gathered themselves together into communities and created a vehicle for social exchange they will inevitably begin to focus and to structure their religious beliefs and practices. The first move will be to shift the object of veneration from inanimate to animate, from rocks and stones to animals, because animate objects succeed inanimate ones in the scale of being. Such image worship is crude and 'bestial', but it represents, nevertheless, a break with the world of unformed, undirected superstition, just as the segmentary system represents a break with the unformed social world of the lowest class of barbarians.

Finally as men move from primitive unhierarchical social unions to the fully articulated society, with a social hierarchy and a settled place of residence, so they move from totemism to true idolatry,[120] and from the middle stage in the scale of creation to the last, from animals to man himself. As man's culture evolves, as his control over his material environment and over himself becomes more complex, as he develops arts and institutions, so his religion approaches in form, if not in content, the true one. Since Christianity depends on revelation it is obvious that no race before the coming of Christ, nor any which has not heard the Gospel, can be fully civilised or possess a fully adequate religion. But many non-Christians – the ancient Greeks and Romans, the modern Chinese – have come very close to it. Acosta's account of the steady rise of all races through the different levels of religious experience available to men is based on the categories available from the traditional description of the scale of nature, and reflects a contemporary insistence that both biological and cultural evolution consists in the acquisition of progressively complex forms.

(This process may also, of course, operate in reverse. If a man were to detach himself from the community to which he belongs by nature then he would become increasingly de-cultured and in both this behaviour and his understanding grow ever closer to the condition of the beast. This, in the eyes of Catholic apologists like Stanislaus Hosius, is what became of heretics. Having forsaken the company of the true Church and with it the company of all true men, they fell ineluctably from Lutheranism to Anabaptism and then to Epicureanism until they came finally to place their trust in magic and in omens.)[121]

The main patristic source which Acosta employs in *De procuranda* to describe the progressive rise of the pagan towards final and inevitable Christianisation was Saint John Damascene. Saint John ascribed the three types of image worship – the worship of natural objects, the worship of animals and the worship of men – to three races of the ancient world which represented for him three different levels of civility. The worship of the elements was, he said, characteristic of the Chaldeans, the worship of animals of the Egyptians (for both Saint John and Acosta, Osiris and Isis were nothing more than a cow and a jackal) and the worship of men of the Greeks.[122] None of these peoples, of course, were 'barbarians' in the sense that Acosta understood the word; but the differences between them, and their relationship to each other, are typologically the same as those between Acosta's own categories of cultural types.

It should be noted, however, that although each stage represents a move forward, all idolatrous peoples carried with them the remnants of their past experience. The missionaries in particular made a clear distinction between the different levels of religious practices they discovered being observed simultaneously, between what they called the Indians' 'superstition' and their 'false religion'.[123]

The transition from one level of religious consciousness to another is mediated, as are all forms of human expression, through the social order. The truth of this is apparent from the euhemeristic explanation of the origins of (true) idolatry Acosta uses in the *Historia*. This is taken from the Book of Wisdom and it goes as follows: A man creates an image of his dead son so that he shall not forget him. Soon he comes to worship the image itself. In the third and final stages he imposes this worship upon the members of his household.[124] The beginnings of idolatry are thus to be found in some form of ancestor worship.

This explanation of the origins of idolatry, like Euhemerus's own, was read as a metaphor. The household is a metonym for the whole society and within that society 'the father' is represented by the 'king' and the long-dead culture hero by the 'son'. By deifying real men, idolaters were, once again, failing to distinguish adequately between two different categories of things, in this case two different types of image. The true image is an image of something which exists, or existed, in the world of the senses: the Christ, the Virgin, the saints and so on. False images or idols – generally referred to as *simulacra*[125] – are representations of things which though they may, like angels and cherubim, be said to have had some kind of existence, are not available for sensory examination. Thus although it was quite proper for a Christian to venerate (but not of course, although the distinction was a fine one, to worship) the wooden image of a saint, it was not proper for him to honour the carved figure of an angel in the same manner.

The Christian use of images was, as the missionaries knew, open to misrepresentation. The story told by one friar, Fernando de Carrera, is typical enough of the predicament they too often found themselves in. One Sunday, Fr. Fernando was faced with having to explain to his flock that the image of Saint Martin in their church was itself neither a god nor a saint and, indeed, that 'neither a bundle nor an image of the saint which was on the altar was Saint Martin himself'. The Indians were not pleased with this piece of information, accused their priest of being a heretic and complained bitterly that they would be the mockery of the neighbouring village for not having a god of their own. Carrera attributes this misunderstanding to the inability of the local priests to explain to the Indians in their own language the difference between their 'gods' and the images of the Christian saints.[126] But the misunderstanding may have been Fr. Fernando's own, for his story depends upon a belief common among missionaries that for the Indians the image *was* the god. Las Casas pointed out, as Jerome had done before him, that since pagans do not swear by a rock or a piece of stone, but in the *name* of their deities,[127] idols cannot be other than symbolic representations. The euhemeristic account of the origins of idolatry, however, presupposed a simple conflation of the image with the creature it represents. Which is why the Spaniards were so keen to cast down idols, believing that they could not be manufactured anew and that the obvious inability of the Indian gods to rise up and defend themselves would be sufficient proof of their vanity.

Idolatry came easily to the unguided pagan, hiding as it did behind what Alexio Vanegas called 'the natural appetite which men have to reproduce themselves'.[128] But the full force of any idolatrous religion could only in Christian eyes be implemented through the machinery of the state. 'This error', Acosta concluded, 'became canonised by law, and so by the command of tyrants and kings, figures and images were worshipped as gods.'[129] Only a highly structured social order could conceive of and maintain a highly complex religious order. The most 'civilised' communities in America were, therefore, as Acosta duly noted, also the most idolatrous.[130] Furthermore, since all the various levels of human progress are reciprocal, barbarian 'kings' who, by definition, ruled as tyrants, could only adequately maintain their power through the manipulation of sacred symbols, by keeping their people, as Acosta phrased it, 'occupied with idolatry'.[131]

The Indians thus lived in fear of their gods, who threatened every deviation from the social norm with dire punishments. The Inca, Acosta observed, practised a form of confession. But as the Inca gods formed a part, not of a spiritual world, but of the merely human social order, all the 'sins' confessed consisted of social misdemeanours. Furthermore, since these gods had no metaphysical existence, the Indians who worshipped them knew nothing of an afterlife. They 'lived in vain hope of some material gain. But the thought of eternal reward never entered their heads.'[132]

Although religion was thought of as the highest of man's cultural achievements, and an integral part of his social world, it was also an area which no Christian, in particular no Jesuit, could regard with entire detachment. For Acosta, with his overriding concern with causation, the only satisfactory explanation for the forms of pagan religious expression was satanic intervention. Only the works of Satan could adequately explain how, as Girolamo Garimberto put it, the Indians could have known about 'laws and customs similar to our own before they had any knowledge of us, or we of them'.[133] Satan's role in the *Historia* is crucial. Acosta had had, or so he believed, personal experience of Satan's power to fill the heads even of Christians like Francisco de la Cruz and Luís López with delirious fantasies. Satan, the Lord of Misrule, worked in the new world as he did in the old, only with a freer hand. He inverted or polluted the natural order of things, taking man's unguided natural reason and diverting it into foul channels where it created evil out of potential good. The image of Amerindian society as a cruel inversion of hallowed norms was a common one.[134] The views of Juan Suárez de Peralta, a resident in Mexico in the 1580s, are ingenious but not unrepresentative. The Indians, he argued, must originally have been 'Ethiopians or Egyptians' since the worlds of both peoples were exact inversions of the natural order. Both have, he claimed, 'the custom that the women do business and deal with trade and other public offices while the men remain at home and weave and embroider. They [the women] urinate standing while the men do so seated; and they have no reluctance to perform their natural deeds in public.'[135] Peralta's observations, which derive in every detail from Herodotus's description of the Egyptians, are quite obviously fictitious. But even the less imaginative observer could point to any number of Indian practices, to the couvade which Cosimo Brunetti offered as conclusive proof of the barbarism of the Arawak,[136] or the transvestite rituals recorded by Oviedo[137] as proof of the general view that the American world was a world turned upside down.

And if the social order was, at so many points, an obvious inversion, how much so was the religious? It was common knowledge that Satan always sought to compete with God: 'and the more saintly and devout the things he [the Devil] makes men do', wrote Pedro Ciruelo, canon of Salamanca cathedral, of Satan's activities in America, 'the greater is the sin against God'.[138] Thus, although the forms of the religion practised by the highest category of barbarians may in many respects have displayed high levels of complexity and hence a degree of civility, they were also strongly marked by inversion or perversion. The whole structure of Mexica religion, claimed Acosta, even to the names of their priests, was a mockery of God.[139] Like the Egyptians before them, the Mexica and the Inca had been led to imitate Moses, Aaron and Micha by using the trappings of the tabernacle to 'compete with the ancient law and usurp its ceremonies'.[140] Satan was capable of conveying to the Indians a distorted account of such things as the Trinity[141] and the Virgin birth.[142] And not only did the Devil convey false information and insinuate himself into what Acosta classifies as 'sacrifices and idolatry', he also 'imitated' confession, communion and the feast of Corpus Christi.[143] The Devil inverted these Christian rites by transforming deeds which God had instituted to secure beneficial ends into evil deeds intended to have unhappy ends. By so doing he tricked the Indian mind into performing the series of crucial category mistakes which are the sources of all forms of pagan religion from simple superstition to true idolatry. Simple inversion of this kind was also accompanied by high levels of real and ritual pollution, by 'one of three things which are, cruelty, filth, slovenliness'. The Mexican 'host' was made of amaranth seeds compounded with human blood. Sacrifices were either of men or of unclean animals. The blood-washed walls of the 'oratories' and the filthy matted hair of the priests all horrified the missionaries because they were the very reverse of the Christian emphasis on cleanliness and sacramental purity. 'All their rituals', wrote Acosta, 'were cruel and harmful. Such as the killing of men and the shedding of blood; or very dirty and repugnant, such as eating and drinking in honour of their idols or, while holding them aloft, urinating in their name and smearing and staining their bodies so hideously.'[144] Filth, real or symbolic, seemed to be everywhere.

All of this, of course, is in keeping with Satan's old image as the *Simia Dei*, the arch-deceiver of mankind.[145] The most dramatic, most offensive, instance of satanic pollution, however, operated at a deeper than ritual level. This was cannibalism. Cannibalism is closely associated with satanic desire, both because it is self-consuming and because it relies, as we have seen, on the same kind of mental error which permits men to worship the wooden images of men as gods.

Acosta approached the subject with Vitoria's *De temperantia* in hand.[146] For him, as for Vitoria, as indeed for Aquinas,[147] cannibalism was viewed as but one part of a category of 'unnatural crimes' which included, most strikingly, acts of sexual deviance such as onanism and sodomy. Both of these are against nature because, as we have seen, they involve, like sodomy, inappropriate sexual partners or, like onanism, a sexual act 'in a vessel not ordained for it'.[148] Indians, like other 'primitives', were frequently accused of being homosexuals and onanists or of practising bestiality. Even when they had access to beautiful women, reported Cieza de León, 'many of them (as I have been reliably informed) publicly and openly practised the nefarious sin of sodomy' while the Arawak, according to Oviedo, even wore jewels depicting 'the diabolical and nefarious act of sodomy'.[149]

Like cannibalism also, unnatural sexual practices were commonly imputed to dangerous outsiders, particularly if those outsiders were unorthodox in their religious beliefs. The highly imaginative fourth-century bishop of Salamis, Saint Epiphanis, described the religious rites of the hated Gnostics as a mixture of unnatural or unproductive sexual acts followed by a cannibal feast. This association between religious deviance and sexual mal-practice is even reflected in the Theodosian code where only sodomy and heresy are punishable by burning, a means of execution intended to rid the community of every vestige of the miscreant.[150]

Cannibalism, onanism and sodomy were, Acosta argued, prohibited at all times, though the failure to eat will result in death through starvation and the failure, for a man, to have sexual intercourse may result in a serious disturbance of the humours.[151] All of these crimes lay so far outside the natural world that even an argument from the most dire necessity could not be applied to them. But Acosta saw another dimension to the subject. For cannibalism, like onanism, like sodomy, is a form of self-pollution. Men, as the doctors well knew, are to a great extent conditioned by what they eat. Those who eat only the food of savages, the roots, nuts, berries, 'that which the earth produces',[152] in Botero's words, will be like savages. Such fare is, as Las Casas had observed, not very good for the human mind.[153] Neither were the bodies of the 'lower' animals; and the Church in Peru made an effort to punish anyone found eating lizards or fleas 'or licking the plates off which they eat'.[154] Every man who ate – even for survival – foods which were, by their nature, inappropriate to his species was guilty of an act of self-defilement.

Such unsavoury food, however, polluted less than did the flesh of men. If a man was to eat one of his fellows, Acosta maintained, his body would become contaminated. Cannibals were, he said, quoting Romans 1.24, given up 'to uncleanness through the lusts of their own hearts, to dishonour their own bodies between themselves'.

It is also the duty of every Christian to love his neighbour *as himself*. In order to fulfil this commandment a man must, however, love himself in the first place. This self-love, or self-respect – to which Acosta dedicates an entire chapter of *De procuranda* – consists precisely in not polluting the body by such acts as cannibalism. Here man-eating is linked once again to crimes of sexual deviance, which are 'sleeping with men, with beasts, even with trees [sic], [sleeping] in the incestuous arms of one's sisters, mother or daughters, acts which among certain barbarians are not only permitted but justified by law'.[155]

It was, Acosta believed, such deviations from natural behaviour that had brought about the downfall of the Peruvian 'empire'.[156] And because their deeds constitute a violation of man's rightful place in the natural world, men who eat men, or lie with beasts or with their sisters, are thought to be capable of a whole string of crimes against the natural order – bloodletting, homicide, theft, deceits, corruptions, infidelities and all the 'other vices' which Acosta took from the formidable catalogue of aberrations provided by the Book of Wisdom (14.22–30) and summarised as 'uncertainty of birth [i.e. of paternity], inconstancy in marriage, adultery and lasciviousness'. All of these are, of course, not only examples of sexual immorality; they are also a threat to the institution of the family and thus to the social fabric as a whole. As such they are said to be 'caused' by idolatry. For just as religious forms are dependent upon, and operate through, the social order, so do men's religious beliefs come to affect the way in which they behave towards their fellow men. Cannibalism, the dissolution of the natural relations between the sexes, the disintegration of the family, all these things – together with such direct assaults on the social fabric as sedition and political unrest – are inversions or perversions of the natural order. The root cause of them all is 'idolatry' because idolatry was the means by which Satan first blinded men to the true shape of God's design for nature. The creation of idols, said Acosta, quoting Wisdom 14.12, 'was the beginning of fornication, and the invention of them was the corruption of life'.[157]

Idolaters – true idolaters that is – would seem, therefore, to be the most depraved, the most barbarous of all men, unclean in body and in spirit. But although the highest category of barbarians such as the Inca and the Mexica were, in Acosta's eyes, certainly the most devout of all the Indian groups in their worship of Satan, the most spectacular in their defiance of the law of nature, their culture was ultimately closer to the civil world of the Christian than that of either of the other two categories. Because, however satanic in form some of the observances of such barbarians may be, their religious order comes closer in structure to the structure of the Christian Church than any other. It has a priesthood, a place of worship, a complex set of rituals and even places that resemble monasteries.[158] For Acosta, no less than for Las Casas, such things were a sign of true reasoning. They may be the creation of the Devil, but the Devil cannot sow in barren soil. His lies are always sacramental, ritualistic. He cannot teach men what to think or to believe; he can only deceive them into reading the book of nature incorrectly, into doing the right things in the wrong way.

Once the satanic rite has been successfully detached from the source of its inspiration, it may be recast as a Christian one. Like Saint Augustine, Acosta clearly saw 'depaganisation' and 'christianisation' as two separate objectives.[159] Once the Indians had been effectively 'depaganised' (by means of the kind of logical arguments offered by Acosta himself and missionary theorists like Diego de Valadés) the very nature of some, at least, of their rites and institutions would enable them to understand the Christian faith the more easily. The teaching of that faith would never be a simple matter; but in choosing to ape some of its basic tenets, Satan had, in effect, greatly facilitated the conversion of the Indians, and, Acosta explained, 'the very things which he [Satan] stole from our law of the Gospel, such as confession and communion and the worship of three in one and other things...enabled those who had accepted the lies to more easily accept the good'.[160]

### 9

As there are three different levels of barbarism in both the social and the religious spheres, so there are three distinct levels of cultural attainment of which barbarians are capable. As man's social environment becomes more complex, so his ability to interpret and adapt the world in which he lives becomes more sophisticated. For Acosta, the inexorable progress of men towards a state of civility through the growth of *scientia* is best measured by the state of their language. Acosta saw language as a source of power in man, a power akin to his ability to dominate and transform his physical environment. The truly civilised man will develop a language commensurate with his cultural abilities just as he will possess a technical culture equipped to supply his material needs. 'Barbarism', as we have seen, was a concept grounded in the linguistic differences between peoples, and this grounding was something which no-one who struggled with the need to provide an adequate definition of the term could afford to forget. In *De procuranda* Acosta had made his initial classification of barbarian peoples in terms of their linguistic skills. In the *Historia* the significance of these skills is examined in some depth. The success of the missionary enterprise evidently depended on the missionaries' ability to communicate with their charges. For this reason, and because language was recognised to be the only sure means of access to the Indian mind, the nature and the status of the native languages were the subjects of a long, often bitter and ultimately inconclusive controversy. Acosta himself makes very little reference to this. But his observations on the role of language in the formation of culture were made in its shadow. It will therefore be helpful to take a brief look at some of the issues involved.

Although some, such as the Jesuit Diego de Torres, thought Indian languages relatively simple in their structure, and others, like the Englishman William Wood, protested that there was, in fact, nothing alien about them at all,[161] most Europeans found the grammatical complexities and semantic unfamiliarity of Indian languages a serious barrier to any understanding of their function. What Ludovico Bertonio described as 'the obscurity of the modes of speech, the circumlocutions of their language, which are very different from ours',[162] drove many missionaries to give up the task of learning them in despair. Acosta's own belief that they were really much simpler than either Hebrew, Greek or Latin carried little conviction.[163] The task of learning such languages was made even more difficult by the fact that the friars who laboured to produce grammars and dictionaries inevitably attempted to force polysynthetic and agglutinative languages into Graeco-Latin morphological patterns. Under such conditions serious misunderstandings were bound to arise.

Not only were Indian languages evidently very complex and in many respects remote from those spoken in Europe; they were also very numerous. Acosta called America 'a forest of language',[164] a place in which tribes, separated from one another by only a few miles, spoke different and mutually unintelligible tongues. These linguistic differences were also, in the view of one Spanish linguist, Bernardo Aldrete, the determinants of political hostility, because 'each district considered itself to be the enemy of whoever did not speak its language'.[165] Confusion was such that in some areas men and women within the same groups even spoke different languages among themselves. Over a century later the great French Jesuit ethnologist, Joseph-François Lafitau, recognised that these were ritual modes of address.[166] But when Miguel Cabello Valboa recorded the phenomenon in the 1580s he assumed that the existence of such languages was further indication of the state of disorder in the Indian world.[167] A society in which husband and wife, mother and father could not communicate with one another was clearly not one in which any degree of true *consortium* could be achieved.

Indian languages may have been numerically wealthy, but they were also thought to be lexically poor. Most of the Europeans who attempted to come to some detailed understanding of their structure, in particular the grammarians and lexicographers, were, if they possessed any theoretical linguistic understanding at all, Modistae. This meant that they accepted the existence of a close relationship, mounting to interdependence, between the structure of reality and the cognitive operations of the human mind, of which language was, of course, the most perfect expression.[168] The poverty or wealth of a language, its ability to provide terms for the things, concrete and abstract, which were thought to exist 'in nature', was seen as a precise indication of its users' intellectual understanding of the world in which they lived. 'According to the Philosopher [Aristotle]...', wrote one grammarian, 'there is nothing by which the mind (*ingenio*) of man may be so well known as the words and languages that he uses, which are the starting point for the concepts of knowledge.'[169]

The apparent absence from so many Indian languages of terms for fundamental abstractions, and their failure to give voice to such seemingly universal notions as (to use Charles de La Condamine's exhaustive list) 'time, duration, space, being, substance, material, body...virtue, justice, liberty, discourse, ingratitude', was seen as an exact measure of 'the little progress which the spirit of these people has made'.[170] And not only did Indian languages possess no terms for such abstractions as these, more important for the missionaries, they lacked, or seemed to lack, other key concepts: 'God', for instance, and 'religion', 'faith', 'cross', 'angel', 'virginity' and 'matrimony'; and they were, as Acosta observed, generally weak on theological and philosophical terms.[171] It was not to be wondered at that races which had so little *scientia* that many of them could not measure time or space should also lack 'certain words which express the mysteries, whose use, even today, is confined to theologians'.[172]

The obvious difficulty of translating the subtleties of Christian theology under such circumstances gave rise to a heated debate over the suitability of the native languages as a vehicle for conversion and instruction. Most of the missionaries who worked in the field – although they warned their colleagues to be careful in their rendering of key terms – were certain that the Indians would only come to a true understanding of the faith through the medium of their own speech for, as one of them put it, one's own language is the only one 'that reconciles the will through contact (*trato*) and communication'.[173] In however minor a way, the Spanish grammarians and lexicographers of the Indian languages saw themselves as working to undo the legacy of Babel. It was only, as Gilberti explained, through patient application to the task of understanding fully the range of what could be said in the Indian languages that it would be possible 'to restore in part the common eloquence of which we were deprived by the arrogance and pride of that building'.[174]

But no matter how well the Europeans might come to understand the Indian languages, the lack of precise terms with which to translate the key concepts of most European discourse was obvious to all. The only solution seemed to be the use of loan words from Spanish or Latin. This did not trouble Acosta because, as he pointed out, all European vernaculars had a high percentage of such words. So long as terms such as *Deus* and *Trinitas* were properly glossed there was no reason why the Indians should not come to understand them as fully as they are now understood by Spaniards.[175] But his confidence was not shared by many of his colleagues. The dangers of confusion were, as I have already mentioned, all too great and all too obvious. The concept of the Trinity presented the greatest difficulties of all. Founded as it was on a paradox – a concept wholly missing from most Indian languages – and barely comprehensible even to the unlearned European, the idea of three separate beings in one was, and remains to this day, largely inaccessible to the Indian mind. The missionaries were aware of their failure to explain adequately this key feature of Christian doctrine and ascribed their failure in large measure to the shortcomings of the linguistic media in which they were obliged to work. The first two parts of the Trinity, 'Father and Son' were, as the Jesuit José de Anchieta explained to Laínez in 1563, easy enough, 'because it is possible to say them in their languages, but for the Holy Spirit we have never found a word nor an adequate circumlocution'.[176]

In an attempt to overcome this difficulty, Anchieta's colleague Manuel da Nóbrega substituted the Tupi word for 'thunder' (*tupā*) for the Holy Ghost – a move which the Huguenot Léry interpreted as a typical Jesuit attempt to use fear to control the newly converted Indians.[177] If it was it did not work. When André Thevet passed through the region some years later he was told by the Tupinamba that *Tupā* was 'the God of the Christians which does good only for the Christians and not for us'. *Tupā*, they explained, had no power over the elements as their gods had and, because of this, they did not worship him 'en aucun façon'.[178]

Nóbrega's attempt and his much publicised failure to find an adequate vehicle for European religious concepts seemed to demonstrate the impossibility of the whole enterprise. Far better, as Bernardo Aldrete explained, to make the Indians learn Spanish. The case of the Romans demonstrated to his mind the advantages, even the inevitability, of such linguistic imperialism.[179] Just as the Indians were now beginning to dress like Spaniards so, in time, they would all come to speak like them and thus, in the opinion of Ortiz de Hinojosa, a doctor of the university of Mexico in 1585, become 'more able and confident in the trade and contacts they have with Spaniards and more capable of discretion in their understanding of Christian doctrine and our Holy Faith, more politic and decorous so that they might come to understand virtue and good customs and to feel what honour is'.[180] If indeed these barbarians were to be properly assimilated into the Christian world they had ultimately to come to reason in a Christian language.

There was a fear, too, that just as an Indian trained in theology might exploit his new knowledge to harm the Church,[181] so, if the Christian message were to be translated into a 'barbarous' tongue, something corrupting would happen to it in the process. Translations would, warned Fernando Zurita, lead to unimaginable – and largely un-detectable – blasphemies. Satan himself had after all (according to Eusebius) spoken to men in 'a collection of noises and barbarous and unintelligible sounds' and the Egyptians were known to have invoked their terrible gods in similar tongues.[182] To most Europeans, in particular to those who could not speak them, Indian languages seemed to belong to that category and, in the words of López Mendel, were 'especially pleasing to the Devil'.[183]

By the early seventeenth century this view had triumphed, at least in official circles. The missionaries insisted on the need to continue their preaching in native languages; but the crown favoured the instruction of Indians in Spanish. 'Having made a close examination', runs the eighteenth law of the sixth book of the *Recopilación de leyes de Indias*, drawn up in 1681, 'of whether, even in the most perfect Indian languages, it is possible to explain well and with propriety the mysteries of the Holy Catholic Faith, it has been agreed that it is not possible without committing great errors, dissonances and imperfections.'[184]

Not only were Indian languages, in the eyes of their detractors, too imperfect to act as a vessel for the Word of God; many of them were hardly even the speech of men. For they belonged not to the realm of reasoned discourse (*locutio*) but to the primitive sources of speech, when men huddled together for mere protection, not *consortium*, and used only such words as were necessary for their immediate survival. Most Indian languages, according to Hinojosa, 'are so inaccessible and difficult that they do not seem to have been created by men, but by nature, with the illiterate voices of birds and brute animals, *which could not be written down in any kind of script*' (my italic).[185] As we have seen, transcription is the all-important characteristic of true language of *scientia*. Since alphabets were created to render articulate sounds in languages which are potentially literate, in Hinojosa's opinion you could no more transcribe an Indian word than you could the cry of a baboon.

Not everyone, however, took so extreme a view. What limitations the

Indian languages were thought to have, as Lafitau later observed, were due less to the inherent defects of Indian semantics than to the missionaries' persistent error in judging Indian languages, as they judged Indian societies, 'by our customs and manners'. Indian semantics were, he pointed out, quite unlike European ones and, had the grammarians been prepared to lay aside their classical models, they might have seen, for instance, that in many Indian languages abstractions have a verbal rather than a nominal form.[186] Lafitau's linguistic knowledge was far removed from anything available to Acosta.

But if Acosta had little understanding of the structural differences between language groups, he, like so many of his companions, could appreciate the succinctness and the range of metaphor available in Quechua and Aymara.[187] Such appreciations were not uncommon. 'In the variety and the beauty of [their languages]', wrote Ignacio de Hoyos Santillana, a canon of Mexico City cathedral, 'no nation can equal these Indians, and in them the ministers of the faith will find the road to the discovery of the nature of these peoples.'[188] The Indian language, in its power as well as in its poverty, offered a road in – indeed for many the only road – to the baffling obscurities of the Amerindian consciousness. As Charles de Brosses explained in his famous *Traité de la formation méchanique des langues* of 1765, the languages of 'savages' were rich in metaphor precisely because such peoples were more dependent on 'passion' than 'reason'. They speak, he said, the 'language of imagination and the passions', a language which, because it is not concerned with *explanation*, with science, depends not on abstract ideas – for these are the modes for rational expression – but on 'material images'.[189]

It was to combat the negative evaluation of Indian languages (and thus of the Indian mind) and in particular that view which, whether it dismissed Indian speech as gibberish or relegated it to the level of what, to the minds of rationalist grammarians, was the 'merely' poetical, that Acosta's near contemporary, the Dominican Domingo de Santo Tomás composed in 1560 one of the most remarkable of Indian grammars. The declared aim of Santo Tomás's Quechua grammar was to prove to the critics of Indian languages they were not 'barbarous' in Quintillian's sense of the word, 'full of defects, without modes, tenses or order or rules of agreement'. Instead he argued they were amenable to the rules of syntax and grammar and 'on a level with the Latin and Spanish [languages] in their arts and artifice'.[190]

Similarly there were those who argued that the very complexity and diversity of Indian languages, which others had seen as a reflection of the high level of disorder in Indian social life and religious observance, was in fact an indication of civility. The Jesuit Francisco Ramírez, for instance, claimed of the language of Michoacán that 'there is none, neither Latin nor Greek, which can be compared with it in artifice and in composition and in the abundance of modes of speech'.[191]

Language was, of course, regarded as the prime vehicle of social expression, the 'instrument of human society',[192] as Vives put it. Semantic disorder, therefore, was evidence of both social and mental disorder. In general, although the uncertainty as to whether language preceded the creation of the social order or vice versa, and the conflict between the Platonic idea of language as an expression of the nature of the things described, and the Aristotelian explanation of the origin of speech in convention, hung over the whole discussion, language was thought of at this period as the vehicle for the expression of forms which already existed in society, and not as the creator of such forms. If, however, all languages are conventional in origin (and most of those who wrote about Amerindian ones were certain that they were) they must, at least in their more complex state, reflect not innate human abilities so much as social preferences and inclinations.

Languages were explicitly tied to the requirements of the society which employed them. 'We cannot imagine', wrote James Beattie in 1783, 'that they whose garments are but a rag and whose lodgings a hole should affect superfluities in their languages.'[193] This, too, is why, John Locke thought, no Indian could count to a thousand, 'Because their language being scanty and accommodated only to the few necessities of a simple needy Life, unacquainted with Trade or Mathematicks, had no Words in it to stand for 1000.'[194] The absence of a word for a thing indicated to Acosta the absence of an understanding of that thing. Indians, who had no access to a belief in the Creator, had no single word for God. Similarly the languages of those tribes who failed to observe the proper social distance between individuals lacked terms of respect and even a means of distinguishing between members of one's own family and outsiders. 'They are barbarians without ability, government, polity or courtesy', wrote one Jesuit of the Xixime, 'not only in deeds but also in words, for in all their language they have no terms for the proper modes of address and they speak to the young and old, the great and the ignoble in the same manner.'[195]

This is also the significance of the Italian Jesuit Giovanni Maffei's seemingly absurd ethnocentric observation that the Brazilians were barbarians because their language lacked three basic elements of the Latin alphabet, the letters *f*, *l* and *r*, and hence could not express the concept *fide, lege, rege*. The point he is making is that the letters are missing because the Indians have no understanding of the *ideas* that they represent,[196] and not that they do not possess loyalty, laws and kings because they cannot formulate such concepts in their language. As the Brazilians live in a world of social and religious obscurity, these three crucial letters are absent from their languages 'by divine dispensation'. Similarly the fact that the peoples of Sinaloa, as one Jesuit observed, lacked all expletives in their languages reflected the essential docility of their society.[197] Unlike Caliban they did not know how to curse because they never had the need.[198]

In Acosta's philosophy of history, the language used to articulate the social order becomes more sophisticated in its means of expression as the society employing it becomes more complex. For Acosta, as for Aquinas, the crucial shift from the 'barbarian' world to that of civilised man accompanied the shift from the spoken to the written language. Acosta indeed had little to say about the semantic structure or lexical density of Indian languages;[199] what concerned him was how close they came to possessing a written script.

Language, said Acosta, is the means which we all employ to 'convey and understand things'. The purpose of the written script is to preserve and transmit this knowledge of 'things' to an intellectual world beyond our own, to 'those absent and those still to be born'.[200] The memory of the individual is a deposit of past information. But this can only be adequately recorded for future generations by writing. The oral transmission of information, though a recognised procedure, was inevitably, in societies so wholly convinced of the primacy of the *text*, regarded with contempt. One of the obvious explanations offered for the superiority of the written over the spoken word was the manner in which information becomes distorted in transmission. In non-literate societies the genealogies of which their history is largely composed are not a precise record of past events but serve as 'mnemonics for social relations'.[201] Certain modifications to the records have to be made from time to time, either because of the change in the structure of the society, or because the constant lengthening of the genealogies requires a process of adjustment so that the perceived length of the past never changes. It was these features which led Spaniards to complain that Indian histories were hopelessly confused and, in Acosta's opinion, 'more like dreams than histories'.[202] The generational shrinkage also meant that they only covered a period of four hundred years before which 'all is pure confusion and darkness'. Because these 'histories' were recognised to fulfil the largely symbolic role of determining social relations in the present they seemed to Europeans to be indistinguishable from myth. And for a man of Acosta's training the failure to distinguish between myth and history was the consequence of the Indians' failure to develop an adequate script.

Some sixteenth-century language theorists maintained that an alphabet must have been revealed by God to Adam. This would have perished with the expulsion from Eden, but although modern scripts were recognised as being human inventions there remained an explicit link between a knowledge of writing and a knowledge of God, partly because a script is the supreme form of *scientia*, partly because it is the prime means by which the consensus on which all knowledge depends is conveyed across time and space. Those nations who, like the Indians, came late to a knowledge of letters, concluded Cabello Valboa, also came late to an understanding of God.[203]

Alphabets constitute a superior form of knowledge because, being based on phonology, only they are able to transcribe actual *words*. For Acosta, as later for Leibnitz, the closer the depiction of the word was to the object in nature which the word described, the more 'primitive' the script, since it is always the first inclination of art to imitate nature. Barbarians, of course, with the possible exception of the Turks and the Arabs, have no true alphabets. But there do exist certain forms of transcription, known among the barbarians, which Acosta saw as representing early stages in the development of a true script. Closest to the alphabetic notation are those writing systems which, though composed of 'cyphers' and 'characters'[204] rather than letters, do contain some alphabetic elements, but consist, for the most part, of elaborate and stylised depictions of things. Such scripts included the ideograms employed by the Chinese and the Japanese, an observation whose significance will become apparent later.

Beneath these semi-alphabetic forms are to be found those systems of signs which do not signify actual *words* at all, but merely attempt to depict the objects of speech, and are thus 'not in reality letters, although they are written'. The true pictographic systems employed by the Mexica belong in this category. 'He who invented them', wrote Acosta, 'did not devise them to represent words, but to represent the thing itself; such signs are not really letters but cyphers and mnemonics, like those that the astronomers use to represent various [zodiacal] signs and planets.' No such system can be employed to convey anything other than simple nouns, 'for one cannot with the same picture indicate the variety of attributes for the sun such as, "the sun is warm" or "he looked at the sun" or "today is sunny" '.[205]

Such a system of transcription relies, as the account of the Mexican picture-books provided by Acosta's informant, Juan de Tovar, made clear, on oral assistance.[206] The symbols on the page could only be translated into speech with the assistance of elaborate rhetorical conventions. The 'reading' of a Mexican book was a ceremonial occasion. The reader spread out the manuscript on the ground before him and as he read he pointed to the events he was describing with two small rods. This kind of mnemonic feat was seen to be closely associated with the ancient European tradition of the theatre of memory and thus only distantly related to true writing, whose function is, of course, to store information which may be recalled by all those who understand the language in which it is written. To 'read' a Mexican codex you need, as the Spaniards who made searching inquiries into how these curious books 'worked' knew, a large amount of prior information, information which perished with the holder unless he was able to transmit it *orally* to a subsequent generation.

The process of translating Indian glyphs into language was thus at best an uncertain one. As one Franciscan historian, Augustín de Vetancurt, whose *Teatro mexicano* owes much to Acosta, noted, Indian 'writings' were not 'fixed', because 'each of the pictures signified at times one thing, at times another'. Furthermore writing was restricted to an elite 'and because of this', he went on, 'it happened that as time went by there was a succession of painters who were not in agreement about the meaning of the characters'.[207]

For Acosta, who nevertheless had great admiration for the Mexican picture-books and the coloured and knotted strings of the Peruvian *quipus*, such 'scripts', in by-passing the condition of rational discourse altogether, had precisely the same relation to the Indians who used them as religious images were decreed to have by the Second Council of Nicae for the illiterate Christian. They were *biblia pauperum*, in Acosta's words 'books for idiots who do not know how to read'.[208] In keeping with this interpretation of Indian picture-scripts, many of the missionaries in America who were troubled by the possibilities of serious error in rendering European concepts into Amerindian languages resorted to an artificial language of symbols. These were to be as close as possible to the Indians' own pictographic systems and would thus, it was hoped, unlike the spoken word, be immediately intelligible.

The first of these languages was devised by Pedro de Gante, a Flemish Franciscan, who, as early as 1523, had established a mission school in Texcoco where his picture-books were in daily use. But the most elaborate theoretical attempt to exploit the indigenous mnemonic systems was Diego de Valadés's *Rhetorica cristiana*, an exhaustive manual on Indian, or more precisely Mexican, culture and on the ways it could be exploited by the missionary in his constant struggle to establish *communicatio* with his charges. Most Indian groups, argued Valadés, although 'rude and uncultured *(crassi et inculti)*' had nevertheless contrived a means of conveying messages through 'arcane modes', using what he calls 'figures of the sense of the mind'. These functioned, or so he thought, as the Egyptian hieroglyphs (which until the late eighteenth century were believed to be purely symbolic). In such systems of representation, animals – because animals are the closest thing in the natural world to man – are used to represent abstract notions. Thus a lion stood for the *idea* of empire, a dove for the *idea* of peace and so on.[209] As these examples demonstrate, this kind of explanation derived from a consideration of the symbols employed in European culture. But Valadés believed that, once a thorough examination of the symbolic codes practised by the Indians had been carried out – once, for instance, the 'meaning' of such animals as the tapir and the crocodile had been discovered – it would be a relatively simple task for the missionary to devise a symbolic vocabulary for such abstractions as the Seven Deadly Sins, the Seven Virtues and so on which would be immediately accessible to the Indian mind, because it would appeal to what Valadés saw as the Indians' characteristic sensitivity to visual stimulae. 'For as they are', he stated, writing of the Indians' response to Gante's picture-books, 'men without letters, with poor memories, and lovers of novelty and painting, this art was very fruitful and successful in explaining the divine Word; for once the sermons were over the Indians would discuss among themselves the figures which had been explained to them.'[210] Both in their outward form and in their function, the new picture catechisms were intended to replace the ancient pictographic scripts.

The state of semi-literacy in which the Mexica and the Inca found themselves was thought by Acosta to be typical of the third and highest category of barbarian. Neither of Acosta's other two categories, however, possesses any kind of script at all, for the *locutio litteralis* like the liberal arts, can only come into being once the community has created within itself a space for leisure and the possibility of the pursuit of higher things. It might plausibly be said then that the Mexica and the Inca had finally reached the stage where their communities were beginning to create the necessary conditions for true *sapientia*. Proof of this belief could be found, for instance, in the ability of these Indian groups to measure time, which Acosta thought of as remarkable precisely because it was the achievement of 'men without letters'.[211]

In each case, the rise from one script to the next corresponds to an increase in the complexity of the culture as a whole. But both the Indians and, to a lesser degree, the Chinese, are still trapped by the limitations of their own cultural world. Their scripts cannot convey to anyone things of which that person has had no prior experience,[212] since their writings are only part of a larger system of communication which depends to a great degree upon shared information. 'An Indian', observed Garcilaso de la Vega, 'who had not learnt by memory and tradition the account of whatever subject was recorded in the *quipu* was as ignorant of such matters as a Spaniard or any other foreigner.'[213] And not only were Chinese ideograms, Mexica pictograms or the knotted and coloured strings of the *quipu* meaningless to anyone who was not already familiar with the text they encoded, they were also unable to represent anything outside the vocabulary of the original language. The Chinese, for instance, were incapable of transcribing the names of the Jesuits whom they encountered and in the end were obliged to give them Chinese names. This Acosta regarded as an absurdity because, for him, names were clearly fixed quantities.[214]

For a diffusionist such as Acosta, cultural progress depended on the accumulation and transmission of information, and language was therefore the means to the creation of man's ever-expanding knowledge of reality. This is why the wisdom of the Chinese consisted, so Acosta believed, entirely in their writing. Once a superior tool, such as the alphabet, had been invented, the whole enterprise would become useless. The most primitive Indian, Acosta claimed, once he had learnt the Latin alphabet, would be able to do things which no mandarin could ever achieve.[215] He would thus be 'wiser'; but only because he, by coming into contact with 'civilised' men, had been inadvertently propelled up the historical continuum to a stage which, left to his own devices, it would have taken him centuries to attain.

Acosta's historical method derives loosely from an old and well-tried descriptive procedure. It consists of an 'overstressed system' in which various sets of elements which are thought to possess a close structural relationship to each other are 'placed' on top of other sets with which they have some category affinity. The most characteristic example of this kind of reasoning, one which goes back to Hippocratic physiology, is to be found in the image of the cosmic harmonies in Saint Isidore of Seville's *De natura rerum*.[216] Here the four elements, the opposing qualities of which they are composed (hot and cold, moist and dry), the four seasons of the year and the four humours of man are all super-imposed one upon another. The point at which their horizontal axes meet is the still point of the turning world, encircling the referents of time (*annus*), space (*mundus*) and man himself. If, however, we read down the vertical axes new sets of 'harmonies' are created: autumn, melancholy, earth, cold; summer, choleric, iron, heat, and so on.

The *Historia* and *De procuranda* both use such overstressing to create an image of the various stages in human evolution. Thus Acosta's three categories of barbarians are compounded of three degrees of social organisation imposed upon three degrees of religious observance and three stages of linguistic development. The first category of barbarian, the Mexica and the Inca, have the most highly organised communities, the most idolatrous and ceremonious religious systems and the highest degree of linguistic proficiency. In the second category are those tribes which have only loose political organisations, a cohesive but as yet unstructured religious system, and no written script, but a developed language. The tribes in the third category have no social organisation worth the name and worship only natural phenomena, while their language not only lacks a script but is still very far from being an adequate instrument of communication. Acosta's method is far from being as homogeneous as this account might suggest. Any work which places such emphasis on the value of experience and the primacy of empirical information, as both the *Historia* and *De procuranda* do, must allow for large areas of inconsistency. Neither do the major shifts in the 'forms of government', religious observance and language all occur at the same time or in the same way. Language may even be said to be the product of a steady evolution rather than the sudden shifts which mark the transition between the three successive stages in social religious organisation. And, of course, it is true of all cultures that phases of the historical past persist into the present. The Inca, the highest of the barbarian Indian cultures, were an idolatrous people with an advanced concept of a creator–deity; but they also worshipped their ancestors, their rulers, lumps of stone, trees, stretches of road and oddly shaped hills.

But if we allow for a large degree of cultural 'lag', an even larger degree of diffusion, Acosta's method of description, his 'philosophical' – as he called it – account of how the different Indian races are to be classified worked because, unlike other histories, with the exception of the *Apologética historia*, it plotted and documented the crucial differences between three separate groups within America itself. It also provided a link between the Amerindian 'barbarians' and those of Asia – something that had never been attempted before. It was, in short, a system of universal ethnology; and it was dependent, as we shall shortly see, upon an account of universal history.

10

Acosta had created, to his own satisfaction, a coherent 'philosophical' account of the Amerindian world based on the most scrupulous examination of the evidence. But some of the 'why' questions still remained unanswered. Differences between Christians and non-Christians are easily explained in terms of the superior *scientia* conferred by Christ on man. But what accounts for the far greater cultural differences between the Chinese, the Inca, the Mexica and the Chichimeca? Like Las Casas, Acosta believed that the answers could be found in some form of historical relativism.

Acosta's only explicitly historiographical statement in either the *Historia* or *De procuranda* consists of a commonplace from the Book of Ecclesiastes; 'the thing that hath been, is that which shall be; and that which is done is that which shall be done'.[217] This would seem to suggest a typically Aristotelian view of history as a series of cycles doomed to repeat themselves throughout time. The evidence of ancient history had shown Acosta that entire cultures – like that of Rome, whose history offered examples of every known form of government – may rise, decline and then fall, to be replaced by a new cycle.[218] The cycles in Acosta's system, however, are not self-enclosing. Man advances by moving from one to the next. In the Aristotelian metaphor, societies operate like biological organisms. They grow up, mature, grow old and die. In a general sense, Acosta's three types of barbarism behave in the same way. Each represents a distinct stage in man's inevitable progress towards the true civility of the Christian world. Each is a discrete form, with its own distinct means of understanding the natural world in which it exists. The dynamics of change lie, of course, in man's teleological condition. For Acosta, the author of *De temporibus novissimis* no less than of the *Historia*, the history of man was, in Augustine's phrase, the *operatio Dei* in time. He saw the cultural evolution of the peoples of America as a steady, if uneven, progress towards the coming of the Spaniards, who brought with them the Word of God, and with the Word, the knowledge men require to live the true, the Christian civil life. Once the union between the two cultures had been effected Indian history, having reached its final stage, would flow on uninterrupted now by evolutionary change 'until the hidden end of time'.

But why do not all men advance through the 'barbarian' phase of their development at the same pace? And how is it that America contains examples of each one of the three 'barbarian' types living in close proximity with each other? Acosta's answer is to be found in the answer to another question. Where did the Indians originally come from? This question formed part of a wider sixteenth- and seventeenth-century preoccupation with human origins, with, for instance, the origins of the Turks whose case, in this as in so much else, was often seen as strikingly similar to that of the Indians. For the Indians, like the Turks, were also thought (as we shall shortly see) to have been the descendants of ancient 'barbarian' tribes, usually the Scythians, themselves the sons of the legendary Magog (Genesis 10.2).[219] In every instance such genealogies were subversive, seeking to explain present cultural traits – as those which claimed that the supposed Jewish origins of the Indians explained their (also supposed) mendacity and timidity – or in terms of some ancient curse – as those which described the Turks as the sons of Ishmael, who 'will be a wild man; his hand will be against every man, and every man's hand against him' (Genesis 16.12), or the Africans as the sons of Ham. In the case of the Indian the problem of finding a suitable genealogy was complicated by the fact of their distance and isolation from the lands of the ancient world. If the Indians were indeed true men, then they had to be the descendants of one of the three sons of Noah, Ham, Japhet and Shem. They must, in other words, have had their origins in Europe and have migrated at some point in the historical past to America. But how and from where?

Acosta had little time for the more conventional solutions to this problem. As we have seen, he did not believe that the Indians were the descendants of the lost tribes of Israel. He also rejected the (for him) inherently more plausible idea that they might be the descendants of the

Carthaginian colony in the Atlantic described by the pseudo-Aristotle in *De mirabilibus auscultationibus*; or that they were the descendants of the survivors of Atlantis, or had drifted to America on rafts. Some few might have sailed from northern Europe; but they could not have constituted a large enough group to populate an entire continent.[220] His own solution was based on the premise that, whatever else they might be, the Indians, like all other non-semitic peoples, were the descendants of the sons of Japhet. Since, furthermore, America contained not only men but also animals such as pumas and jaguars which the Indians could never have brought with them in rafts, both they and all the other animal species in America must have come overland.[221] Acosta's theory is simple and economic.[222] Since he knew nothing about the configuration of the northern landmass of America but had every reason to believe that it extended for a great distance, he postulated the existence of a landbridge between Europe and America across what is now the Bering Strait. The Indians had, he thought, migrated across 'Tartary' to modern Alaska and then begun their long trek south, down the continent of America in search of suitable settlement areas.

A proof of this hypothesis could, Acosta believed, be found in the Indians' own account of their past. Like most intellectuals of his day, Acosta believed that a people's mythology was an attempt to provide a coherent explanation of their tribal origins. Because of the defectiveness of oral transmission and the human tendency to translate all events into symbolic acts, real 'history', unless it was preserved in a textual form, soon degenerated into mythopoeic fable. Thus both the Inca and the Mexica preserved, in mythological form, a garbled version of their nomadic origins.[223] Both claimed to be descended from one of a number of brothers who, in the beginning of the world, had emerged from a cave, located in some remote region to the north. These brothers, as Tovar observed, stood for the various clans of which each tribe was composed.[224] Both the Inca and the Mexica were led away from their first homes in search of a promised land; and both finally settled in fertile valley regions. The chieftains who had led them on this migration then became, in the manner of barbarians, their gods.[225]

Acosta himself gave this Indian migration no location in historical time although later writers, such as the Barnabite chronologist Agostino Tornielli and the jurist Juan de Solórzano Pereyra who drew heavily on his work, attempted to do so.[226] Acosta, to judge by the remarks on the possible extent of time in *De temporibus*, was suspicious of such calculations, calculations which could not be verified by reference to present conditions or to known facts about the past. The very remote past would always be like the future: 'however much we may speculate, it is always greater than our feeble minds can imagine'.²²⁷ In the *Historia*, the migration is a device used to explain the diversity of cultural forms to be found in America. It is also worth observing how close it is in many respects to Herodotus's account of the history of the Scythians, a race with whom the Indians were frequently compared. For just as the Indians migrated from Asia to America, so the Scythians were said to have migrated from Asia to Europe, and just as the Indians are said by Acosta to be divided into settled 'monarchical' groups, settled but essentially leaderless groups and nomads, so the Scythians were divided by Herodotus into the 'Royal Scythians', the agriculturalists and the nomads.²²⁸

Acosta's Bering Strait theory had the advantage of being not only largely true, but also of providing the Indians with a place in the pre-history of the peoples of Asia. For the theory makes the Indians the final settlers in a prolonged migration of peoples. The cultural similarities between Indians and Chinese, their forms of writing, the behaviour of their priests²²⁹ and even, as Solórzano Pereyra noted, their physical similarities,²³⁰ could thus be explained in terms of a common cultural heritage. The dissimilarities between them, on the other hand, the facts that the Asiatic barbarians were more advanced than any Indian and that the Mexica far outstripped the Chichimeca, could be explained in terms of the deleterious effect of movement upon peoples. For migratory groups cannot create cities nor any form of civil association for the simple reason that civil association depends upon temporal continuity, upon the creation of a social space with its appropriate social and religious institutions and the cultural forms which accompany them. If, indeed, the civil life is to be largely defined as a life lived in cities, then it is obvious that peoples who live in tents, who are pastoralists or even hunter–gatherers rather than agriculturalists, will be unable to develop a true community.

Nomadism was consequently held to be inimical to every aspect of civilised life; and the Spaniards therefore did their best to prevent the Indians from moving very far from the areas in which they were settled. It was also considered a threat to any form of constructive religious organisation and one Jesuit even refused baptism to a group of Tupinamba because 'in addition to having no king whom they obey, their houses are not fixed [in one place], so that they move them and themselves when and where they please'.²³¹

The long migration of the peoples who were eventually to become the Chinese, the Japanese, the 'Tartars' and finally the Indians would not only have prevented them from increasing their stock of knowledge, of improving their way of life; it would also have erased what little they had once known. As they travelled westward their culture inevitably degenerated.

After they had left their well constituted and civilised (*culta et bene morata*) republics in the old world [commented Solórzano Pereyra] they had forgotten, before they reached the distant regions of the new, most [of their old life], and what remained was eroded with time, leaving their descendants with hardly a trace of manhood but only the physical appearance of men.[232]

Primitive 'natural man', for Acosta no less than for Hobbes, lives within us all. Only a fully civilised life keeps him quiescent, only such a life allows the rational soul to fully dominate the passions. Drive a civilised people from their settled homes and they will, within a short space of time, return to the savagery of their first ancestors. The idea was a popular and enduring one. Mathew Hale, for instance, pondering in 1677 the same problem as Acosta had done, concluded that the Indians must have been migrant for five hundred years and that after such a time, 'there must in all probability happen a great forgetfulness of their Original, and a great degeneration from the Primitive Civility, Religion and Custom of those places from whence they were derived'.[233] Man is always but a few steps away from his origins.

When, at last, the Indians settled again they had to slowly reconstitute what they had once known.[234] If knowledge depends on the consensus, and civilisation was the product of prolonged contact between peoples, it is evident that a race like the Indians, which because of the distances they had had to cover had been migratory for far longer than any other race and in their continental isolation had been denied all contact with other groups, would be backward in relation to the rest of mankind. By the middle of the seventeenth century, clear empirical proof which would have delighted Acosta of the deleterious effect of isolation upon human groups was readily available in Europe. In 1626 the Dominican Gregorio López, in the course of a lengthy attempt to discover whether or not the Indians had been visited by Christian evangelists before the coming of the Spaniards, cited the case of a group of Visigoths who, in order to avoid conversion to Islam after the Arab invasion of the Peninsula, had fled into the mountains near Almuñeca. There, in the course of time, the effect of isolation and of a mountain environment slowly eroded their culture until they had ceased to be Christians in belief and 'in their way of life (*modo de vivir*)' and all they preserved of their old religion was 'a bell and a few other symbols'.[235]

For Solórzano Pereyra there was an even more dramatic piece of evidence to hand. In the mountains of Las Batuecas, a region in the modern province of Salamanca, another group of Christians had taken refuge from the Muslim invader. There they had remained until they were discovered in the sixteenth century by the Duke of Alba. These peoples were wild, garbled their speech, worshipped the Devil, wore no clothes and possessed no technical skills whatsoever.[236] The story aroused a great deal of interest, was the subject of a play by Lope de Vega and continued to be discussed as evidence of the associative theory of culture down to the nineteenth century.

The peoples of Las Batuecas, no less than Gregorio López's wild men of Almuñeca, as Feijoo later realised, inhabited an imaginary country, a place where, like the lands of America, men were savage because they were cut off from the company of their fellows.[237] But for those like Solórzano Pereyra who accepted such stories as fact, the condition of the Batuecans seemed to demonstrate the universality of the human response to certain cultural conditions, the proof that Indians were only unlike Spaniards in not having been reared for generations as Spaniards.

Acosta's migration theory suggested that the differences between the types of 'barbarians' to be found in both Asia and America could be explained in terms of the amount of time they had spent in constant movement in isolated bands. The most primitive of these peoples, the third category of barbarians, were either the most recent arrivals in America or, as Lafitau would later argue, those who had been forced by larger or more powerful groups to keep moving, or to settle in the highlands or other areas unfit for the development of human culture.[238] The 'segmentary' American tribes – the second category of barbarian – belong to a slightly earlier phase of the migration, while the Mexica and the Inca, who in the *Historia* make up the first category of barbarian, belong to the earliest phase. The semi-civilised peoples of Asia, China and Japan (in *De procuranda* they belong to the first category of barbarian) were the very first to have settled and are consequently much closer to the Europeans than any other group of barbarians.

Acosta's interpretation of Amerindian culture was enormously influential. *De procuranda* became the standard work on its subject and

Acosta's approach something of an orthodoxy. It was not only used as a textbook by his own order in places as far from the Americas as Calabria and Asturias, North Africa and the Philippines; it was also employed as a model by members of other orders, such as the Carmelite Tomás de Jesú, whose *De procuranda salute omnium gentium* (1613) owes far more than its title to Acosta. The *Historia natural y moral de las Indias* achieved even wider renown. By 1604 – only fourteen years after its appearance – it had already gone through several editions in Spanish and Latin and had been translated into Italian, German, Dutch, French and English. It was undoubtedly the most widely read account of the Spanish Indies to appear before the publication in 1781 of Francisco Clavigero's *Historia antigua de Mexico*, and its influence can be seen in such otherwise dissimilar works as the Augustinian Antonio de Calancha's *Crónica moralizada del orden de San Augustín en el Perú* (1639–53) and Juan de Torquemada's *Monarchía indiana* (1615).

Acosta's insistence that barbarism described not one but several different cultural types, that peoples could be graded, so to speak, for civility or barbarism by examining their political institutions, religious beliefs and linguistic sophistication, and that any pronouncement about the nature of 'the other' must be rooted in hard evidence, had a direct influence on a number of writers who themselves had no particular concern with missionary work. Giovanni Botero borrowed and adapted Acosta's system of classification, so too did Solórzano Pereyra and the Frenchman Pierre d'Avity, the author of *Les empires, royaumes, estats, seigneuries, duchez et principautez du monde*, one of the most widely read ethnographical encyclopaedias of the seventeenth century. D'Avity's system omits language, divides social organisation up into habitation and government and adds both diet and nakedness as classifiers. But though more complex and, since d'Avity had never met a 'savage' face to face, a good deal more speculative than Acosta's rather more rough and ready divisions, the enterprise is still essentially the same.[239]

Interest in the possibility of classifying barbarians in this manner was matched by an equal interest in the possibility that mass migrations during the prehistorical period of human history might explain the wide diversity in cultural types. During the seventeenth century theories of migration and of the origins of the American Indians became the subject of widespread debate which involved such men as Grotius and Fontenelle as well as an army of lesser intellects such as Peter Heylyn,

Henri Estienne, Pierre-Daniel Huet, Isaac Vossius. The writer who made the most imaginative use of Acosta's ideas, who had himself first-hand experience of the Indians and, like Acosta, insisted that only what is now called fieldwork could equip the ethnologist for his task was the Jesuit Joseph-François Lafitau. Lafitau's *Moeurs des sauvages amériquains compareés aux moeurs des premiers temps* (1724) – which is based on the novel supposition that since the Indians have been, so to speak, frozen in time by virtue of their long migrations, their culture may be used to illustrate the past of the peoples of Europe – had a considerable impact on the anthropological literature of the eighteenth and even the nineteenth centuries. Lafitau's remarkable work makes explicit what is sometimes only implicit in Acosta's texts, that all cultures are systems of symbolic representations which constitute the means of communication between individuals within societies. For Lafitau man was what Ernst Cassirer referred to as an *animal symbolicum*,[240] and the *Moeurs* therefore sought to explain the representational, the symbolic function of such specific cultural phenomena as religion, burial rites, games, warfare and language itself – areas of human activity which were thought to hold the key to the understanding of the 'savage mind' both present and past.

In both its methods and its ultimate ambition Lafitau's work is far removed from Acosta's *Historia*. But the two books belong to the same kind of enterprise. Both claim to offer a 'philosophical' account of the Amerindian world and both claim that this account will illuminate far more than a mere 'barbarian' culture. Both are comparative and both draw their strength from the experience and observational powers of their authors. Both, also, were written by Jesuits.

The cast of Lafitau's mind, post-Cartesian and concerned with the need to refute with empirical evidence the claims of the atheists, is quite unlike that of his predecessor. But although it would be to falsify the evidence to attempt to describe a simple 'texual' progression from Acosta to Lafitau, it is possible to see how Acosta's writings demonstrated the possibility that patterns of human behaviour were due to specific cultural conditions which could be classified and described in terms that were both historical and in some degree relative. As one contemporary reviewer of the *Moeurs* observed, for Lafitau, 'distances in space were analogous to distances in time',[241] and that therefore to 'know' the Indians brought man one step closer to knowing the past of his own culture.

The road from the speculations of John Mair and Palacios Rubios to the observations of Acosta and Lafitau is a long one. We have moved from one mode of discourse to another, from texts which relied heavily upon citation and allusion and were composed for audiences which were specific, limited and, to some degree, participant in the writer's 'speech act', to texts written for far wider and far more diffuse audiences, texts which were descriptive rather than discursive. We have moved, too, from texts written by men who had no first-hand experience of the peoples they were seeking to classify, to those written by men who did and who insisted, furthermore, that, in the end, only such experience could guarantee the accuracy of ethnological observation.

The kind of enterprise on which Vitoria was engaged and that pursued by Acosta were evidently very different. But, as we have seen, Acosta's ethnological descriptions relied heavily upon a substructure of theory, a conceptual image of the workings of 'the machine of this world', adumbrated by Vitoria and his pupils. It would, of course, be wrong to see Acosta, and beyond Acosta, Lafitau and de Brosses, as in any direct sense the intellectual heirs of the Salamanca theologians. But Vitoria and his pupils did provide Acosta with a coherent and authoritative anthropology on to which he could chart his own observations of the American world. And by so doing they succeeded, in a perhaps unforeseen way, in burying the first crude image of the American Indian as an unreasoning creature of passion, non-cultural 'natural man', and thus made some kind of comparative ethnology, and ultimately some measure of historical relativism, inescapable.

# Notes

Translations from the works of Aristotle are based upon the versions provided in *The works of Aristotle translated into English*, ed. W. D. Ross (Oxford, 1908–52), 12 vols. Translations from other classical texts are those given in the Loeb Classical Library. All other translations are my own.

## Introduction

1. Foucault, 1970, p. 51.
2. See p. 66 below.
3. Carro, 1951, p. xiv.

## 1   The problem of recognition

1. O'Crovley, 'Idea compendiosa', f. 166ʳ.
2. Darnton, 1970, pp. 12–13.
3. Amazons were a popular fantasy whose description by Francesco de Orellana was so convincing that their name, not his, was given to the river he was the first to navigate. Not all observers, however, were quite so naive. See, for instance, Girava, 1570, p. 227: 'en las Islas deste rio [the Amazon] se dezia que avia visto mugeres que pellavan las quales llamavan Amazonas. Pero es burla porque nunca las huvo ni las ay.' On pygmies and giants see Friederici, 1973, pp. 177–81.
4. On the Fountain of Eternal Youth see Olschki, 1941a. Amerigo Vespucci recorded having seen Indian women who never aged, whose breasts never fell and whose bellies, even after many childbirths, 'were in no way different from those of virgins' (Vespucci, 1966, p. 88). He may have been drawing on the account of the Hyperboreans made famous by Pliny (*Natural history*, 4.589–91) and Pomponius Mela (*Chorographia*, 3.36–7). Tales of the extreme longevity of the Indians were still being repeated in the seventeenth century. Even Charles Rochefort, who had had first-hand experience of the Arawak, claimed that there were Indians whose average life-span was 'one hundred and fifty years and sometimes more', and he recorded that Laudonière's expedition to Florida in 1564 had encountered an Indian three hundred years old. Rochefort, 1658, pp. 502–3.
5. See Olschki, 1937 and 1941b, and Randles, 1959.
6. On Columbus's references to Africans and Canarians see Cioranescu, 1959, pp. 15–25.
7. Columbus, 1930, 1, p. 15, and 1960, pp. 52, 100. There are interesting observations on the stories Columbus was told about the 'cannibals' in Hulme, 1978; and see pp. 80–7 below.
8. See e.g. Oviedo, 1956, who saw nightingales (p. 185), tigers (p. 143), lions

(p. 150) and so on. Only with such creatures as the tapir (p. 148) did he resort to Indian names.

9. Armstrong, 1961, p. 132.
10. Acosta, 1962, p. 203. The inadequacies of such crude methods of classification soon became apparent to the botanists. Ulisse Aldrovandi even sought the backing of Cosimo de' Medici in 1569 for a scientific expedition to America. See Olmi, 1976, and Tugnoli Pataro, 1979.
11. *Carta del licenciado Alonso Zuazo al padre Fray Luis de Figueroa prior de la Mejorada* (dated Santiago de Cuba, 14 November 1521) in García Icazbalceta, 1858, 1, pp. 358–67.
12. Oviedo, 1535, f. xci$^v$. The bulk of Oviedo's great history remained unpublished during his lifetime. I have used the earliest printed edition of the *primera parte* (which includes all of Oviedo's ethnographical observations) because that, rather than the complete work, represents what the contemporary reader had access to, and because later editions have introduced textual complications which do not concern me here. On the printing history of the work see Gerbi, 1975, pp. 168–74.
13. Stannard, 1966, pp. 1–21.
14. See Edward F. Tuttle, 'Borrowing versus semantic shift. New World nomenclature in European languages' in Chiapelli, 1976, 2, pp. 595–611.
15. There is no satisfactory study of medieval classification of this type but see, in general, Glacken, 1967, pp. 254–86, and Hodgen, 1964, pp. 17–107.

## 2 The image of the barbarian

1. This was the common etymology of the word. See e.g. *Primera crónica general*, 1955, 1, pp. 27, 157. It also appears on sixteenth-century maps. See Skelton, 1958, pp. 45, 60.
2. For the Irish see Giraldus Cambrensis, 1867, p. 150, and for the Normans, Kerr, 1958, p. 224. There are two useful histories of the changing meanings of the term 'barbarian': Jones, 1971, and de Mattei, 1939. There are also some observations in Chabod, 1977, pp. 28–33.
3. Baldry, 1965, pp. 20–4.
4. See e.g. Strabo (*Geography*, 14.2.27–8), who claims that the word was onomatopoeic: the *barbaroi* were a people who spoke 'barbar'. But he was also aware of a cultural, if not racial, distinction between Greeks and barbarians, quoting Thucydides, 1.3 on Homer, who 'did not use the term [barbaros] because the Hellenes had not yet been distinguished under one name as opposed to them'.
5. The earliest extant account of the origins of language, and of its role in the formation of human societies, is Diodorus Siculus (*The library of history*, 18.2–3). It is discussed by Cole, 1967, pp. 60–9. Cf. Aristotle, *Rhet.* 1355 b 1; '*logos*, language, is more characteristic of man than the use of the body'.
6. See Cole, 1967, p. 133, and Isocrates (*Panegyricus*, 50); 'and she [Athens] has brought it about that the name "Hellenes" suggests no longer a race but an intelligence'.
7. Clark, 1975, p. 25. For Plato, even women appeared to be almost a separate species, *Timaeus*, 42 a–b.
8. See Lévi-Strauss, 1969, p. 46: 'a very great number of primitive tribes simply refer to themselves by the term for "men" in their language, showing that in their eyes an essential characteristic of man disappears outside the limits of the group'.

9. Molina, 1571, f. 90ᵛ. Siméon (1885, p. 216) renders *maceualli* (now usually spelt *macehual*) as 'vassal, homme du peuple, paysan, sujet', but his definitions are generally derived from Molina.

10. Columbus, 1930, 1, p. 11. Vega, 1943, 1, 269, dicusses the meanings of the word *viracocha*. Randles, 1968, p. 88.

11 See e.g. Aristotle, *Hist. an.* 490 b 16–19, and Baldry, 1965, *passim*.

12. It was surely something like this that Francisco Tamar had in mind when, at the end of an unremarkable list of their vices, he described the Indians as being 'of little memory'. Boemus, 1586, f. 253ʳ.

13. See Hardie, 1968, pp. 129–51.

14. These are all references to the conditions of the natural slave; but, as we shall see (p. 47 below) the natural slave and the *barbaros* are, for Aristotle, one and the same creature.

15. On the problematic links between the city and the *polis* see Weill, 1960, pp. 327–415.

16. See Guthrie, 1957, pp. 8–94.

17. Tyranny is, by definition, a lordship over slaves. See *Pol.* 1285 a 20ff. and *NE*, 1160 b 30.

18. *De officiis*, 1.11–14 and 2.11–15; Lactantius, *Divinae institutiones*, 6.10; Isidore, *Etymolgiae*, 15.2.5–6; St Augustine, *De civitate Dei*, bks 14–18 *passim*.

19. See Aquinas, Ia IIae q. 100 art. 5. This, however, was not a universal view. Dante, William of Ockham and Marsilius of Padua, to name but three major figures, all regarded the *congregatio fidelium* as a community of believers within a larger political unit, the *communitas mortalium*. See Wilks, 1964, pp. 105–6. The writers I shall be discussing, however, owed little to this tradition.

20. See Martin of Braga, 1950, pp. 200–3.

21. Ullmann, 1977, p. 14.

22. Eusebius, 1979, 1, p. 105.

23. Gregory the Great, 1884–5, 2, p. 681. Originally the term *paganus* meant a countryman (or a civilian as opposed to a soldier: Ulpian, *Digest*, 39.5.7.6.). It was first used to describe an unbeliever, possibly because the fiercest resistance to Christianity came from the countryside (Mohtmann, 1952, pp. 109–21). But it still retained, for all Christians, the implication of incivility and *rusticitas*. This has been brilliantly analysed in Brown, 1977, pp. 8–10, who concludes that *rusticitas* amounted to 'a refusal to see the world as intelligible'.

24. See e.g. Giménez Fernández, 1944, p. 173. For the grammarians, of course, the *barbari* were merely those who wrote a 'barbarous' language. Curtius, 1953, pp. 43–4.

25. The most often quoted source for this idea (used here by Albertus) is Cicero, *De inventione* 1.7. See the observations in Tuck, 1979, pp. 33–4.

26. This translates *koinōnia*, the essential connection between individuals within the community.

27. Albertus Magnus, 1890–9, 8, p. 10 (*Politicorum*, bk 1, ch. 1, paras. i–k).

28. *Ibid.*, 7, p. 464 (*Ethicorum*, bk 7, tract. 1, ch. 1). The reference appears to be to Cicero, *De inventione*, 1.1–2.2–3, discussing the prehistory of man. The quotation, however, is inaccurate.

29. See M. I. Finley, 'Aristotle and economic analysis' in Barnes *et al.*, 1977, pp. 140–58 at p. 144.

30. On the wild men see Bernheimer, 1952. The distinction lowland/highland is to be found in Plato, *Laws*, 3, 681 d–e.

31. Janson, 1952, pp. 76–106.

32. *Summa contra gentiles*, 2.68. See Lovejoy, 1948, for a discussion of the Great Chain of Being.

33. *Ibid.*

34. *Ibid.*

35. Repeated by Helmont, 1648, p. 25. St Isidore thought that such fauns were really wild men (*Etymologiae*, 2.3.22.). Helmont also claimed that he had been told by Mercator of the existence of mummified dwarfs which he took to be the remains of pygmies (*ibid.*, p. 679). I owe these references to Dr Alice Brown.

36. Albertus Magnus, 1916–20, 16.1332.

37. Paracelsus, 1603, 9: *Liber de nymphis, sylphis, pygmaeis et salamandris*, p. 35. Indians, he thought, were probably without souls, certainly lacked reason and 'talk like parrots' (*ibid.*, 20, p. 19). Cesalpino, 1571, pp. 92–7, and see Gliozzi, 1977, pp. 306–12.

38. See Gliozzi, 1977, pp. 535–66, and Popkin, 1976.

39. Martín del Río, 1652, p. 230. The same objections are made by Solórzano Pereyra, 1648, pp. 18–19.

40. Quoted by Mexía de Ovando, 'Libro memorial', p. 87.

41. Las Casas, 1975, ff. 13$^v$–14$^r$.

42. Martyr, 1530a, f. xxxvii$^r$. Letter to Pomponio Mela, 21 December 1494.

43. *Ibid.*, f. xlix$^v$. Letter to Pomponio Mela, 12 May 1499.

44. Martyr, 1530b, f. vi$^v$. Although by this date Martyr had seen the ethnographical report of Ramón Pané, the Hieronymite left behind on Hispaniola by Columbus after his second voyage, and had incorporated much of it into the text of *De orbe novo*, the only modification he was willing to make to his neo-Platonic image at this stage was the recognition that 'even in the Golden Age men must have fought wars' (*ibid.*, f. vi$^v$).

45. With reference to their marriage laws see Oviedo, 1535, f. xlix$^v$.

46. *Ibid.*, ff. 1$^r$, lxviii$^v$.

47. Oviedo, *ibid.*, f. xlix$^v$, identifies polyandry among the Arawak on the evidence of Tostado, 1507, f. xxxviii$^r$, who claimed, citing Celsus, that 'there was once a time when it was the custom among the English that six of them should marry jointly with one woman. This law was more than bestial and we know of no people who observe it today.'

48. Pico della Mirandola, 1572–3, 2: *De examen vanitatis doctrinae gentium*, p. 861, and Schill, 1929, pp. 15–18.

49. Oviedo, 1535, f. 1$^r$.

50. Vitoria, 1960, p. 150. Cf. Suárez, 1971, 1, p. 4: 'Deinde theologicum est negotium conscientiis prospicere viatorum…ergo et legis inspectio, quatenus est conscientiae vinculum, ad theologum pertinebit.'

51. See Curtius, 1953, pp. 319–26, and the brilliant observations by Ginzburg, 1979.

3 *The theory of natural slavery*

1. Neither the role of the royal confessor nor that of the *junta* has been studied. My comments are based on the records of the Burgos *junta* of 1512 (see pp. 47–50 below) and the Valladolid debates discussed in chapter 5.

2. In a letter dated 18 March [1546] to Miguel de Arcos, Dominican provincial

of Andalusia. BUS, MS 333–166, f. xviᵛ, and printed in Beltrán de Heredia, 1931, p. 174. On the *junta* which assembled at the request of Philip II to discuss the possibility of moderating the heresy laws in the Netherlands, and whose decisions were overruled because they were in favour of moderation, see Parker, 1979, pp. 64–5.

3. See p. 66 below.
4. Suárez, 1971, 1, p. 5.
5. See p. 66 below.
6. C.R. *en respuesta al almirante y oficiales reales* [Burgos 20 March] 1512, printed in Chacón y Calvo, 1929, p. 429.
7. Santa Cruz, 1951, 1, p. 354.
8. These are: *Inter cetera* and *Eximie devotionis*, both of 3 May, *Piis fidelium* (23 June), *Inter cetera* (28[?] June), *Dudum siquidem* (25 September). The best printed versions are provided by Giménez Fernández, 1944, pp. 173–426.
9. *Ibid.*, p. 181. I have followed the text of *Inter cetera* of 3 May.
10. See, for instance, Las Casas, 1552a, ff. Iiiiʳ–iiiiᵛ, and Góngora, 1975, pp. 33–40.
11. Giménez Fernández, 1944, p. 362 (*Eximie devotionis* 3–7).
12. *Romanus pontifex*. It was issued on 8 January 1455 and is printed in *Monumenta henricina*, 1960–74, 12, pp. 71–9.
13. *Romanus pontifex* (p. 75) refers to the inhabitants of Africa as 'sarracenos et paganos aliosque Christi inimicos ubicumque constitutos'.
14. Giménez Fernández, 1944, p. 181. I have followed the version given in *Inter cetera* of 3 May. For Columbus's description see Columbus, 1930, 1, pp. 6–11.
15. A general account of these events is provided by Hanke, 1965, pp. 17–22. The only source we have is Las Casas, 1951, 2, pp. 441–4.
16. Las Casas, 1951, 2, p. 443.
17. Chacón y Calvo, 1929, pp. 431, 446.
18. Las Casas, 1951, 2, p. 445.
19. Chacón y Calvo, 1929, p. 447.
20. *Cédula* of April 1495, printed in *CDH*, 1, p. 2.
21. Polybius, *History*, 4.38.4. See Davis, 1961, pp. 96–7.
22. Chacón y Calvo, 1929, pp. 436 and 445–6. Although Ferdinand was uneasy about the possible consequences of whites marrying with Indians (see *CDH*, 1, p. xviii) nothing seems to have come of this project.
23. See Cortés, 1964. Some new information is given in Texeira da Mota, forthcoming, and on Seville see Collantes de Terán Sánchez, 1972.
24. See Russell, 1971.
25. Soto, 1568, ff. 102ᵛ–103ʳ; Ledesma, 1560. See also Saunders, 1982, pp. 42–4, Boxer, 1978, p. 32, and Maxwell, 1975, p. 67.
26. Las Casas, 1951, 2, p. 177, and see Kamen, 1971. The use of Blacks to alleviate the misery of the Indians was still being advocated as late as the 1580s. A report (*informe*) of 1581 by the *audiencia* (local court) of Santa Fe paints a dismal picture of the Indians' fate and urges the king to buy Blacks: 'que podria S. Majestad...comprar los negros de cabo verdo muy baratos y embiarlos en las Indias...'. AGI, Audiencia, Santa Fe 1, ramo 1, no. 28.
27. *Carta de Fray Francisco de Vitoria al padre Fray Bernardino de Vique acerca de los esclavos que trafican los portugueses y sobre el proceder de escribanos*, BUS, MS 333–166–1, f. xvʳ⁻ᵛ, and printed in Beltrán de Heredia, 1931, p. 174. Indians were also enslaved in so-called 'just wars' though the crown made periodic attempts to put a stop to the practice. See e.g. the

*provisión* of 2 August 1530 (*CDH*, 1, pp. 134–6). The alleged cannibalism of certain Indian tribes was the most common justification offered for such 'wars' and was frequently accepted as legitimate. See e.g. the *provisión* of 1531 permitting Indians of Guatemala and the Caribs to be enslaved (*CDH*, 1, p. 142).

28. Quoted by Morelli, 1791, p. 249.
29. Albornoz, 1573, f. 130ᵛ.
30. *Carta...al padre Fray Bernardino de Vique*, f. xvʳ, printed in Beltrán de Heredia, 1931, p. 174.
31. Letter to Miguel de Arcos in Vitoria, 1967, pp. 136–9.
32. *Instrucción* of September 1501 in *CDH*, 1, p. 5.
33. *Cédula* of 2 December 1501 in *CDH*, 1, pp. 7–8.
34. Letter to the king, signed but not dated. AGI, Patronato, 184, ramo 26, f. 1ʳ.
35. The Indians were deemed to be free in 1508 and *naborias* (forced labourers) in 1509; on this and the slave trade among the islands of the Caribbean see Otte, 1975.
36. *Cédula* to Diego Colón dated 21 July 1511, *CDH*, I, p. 29.
37. There is e.g. a letter from Tello de Sandoval to the king dated November 1543, complaining that 'los indios que V[uestra] M[ajestad] mando se llevasen a sus tierras se quedan muchos dellos por averlos sus dueños llevado fuera de sevilla, no obstante el mando y embargo que les abia sido hecho'. AGI, Indiferente general, 1095, ramo 6, no. 161. Sandoval was still trying in 1544 to carry out 'con cumplimiento delo que el licenciado Gregorio López del Consejo de V[uestra] M[ajestad] dexo proveido tocante a los indios' (*ibid.*). The problem of illegal slaving was not confined to America; Filipinos were also sold and shipped to Spain. As late as 1596, for instance, Miguel de Benavides, bishop of Manila, was paid 800 *reales* for the cost of shipping home a Filipino 'Indian'. AGI, Audiencia, Filipinas, 1.
38. One Doctor Hernández reported to the crown in September 1547 that the Indians living in Seville were content, 'especialmente siendo libres porque ganavan aqui mas en una semana que alla en un año y estavan mas seguros'. AGI, Indiferente general, 1093, ramo 6, no. 101. The Indians confounded the judges by arguing that *as* they were free they chose to exercise their freedom by not returning home.
39. Mörner, 1970, pp. 21–7.
40. *CDH*, 1, pp. 39–41. The complete text of the Laws are printed in *ibid.*, pp. 38–57.
41. This has been studied with reference to the Yucatán by Clendinnen, 1980.
42. On the social organisation of the Arawak see Stewart, 1930, 4, pp. 557–9. Some degree of matrilocality seems to be confirmed by the report of Bernardino de Manzanedo in 1517: 'Quando un yndio se casare con una yndia esta tal casa pertenesce a la familia de donde la muger hera.' *Memorial de fray Bernardino de Manzanedo sobre el buen régimen y gobierno de los indios*, in Serrano y Sanz, 1918, 1, p. dlxv. In addition to their attempts to make the Arawak monogamous and patrilocal, the Spaniards obliged them to dress like Europeans (*CDH*, 1, p. 50) and attempted to make them comply with European economic demands.
43. Confessors were constantly reminded to question all male confessants if they had assisted a woman to abort. See e.g. Vetancurt, 1673, f. O2ʳ.
44. 'Naturalmente son gente sin piedad, no tienen verguença de costa alguna, son de pessimos deseos y obras y de ninguna buena inclinacion.' Oviedo,

1535, f. lviii$^v$. The Franciscan Tomás Ortiz reported that 'con los enfermos no tienen piedad ninguna [si] esta grave el enfermo aun que sea su pariente o vezino, le desampran o llevan a los montes a morir'. *Estas son las propriedades delos Yndios por donde no merescen liberdades* in Martyr, 1530b, f. xcv$^r$. More sympathetic observers, like the Frenchman Marc Lescarbot, assumed that the practice of abandoning the old and the dying was an inevitable function of a nomadic society: 'Car ce peuple estant vagabond et ne pouvant toujours vivre en une place, ils ne peuvent traîner après eux leurs pères ou amis vieillards ou malades.' Lescarbot, 1612, p. 19.

45. Cook, 1976, pp. 135-57.

46. The case of the Ik is described by Turnbull, 1972. On the rather different situation in Central Mexico where movement between 'urban centres' may have been a feature of pre-conquest life see Lockhart 1979.

47. Warren, 1963, p. 34. Pedro de Gante had complained in 1552 that forcing Indians to abandon their ancestral homes would destroy them all within forty years; *Cartas de Indias*, 1877, pp. 95-6, and cf. the reports to the Council of the Indies in 'Relaciones y paresceres' which already provides ample evidence of a population decline following forced migrations.

48. Hanke, 1959, p. 15. Las Casas's account of the Laws, which is generally favourable, is to be found in Las Casas, 1951, 3, 112-52, *passim*.

49. 'Si no le da un golpe no puede mandar sus carnes.' Reported in Anon, 'Sobre la reformacion', f. 4$^r$.

50. The Inquisition in Mexico tried many such cases; e.g. Juan de Pedraza of Granada, Nicaragua, who urinated on the cross (AGN, Inquisición, vol. 56, no. 1) and Diego Hernández de Sahagún, who attempted to stab an image of the Virgin with a knife (*ibid.*, vol. 125, nos. 38, 58).

51. Cf. the comments of Nicholas Canny on the role of the English in sixteenth-century Ireland, in Canny, 1978.

52. The Franciscans on one occasion refused absolution to *encomenderos* until they had asked 'perdon universal a todos los Indios por lo que les avian agraviado'. Letter from Diego de Avellaneda, Jesuit provincial of Andalusia, dated July 1563, ARSI, MS Hisp. 100, f. 238. *Encomenderos* who failed to provide proper instruction for their Indians were also described by one Augustinian friar as 'herejes o sospechosos en la fe' and denied absolution. AGI, Patronato, 252, ramo 20, f. 1$^r$; and see Las Casas's advice in his notorious *confesionario*, Las Casas, 1552b, ff. Aii$^r$–iii$^v$.

53. Las Casas, 1951, 3, pp. 113, 199. This concern for the spiritual welfare of Spaniards engaged in persecuting Indians seems to have been widespread. One Franciscan, Francisco de Dios, even went so far as to say, 'que si Dios no hacia justicia con los españoles perderia la fe'. AGN, Inquisición, vol. 125, no. 32, f. 1$^r$.

54. Cajetan, 1897, 9, p. 94, commenting on Aquinas, IIa IIae q. 66 art. 8.

55. See Gibson, 1977.

56. Aquinas, Ia, IIae q. 10 art. 1, and see Caperan, 1912, which, though old, is still a useful survey.

57. Lafaye, 1974, esp. pp. 238-75.

58. See Renaudet, 1953, and Skinner, 1978, 2, pp. 45-7.

59. *Tetrabiblos*, 2.2.

60. Mair, 1519a, f. clxxxvij$^r$.

61. Mair's reading of Ptolemy was, however, wildly inaccurate for, as Las Casas later pointed out, the Indians did not live 'beneath the Poles' but close to the equator which, on Ptolemy's own reckoning, was a most propitious place

to grow up. Las Casas, 1975, ff. 236–7$^r$. The same observations were made by López (1848, 1, p. 485).

62. Mair, 1706, 2, cols. 1145–64, and see Oakley, 1962.
63. Chenu, 1946.
64. Durkhan, 1950.
65. Las Casas, 1951, 3, p. 343.
66. Mair, 1519b, f. Aii$^r$.
67. Mair, 1892, p. 449.
68. Mair, 1519a f. l$^v$. Such comparisons between the advancement of science and the discoveries in Africa and America soon became a commonplace; see e.g. Campanella, 1636, p. 6, who claims that denying that theology had made significant advances since the days of the New Testament was like denying the reality of the overseas explorations and the new knowledge of the heavens.
69. Chrysostom believed that the origins of slavery were to be found in mere human greed (*In espistolam ad Ephesios homilia*, 6.22.2, printed in *PG*, 62, pp. 156–8); and see Jonkers, 1934.
70. *Digest*, 1.5.4.1. Cf. Justinian, *Institutes*, 1.3.2.
71. Justinian, *Institutes*, 1.3.3.
72. 'A servant of servants shall he be unto his brethren. Blessed be the Lord God of Shem and let Canaan be his servant.' Genesis 9.25–6. There are some interesting observations on the use of the Ham legend to classify Blacks in McKee, 1980.
73. Man himself is, of course, built to the same specifications as the universe, having his head up and his legs on the ground, 'Where they ought to be', *Hist. an* 494 a 26f.
74. This aspect of Aristotle's thought is discussed in Fortenbaugh, 1975, pp. 23–57.
75. Matienzo, 1967, pp. 17–18. Matienzo also believed that the physical strength of the Indians was evidence of their lack of *ratio* (see pp. 45–6 below). *Ibid.*, pp. 16–17, and Elliott, 1972, p. 11. For an account of the life and work of this important figure see Lohmann Villena, 1966.
76. 'Prohairesis is intellect associated with psychological drive or psychological drive associated with intellect, and as such is a source of action in the human being.' This version is the one given by Adkins, 1970, p. 212.
77. See Clark, 1975, p. 27.
78. RAH, Jesuitas, 73 (9–3647), item 85. (Diego de Avendaño, 1668, p. 201), makes the same observation on the reliability of Indians as witnesses. So too does Solórzano Pereyra, 1648, p. 235.
79. These, however, were frequently favourable even when they came from observers such as Oviedo. See e.g. Oviedo, 1956, p. 16; and cf. Landa, 1975, p. 89; 'The Indian women of Yucatán are generally better-looking than Spanish women, and bigger and well-built, but not so large-thighed as Negresses.'
80. Las Casas, 1967, 1, p. 181. This text is discussed at length in chapter 6.
81. *Parecer de un hombre docto cerca del servicio personal de los indios presentado a la magestad catolica por don Alonso de Onate* (Madrid, 1600), quoted by Elliott, 1970, p. 44. I am grateful to Professor Elliott for having lent me his notes on this document. Cf. Matienzo, 1967, p. 17: 'Ansí se ve en que estos indios son muy recios de cuerpo, mucho mas que los españoles, y sufren mas que ellos, pues se ve que traen cargas a cuestas de una y dos arrobas y caminan con ellas muy sin pena.' Oviedo's view that the Indians

had heads three times thicker than those of Europeans belongs to the same tradition: 'y ansí como tienen el casco grueso, ansí tiene el entendimiento bestial'. Oviedo, 1535, f. xliiii$^v$.

82. According to Aristotle, however, it is also the case that every human being contains the potential for becoming an animal – and therefore, presumably, also a natural slave – for every living thing 'contains a series, each successive term of which potentially contains its predecessors' (*De anima*, 414 b 30), and the semen of the male carries within it the traits of the most remote of its ancestors (*De gen. an.* 768 a 2ff.). It might therefore be possible to say that a man may slip down the biological continuum or, in other words, degenerate.

83. Justinian, *Institutes*, 1.3.3.

84. Covarrubias, 'De iustitia', f. 39$^v$.

85. 'Servus enim est quasi instrumentum animatum, sicut e converso, instrumentum est quasi servus inanimatus.' Aquinas, 1964, p. 1447, para. 1699 (lectio, 7.1.9.).

86. Mercado, 1571, f. 108$^r$.

87. 'Siempre tuve mucha devoción a este orden', he told the provincial Alonso de Loaysa. Chacón y Calvo, 1929, p. 430.

88. The only full account we have of this meeting is provided by Las Casas, 1951, 2, 452ff., according to whom the chief participants were: the Dominicans Tomás Durán and Pedro de Covarrubias; Bernardo de Mesa, a member of the royal household and later bishop of Cuba; the *licenciado* Gil Gregorio, the civilian jurist Juan López de Palacios Rubios; the canonist Matías de Paz; Francisco de Sosa, who later became bishop of Almería. Pedro Mexía de Ovando ('Libro memorial', p. 66) adds the names of two others, Tomás de Matienzo, a royal confessor and the author of a report, now lost, on the treatment of the Indians (Las Casas, 1951, 3, p. 109), and the Dominican Alonso de Bastilla. The whole affair was presided over by two representatives of the Royal Council, Luis de Zapata and a *licenciado* called Santiago, and possibly by one Hernando de Vega and another *licenciado* by the name of Moxica.

89. Both are quoted by Las Casas, 1951, 2, pp. 458–62 (Mesa) and 471–3 (Gregorio). There is a manuscript copy in a contemporary hand of the *parecer* of Gil Gregorio (which supplies his first name) in RAH, 9–17–93688, item 33. All subsequent references will be to the manuscript, although the differences between this version and that of Las Casas are not very great.

90. 'Donde paresce que por la malicia y barbarica disposicion del pueblo se pueden y deben guvernar cuomo siervos'. 'Parecer de Gil Gregorio', f. 1$^v$.

91. 'Son siervos y barbaros que son aquellos que faltan en el juizio y entendymento cuomo son estos yndios que segund todos dizen son cuomo animales que hablan'. *Ibid.*

92. *Ibid.*

93. 'Inter omnes autem homines, qui plus habent de ratione motus sunt reges et principes et omnes qui praesunt, sive in gubernando sive in iudicando sive in defendendo, et sic de aliis actibus qui ad curam regiminis pertinent.' Aquinas, 1954, p. 297, para. 929.

94. 'Parecer de Gil Gregorio', f. 2$^r$.

95. *Ibid.* Mesa confirmed Gregorio's opinion on this point: 'la libertad absoluta daña a los indios por su mala disposicion'. Las Casas, 1951, 2, p. 561.

96. 'Que no fuessen asi siervos que se pudieren vender y que ninguna persona consi pudiessen poseer, pero en disponer y mandar que serviesen a los

cristianos quiso la Reyna ponerlos en una servydumbre qualificada cuomo es esta lo qual les convenga pues la total libertad les dañava.' 'Parecer de Gil Gregorio', f. 2$^r$.

97. Las Casas, 1951, 2, p. 459.
98. *Ibid.*, pp. 459–60.
99. *Ibid.*, pp. 461–2.
100. *Ibid.*, p. 462.
101. In seeking the opinions of both a civil and a canon lawyer Ferdinand was following an established procedure, and one that had been used before in similar circumstances by the papacy. In the 1430s Eugenius IV had sought the advice of two Bolognese lawyers, the canonist Antonio de Rosellis and the civilian Antonio Minucci da Pratovecchio, on whether or not it was legitimate for the Portuguese to send armies into the Canary Islands. Both texts have been printed in *Monumenta henricina*, 1960–74, 5, pp. 287–320, 322–43. See also Russell, 1978, and Muldoon, 1980, pp. 124–31.
102. Palacios Rubios, 'De insulanis', and Paz, 1933. Both works have been published in translation in Zavala, 1954. For convenience I have given page references to the translation of 'De insulanis' in square brackets following the manuscript references.
103. His extant works are listed in Zavala, 1954, pp. 269–87.
104. Recorded in Antonio, 1783, 1, p. 719. I say 'perhaps' because the reference may be to 'De insulanis' under another name. I have found no further trace of either this work or the commentary on the *Politics*.
105. See Hanke, 1938.
106. *CDI*, 7, pp. 24–5.
107. Palacios Rubios, 'De insulanis', f. 4$^r$ [p. 9].
108. 'Homines rationales mansueti, pacifici et fidei nostrae capaces reperti sunt'. *Ibid.*
109. 'Unde apud eos ius primaevum libertatem et ingenuitatem hominibus concedens nondum fuit immutatum, immo semper duravit.' *Ibid.*, f. 13$^r$ [p. 32].
110. Ia IIae q. 103 arts. 1–4. The 'age of the natural law' was thought of as the age before the Flood and as somehow identical to the classical Golden Age. The idea that the Indians were living in their own 'age of the natural law' was a common one. See, for instance, the observations of Alessandro Geraldini, a companion of Columbus and bishop of Santo Domingo from 1520 to 1525 (Geraldini, 1631, p. 220): 'in lege naturae vivebant. Nullam alicui vim inferebant matrimonia observabant. Summum Ius aequi, et boni menti innocuae affixum nullo vinculo sed quodam animi bono erat.'
111. Palacios Rubios, 'De insulanis', f. 4$^r$ [p. 9].
112. Lovejoy and Boas, 1935, pp. 1–22.
113. Aquinas, Ia IIae q. 102 art. 6. Vitoria, 1960, p. 1018. For a discussion of these *topoi* see pp. 88–9 below.
114. The opposite view is taken by Juan de Palafox y Mendoza: 'la cortesía es grandíssima porque todos ellos son muy observantes en las cerimonias de reverencia y veneración a los Superiores'. Palafox y Mendoza, 1650, p. 82.
115. Palacios Rubios, 'De insulanis', f. 4$^r$ [p. 10]. The belief that Indian women were sexually more obliging than European ones was a common fantasy, based on texts such as the letter *Mundus novus* attributed to Vespucci. See Vespucci, 1966, p. 88.
116. Palacios Rubios, 'De insulanis', f. 4$^v$ [p. 10]. Oviedo, 1535, f. xlix$^v$.
117. Promiscuity, like polygyny (and, indeed, polyandry of which Indians were

sometimes accused), was said to be 'against nature' on the grounds that it was in the nature of the human animal to mate with only one person 'cum qua permaneat, non per modicum tempus sed diu, vel etiam per totam vitam'. Aquinas, IIa IIae q. 154 art. 2.

118. 'Alii tamen pauci legis naturae percepta servabant; et unum colentes venerantesque deum, quodam rationis lumine illustrati, naturaliter cognoscebant bonum esse faciendum, malo vero vitandum.' Palacios Rubios, 'De insulanis', ff. 4$^v$–5$^r$ [p. 11].

119. 'Per boves enim et pecora campi intellegimus infideles, praesertim sarracenos, qui tanquam bestiae ratione carentes relicto vero Deo collunt idola.' *Ibid.* f. 36$^v$.

120. This is discussed in *ibid.*, ff. 4$^v$–7$^r$ [pp. 11–16].

121. *Ibid.*, f. 10$^r$ [p. 24].

122. *Ibid.*, f. 11$^r$ [p. 25].

123. *Ibid.*, echoing *Pol.* 1254 a 20ff.

124. Aquinas, Ia IIae q. 96 art. 4.

125. Ca' da Mosto, 1966, p. 52.

126. Palacios Rubios, 'De insulanis', f. 11$^v$ [p. 26]. This is the familiar Aristotelian premise, *natura nihil fecit frustra*, see p. 94 below.

127. 'Tamen aliqui eorum ita sunt inepti et imbecilles, qui se nullo modo gubernare sci[u]nt; quapropter largo modo possunt dici servi, quasi nati ad serviendum, non autem ad imperandum'. *Ibid.*, f. 15$^v$ [p. 37].

128. *Ibid.*

129. See Maclean, 1980, pp. 50–1.

130. *Memorial de fray Bernardino de Manzanedo sobre el buen régimen y gobierno de los indios*, in Serrano y Sanz, 1918, 1, p. dlxviii.

131. Soto, 1568, ff. 102$^v$–103$^r$.

132. Palacios Rubios, 'De insulanis', f. 15$^v$ [p. 38].

133. This is a Stoic and Christian belief, not an Aristotelian one. See Cicero, *De natura deorum*, 2.3, who attributes the view to Zeno; and see in general Passmore, 1970, p. 54.

## 4 From nature's slaves to nature's children

1. See e.g. Schlaifer, 1936, p. 193.

2. These are described in Ybot, 1948.

3. Las Casas, 1951, 3, p. 348. Quevedo himself wrote a treatise on natural slavery which has not survived. A passage from it is, however, quoted by Las Casas, *ibid.*, pp. 345–6. This sets out the relationship between the Indian and his master in much the same terms as those used by Gregorio and Mesa. The debate between Las Casas and the bishop is described in Morelli, 1791, pp. 239–40, who may have had access to Quevedo's treatise.

4. Bibliographical details for all these are to be found in Harrisse, 1958, pp. 202–340.

5. Oviedo's *Historia* is the notable exception; but even this contains relatively little material on the Indians themselves – only some twenty-eight folios of the original *primera parte*.

6. 'Senza forma di governo, privo d'ogni lume di religione, enteramente lontano d'ogni commercio, non puol' essere materia di troppo grandi speculazione.' Brunetti, 'Lettera', f. 89$^v$, also cited by Landucci, 1972, p. 16.

7. See Pagden, 1981.

8. Cano, 1569, p. 670.

9. For this period of Vitoria's life see Villoslada, 1938, pp. 101–4, 258–79.
10. Vitoria, 1934, 1, p. ix.
11. 'Erasmus ex grammatica fecit se theologus.' Vitoria, 1934, 1, p. xxxi. On the Valladolid *juntas* see Bataillon, 1966, pp. 226–78. One modern scholar to have demolished the 'humanist' myth (repeated e.g. in Hamilton, 1963, p. 174) is Skinner, 1978, 1, p. 141.
12. Cano, 'De dominio indorum', f. 30$^r$.
13. The phrase is, of course, an anachronism, but see Soto, 1568, f. 7$^v$.
14. This is Saint Augustine's phrase (*Confessions*, bk 2, ch. 4) and was the most widely used description of the natural law. See e.g. Vitoria, 1934, 1, p. 11. The natural law belongs to those categories of things implanted by God in all creatures to allow them to encompass their ends. See e.g. Soto, 1568, f. 7$^v$. In the account of the natural law which follows I have drawn heavily on Soto's formulation because it is the clearest available summary of the views of the Salamanca theologians.
15. Soto, 1568, f. 11$^r$.
16. Vitoria, 1960, p. 1010.
17. See Crowie, 1956.
18. See Vitoria, 1960, p. 184.
19. Soto, 1568, f. 11$^r$.
20. Vitoria, 1960, p. 1099. Cf. Soto, 1568, f. 11$^r$, and Suárez, 1971, 3, p. 79.
21. Hart, 1961, p. 183.
22. Mesnard, 1951, p. 626.
23. Vitoria, 1960, pp. 1234–49.
24. Vitoria, 1934, 1, p. 8, and 1932, 3, p. 11.
25. Vitoria, 1932–52, 3, p. 11.
26. 'Hoc est scire, scilicet, quod omnes assentiantur.' Vitoria, 1934, 1, p. 10.
27. Ullmann, 1960.
28. *Ibid.*
29. Mersch, 1944, 1, pp. 120–7.
30. Bodin, 1650, p. 322, and quoted by Elliott, 1970, p. 53.
31. Geertz, 1968, p. 97.
32. Vitoria, 1967, p. 10.
33. *Ibid.*, p. 98.
34. See Miaja de la Muela, 1965.
35. Vitoria, 1932, 6, pp. 501–3. On the question of the rights of Christian princes to occupy the territories of pagans see *ibid.*, 3, pp. 63–81. The development of Vitoria's reflections on the Indian question is discussed by Reginaldo di Agostino Iannarone in *Génesis del pensamiento colonial de Francisco de Vitoria* in Vitoria, 1967, pp. xxxi–xli.
36. *Carta de Francisco de Vitoria al P. Arcos sobre negocios de Indias*, printed in Vitoria, 1967, pp. 136–9.
37. On the textual relations between this *relectio* and Vitoria's lecture course for 1526–9 see the introduction by Teófilo Urdanoz in Vitoria, 1960, pp. 997–9.
38. Getino, 1930, pp. 148, 152–3.
39. Vitoria was not, however, the only professor to discuss the subject openly. Soto touched on the problem in a *relectio* 'De dominio' in 1534 or 1535 (Soto, 1964). He also wrote a treatise, now lost, on evangelisation which must have been composed before 1553. 'Sed de hoc latius in libello nostro De ratione promulgandi Evangelium ubi de dominio et iure quod catholici reges in novum orbem oceanicum fugantur amplior patebit dicendi locus.' Soto, 1568, f. 103$^v$.

40. Vitoria, 1967, p. 5.
41. *Ibid.*
42. *Ibid.*, p. 10.
43. *Ibid.*
44. *Ibid.*, p. 11. He makes the point that, for example, although jurists may be able to decide whether a contract is legally binding, they cannot say whether it is morally so (pp. 6–7). The whole introduction to this *relectio* is, in fact, an assertion of the need for a correct division between different systems of knowledge.
45. *Ibid.*, p. 10.
46. Soto, 1568, ff. 7ᵛ–8ʳ.
47. See Aquinas, Ia IIae q. 91 arts, 1, 2.
48. Vitoria, 1967, p. 14.
49. *Ibid.*, pp. 14–15. See Skinner, 1978, 1, p. 169.
50. Vitoria, 1967, p. 13.
51. *Ibid.*
52. *Ibid.*, p. 27.
53. *Ibid.*, pp. 138–9.
54. Domingo de Cuevas and Juan de Salinas, 'De insulanis', printed in Vitoria, 1967, pp. 196–218 at p. 199. This fragment is based upon lectures by Vitoria and may repeat lost sections of *De indis*.
55. Soto, 1568, ff. 1ʳ, 11ʳ.
56. Vitoria, 1967, p. 29. For the significance of the word *ordo* in the Augustinian sense in which it is here used by Vitoria see Markus, 1970, pp. 76–9.
57. See Curtius, 1953, p. 70, whose English translator renders this as 'storehouses of trains of thought'.
58. Soto, 1568, f. 6ʳ–ᵛ.
59. See e.g. Vitoria, 1960, pp. 156–7.
60. *Ibid.*, p. 158, citing *Physics*, 250 b 11. Cf. Soto, 1568, ff. 10ᵛ–11ʳ. Man by nature seeks for a knowledge of God and through this derives his urge to participate in virtue which can, of course, only be acquired within the community.
61. Vitoria, 1960, p. 155.
62. Soto, 1568, ff. 10ᵛ–11ʳ.
63. *Ibid.*, f. 6ʳ.
64. Suárez, 1971, 1, p. 109. Cf. Soto, 1568, f. 6ᵛ.
65. Most Christians would have agreed with Augustine (*De civitate Dei*, bk 15, ch. 8; *PL*, 41, p. 446) that the physical existence of a walled enclosure is not important. But, of course, the presence of walled cities is itself a sign of civility. This subject has been discussed with reference to Aristotle in Weill, 1960, pp. 367–415.
66. See e.g. *Pol.* 1252 b 12ff., *NE*, 1162 a 19–24, and *Oec.* 1343 b 15ff.
67. Vitoria, 1960, p. 154. The account of human prehistory as a development from the tribe to the phratry and finally to the *polis* was a common one in antiquity. See e.g. Plato, *Laws*, 3.680–1, and *Pol.* 1252 b 12ff. The matter is discussed in detail in Cole, 1967, pp. 97–106.
68. Vitoria, 1960, p. 157.
69. See e.g. Vitoria, 1960, pp. 156–7. The invention of the city was also attributed by Pliny (*Natural history*, 7.56.194) to Cecrops, the legendary builder of the Acropolis, and by Augustine (on the evidence of Genesis 4) to Cain (*De civitate Dei*, bk 15, ch. 5).
70. Vitoria, 1960, p. 156.

71. 'He who is sufficient unto himself must be either a beast or a god.' *Pol.* 1253 a 27–30. See Soto, 1568, f. 6ʳ.

72. Giraldus Cambrensis, 1867, p. 151. This was, of course, a widespread attitude. See, for instance, João de Castro on the 'Ethiopians' who had no agriculture and lived in caves rather than cities, which is evidence of 'falta de engenho e arte dos moradores' (Castro, 1964, pp. 20–1). Nor was it restricted to Christians. The fifteenth-century Tunisian historian Ibn Khaldûn speaks of Black Africans as being 'close to dumb animals...they dwell in caves and thickets, eat herbs, live in savage isolation, do not congregate and eat each other. The same applies to the Slavs.' Ibn Khaldûn, 1958, 1, pp. 168–9. The association between a city-less way of life and cannibalism is also conventional.

73. Botero, 1665, p. 8. Cf. Luis de León, who believed that the Indians had little chance of development so long as they lived in scattered communities without cities. (Léon, 1892, 3, p. 162.)

74. Cortés, 1972, p. 102.

75. Motolinía, 1971, p. 201.

76. Vega, 1943, 1, p. 8.

77. Landa pointed out that on the evidence of the garments worn by the figures in the friezes on Maya buildings, 'it is untrue to say that these buildings were built by other nations to whom the Indians were subject'. Landa, 1975, pp. 126–7. But as late as 1650, Antonio de León Pinelo was still trying to demonstrate that they were really the work of a vanished race of giants. León Pinelo, 1943, 1, pp. 241–53.

78. 'Aquestas indianas gentes vivían socialmente como hombres racionales en ayuntamientos grandes que llamamos villas y ciudades, poniendo en obra aquella inclinación natural...conviene a saber, vivir en compañía.' Las Casas, 1967, 1, p. 304.

79. See e.g. *NE*, 1162 a 19–27, and *EE*, 1242 a 23–8. Monogamy is the natural inclination of man because the end of sexual association is the creation of the family.

80. Vitoria, 1967, p. 106.

81. Soto, 1568, ff. 5ᵛ–6ʳ, arguing on the basis of *NE*, 1103 a 23–6, that habituation always leads to virtue and that the creation of a virtuous citizen is, of course, the ultimate purpose of the law (*NE*, 1179 b 31–2).

82. See e.g. Cortés, 1972, pp. 84–5, 109–12, and Motolinía, 1971, pp. 335–8.

83. Palafox y Mendoza, 1650, pp. 83, 85.

84. Santillán, 1968, p. 104.

85. See Aquinas, *Prima pars*, q. 19 art. 4 ad. 4, and q. 79 art. 4; IIa IIae q. 179 art. 2; and *Summa contra gentiles*, 1.72; 2.92; 3.44 and 77, and the discussion on intellectual acts in the commentary on the *De anima*, Aquinas, 1925, paras. 720–7.

86. Las Casas, 1967, 2, p. 531.

87. Acosta, 1962, p. 298.

88. See Aquinas, Ia IIae q. 102 art. 6. This idea is, of course, inherent in the classical account of prehistory which describes cultural evolution in terms of, among other things, the increasing complexity in the *varietas artium*. See Cole, 1967, pp. 39–41.

89. Vitoria, 1960, pp. 1018–19.

90. Hobbes, 1968, p. 186.

91. Vitoria, 1960, p. 1019. Cf. Aquinas, Ia IIae q. 103 arts. 1–4.

92. Diodorus Siculus, *The library of history*, 1.8.5–6.

93. All arts are potencies. *Meta.* 1046 a 36 – b 11. See Cole, 1967, pp. 36–7.
94. Charron, 1604, pp. 322–3.
95. See Rossi, 1971, pp. 139–41, and Close, 1969.
96. Soto, 1568, f. 13ᵛ.
97. *MB*, 1, p. 136.
98. Hurtado, 'Declaracion', f. 1ᵛ.
99. *Cartas de Indias*, 1877, pp. 64–5.
100. Motolinía, 1971, pp. 235–9. Cf. Sahagún, 1956, 3, p. 158. Indians are skilled in both the mechanical arts (which here include geometry and building as well as the traditional 'vile' professions of shoemaking and tailoring) and the liberal arts.
101. Cicero, *De officiis*, 2.13 and 15. Seneca, *Epistles*, 90.15–26.
102. See Mauss, 1967.
103. See e.g. Durán, 1967, 1, p. 69, and Landa, 1975, p. 68. It is clear that both the Maya and certain Nahua groups practised a form of potlatch, an elaborate ritual of gift exchange, and sometimes the ostentatious 'sacrifice' of personal property common among tribes of the American North West. See Mauss, 1967, pp. 31–7.
104. Weill, 1954, p. 215. Cf. his observation that 'le droit de réciprocité maintient la société civile... Cette réciprocité entre les rapports fait subsister la cité.'
105. Polyani, 1968, pp. 148–74, and see the critique by North, 1977.
106. Tovar, 1972, p. 9.
107. Vitoria, 1960, pp. 155–6.
108. Vitoria, 1967, pp. 79–81. Cf. *EE*, 1242 b 23–5. Both the *polis* itself and all international alliances depend on political friendship (*politikē philia*) which in turn depends on the exchange of goods. See also Aquinas, Ia IIae q. 96 arts. 2, 8.
109. 'Ergo videtur quod amicitia ad omnes homines sit de iure naturali, et quod contra naturam est vitare consortium hominum innoxiorum.' Vitoria, 1967, p. 79.
110. *Ibid.*
111. *Ibid.*, citing *Aeneid*, 1.538–40. Cf. Baldry, 1965, p. 194.
112. Vitoria, 1967, p. 80.
113. Covarrubias, 'De iustitia belli', f. 42ʳ.
114. See e.g. Cortés, 1972, pp. 103–4. For Girava (1570, p. 198), citing Xenophon (*Cyropaedia*, 8.2.5.), organised markets were the crucial evidence for the civility of the Mexica.
115. Motolinía, 1971, pp. 39, 41, 68, and Sahagún, 1956, 3, pp. 15–64, 68–9.
116. Le Roy, 1576, f. 25ʳ.
117. Thevet, 1953, p. 264.
118. Sahagún, 1956, 3, p. 159, and Ricard, 1933, pp. 33–49.
119. Las Casas, 1967, 2, p. 255.
120. Columbus, 1930, 1, p. 13.
121. Las Casas (1967, 2, p. 42), spoke of '[los] tres artículos que contiene la religión, conviene a saber: los dioses, los templos y los ministros y grados sacerdotales'.
122. *Ibid.* 1, pp. 369–80, 680–97; 2, pp. 19–293.
123. See e.g. Zorita, 1909, pp. 136–8.
124. See e.g. Quiroga, 1922, p. 50: 'si supieses que religiosos eran estos infieles desta tierra, y que cultores de sus dioses sino eraran; que observadores de sus ritos!...Confunde esto por cierto, si lo quieres contemplar, a nuestra tibieça y poca christiandad.'
125. See e.g. Las Casas, 1967, 2, pp. 29–32, 330–2, and Acosta, 1954, pp. 240–2.

126. 'E ya que anduvieron todas errados, fueron en sus desavios mas cercanos...
     de razón.' Las Casas, 1967, 2, p. 242.
127. Covarrubias, 'De iustitia belli', f. 40$^r$.
128. Vitoria, 1967, p. 97.
129. *Ibid.*
130. During his course on the *Secunda secundae* in 1533–4, Vitoria had observed
     'Omnia ista confirmantur, quia omnes doctores conveniunt quod actus
     bonus est quod est conformis legi, et malus quod est difformis. Sed conformis
     vel difformis legi est etiam conformis vel difformis rationi.' Vitoria, 1952,
     p. 12; and see Aquinas, *In quartum sententiarum librum*, dist. 33 art. 1.
     Man is, of course, the only creature capable of understanding causality and
     because of this his natural understanding of things (*naturalis conceptio*) is
     always directed towards the moral good. It might, therefore, be argued that
     men who created unnatural laws lacked such understanding and were thus
     either perverse or not real men. As we shall see, there was, however, an
     alternative explanation for seemingly aberrant patterns of behaviour.
131. Vitoria, 1967, pp. 93–4.
132. *Odyssey*, 9.106f. and 10, 82ff. Martyr, 1530a, f. xxxv$^r$.
133. *Pol.* 1338 b 19 and *NE*, 1148 b 19ff.; Herodotus, *History*, 4.106 and 2.10;
     Pliny, *Natural history*, 7.1.8–11; Strabo, *Geography*, 4.5.4. (on the Irish);
     Jerome, *Adversus Jovinianum*, 2.7.
134. Isidore, *Etymologiae*, 9.2;15.3; and Tertullian, *Adversus Marcionem*, 1.1.
135. Columbus, 1930, 1, p. 15. There are some interesting observations of
     Columbus's understanding of the stories he was told by the Arawak in
     Hulme, 1978.
136. Columbus, 1960, p. 52.
137. *Ibid.*, p. 200.
138. See e.g. Torquemada, 1723, 1, 34–6, who believed that mammoth bones
     were the bones of giants.
139. Columbus, 1930, 1, p. 17.
140. Kupperman, 1980, p. 43.
141. Evans-Pritchard, 1965, p. 137, and Friedman, 1981, pp. 70–5.
142. For the use of dogs as images of unselective consumption see Morse, forth-
     coming.
143. Columbus, 1960, p. 52.
144. Azande kings were described by European explorers as 'burning with a
     desire to eat human flesh' (Evans-Pritchard, 1965, p. 145). On the Iroquois
     see Chodowiec, 1972.
145. Livy, *History*, 38.8–19.
146. Cohn, 1976, pp. 1–2.
147. Ca' da Mosto, 1966, p. 85.
148. Arens, 1979, p. 12.
149. For the Xixime see p. 87 below, on the Guarani, Chase Sardi, 1964,
     and on the Maya, López Mendel, 1612, f. 235$^v$.
150. Standen, 1557.
151. Leite, 1954, 2, p. 113, José de Anchieta from São Paolo de Piratininga,
     1 September 1554.
152. This has not survived, but it would seem to have been written in order to
     dissuade Christians from adopting the custom. Leite, 1954, 3, p. 77, and see
     *ibid.*, p. 468.
153. *MB*, 1, p. 137; the reference is to Saint John, 8.44.
154. See Arens, 1979. Professor Arens maintains that it is rarely, if ever, possible

to substantiate accusations of cannibalism and that such accusations serve only to provide moral legitimacy for otherwise illegitimate activities. No European account of cannibalism will, he claims, stand up to critical examination. Either the supposed witness turns out not to have been present at the crucial moment when the victim was eaten or his account is, on internal evidence, unreliable as an ethnographical report. Although Professor Arens's argument is based solely on printed sources which are easily available in English, his hypothesis, in so far as it applies to the Amerindians, also holds true for the large body of documentary material on cannibalism. I, at least, have not found a single eye-witness account of a cannibal feast nor, indeed a single description which does not rely on elements taken from classical accounts of anthropophagy. In every case it is always assumed that cannibalism follows naturally from human sacrifice (see pp. 89–90) below); and since many Indian tribes did practise human sacrifice, this is held to be sufficient proof that they were also man-eaters.

155. Las Casas, 1958, p. 385.
156. Torraca, 1949–50, p. 117.
157. Montaigne, 1962, 1, pp. 238–9.
158. Davis, 1975, p. 324, and Le Roy Ladurie, 1966, 1, p. 398.
159. Pauw, 1770, 1, p. 217.
160. José de Anchieta to Diego Laynes, San Vicente, 8 January 1565, in *MB*, 4, p. 129; and cf. Antonio Blásquez from Bahia, 10 June 1557, in Leite, 1954, 2, p. 384, on the advisability of allowing the Tupinamba to go on killing their enemies if they could be persuaded not to eat them.
161. See Harris, 1977.
162. Aguiano, 1706, pp. 30–1.
163. López Mendel, 1612, f. 235$^v$.
164. *CDI*, 23, p. 356. A few people, such as Girava, assumed that cannibalism possessed a ritual purpose, and that the Amerindians were exo-cannibals: 'y así tiene por religión comer a sus enemigos mas no a sus amigos'. Girava, 1570, p. 197.
165. 'Nationes viventes civiliter et non inhumaniter'. Vitoria, 1960, p. 1036.
166. *Ibid.*, p. 1027, with a reference to the 'Thystean feast'; 'Imo apud gentiles tanquam infandum scelus habebatur. Unde et christianis hoc facinus a paganis imponebatur quod in nocturnis sacrificiis infantes occisos comederent.'
167. *Ibid.*
168. See Pagden, 1982.
169. This term was first used by Gilbert Ryle, 1963, p. 17: '[a category mistake] represents the facts of mental life as if they belonged to one logical type or category (or range of types or categories) when they actually belong to another'.
170. Vitoria, 1960, p. 1011.
171. *Ibid.*, p. 1035.
172. *Ibid.*, p. 1028.
173. 'Quia alimentum ordinatur ad id cuius est alimentum, et per consequens debet esse ignobilius eo. Ergo homo non est alimentum hominis.' *Ibid.*, p. 1027.
174. See Aquinas, IIa IIae q. 142 art. 4 ad. 3: 'Et tamen etiam illa videntur reduci ad genus intemperantiae secundum quendam excessum: sicut si aliquis delectetur in comestione carnium humanarum, aut in coitu bestiarum aut masculorum.' See pp. 176–7 below.

175. Soto, 1568, ff. 10$^v$–11$^r$.
176. *Ibid.*, ff. 11$^v$–12$^r$. Sodomy is against man's animal nature because it denies the principle of generation.
177. See e.g. Báñez, 1595, p. 79.
178. Vitoria, 1967, p. 97.
179. For Vitoria food taboos which had no obvious ceremonial function nor served to articulate some mystery (such as eating fish on Fridays) were moral precepts. See e.g. Vitoria, 1960, p. 1009, on the abominations of Leviticus.
180. AGN, Jesuitas, 3, item 16. Cf. Tomás Ortiz: 'comen piojos y arañas y gusanos crudos do quiera que los hallan'. *Estas son las propriedades delos yndios por donde no merescen liberdades*, printed in Martyr, 1530b, f. xcv$^r$.
181. See Girava, 1570, p. 199. Johann Alstedt cited unselective food consumption as evidence for the barbarism of the Canarians and the Amerindians. Alstedt, 1620, p. 2143.
182. Cárdenas, 1591, p. 201.
183. Matienzo, 1967, p. 17.
184. Plano Carpini, 1929, 47–8.
185. George of Ostia, 1974, p. 27.
186. Pliny, *Natural history*, 5.8.45; and see Fernández de Enciso, 1519, f. Eviii$^v$.
187. 'Esus autem carnium ad quasdam delicias et curiositatem vivendi'. Vitoria, 1960, p. 1018.
188. 'Et hoc ideo quia a terra nascentia magis pertinent ad simplicitatem vitae.' *Ibid.*
189. *Ibid.*, pp. 1018–19 discussing Aquinas, Ia IIae q. 102 art. 6 ad 2. Vitoria argues that if men before the Flood abstained from eating meat, this was by custom, not divine decree.
190. See e.g. Tertullian, *Liber de corona*, ch. 4 (*PL*, 2, p. 80), who warns that if a crumb of the sacramental bread or a drop of the wine were to be dropped Christ's body would, as he put it, be 'harassed'. A Franciscan called Maturino Gilberti was tried for blasphemy by the Mexican Inquisition for attempting to teach Indians the significance of transubstantiation by only consecrating one of several wafers and then throwing the remainder on the floor and treading on them. What the Indians made of this performance is not recorded. Gilberti's Tarascan grammar was also rounded up by the Inquisition on the grounds that it might be similarly unorthodox. But it was not (Gilberti, 1558). AGN, Inquisición, vol. 43, Nos. 6, 20, and vol. 72, no. 35.
191. Aquinas, Ia IIae q. 101. Discussed by Vitoria, 1960, p. 1012.
192. Vitoria, 1586, f. 38$^v$.
193. The idea that cooking is a significant stage in man's cultural evolution is an ancient one which may have its origin in Hippocrates. See Cole 1967, p. 7, and Miller, 1955.
194. 'Ostendit [Caietanus] naturalem usum comedendi carnes, scilicet, non crudas, sed coctas, aliud est enim barbarum et ferale.' Vitoria, 1960, p. 1026.
195. Las Casas, 1967, 1, p. 470.
196. See Loeb, 1923, pp. 5–11.
197. Vitoria, 1960, p. 1033.
198. 'Item, ipse Redemptor noster seipsum sacrificavit in cruce.' *Ibid.*, p. 1032. On the disturbing similarities between the death of Christ and human sacrifices by pagans, especially the Druids, see Walker, 1972, p. 74–5.
199. Las Casas, 1975, f. 161$^{r-v}$. The subject is discussed at length in Las Casas, 1967, 2, pp. 187–257; and see pp. 143–4 below.

200. Vitoria, 1960, p. 1037, citing Aquinas, Ia IIae q. 88 art. 2, in turn citing Jerome. Aquinas makes the point that Jephthah's vow to sacrifice the first thing he encountered on his return home was foolish since something unfit (*non immolativum*) might come to greet him, either something human (as indeed was the case) and thus too 'high' or an unworthy animal such as an ass which would have been too 'low'.

201. Vitoria, 1960, p. 1035.

202. Vitoria, 1967, p. 97.

203. Montesquieu, 1758, 1, p. 387.

204. Anders and Heitkamp, 1972, and Panofsky, 1945, 1, p. 209.

205. Locke, 1975, p. 646. Juan Ginés de Sepúlveda (see pp. 109–18 below) argued that the conquest of America could be justified in terms of an exchange of gold and silver for the vastly more useful iron. Sepúlveda, 1951, p. 78. The idea that the land of America was, in some sense, deficient became a subject of heated debate in the eighteenth century (discussed in Gerbi, 1973); but it was also the case that many Europeans believed America to be a source of great wealth and the Indians' inability to exploit it a sign of their barbarity. See e.g. Valadés, 1579, p. 226, and Kupperman, 1979.

206. Monardes, 1574, ff. 159ᵛ–160ʳ. Cf. Solórzano Pereyra, 1648, p. 948, who claims that the Indians did not understand the purpose to which metals could be put until the Europeans taught them, and the observation of Francisco Medes in 1671 that the inhabitants of the Caroline Islands could paint their bodies 'que espanta como gentes que no conocieron hierro ni oro ni plata ayan podido pintar assí un cuerpo humano'. Lamalle, 1980, p. 410.

207. Landa, 1975, p. 39, and Acosta, 1962, p. 297.

208. Soto, 1568, f. 13ᵛ. Cf. *Meta.* 981 b 13ff., and Clark, 1975, p. 106.

209. Maldonado, 1549, f. 63ʳ, and quoted by Rico, 1978, p. 906.

210. *Ibid.*

211. *Ibid.*, f. 63ᵛ; Rico, 1978, p. 907.

212. 'El cardenal me contestó que yo estaba engañado, que los indios no eran mas que unos papagayos.' *Memorial de Bernardino de Minaya*, c. 1535, printed in Hanke, 1968, p. 76.

213. Vitoria, 1967, p. 30.

214. *Ibid.*

215. E.g. *Pol.* 1523 a 8; *De part. an.* 961 b 4; *De gen. an.* 736 b 30, 741 b 5, 744 a 37.

216. 'De insulanis' in Vitoria, 1967, p. 199.

217. See Sorabji, 1974, pp. 124–9.

218. Aquinas, Ia IIae q. 5 art. 1; *Prima pars*, q. 93 art. 3 ad. 3; and see the observations by Kenny, 1964, p. 71.

219. Vitoria, 1960, p. 1099.

220. Vitoria, 1932–52, 3, p. 11, and 1934, 1, p. 8.

221. Clark, 1975, p. 25.

222. Vitoria, 1932–52, 3, p. 11.

223. Cano, 'De dominio indorum', 32ʳ⁻ᵛ.

224. *Ibid.* Cf. Soto, 1568, ff. 102ᵛ–103ʳ.

225. Covarrubias, 'De iustitia belli', f. 40ʳ. This insistence that 'barbarians' and natural slaves are only those who live *wholly* uncivil lives was repeated by all Vitoria's successors. See e.g. Francisco Suárez, for whom the barbarians were those 'qui nullam habent humanam politiam et nudi prorsus incedunt carnibus vescuntur humani'. Not all infidels are barbarians, he went on,

because many are clearly more able than Christians. Suárez, 1954, 2, pp. 156–7.

226. Suárez, 1621, p. 630. If such men were ever to be found, 'tunc enim non titulo religionis sed titulo, ut ita dicam, defensionis humanae naturae'.

227. 'Sed nunquam fuit inventa talis natio.' Peña, 'Compendium', f. 156ᵛ.

228. Báñez, 1595, p. 79; Ledesma, 1560, f. 255ʳ; Suárez, 1621, p. 630.

229. 'We may conclude that Aristotle's view of slavery is neither psychologically foolish nor morally repulsive. Of course, there are no natural slaves in the world, so the view remains theoretical.' Fortenbaugh, 1977, p. 131.

230. Vitoria, 1967, p. 30.

231. Voltaire, 1963, 1, pp. 22–3.

232. Noue, 1967, pp. 606–7.

233. Solórzano Pereyra, 1648, p. 235, also classed Indians, because of their supposed reluctance to work, together with vagabonds and beggars.

234. See e.g. the *licenciado* Herrera to Dionysio Vázquez, 20 September 1568: 'no ay indias donde vuestros ministros van por tantos peligros de agua y otros miserias que tengan mas necesidad de entender la palabra de Dios que estas asturias'. ARSI, MS Hisp. 109, f. 53ᵛ. See also *ibid.*, f. 55ʳ; Hisp. 100, f. 238ᵛ; Hisp. 102, f. 330ʳ⁻ᵛ; Hisp. 119, f. 218ᵛ; Lus. 70, f. 36ᵛ. On the Italian material see Prosperi, forthcoming, and Venturi, 1952, 1, p. 324. The Italian *mezzogiorno* was frequently referred to as 'Indie de quaggiù'. Ginzburg, 1972, p. 657.

235. Leonard Kessel, to Francisco Borja, speaks of preaching in the Netherlands 'in qua indios qui a calvinistis fuerunt seducti videntur redire ad Ecclesiam Catholicam'. ARSI, MS Gem. 140 ff. 44ᵛ–45ʳ.

236. In 1517, for instance, the Jeronymite governors of Hispaniola had carried out the first of many inquiries into the 'capacity' of the Indians. The main question which they put to the colonists on the subject was: would the Indians be capable, if given their freedom, of working their land 'in accordance with the manner followed by a peasant in Castile?' *Ynformación que los reverendos padres de Sant Xerónimo tomaron de los dichos testigos*, printed in *CDI*, 34, pp. 199–229 at 207. The inquiry was repeated with much the same questionnaire in Cuba in 1533. 'Testimonio de lo que se hizo en la villa de Bayamo en favor y por la libertad de los yndios', AGI, Patronato 231, no. 3, *ramo único*.

237. Veracruz, 1968, 2, p. 372.

238. Soto, 1965, p. 26. The authority cited by Soto, however, is *De part. an.* 961 b 4, where the body/soul distinction is made in biological not psychological terms.

239. Printed in Hera, 1956.

240. Soto, 1568, f. 12ʳ.

241. Durán, 1967, 1, p. 4.

242. Everything in Indian life was uncontrolled and contradictory. The Indian was a creature of extremes, with no understanding of the mean which was, for the Aristotelians, always the most perfect. 'El natural de los Indios', wrote one seventeenth-century observer, 'por la mayor parte es todo estremos: porque o son demasiadamente timidos, o totalmente fieras.' Acosta, 'El doctor Miguel de Acosta Granada [sic], presbytero, canonigo de la catedral del nuevo reino de Granada'.

243. 'Possunt enim barbari tanta morum vitiositate perverti atque errorem perversitatibus offuscari, ut pro peccatis non ducant, quae lex naturae vetat.' Soto, 1568, f. 13ʳ.

244. 'Sunt enim (ut a fide dignis accepimus) reperti inter illos mortales Novi orbis qui nefandam turpitudinem contra naturam non solum impune permittebant verum nulla culpa denotabant.' *Ibid.*

245. It was said that Lycurgus reared two dogs from the same litter, one for hunting, the other as a pet, and that when they reached adulthood they had acquired entirely different natures. It was a much discussed case; see, for instance, the observations by La Primaudaye, 1580, f. 243$^{r-v}$.

246. Vitoria, 1960, p. 104. He is discussing the Greek Church's prohibition against the consumption of the blood or flesh of drowned animals. The fact that such a precept, for which he could find no explanation in natural law, *is* a custom gives it its authority. See also Aquinas, Ia IIae q. 103 art. 2, and the observations of Las Casas, 1975, f. 149$^v$.

247. Bodin, 1650, p. 147, and Las Casas, 1942, p. 92, citing *De mem.* 451 b 10ff.

248. Soto, 1568, f. 12$^r$.

249. 'Omnium quae a lege naturae fluunt, naturalis ratio reddi potest: non autem omnium quae a mairoribus constituta sunt.' *Ibid.*, f. 14$^r$.

250. Aquinas, Ia IIae q. 19 art. 5 ad. 6. Cf. *In secundum sententiarum*, dist. 39, q. 3 ad. 3.

251. Anon., 'Voyages des isles de l'Amérique', f. 13$^v$. Cf. the observations of one observer that 'son estos naturales casi indiferentes en materias de religion', but they are firmly attached to 'las illusiones y fabulas de su gentilismo solo porque viene de sus maiores'. Anon., 'Estado actual del catholismo [sic]', f. 8$^v$.

252. Torquemada, 1723, 2, pp. 131–2.

253. Las Casas, 1942, p. 72.

254. Palacios Rubios, 'De insulanis', f. 14$^r$, and Zavala, 1954, p. 34.

255. Soto, 1568, f. 12$^v$.

256. See, for instance, the wholly typical reaction of Francesco Guicciardini to the information he received from America. The Indians, he said, because they had 'non scienza, non esperienza alcuna delle cose' were 'non altrimenti che animali mansueti'. Guicciardini, 1929, 2, p. 131. For this and other Italian responses to the discoveries see Romeo, 1954.

257. *NE*, 1139 b 14–35; 1140 b 31ff.; Aquinas, 1969, p. 341, lines 101–16 (lib. 6, lect. 3).

258. Aquinas, Ia IIae q. 54 art. 4 ad. 3. See Maurer, 1974.

259. Arriaga, 1968, p. 218.

260. Acosta, 1590a, p. 59.

261. Las Casas, 1942, p. 52.

262. Bertonio, 1612, f. A3$^v$.

263. Augustín de Vetancurt warned missionaries that an unguarded question 'en esta gente sera abrir los ojos a la malicia'. Vetancurt, 1673, f. 02$^r$. On the debate over the advisability of educating Indians see Labayes, 1958, and on the analogous question of the Spaniards' unwillingness to create a native clergy in America, Boxer, 1978, pp. 14–22.

264. Silva, 1621, f. 43$^r$. There is an earlier version of this work as a printed broadsheet dated 1613 in BNM, MS 13239.

265. *Ibid.*, f. 23$^r$.

266. Minaya to Julián Garcés, 1536, printed in Cruz y Moya, 1955, p. 46.

267. Children do not 'have' the natural law any more than they 'have' the habit of acquiring virtue. These things come later with the growth of the logical soul. Vitoria, 1952, p. 25.

268. Vitoria, 1967, p. 28, citing Galatians 4.1.

269. Báñez, 1595, p. 79. 'Et eadem ratione dominium naturale quod respondet isti servituti non est proprie dicendum dominium nisi en generali quadem significatione et ampla acceptione.' Soto, 1568, ff. 102ᵛ–103ʳ. Similarly, Vázquez de Menchaca, 1668, p. 52, and Covarrubias: 'At servitus, quam diximus natura ipsa constituti, non pertinet ad coactionem nec necessitatem, nec dominium sed ad honorem et reverentiam, senioribus a junioribus; generosis ab ignobilis, parentibus a filiis, marito ab uxore debitam.' Covarrubias, 1679, 1, p. 685.

270. Plamenatz, 1963, 2, p. 213.

271. Vitoria, 1960, pp. 161–4. The *regia potestas* derives from the natural law. The republic transfers its authority to its rulers but does not confer power upon them. 'Quamvis enim a respublica constituatur (creat namque respublica regem) non potestatem, sed propriam auctoritatem in regem transfert.' *Ibid.*, p. 164. For a more detailed study of this point see Mesnard, 1951, pp. 620–39.

272. Suárez, 1613, p. 225.

273. Vitoria, 1967, p. 198.

274. Cano, 'De dominio indorum', f. 31ᵛ.

275. See e.g. *Códice franciscano*, 1941, p. 59: 'porque ellos son como niños, y para bien regirse hanse de haber con ellos como con los niños los maestros de las escuelas'. And *Códice Mendieta*, 1892, 2, p. 28: 'Considero que puestos en subjección de los españoles, totalmente acobardaon y amilanaron y perdieron el estilo de su gobierno, no tomanda tampoco el de los españoles, porque aún no es para ver [sic], y quedaron en el estado, capacidad y talento como de los muchachos como de nueve a diez anos, necesitados de ser regidos por tutores o curadores como menores de edad.'

276. The *encomendero* was Sarmiento de Gamboa. See Bataillon, 1965, pp. 291–308, who demolishes the absurd notion of Alonso Getino (1930, p. 168) that Charles V was so touched in his conscience by Vitoria's words that he contemplated abandoning the Indies.

277. Printed in Getino, 1930, pp. 150–1.

278. The *relectio* itself does not survive, but as *relectiones* were usually closely related to a lecture course, the Vatican manuscript (Carranza, 'Annotationes in 2a 2ae') probably represents an earlier or summarised version of it.

279. 'Cum iam non indigeant tutore Rex Hispaniarum debet relinquere indos in sua prima et propria libertate.' *Ibid.*, f. 53ʳ. In considering this title Carranza was rather more circumspect: 'De his [the arguments that Indians should be tutored and then freed] sunt argumenta pro utraque parte, sed ego nullo ponere tamen in summa resolutionem dixi.' *Ibid.*, f. 54ʳ.

280. Cano, 'De dominio indorum', f. 30ʳ.

281. See p. 110 above.

282. See p. 36 above.

283. Las Casas, 1975, f. 241ʳ⁻ᵛ. Las Casas's residence at San Gregorio is discussed in González Monteagudo, 1975.

284. Las Casas's friendship with Carranza is discussed by Tellechea Idígoras, 1959; for his relationship with Cano see Pereña, 1956, pp. 258–62.

5  *The rhetorician and the theologians:*
    *Juan Ginés de Sepúlveda and his dialogue*, Democrates secundus

  1. It was first published by M. Menéndez y Pelayo in 1892 with the title *Democrates, alter sive de justis causis belli apud indos* in *Boletín de la Real*

*Academia*, 21, pp. 257–369. I have used the edition by Angel Losada (Sepúlveda, 1951). The most detailed account of Sepúlveda's life is provided by Losada (1959) and by the *De vita et scriptis Jo. Genesii Sepulvedae cordubensis comentarius* in Sepúlveda, 1780, 1, pp. i–cxii.

2. He referred to him as 'Petrus Pomponatius praeceptor meus, familiaris tuus' in the dedicatory epistle to Alberto Pio of his translation of the *Parva naturalia*, Sepúlveda, 1552, f. AA5$^v$.

3. His works are listed by Losada, 1959, pp. 329–402.

4. He seems indeed to have shared the view of many conservative churchmen that the study of classical learning had prepared the way for Luther. See *De fato et libero arbitrio contra Luterum* in Sepúlveda, 1780, 4, p. 470.

5. Bataillon, 1966, p. 409.

6. An account of the events is given in a letter from the Comendador Mayor of the order of Santiago, Juan de Zúñiga, to the king, it is printed in Marcos, 1947, pp. 51–3. The decision of Alcalá is recorded by Alvaro Gómez de Castro, 1569, fl. 226$^v$–7$^r$.

7. 'quod late probant et optime Genesius a Sepúlveda in libri 1 de *Justitia belli adversus Indos*'. Covarrubias, 1547–8, f. 41$^v$.

8. Sepúlveda, 1780, 4, p. 330.

9. Sepúlveda, 'Cartas'. I am grateful to Dr David Lagomarsino for having provided me with a xerox copy and his transcription of this valuable document. The text reads: 'i asi mi libro fue aprouado por todos quantos doctos lo leyeron sin passion antes que el obispo de chapa [sic] tomasse la mano de vrdir la tela que vrdio en salamanca y alcala con mañas suyas y fauores de otros aquien pesaua que io oviesse diclarado la verdad contra lo que ellos avian aconsijado o escripto'.

10. 'Yo he entendido que su Majestad manda que se haga junta de letrados que determinen la manera que se ha de tener para hazer la conquista de indias y que los theologos sean frai bartholome de miranda [Carranza] y frai domingo de soto y frai melchior cano, y estoi espantado de quien tal consejo dio a su Majestad porque no se podian nombrar en españa otros mas contrarios al proposito de su Majestad para su onrra y consientia y hazer lo que conuiene a la conuirsion de aquellas gentes.' *Ibid*. For a more detailed account of the struggle between Sepúlveda and the universities see Pagden, 1981.

11. *Jo Genesius Sepulveda doctor theologus Melchiori Cano doctori theo.*, in Sepúlveda, 1780, 3, pp. 1–20. The correspondence between Sepúlveda and Cano is paginated separately.

12. *Ibid.*, pp. 34–5.

13. *Ibid.*, p. 59.

14. In a letter to Francisco Argote of 1552, in Sepúlveda, 1780, 3, pp. 287–8.

15. Fernández-Santamaria, 1977, p. 211.

16. Losada, 1959, pp. 38–9.

17. Austin, 1962, p. 116, and see Skinner, 1970, 1972.

18. *Apologia Ioannis Genesii Sepulvedae pro libro de iustis belli causis.* I have used the edition printed in Sepúlveda, 1780, 4, pp. 329–51.

19. *Ibid.*, p. 330. In a letter of 1546 to Antonio Augustín, who was a great admirer of *Democrates secundus* and wrote a preface to the *Apologia*, he spoke of the work as a 'summam in more scholasticum'. Sepúlveda, 1780, 3, p. 249.

20. *Ibid.*

21. *Ibid.*, pp. 332–4.

22. *Ibid.*

23. Winch, 1967.
24. Cano, 1569, pp. 531–2. Sepúlveda also defended his use of Aristotle in *Democrates primus*; see Mechoulan, 1974, pp. 91–7.
25. Sepúlveda, 1780, 3, pp. 246–7.
26. Sepúlveda, 'Carta': 'ellos trabajan de diminuir la auctoridad de mi libro diziendo que yo he estudiado mas en lenguas que en theologia'.
27. Cano, 1569, p. 555.
28. See Sepúlveda, 1951, p. 2, where the link is made explicit.
29. See Prosperi, 1977–8, pp. 510–15.
30. Sepúlveda, 'Cartas': 'Porque sepa vuestra señoria que lo que los que antes de mi escriuieron en esta materia delas indias fueron estos tres [Carranza, Soto and Cano] y frai francisco de vitoria y el magistral gaetano todos frailes de santo domingo y todos escriuieron diziendo o dando a entender que esta conquista es injusta.'
31. *De civitate Dei*, bk 9, ch. 18, and see Clark, 1980.
32. Sepúlveda, 1951, p. 20.
33. *Ibid.*, p. 122. Democrates is here describing the correct treatment for the *servus*.
34. *Ibid.*, p. 20.
35. *Ibid.*, p. 21.
36. *Ibid.*, p. 120. Democrates discourses at length on the similarity in structure between the household and the state, the implication being that the Indian is to the larger Spanish community in the Indies what the domestic servant is to the individual household.
37. Fortenbaugh, 1975, pp. 23–44.
38. Sepúlveda, 1951, pp. 20–1.
39. Cf. *ibid.*, p. 123.
40. The word *humanus* is also used merely to mean 'polite' or 'civilised' and as a synonym for 'urbanus' (i.e. the virtues associated with the life lived in cities; see e.g. Cicero *De senectute*, 17.59). But it is evident from the context that Sepúlveda wishes to suggest that the Indians are also something less than real men.
41. Sepúlveda, 1951, p. 120.
42. Fortenbaugh, 1975, p. 55.
43. Sepúlveda, 1951, p. 36.
44. *Ibid.*, p. 22.
45. *Ibid.*, p. 33. The final phrase, 'denique quam Simiae propre dixerim ad hominibus', has been erased from the manuscript in the Biblioteca del Palacio (Madrid) used by Angel Losada for his edition. The erasure, however, was certainly not done by the scribe and I doubt that it represents a modification to the text. Had Sepúlveda wished to moderate his language, as Losada seems to think, it is unlikely that he would have left the passages quoted below unaltered.
46. *Ibid.*, p. 35.
47. *Ibid.*
48. *Ibid.*, p. 36.
49. *Ibid.*
50. *Ibid.*, p. 38.
51. *Ibid.*, pp. 38–9.
52. *Ibid.*, p. 35. Sepúlveda's taste for shocking and defamatory imagery is evident elsewhere. In his life of Cardinal Gil de Albornoz, for instance, he accused the fourteenth-century Franciscan Fraticelli of crimes – nocturnal

orgies, the slaughter and consumption of children, etc. – imputed to the mid-fifteenth-century group of the same name. See Cohn, 1976, p. 53.

53. Quoted by Bataillon, 1966, p. 663.

6 *A programme for comparative ethnology (1) Bartolomé de Las Casas*

1. Las Casas, 1975, f. 11ʳ.
2. *Ibid.*, f. 2ᵛ. Las Casas speaks of having seen a vernacular version of a work entitled 'De justis belli causis'. This is Sepúlveda's *Apologia*, three vernacular versions of which were distributed among members of the court (Las Casas, 1552c, f. Aiiᵛ.). Elsewhere he speaks of 'alia quedam prolixius in codice latino quem mihi nondum videre contingit inculcare'. Las Casas, 1975, f. 7ᵛ.
3. The circumstances of the debate have been described in detail by Losada, 1959, pp. 209–11. Sepúlveda was, of course, outraged by the choice of judges (see p. 110 above) and suggested in his letter to Granvelle that they be substituted by Luis de Carvajal, Luis de Villalonga, Alfonso de Castro and Alvaro Moscoso whom he described as 'doctos clerigos y frailes que sin pasion hablan en esta materia' and all of whom had, of course, applauded his work. 'Carta'.
4. Las Casas, 1552c, f. AAiiʳ.
5. Las Casas, 1552c. It was pirated in the year of its publication and reprinted in Paris in 1646 as part of the French propaganda campaign against Spain.
6. See Edmundo O'Gorman, 'El señor Lewis Hanke y la apologética' in Las Casas, 1967, 1, pp clxvii–clxix, and Hanke, 1974, pp. 74–9, 173–6.
7. E.g. Las Casas, 1975, ff. 23ʳ, 24ʳ⁻ᵛ, 177ʳ, 243ᵛ and 253ʳ; and see the comments by Losada in Hanke, 1974, p. 108.
8. This is addressed to the Royal Council and is, in effect, a request for a licence to print. For some reason the original has been omitted from Losada's facsimile.
9. Las Casas, 1975, f. 24ʳ.
10. Las Casas, 1967, 2, pp. 637–54. There are other parallels, e.g. the refutation of the theory that the Indians are natural slaves on the grounds discussed on pp. 133–4 below and repeated in the *Apologética historia*, Las Casas, 1967, 1, pp. 259–60.
11. Cf. Las Casas, 1975, f. 182ʳ⁻ᵛ and 212ᵛ, on the fact that the Indians constitute, for the Church, a new problem which cannot be accommodated within the older structure of legislation concerning pagans.
12. Covarrubias, 1943, p. 194.
13. Cortés, 1972, p. 108.
14. Zorita, 1963, pp. 100–3.
15. Cano, 'De dominio indorum', f. 31ʳ. This type of argument was widely used in the seventeenth century. See the comments by Vivanti, 1962, p. 238.
16. Peña, 'Compendium', f. 156ᵛ. Cf. Las Casas, 1552c, f. cᵛ.
17. Covarrubias, 'De iustitia belli', f. 40ʳ.
18. Las Casas, 1975, f. 13ᵛ. Cf. f. 22ʳ where Las Casas claims that the first three of his categories of barbarians are taken from four of Aquinas's works, the commentary on Aristotle's *Politics* and the commentaries on Romans 1, Corinthians and Colossians. The substance of his thesis and the identification of the different types of barbarism, however, derive entirely from the commentary on the *Politics*.

19. Las Casas, 1975, f. 13$^v$, and 1967, 2, p. 638, where such peoples are described as being 'ciegos de pasión'.
20. *Ibid.*, f. 14$^r$.
21. *Ibid.*, f. 13$^v$.
22. *Ibid.*, f. 14$^{r-v}$. Las Casas claims, citing *NE*, 1145 a 25ff., that this is the category to which Aristotle is referring when he says that 'bestiality is the greatest among the barbarians (*maxime aut in barbaris est bestialiter*)'. What Aristotle in fact says is that such men are *commoner* among barbarians, in the Grosseteste translation which Las Casas seems to have been using; 'sic et bestialis in hominibus rarus. Maxime autem in Barbaris est.' Gauthier, 1972, p. 271. Nearly all Las Casas's citations from Aristotle and Aquinas are similarly modified to suit his purpose.
23. Wokler, 1978, pp. 107–14.
24. See e.g. *De int.* 16 a 19–20; 'a name is a spoken sound made significant by convention without time, none of whose parts is significant in separation'. Ackrill, 1963, p. 117. Aristotle is refuting the view of Plato (*Cratylus* 397 A–425 E) that the names for things exist in nature and reflect the essence of those things. In general see Larkin, 1971, pp. 22–3.
25. Helmont, 1667, *passim*, supposed that the Hebrew alphabet was a visual transcription of the natural, God-given speech of man. The belief in the primacy of Hebrew over all the other languages was a common one in the sixteenth and seventeenth centuries.
26. Vives 1785, 6: *De tradendis disciplinis*, p. 299.
27. *Ibid.*
28. Quoted in Berlin, 1976, p. 136.
29. Aquinas, 1971, p. A74.
30. Aquinas, 1953, 1, pp. 14, 18, 154, 394.
31. 'Et secundum hoc illi qui suum inuicem sermonem non intelligunt barbari ad se ipsos dici possunt.' Aquinas, 1971, p. A75.
32. Pocock, 1973, p. 33.
33. Las Casas, 1967, 2, p. 653.
34. *Ibid.*, p. 637.
35. This is also, of course, a sign of their barbarism. Sepúlveda, 1780, 4, p. 360.
36. 'It [Latin] was clearly understood to belong to a world different from that populated by ordinary mankind'. Ullmann, 1977, p. 70.
37. Las Casas, 1975, f. 14$^v$.
38. Aquinas, 1971, p. A75.
39. Mersenne, 1634, pp. 135–8.
40. Le Roy, 1576, f. c$^r$.
41. Sepúlveda, 1951, p. 35. In his *De regno et regis officio* Sepúlveda again decried the Indian as 'gente...incultas et barbaras quae litterarum nullam prorsus notitiam, numorum usum habebant'. Sepúlveda, 1780, 4, p. 100. The addition of 'money' is in keeping with the common view that barbarous people are without any means of exchange.
42. Aquinas, 1971, p. A75. Cf. Gregory the Great, *Moralia*, bk 27, ch. 2 (*PL*, 76, p. 411): 'ecce lingua Britanniae, quae nil aliud noverat, quam barbarum frendere, jam dudum in divinis laudibus Hebraeum coepit Alleluia resonare', which is repeated in Bede, 1969, p. 130, and must surely be the passage to which Aquinas is referring. The same reference is employed by Alonso de Madrigal ('El Tostado'), who defines barbarians as 'los que no tienen artes o sciencias tornados en su lengua...en otra manera dezimos barbaros alos

que no tienen complimentos de leyes razonables para todos los negocios y cosas de la vida'. Tostado, 1507, f. xxxviii$^r$.

43. Las Casas, 1975, f. 22$^{r-v}$. Cf. f. 15$^v$.

44. *Pol.* 1284 b 35ff. The Moerbeke translation, which Las Casas appears to be using, runs: 'Quia enim magis serviles moribus sunt natura barbari quidem graecis.' (Printed in Aquinas, 1951, p. 168.) This is, again, a deliberate distortion of Aristotle's text since those who are 'barbarians by nature' must, in this context, also be 'slaves by nature'. Las Casas, however, repeated his reading before Sepúlveda and accused his opponent of failing to understand Aquinas and 'disimulando' with Aristotle (Las Casas, 1552c f. [E8$^v$].)

45. 'Habent autem haec omnia potentiam similem tyrannis, sunt tamen secundum legem et paterna', in Aquinas, 1951, p. 168, and cited by Las Casas, 1975, f. 22$^v$.

46. Las Casas, 1967, 2, pp. 636, 563, 305.

47. Las Casas, 1975, f. 16$^r$.

48. *Ibid.*

49. *Ibid.*, ff. 16$^v$–17$^r$.

50. *Ibid.*, f. 16$^r$.

51. 'Itaque natura plerumque quod optimum et perfectum est gignit productique.' *Ibid.*, f. 17$^r$.

52. *Ibid.*, f. 17$^v$.

53. *Ibid.* The reference is to *De civitate Dei*, bk 16, ch. 8. (*PL*, 41, pp. 485–6).

54. Las Casas, 1975, f. 17$^v$. Las Casas cites Aquinas, 1925, para. 811, as his authority.

55. *De civitate Dei*, bk 16, ch. 8 (*PL*, 41, p. 486).

56. *Prima pars*, q. 23 art. 7 ad. 3. Cited incorrectly by Las Casas, 1975, ff. 18$^{r-v}$.

57. *Ibid.*, f. 19$^r$. The whole argument is repeated in Las Casas, 1967, 1, pp. 259–60, and, according to Las Casas, 1975, f. 20$^r$, in the now lost first book of his treatise *De unico vocationis modo gentium ad veram religionem*.

58. Las Casas, 1975, f. 28$^r$.

59. Las Casas, 1967, 2, p. 92.

60. This, at least, is the main thrust of the argument in Las Casas, 1975, ff. 28$^r$–29$^v$, although Las Casas denies that it can ever be a just cause for conquest. *Ibid.*, ff. 32$^v$–43$^v$.

61. Las Casas, 1967, 1, p. 239. Aquinas, 1925, para. 127.

62. Las Casas, 1967, 1, p. 239.

63. Soto, 1568, f. 6$^r$.

64. Sepúlveda, 1951, pp. 36–7.

65. Las Casas, 1967, 2, p. 531, where, for example, the buildings of the Inca are cited as evidence of their creators' 'prudencia y buena policía'.

66. *Ibid.*, p. 240.

67. *Ibid.*, p. 242, citing *Pol.* 1328 b 15ff.

68. *Ibid.*, p. 248; and for the possible reasons for men failing to create cities see *ibid.*, pp. 245–7.

69. Las Casas, 1975, f. 22$^v$.

70. Las Casas, 1967, 2, pp. 34–5, citing *Pol.* 1331 a 30ff.; and see the observations of Huxley, 1980.

71. Sepúlveda, 1951, p. 36–7.

72. 'Habitus est intellectus operativus', that is, is a function of the rational soul. Las Casas, 1975, f. 24$^r$.

73. *Ibid.*, ff. 24$^v$–25$^r$.

74. *Ibid.*, f. 240ʳ.
75. Aquinas, 1971, p. A75.
76. A brief account of this theory is provided by Walbank, 1957, 1, pp. 465–6, and Heiberg, 1920. For the early-modern period see Tooley, 1953.
77. Quine, 1966, p. 242.
78. Las Casas, 1967, 1, p. 118. See Aquinas, Ia IIae q. 9 art. 5; and on the power of the human will to overcome the influence of the environment, *Prima pars*, q. 115 art. 6. Cf. Las Casas, 1967, 1, p. 116, and Aquinas, 1951, para. 1118.
79. Cognitive acts are sensational in origin. See Richard Sorabji, 'Body and soul in Aristotle', in Barnes, Schofield and Sorabji, 1977, 4, pp. 42–64. Las Casas's own references (1967, 1, p. 177) are to *De anima*, 427 a 16–27 b 26, and Aquinas, 1925, para. 617.
80. Las Casas, 1967, 1, p. 116. This is a somewhat loose translation of the convoluted original.
81. Bodin, 1608, p. 680.
82. Las Casas, 1967, 1, p. 122.
83. *Ibid.*, 1, p. 123.
84. Leibnitz, 1718, pp. 37–8. Leibnitz employed the theory of climates to explain the 'différence merveilleuse' between the various tribes in America. The anonymous traveller to whom he refers is probably the 'fameux voyageur' who contributed a classification of peoples to the *Journal des sçavans*, 12 (1684), pp. 148–55.
85. Las Casas, 1967, 1, pp. 15–103. Hispaniola is offered as something of a model for the whole of America; see *ibid.*, 1, p. 115.
86. *Ibid.*, 1, p. 117.
87. *Ibid.*, 1, p. 207.
88. *Ibid.*, 1, p. 249, citing *De inventione*, 1,2–3.
89. 'Ut iam universus hic mundus sit una civitas communis deorum atque hominum existimanda'. *De legibus*, 1.23.
90. Las Casas, 1967, 1, pp. 257–8, citing *De legibus*, 1, 22–4.
91. Las Casas, 1967, 1, p. 250.
92. *Ibid.*, 2, pp. 256, 224, 221.
93. Pocock, 1977, p. 243.
94. Las Casas, 1967, 1, pp. 250–1.
95. *Ibid.*, p. 249.
96. *Ibid.*, p. 253, and cf. p. 256 where Las Casas cites the list of inventions in *Pol.* 1329 b 5ff.
97. Las Casas, 1967, 1, pp. 253–5.
98. See e.g. the observations of Bernardino de Sahagún on Quetzalcoatl: 'Está el negocio de este rey entre estos naturales como el del rey Arthus entre los ingleses.' Sahagún, 1956, 2, p. 281.
99. For Acosta see pp. 178–9 below; for Garcilaso, Miró Quesada, 1971, pp. 214–22.
100. Las Casas, 1967, 1, p. 258; cf. *ibid.*, p. 130.
101. *Ibid.*, p. 256.
102. *Ibid.*, p. 248.
103. Sepúlveda, 1951, p. 37.
104. Las Casas, 1975, f. 152ʳ; cf. 1552c, f. Gᵛ. Las Casas is referring to *Topics*, 100 a 30–b 20 and *Rhet.* 1356 b 12ff. An opinion is 'probable' when it is held by the majority of the learned men in the community. Clearly, however, Aristotle does not discuss the possibility of a probable *error*.

105. Las Casas, 1552c f. G$^v$.
106. *Ibid.*, ff. [Fviii$^v$]–G$^r$.
107. Las Casas, 1967, 2, pp. 252–3. Comparison between Indian sacrifices and those of the ancient British and the Scots were also made by English settlers in North America, Kupperman, 1980, pp. 68–9.

7 *A programme for comparative ethnology (2) José de Acosta*

1. See Edmundo O'Gorman, 'La *Apologética historia*, su génesis y elaboración, su estructura y su sentido', in Las Casas, 1967, p. xxv.
2. The royal censors did their best, however, after the Valladolid debate to prevent any further discussion on the Indian question. A decree (*cédula*) of 1556 forbade any book on the Indies to be printed without a royal licence; and in 1560 the crown ordered a round-up of all books 'que traten de cosas de Indias'. Encinas, 1596, 1, pp. 227–8.
3. See Lopeteguí, 1942, pp. 185–8.
4. This brief biographical account is taken largely from Lopeteguí, 1942, which is the closest thing to a biography of Acosta yet written.
5. Alcázar, 1710, 2, p. 201.
6. See e.g. the letter of Juan de Atienza to Aquaviva, 1583: 'El padre Joseph de Acosta tiene mas salud que los años atras; aunque el estar sujeto a melancolías le es natural.' *MP*, 3, p. 255.
7. The records of Cruz's trial are in the Archivo Histórico Nacional (Madrid), legajo 1650. A small part of this documentation (which runs to over 2000 folios) is printed in Medina, 1956, 1, pp. 63–124.
8. Bataillon, 1965, pp. 309–24.
9. Acosta, 1588. This work consists of confessions in Quechua and Aymara with glosses in Spanish. Acosta was probably the author of the introduction and the glosses.
10. A bibliography is provided by O'Gorman in Acosta, 1962, pp. lxi–lxiv.
11. Acosta, 1962, p. 13.
12. *Ibid.*, p. 278.
13. *Ibid.*, p. 14; and cf. p. 319.
14. I owe this quotation and the substance of all my observations on imaginary worlds and on counterfactual reasoning in general to an unpublished paper by Geoffrey Hawthorn given to Clifford Geertz's Social Science seminar at the Institute for Advanced Study in 1979.
15. Acosta, 1962, p. 319.
16. *Ibid.*, p. 288.
17. *Ibid.*, p. 13.
18. Acosta, 1598, f. Aiii$^v$.
19. Acosta, 1962, p. 87.
20. *Ibid.*, p. 13.
21. *Ibid.*, p. 87.
22. Humboldt, 1836–9, 2, pp. 315, 341.
23. 'Para Oviedo el mundo no era la obra de un Logos: la naturaleza es un perpetuo milagro, en ella no hay ley o, si existe, no nos es asequible.' Alvarez López, 1943, p. 307.
24. Acosta, 1962, p. 13.
25. *Ibid.*, p. 9.
26. *Ibid.*, p. 13.
27. *Ibid.*, p. 33.

28. Jarcho, 1959.
29. Acosta, 1962, p. 77.
30. For a different view based, it would seem, on a very rapid reading of the *Historia*, see Maravall, 1966, p. 446.
31. Acosta, 1962, p. 67.
32. *Ibid.*, p. 30. St Augustine, *De civitate Dei*, bk 16, ch. 9 (*PL*, 41, pp. 487-8).
33. Acosta, 1962, pp. 77-8.
34. Acosta, 1596, p. 517.
35. Quiroga, 1922, p. 52.
36. Acosta, 1590b, p. 154.
37. Acosta, 1962, p. 27, quoting *Divinae institutiones*, 3.24 (*PL*, 6, pp. 426-7). Acosta's own reference, however, is wrong.
38. Acosta, 1962, p. 28.
39. *Ibid.*, p. 13.
40. *Ibid.*, p. 29.
41. *Ibid.*, p. 28. Acosta's cosmography was strictly Ptolemaic. It is unlikely that he would have had much opportunity in a Jesuit college to consult Copernicus's *De revolutionibus orbium caelestium*, although it had first appeared in 1543.
42. Acosta, 1962, pp. 60-1, and cf. pp. 44-5. See also Maluenda, 1604, pp. 151-4, who echoes much of Acosta's argument. The subject is also discussed in Kottman, 1975.
43. Acosta, 1962, p. 319.
44. See Leite, 1953.
45. Nóbrega, 1954, p. 53.
46. Gibson, 1964, pp. 100-1.
47. Gilberti, 1558, p. 11.
48. Arriaga, 1968, p. 219.
49. Bellarmino, 1688, p. 12.
50. Acosta, 1962, p. 319.
51. See, in addition to the comments below, his remarks in *De procuranda* (Acosta, 1596, p. 338) that although the Spartans were cured of drunkenness by the mere sight of a drunken man, the Indians required firmer treatment, because 'mores sunt et ingenium natura ipsa servile'; that if they are sometimes reluctant to accept *beneficium*, 'causa est naturae ipsorum imbellicitas et timiditas' (*ibid.*, p. 416); and that they are alien to any kind of *consortium*. Although all these remarks are general and do not apply to all Indians equally, it is absurd to claim, as J. A. Maravall has done, that in Acosta, 'la tendencia a la idealización del salvaje es muy marcado como en la major parte de nuestros escritores del siglo xvi'. Maravall, 1966, p. 450.
52. Acosta, 1596, p. 146.
53. *Ibid.*, p. 231.
54. *Ibid.*, p. 119.
55. *Ibid.*, p. 119. St John Chrysostom, *In epistolam primam ad Timotheum commentarius*, 2.4 (*PG*, 62, p. 685).
56. Acosta, 1596, pp. 100-1.
57. St John Chrysostom, *In epistolam primam*, 2.4 (*PG*, 62, p. 685), and later cited by Acosta, 1596, p. 151.
58. Acosta, 1596, pp. 137-8.
59. *Ibid.*, p. 139.
60. *Ibid.*, pp. 232-42. Despite the strong similarities in argument between this

passage in *De procuranda* and the *De indis*, Acosta does not here refer directly to Vitoria.

61. *Ibid.*, p. 209. There is also here an echo of Vitoria's analogy between the Indian nations and a land abandoned by the entire male population. See pp. 105–6 above.
62. *Ibid.*, pp. 199, 204.
63. *Ibid.*, pp. 203–4, 149–50.
64. *Ibid.*, pp. 150, 324, citing *NE*, 1145 b 10ff. and 1157 a 11ff.
65. *Littera annua* of 1577 to Everado Mercuriano in Rome, *MP*, 2, p. 228.
66. Acosta, 1596, p. 150.
67. Acosta, 1962, p. 266.
68. Acosta, 1588, ff. A2$^v$–3$^r$.
69. Acosta, 1596, p. 246.
70. *Ibid.*, p. 150; cf. Solórzano Pereyra, 1629–39, 1, p. 114.
71. Pontano, 1518, *De servitute*, f. 24$^v$.
72. Acosta, 1596, pp. 150–1.
73. See Prosperi, forthcoming.
74. Acosta, 1596, p. 209.
75. 'Barbarus non natura sed studio et moribus talis est; puer et amens non studio sed natura.' *Ibid.*
76. Extract from the rules drawn up for the 'Colegio de caciques' in Lima c. 1576. ARSI, MS Congr. 42, f. 266$^r$. I would like to thank Dr N. Griffin for providing me with a transcript of this document. Cf. the comments of Pedro de Quiroga (1922, p. 53): 'ya salio esta tierra de la niñeç y la puericia y dio salto en la vejeç'.
77. Acosta, 1596, p. 103.
78. *Ibid.*, pp. 99, 102.
79. *Ibid.*, p. 104.
80. *Ibid.*, p. 105.
81. Acosta, 1962, p. 286. There were Chinese books in the library of the Escorial by the mid-1580s and the use of ideograms had already been described in 1569 in Gaspar da Cruz's *Tractado em que se cotam muito por estēso as cousas da China*. Knowledge of Chinese culture was also circulated widely among Jesuits during this period. Acosta clearly possessed an extensive knowledge of, and a keen interest in, the Asiatic peoples. See Boxer, 1953, pp. 47–230, and Lach, 1965, 1, pp. 776, 803.
82. Ricci, 1911–13, 1, p. 426.
83. See Rossi, 1971, pp. 143–4. The Chinese, however, refused to accept that there was any necessary connection between European technology, whose benefits were obvious to them, and the Christian religion. See Needham, 1959, 3, p. 449.
84. Acosta, 1596, pp. 105–6.
85. *Ibid.*, p. 107. This type includes not only the Mexica and the Inca, but also the Araucana and the Tucapel of Chile. See, however, p. 166 below.
86. *Ibid.*, p. 483.
87. Acosta, 1962, p. 281.
88. 'Las leyes y costumbres y modo de gouernar que ellos tienen en sus tierras que no es contrario a la ley christiana y natural no es bien quitarsele [sic] ni conbiene hazerles españoles en todo porque demas de ser muy dificil y que sera ocasion de dexarlo todo, es gran perjuizio para su gouierno y Rep[ublica] dellos.' ARSI, MS Congr. 42, f. 266$^r$.
89. Acosta, 1596, p. 108.

90. *Ibid.*, p. 205.
91. Solórzano Pereyra, 1629–39, 1, p. 126.
92. *Ibid.*, p. 299.
93. Acosta, 1962, p. 293; cf. p. 304.
94. *Parecer sobre la guerra de China* [Mexico 1587], printed in Acosta, 1954, p. 333.
95. Acosta, 1962, p. 337.
96. Mexía de Ovando, 'Libro memorial', p. 64.
97. Acosta, 1962, p. 305.
98. I use this term as it is used in Fortes and Evans-Pritchard, 1946, to describe a society with no central political authority, which maintains political cohesion by each 'segment' (a lineage or territorial group) 'nesting' inside another in complementary opposition. This should not be confused with Durkheim's use of the term (*De la division de travail social*, Paris, 1893), in which a segmentary system is one composed of a number of segments or clans, in a society where there is no organised division of labour. We know almost nothing about the real social organisation of the peoples Acosta describes, and the term 'segmentary system' should thus be regarded as a convenience. It is clearly not intended to imply any similarity between Amerindian and African groups.
99. Landa, 1975, pp. 85–6.
100. Acosta, 1962, p. 293.
101. *Ibid.*, p. 320. Cf. the description provided by Acosta's informant in Mexico, Juan de Tovar, 1972, p. 9.
102. Acosta, 1962, p. 320.
103. See e.g. Esteban de Páez, *littera annua* of 1596 on the Chichimeca who elected rulers in time of war, *MM*, 5, p. 450, and Anon., 'Mision y entrada', f. 82$^v$: 'Porque el curaca es solo para la guerra que en ella dizen que obedecen con gran puntualidad'. The same observations are made of the peoples of Sinaloa by Gonzalo de Tapia in 1592, *MM*, 5, p. 7.
104. 'Noticia de los chichimecas', f. 1$^v$.
105. 'Crian sus hijos con harto trabajo, porque como non tienen casa y andan de unas partes en otras muchas vezes les acontecia parir camiando y aun con los [?] colgando y comiendo sangre caminan (como si fuesen una oueja o cabra)'. *Ibid.*, f. 6$^v$.
106. Acosta, 1962, p. 228, and 1596, p. 179.
107. See Prosperi, 1976.
108. Acosta, 1596, p. 469.
109. For a discussion of the differences between *religio* and *superstitio* in the ancient world see Momigliano, 1977, pp. 144–5. And see Luis de Granada, 1588, p. 138, who lists several types of religions in which those that are mere 'supersticiones' are clearly distinguished from those that are 'vanas' but none the less organised and systematised.
110. Léry, 1594, p. 259.
111. Mandeville, 1919–23, 1, p. 109.
112. Mexía, 'Relación'.
113. Tylor, 1871, 1, p. 112.
114. Gregory the Great, 1891–9, 1, p. 262.
115. Valadés, 1579, pp. 172–3.
116. Acosta, 1962, p. 225. For further examples see Rowe, 1960. Similar methods of conversion had been in use for centuries. See Sullivan, 1953, for the techniques employed by Carolingian missionaries.

117. Botero, 1605, p. 43.
118. *Ibid.*, p. 2.
119. Acosta, 1596, p. 246.
120. It should be noted, however, that 'idolatry' is a compound of *idolo* and *latria* and means simply 'the worship of an image'. On the basis of this Aquinas argued that any form of religion which focused on the physical representation of the deity was effectively a form of idolatry (IIa IIae q. 94 art. 1). Acosta, who is himself somewhat loose in his use of the term, initially divides idolatry into three general categories: the worship of real things – of trees, stones, the elements, etc.; the worship of things that are 'pure or human invention...such as Mercury and Pallas'; and the worship of things that were once real but are no longer, such as the dead (Acosta, 1962, p. 219). Elsewhere, however, he says, 'digo de la idolatría que propriamente es adorar ídolos e imágenes'. *Ibid.*, p. 226.
121. Hosius, 1559, f. 24$^r$.
122. St John Damascene, *Barlaam and Ioasaph*, 28.240–50.
123. Anon., 'De las costumbres antiguas', ff. 57–8: 'dexando aparte lo que toca a su religion falsa, sus dioses sus sacrificos y sus templos y sepulchros y oratorios y sacerdotes y hechizeros lo que es superstition desprendianlo desde niños, porque mirauan en todos sus ados y en sus meneos y casi en todos ellos halluan misterio que reparar de bueno o malo'.
124. Wisdom 14.15–21. Acosta, 1962, p. 226, and 1596, p. 471. The same text was also employed by Las Casas, 1967, 2, p. 569.
125. Bellarmino, 1590, pp. 2018–19.
126. Carrera, 1644, f. *7$^r$–8$^v$.
127. Las Casas, 1958, p. 47, quoting St Jerome's commentary on Psalm 92.
128. Vanegas, 1583, f. 283$^r$.
129. Acosta, 1962, p. 226. For Aquinas the most probable originator of idolatry was Nimrod, who is also accredited with being the creator of the first city (IIa IIae q. art. 4).
130. Acosta, 1596, p. 474.
131. Acosta, 1962, p. 242.
132. *Ibid.*, pp. 260–7.
133. Garimberto, 1959, p. 115, and see Bataillon, 1959.
134. See *Satan*, 1948, p. 170, and Clark, 1980.
135. Suárez de Peralta, 1949, p. 5. Cf. Herodotus, *History*, 2.35. The same device, that is the assumption that as there exists some measure of geographical inversion (in the case of the Egyptians it is the fact that Herodotus believed the Nile to flow *upstream*) there must also exist cultural inversion, is employed by Francesco Carletti when describing the Japanese whose customs, he says, are opposed to those of the Europeans, 'come essi sono contraposti a noi nel sitio della loro terra'. Carletti, 1958, p. 143.
136. Brunetti, 'Lettera', f. 95$^v$. The other proofs of 'son fuor di modo barbari' are the social status they attach to prisoners, and their cannibalism.
137. Oviedo, 1535, f. xlviii$^v$.
138. Ciruelo, 1628, p. 183.
139. Acosta, 1962, p. 239.
140. *Ibid.*, p. 235.
141. *Ibid.*, p. 268.
142. See Echanove, 1955–6, p. 525, quoting from a Jesuit *littera annua* of 1602 on an Aymara myth. When the Indians were told about Christ and the

Virgin, 'decian que era verdad y todo lo aplicaban a su Juñupa, y en lugar de reverenciar y adorar a Christo, adoraban a su maldito Juñupa'.

143. Acosta, 1962, pp. 255–6.
144. Acosta, 1962, pp. 266–7.
145. On Satan's image in the sixteenth century see Delumeau, 1978, pp. 232–53.
146. Acosta, 1596, p. 485. He makes, however, only this one direct reference to Vitoria's text.
147. See pp. 85–6 above.
148. Gerson, 1706, 3, p. 95. For Aquinas's view of 'unnatural' sexual practices see Bailey, 1955, pp. 116–18.
149. Cieza de León, 1924, p. 163; Oviedo, 1535, f. xlvii$^{r-v}$. On the accusations made against other 'primitives' see Karsch-Haack, 1911, whose list is formidable, from the Melanesians to the peoples of the Congo, from the Hottentots of South Africa to the Eskimos of Alaska, from the Mongols to the Huron of northern Canada. I am grateful for Dr Paul Cartledge for drawing my attention to this remarkable book.
150. Noonan, 1966, pp. 95–6,
151. Acosta, 1596, p. 485.
152. Botero, 1605, p. 44.
153. Las Casas, 1967, 2, p. 206.
154. Porras, 'Instruccion', f. 64.
155. Acosta, 1596, p. 486.
156. Acosta, 1962, pp. 294–5.
157. Acosta, 1596, p. 486.
158. *Ibid.*, pp. 242–4.
159. See Kahl, 1961, p. 56.
160. Acosta, 1962, p. 376.
161. Torres, 1603, pp. 8–9; Wood, 1634, p. 92.
162. Bertonio, 1612, f. *A2$^r$.
163. Acosta, 1596, p. 382. One of the reasons given for their simplicity was the relative lack of inflexions in Quechua.
164. *Ibid.*, p. 379; and cf. p. 121.
165. Aldrete, 1606, p. 144.
166. Lafitau, 1724, 1, p. 55.
167. Cabello Valboa, 1951, pp. 104–5.
168. Bursill-Hall, 1972, p. 29.
169. Santo Tomás, 1560, f. A5$^r$.
170. La Condamine, 1745, p. 54.
171. Acosta, 1596, p. 383.
172. Anon. 'Estado actual del catholismo [sic]', f. 4$^r$.
173. Carrera, 1644, f. A6$^r$.
174. Gilberti, 1558, p. 3.
175. Acosta, 1962, p. 220.
176. In *MB*, 3, pp. 559–60.
177. Nóbrega, 1955, p. 62; Léry, 1594, p. 262.
178. Thevet, 1953, p. 364.
179. Aldrete, 1606, p. 146.
180. Hinojosa, 1963, p. 299.
181. This, according to Torquemada (1723, 3, p. 115), was a common fear, though he dismisses it as absurd.
182. Zurita, 1586, f. 118$^{r-v}$. Eusebius, 1979, p. 83; and on the Egyptians see Festugière, 1944, 1, p. 26.

183. López Mendel, 1612; f. 235$^v$.
184. *Recopilación*, 1681, f. 190$^r$.
185. Hinojosa, 1963, p. 200.
186. Lafitau, 1724, 2, pp. 484–6.
187. Acosta, 1596, p. 382.
188. In Vetancurt, 1673, A1$^r$.
189. Brosses, 1765, pp. 32–3.
190. Santo Tomás, 1560, f. A5$^r$. Acosta evidently relied heavily on this text to which he refers twice in *De procuranda* (1596, pp. 155, 382). For Santo Tomás's intellectual affiliations with Las Casas see Mahn-Lot, 1973, 2, pp. 353–65.
191. *Relación sobre la residencia de Michoacán*, 1585, *MM*, 2, p. 492.
192. Vives, 1785, 6: *De tradendis disciplinis*, p. 298.
193. Beattie, 1783, p. 271.
194. Locke, 1975, p. 207.
195. AGN, Jesuitas, III–15, no. 33.
196. Maffei, 1589, p. 32.
197. *Littera annua* of 31 March 1593, signed 'Petrus Diaz', in *MM*, 5, p. 91.
198. Stephen J. Greenblatt, 'Learning to curse. Aspects of linguistic colonialism in the sixteenth century' in Chiapelli, 1976, 2, pp. 561–80.
199. What he does say is in Acosta, 1596, pp. 382–3.
200. Acosta, 1962, p. 284. Cf. Le Roy, 1576, f. c$^r$, who describes the importance of letters in almost identical terms.
201. Goody and Watt, 1968, pp. 31–3.
202. Acosta, 1962, pp. 63–4.
203. Cabello Valboa, 1951, pp. 88–90.
204. Acosta, 1962, p. 285.
205. *Ibid.*, p. 284.
206. Acosta wrote to Juan de Tovar asking him how the Indian could 'conservar por tanto tiempo la memoria de tantas y tan varias cosas' without the use of writing. In his reply Tovar gave an account of the 'reading' of a Mexican book which was accompanied by elaborate rhetorical exercises. Tovar, 1972, pp. 3–5.
207. Vetancurt, 1698, part 2, p. 1.
208. Acosta, 1962, p. 284.
209. Valadés, 1579, pp. 93–6.
210. *Ibid.*, p. 95.
211. Acosta, 1962, p. 283.
212. *Ibid.*, p. 288.
213. Vega, 1943, 2, p. 76.
214. Acosta, 1962, p. 287.
215. *Ibid.*, p. 288.
216. Ch. 7 (*PL*, 83, pp. 974–5).
217. Acosta, 1962, p. 319; Ecclesiastes 1.9.
218. *Ibid.*, p. 337.
219. See Heath, 1979.
220. On the debate over the origins of the Indians see Gliozzi, 1977, pp. 371–513.
221. Acosta, 1962, p. 57. Further evidence is provided by the absence of inhabitants on the island of Bermuda since these would have been too far from the mainland for primitive navigators.
222. He was not, however, the first to suggest the idea. A landbridge appears in

the planisphere of Giacomo Gastaldi of 1550 but its existence was rejected by both Ortelius and Mercator. Penrose, 1952, p. 261.

223. Acosta, 1962, pp. 320–1 and 324.
224. Tovar, 1972, p. 10.
225. Acosta, 1962, pp. 324–30, on Huitzilopochitl, the tutelary deity of the Mexica.
226. Solórzano Pereyra, 1648, p. 21; on Tornielli see Gliozzi, 1977, pp. 160–1.
227. Acosta, 1590b, p. 154.
228. Hartog, 1980, pp. 207–18.
229. Acosta, 1962, p. 242.
230. 'Es mucha la semejanca que ay entre los de ambas Indias en talle condición ritos y costumbres.' Solórzano Pereyra, 1648, p. 21.
231. José de Azpilcueta to the lay brothers of Coimbra, March 1550, in *MB*, 1, p. 181.
232. Solórzano Pereyra, 1629–39, 1, p. 144.
233. Hale, 1667, p. 197.
234. Acosta, 1962, p. 63.
235. López, 1626, ff. 19$^v$–20$^v$.
236. Solórzano Pereyra, 1648, p. 18.
237. Menéndez y Pelayo, 1949, 5, pp. 356–77.
238. Lafitau, 1724, 1, pp. 33–42.
239. D'Avity, 1614, pp. 245–6.
240. Cassirer, 1944, pp. 26–7.
241. *Mémoires de Trevoux*, 1724, p. 1569.

# Bibliography

*Manuscripts*

Acosta, Miguel de. 'El doctor Miguel de Acosta Granada [sic] presbytero canonigo de la catedral del nuevo reino de Granada.' (n.d., late sixteenth century), RAH, Jesuitas, 122 [9–3695], item 3

Anon. 'De las costumbres antiguas de los naturales del Piru' (n.d., early seventeenth century), BNM, MS 3177

Anon. 'Estado actual del catholismo [sic] politica y economia de los naturales del Peru' (n.d., late sixteenth century), RAH, MS 9–9–3, 1722

Anon. 'Mision y entrada de los indios Chiriguanes de la cordillera' (n.d., late sixteenth century), RAH, MS 93654

Anon. 'Sobre la reformacion de los naturales de las yndias que propuso Isidro Sanchez de la Mota y Aguiar' (n.d., late sixteenth century), AGI, Patronato, leg. 171, no. 2, doc. 11

Anon. 'Voyages des isles de l'Amerique en l'annee 1681', BNF, MS Magl. xiii–58

Brunetti, Cosimo. 'Lettera di Cosimo Brunetti a Cosimo de' Medici', BNF, MS Gal. 280.

Cano, Melchor. 'De dominio indorum', in BV, MS Lat. 4648 (Part of this manuscript is printed in Pereña, 1956, pp. 90–146.)

Carranza, Bartolomé de. 'Incipiunt annotationes in 2a 2ae D. Thomae per reverendum patrem fr. B.M. magistrum meritissimum', in BV, MS Lat. 4645 (Part of this manuscript is printed in Pereña, 1959, pp. 38–56.)

Casas, Gonzalo de las. 'Noticias de los chichimecas y justicia de la guerra que se les ha hecho por los españoles', Biblioteca de El Escorial, MS K. iii, 8

Covarrubias, Diego de. 'De iustitia belli adversus indos', Salamanca University Library, MS M. 2043 (Part of this manuscript is printed in Pereña, 1956, pp. 184–230.)

Gregorio, Gil. 'Parecer de Gil Gregorio' (1512), RAH, MS 9–17–93688, item 33

Hurtado, Jacinto. 'Declaracion que hiço el P. Fr. Jacinto Hurtado, franciscano, estando para morir de algunos puntos tocantes a la conversion de los indios de la Provincia de Choco' (n.d., sixteenth century), BNM, MS 19.699, no. 3

López Mendel, Tomás. 'Tratado cuyo titulo es, De los tres elementos; aire agua i tierra en que se trata de las cosas que en cada uno dellos, acerca de las Indias, naturaleza engendra y produce communes con las de aca' (1612), RAH, Colección de Don Juan Bautista Muñoz, MS 275

Mexía, Pedro de. 'Relacion que hace el obispo de Chiapa Fr. Pedro de Mexia sobre la residencia en sus idolatrias de los indios de aquel pais despues de 30 años de christianos' (n.d., late sixteenth century), AGI, Patronato, leg. 183, no. 1, ramo 11

Mexía de Ovando, Pedro. 'Libro memorial de las cosas memorables que los Reyes de España y Consejo Supremo y Real de Indias han proveido para el govierno politico del nuevo mundo' (n.d., later sixteenth century), BNM, MS 3182.

O'Crovely, Pedro Alonso. 'Idea compendiosa del reyno de la Nueva España (1774), BNM, MS 4532

Palacios Rubios, Juan López de. 'Libellus de insulanis oceanis quas vulgus Indias apelat per Ioannem Lopez de Palacios Ruvios decretorum doctorem regiumque consiliarum editus' (1513), BNM, MS 17641

Peña, Juan de la. 'Compendium seu memoriale questionum ac difficilium rerum quae in hac parte [Ia IIae] continentur' (1561–2), BV, MS Ottob. Lat. 1046 (Part of this manuscript is printed in Pereña, 1956, pp. 268–304.)

Porras, Diego de. 'Instruccion hecha por fray Diego de Porras para los sacerdotes del Peru' (n.d., late sixteenth century), AGI, Patronato, leg. 231, no. 7

'Relaciones y paresceres sobre cosas de yndias dadas en Granada' (1526). AGI, Patronato, leg. 170, ramo 26

Sepúlveda, Juan Ginés de. 'El doctor Sepúlveda al obispo de Arras' (1550), BPM, MS 2324, from the series Cartas al obispo de Arras

## Printed works

This is a list of all the works cited in the endnotes. For ease of reference no distinctions have been made between secondary and primary sources.

Ackrill, J. L. ed. 1963. *Aristotle's Categories and De Interpretatione*, Oxford

Acosta, José de. 1588. *Confesionario para los curas de indios*, Lima

   1590a. *De Christo revelato*, Rome

   1590b. *De temporibus novissimis*, Rome

   1596. *De natura novi orbis libris duo, et De promulgatione evangelii apud indos, sive, De procuranda indorum salute libri sex*, Cologne

   1598. *Histoire naturelle et morale des indes tant orientales qu'occidentales. Traduite en français par Robert Regnault*, Paris

   1954. *Obras del P. José de Acosta*, ed. Francisco Mateos, Biblioteca de autores españoles, 73, Madrid

   1962. *Historia natural y moral de las Indias* (1590), ed. Edmundo O'Gorman, Mexico

Adkins, A. D. W. H. 1970. *From the one to the many*, London

Aguiano, Matheo de. 1706. *Epítome historial y conquista espiritual del imperio abyssinio en Etiopia la alta*, Madrid

Albertus Magnus (St Albert the Great, Bishop of Ratisbon). 1890–9. *B. Alberti Magni opera omnia*, ed. Augusti Borgnet, Paris. 38 vols.

   1916–20. *De animalibus*, ed. Herman Stadler, Beiträge zur Geschichte der Philosophie des Mittelalters, 15–16, Münster

Albornoz, Bartolomé de. 1573. *Arte de los contractos*, Valencia

Alcázar, Bartolomé de. 1710. *Cronohistoria de la compañía de Jesús en la provincia de Toledo*, Madrid

Aldrete, Bernardo. 1606. *Del origen y principio de la lengua castellana o romance que oi se usa en España*, Rome

Alstedt, Johann. 1620. *Cursus philosophicus encyclopaedia libri XXVII*, Herborn

Alvarez López, Enrique. 1943. 'La filosofía natural en el P. José de Acosta', *Revista de Indias*, 4, pp. 306–8

Anders, F. and D. Heitkamp. 1972. *Mexico and the Medici*, Florence

Antonio, Nicolás. 1783. *Bibliotheca hispana nova; sive hispanorum scriptorum qui ab anno 1500 ad 1684 floruere notitia*, Madrid

## BIBLIOGRAPHY

Aquinas, St Thomas. 1925. *Sancti Thomae Aquinatis in Aristotelis librum De anima commentarium*, ed. M. Pirota, Turin
1951. *Sancti Thomae in libros Politicorum Aristotelis expositio*, ed. R. M. Spiazzi, Rome–Turin
1953. *Super epistolas S. Pauli lectura*, ed. P. Raphael Cai, Rome
1954. *De regimine principum ad regem Cypri*, in *Divi Thomae Aquinatis, opuscula philosophica*, ed. R. M. Spiazzi, Rome–Turin
1964. *In decem libros ad Nicomachum expositio*, ed. R. M. Spiazzi, Rome–Turin
1969. *Sententia libri Ethicorum*, Rome
1971. *Sententia libri Politicorum*, ed. H. F. Dondaine and L.-J. Bataillon, Rome. Vol. 48 of the Leonine edition of the *Opera omnia*
Arens, W. 1979. *The man-eating myth. Anthropology and anthropophagy*, New York
Armstrong, D. A. 1961. *Perception and the physical world*, London
Arriaga, Pablo José de. 1968. *Extirpación de la idolatría del Perú* (1621), Biblioteca de autores españoles, 209, Madrid
Austin, J. L. 1962. *How to do things with words*, ed. J. O. Urmson, Oxford
Avendaño, Diego de. 1668. *Thesauris indicus, seu generalis instructor pro regimine conscientiae. in iis quae ad Indias spectant*, Antwerp
Axtell, James. 1972. 'The scholastic philosophy in the wilderness', *William and Mary quarterly*, 29, pp. 344–66
Bailey, D. S. 1955. *Homosexuality in the western Christian tradition*, London
Baldry, H. C. 1965. *The unity of mankind in Greek thought*, Cambridge
Báñez, Domingo. 1595. *Decisiones de iustitia et iure*, Venice
Barnes, J., M. Schofield and R. Sorabji, eds. 1977. *Articles on Aristotle*, London. 2, *Politics and ethics*; 4, *Aesthetics and psychology*
Bataillon, Marcel. 1959. 'Montaigne et les conquérants de l'or', *Studi francesi*, 3, pp. 353–67
1965. *Etudes sur Bartolomé de Las Casas*, Paris
1966. *Erasmo y España*, Mexico
Beattie, James. 1783. *Dissertations moral and critical*, London
Becmann, J. G. 1673. *Historia orbis terrarum geographica et civilis*, Amsterdam
Bede, The Venerable (c. 672–c. 735). 1969. *Historia ecclesiastica*, ed. Bertram Colgrave and R. A. B. Mynors, Oxford
Bellarmino, Roberto. 1590. *De controversiis Christianae*, Ingolstadt
1688. *Declaración copiosa de la doctrina christiana traducida de lengua castellana en lengua Ylloca por Fr. Francisco López*, Manila
Beltrán de Heredia, V. 1931. 'Colección de dictámenes inéditos', *Ciencia tomista*, 43, pp. 27–50, 169–80
Berlin, I. 1976. *Vico and Herder. Two studies in the history of ideas*, London
Bernheimer, R. 1952. *Wild men in the middle ages*, Cambridge, Mass.
Bertonio, Ludovico. 1612. *Vocabulario de la lengua Aymara*, Juli, Peru
Bodin, Jean. 1608. *Six livres de la république*, Geneva
1650. *Methodus ad facilem historiarum cognitionem*, Amsterdam
Boemus, Joannes. 1586. *El libro de las costumbres de todos las gentes del mundo y de las Indias. Traduzido y complido por Francisco Thamara*, Antwerp
Botero, Giovanni. 1605. *Le relationi universali*, Venice
1665. *Origine urbium, earum excellentia et augendi ratione*, Helmstadt
Boxer, C. R. 1953. *South China in the sixteenth century*, London
1978. *The Church militant and Iberian expansion 1440–1770*, Baltimore–London

Brosses, Charles de. 1765. *Traité de la formation méchanique des langues*, Paris

Brown, Peter. 1977. *Relics and social status in the age of Gregory of Tours*, Reading

Bursill-Hall, G. L. 1972. 'Introduction' to Thomas of Erfurt, *Grammatica speculativa*, London

Cabello Valbao, Miguel. 1951. *Miscelánea anthártica. Una historia del Perú antiguo* [1586], ed. Luis E. Valcárcel

Ca' da Mosto, Alvise da. 1966. *Le navigazioni atlantiche del veneziano Alvise da Mosto* (1455–6), ed. Tullia Gasparini Leporace, *Il nuovo Ramusio*, 5, Rome

Cajetan, Cardinal (Tommaso de Vio). 1897. Commentary on St Thomas Aquinas, *Summa theologica*, in *Sancti Thomae Aquinatis doctoris angelica opera omnia cum commentaris Thomae de Vio Caetani*, vols. 4–12; Rome, 1888–1906

Campanella, Tommaso. 1636. *De gentilismo non retirendo quaestio unica*, Paris

Canny, Nicholas. 1978. 'The permissive frontier. Problems of social control in the English settlements in Ireland and Virginia 1550–1650', in K. R. Andrews, N. Canny and P. E. H. Hair, eds., *The westward enterprise. English activities in Ireland, the Atlantic and America 1480-1650*, pp. 17–44, Liverpool

Cano, Melchor. 1569. *De locis theologicis*, Louvain

Caperan, Louis. 1912. *Le problème du salut des infidèles. Essai historique*, Paris

Cárdenas, Juan de. 1591. *Problemas y secretos maravillosos de las Indias*, Mexico

Carletti, Francesco. 1958. *Ragionamenti del mio viaggio intorno al mondo*, Turin

Carreño, A. 1974. 'Una guerra *sine dolo et fraude*. El P. Las Casas y la lucha por la dignidad del indio en el siglo XVI', *Cuadernos americanos*, 34, pp. 119–39

Carrera, Fernando de. 1644. *Arte de la lengua yunga de los valles del obispado del Perú*, Lima

Carro, Venancio. 1951. *La teología y los teólogos–juristas españoles ante la conquista de América*, Salamanca

*Cartas de Indias.* 1877. Madrid

Casas, Bartolomé de Las, *see* Las Casas, Bartolomé de

Cassirer, Ernst. 1944. *An essay on man*, New Haven

Castro, João de. 1964. *Roteiro de Goa a Suez ou do Mar Roxo* (c. 1541) Lisbon

Cesalpino, Andrea. 1571. *Peripateticarum quaestionum libri quinque*, Venice

Chabod, Federico. 1967. *Scritti sul rinascimento*, Turin

1977. *Storia dell'idea d'Europa*, Rome–Bari

Chacón y Calvo, José María. 1929. *Cedulario cubano*, Madrid

Charron, Pierre, 1604. *De la sagesse*, Paris

Chase Sardi, Miguel. 1964. *Avaporu. Algunas fuentes documentales para el estudio de la antropofagía guarani*, Asunción, Paraguay

Chenu, M. D. 1946. 'L'humanisme et la réforme au collège de Saint Jacques', *Archives d'histoire dominicaine*, 1, pp. 130–54

Chiapelli, F., ed. 1976. *First images of America. The impact of the new world on the old*, Berkeley–Los Angeles. 2 vols.

Chodowiec, Urszula. 1972. 'La hantise et la pratique. Le cannibalisme iroquois', in *Destins du cannibalisme*. Nouvelle revue du psychanalyse, 6, pp. 55–69

Cieza de León, Pedro. 1924. *La crónica general del Perú* (1553), ed. Horacio H. Urteaga, Lima

Cioranescu, A. 1959. *Colón y Canarias*, La Laguna

Ciruelo, Pedro. 1628. *Tratado en el qual se repruevan todas las supersticiones y hechizerias*, Barcelona

Clark, Stephen R. L. 1975. *Aristotle's man. Speculations upon Aristotelian anthropology*, Oxford

Clark, Stuart. 1980. 'Inversion, misrule and the meaning of witchcraft', *Past and present*, 87, pp. 98–127

Clendinnen, Inga. 1980. 'Landscape and world view in the survival of Yucatec Maya culture under Spanish conquest', *Comparative studies in society and history*, 22, pp. 374–93

Close, Anthony. 1969. 'Commonplace theories of art and nature in classical antiquity and the renaissance', *Journal of the history of ideas*, 30, pp. 467–86

*Códice franciscano*. 1941. Madrid

*Códice Mendieta*. 1892. Mexico

Cohn, Norman. 1976. *Europe's inner demons*, St Albans

Cole, Thomas. 1967. *Democritus and the sources of Greek anthropology*, Cleveland, Ohio

Collantes de Terán Sánchez, Antonio. 1972. 'Contribución al estudio de los esclavos en la Sevilla medieval', in *Homenaje al profesor Carriazo*, 2, pp. 109–22. Seville, 3 vols.

Columbus, Christopher. 1930. *Selected documents illustrating the four voyages of Columbus (1493–1505)*, ed. Cecil Jane, London. 2 vols.

  1960. *The journal of Christopher Columbus*, trans. Cecil Jane, revised and annotated by L. A. Vigneras, London

Cook, Sherbourne F. 1976. *The conflict between the California Indian and white civilization*, Berkeley–Los Angeles

Cortés, Hernán. 1972. *Letters from Mexico (1520–6)*, trans. and ed. A. R. Pagden, Oxford

Cortés, Vicenta. 1964. *La esclavitud en Valencia durante el reinado de los Reyes Católicos (1479–1516)*, Valencia

Covarrubias, Diego de. 1679. *Opera omnia*, Geneva. 2 vols.

Covarrubias, Sebastián de. 1943. *Tesoro de la lengua castellana o española* (1611), ed. Martín de Riquer, Barcelona

Crowie, M. B. 1956. 'The term "synderesis" and the scholastics', *Irish theological quarterly*, 23, pp. 151–64

Cruz y Moya, Juan José de la. 1955. *Historia de la sancta y apostólica provincia de Santiago de predicadores de México en la Nueva España, 1756–57*, Mexico. 2 vols.

Curtius, E. R. 1953. *European literature in the late middle ages*, trans. William Trask, London

Darnton, Robert. 1970. *Mesmerism*, New York

Davis, David Brion. 1961. *The problem of slavery in western culture*, Ithaca, NY

Davis, Natalie Zemon. 1975. *Society and culture in early modern France*, London

D'Avity, Pierre. 1614. *Les empires, royaumes, estats, seigneuries, duchez et principautez du monde*, St Omer

Delumeau, Jean. 1978. *La peur en occident (XIVᵉ–XVIIIᵉ siècles)*, Paris

De Mattei, R. 1939. 'Sul concetto di barbaro e barbarie nel medioevo', in *Studi di storia e diritto en onore di Enrico Besta*, 4, pp. 485–98, Milan

Durán, Diego. 1967. *Historia de las Indias de Nueva España y islas [sic] de tierra firme (1570–9)*, ed. Angel María Garibay, Mexico

Durkhan, J. 1950. 'John Major after four hundred years', *The Innes review*, 1, pp. 131–57

Echanove, Alfonso. 1955–6. 'Origen y evolución de la idea jesuítica de "reducciones" en las missiones del virreinato del Perú', *Missionalia hispánica*, 12, pp. 95–144; 13, pp. 497–50

Elliott, J. H. 1970. *The old world and the new, 1492–1650*, Cambridge.

1972. 'The discovery of America and the discovery of man', *Proceedings of the British Academy*, 58, pp. 4–27

Encinas, Diego de. 1596. *Provisiones, cédulas, capítulos de ordenanças, instrucciones y cartas*, Madrid

Eusebius of Caesarea (c. 260–c. 339). 1979. *La préparation évangelique*, bks 4–5, ed. Odile Zink, Paris

Evans-Pritchard, E. E. 1965. 'Zande cannibalism', in *The position of women in primitive societies, and other essays in social anthropology*, London

Fernández de Enciso, Martín. 1519. *Suma de geographia*, Seville

Fernández de Oviedo, Gonzalo, *see* Oviedo, Gonzalo Fernández de

Fernández-Santamaria, J. A. 1977. *The state, war and peace. Spanish political thought in the renaissance, 1516–1559*, Cambridge

Festugière, A. J. 1944. *La révélation d'Hermès trismégiste*, Paris, 4 vols.

Fortenbaugh, W. W. 1975. *Aristotle on emotion*, London
    1977. 'Aristotle on slaves and women', in Barnes, Schofield and Sorabji eds., 1977, pp. 135–9

Fortes, M. and E. E. Evans-Pritchard. 1946. *African political systems*, Oxford

Foucault, Michel. 1970. *The order of things* (translation of *Les mots et les choses*), London

Friederici, G. 1973. *El carácter del descubrimiento y conquista de América*, Mexico

Friedman, John Block. 1981. *The monstrous races in medieval art and thought*, Cambridge, Mass.

García Icazbalceta, Joaquín. 1858. *Documentos para la historia de México*, Mexico

Garcilaso de la Vega, *see* Vega, Garcilaso de la

Garimberto, Girolamo. 1959. *Problemi naturali* (1549), Venice

Gauthier, R. A., ed. 1972. *Ethica nicomachea*. Aristoteles latinus, 26: 1–3, Leiden–Brussels

Geertz, Clifford. 1968. *Islam observed. Religious development in Morocco and Indonesia*, Chicago–London

George of Ostia. 1974. *Georgi episcopis ostiensis epistola ad Hadrianum papam*, in *Epistolae Karolini aevi*, Monumenta germaniae historica, Berlin

Geraldini, Alessandro. 1631. *Itinerarium ad regiones sub aequinoctiali plaga constitutas*, Rome

Gerbi, Antonello. 1973. *The dispute of the New World*, Pittsburgh
    1975. *La natura delle indie nove*, Milan

Gerson, Jean de. 1706. *Opera omnia*, Antwerp. 5 vols.

Getino, Alonso. 1930. *El maestro Fray Francisco de Vitoria*, Madrid

Gibson, Charles. 1964. *The Aztecs under Spanish rule*, Stanford–London
    1977. 'Reconquista or conquista', in *Homage to Irving Leonard. Essays on Hispanic art, history and literature*, ed. R. Chang-Rodríguez and D. A. Yates, pp. 17–28, New York

Gilberti, Maturino. 1558. *Arte de la lengua de Michoacán*, Mexico

Giménez Fernández, Manuel. 1944. 'Nuevas consideraciones sobre la historia y el sentido de las letras alejandrinas de 1493 referentes a las Indias', *Anuario de estudios americanos*, 1, pp. 173–429

Ginzburg, Carlo. 1972. 'Folklore, magia, religione', in *Storia d'Italia*, 1, Turin, pp. 603–76
    1979. 'Spie. Radici di un paradigma indiziario', in *Crisi della ragione*, ed. Aldo Gargani, Turin, pp. 59–106

Giraldus Cambrensis (Gerald of Wales). 1867. *Topographia hibernica*, ed. James F. Dimock, Rolls series, 21e, London

BIBLIOGRAPHY

Girava, Gerónimo. 1570. *La cosmographia y geographia*, Venice
Glacken, C. J. 1967. *Traces on the Rhodian shore. Nature and culture in western thought from ancient times to the end of the eighteenth century*, Berkeley
Gliozzi, Giuliano. 1977. *Adamo e il nuovo mundo*, Florence
Gómez de Castro, Alvaro. 1569. *De rebus gestis a Francisco Ximenio Cisnerio*, Alcalá de Henares
Góngora, Mario. 1975. *Studies in the colonial history of Spanish America*, Cambridge
González Monteagudo, Monio Melinda. 1975. 'El padre Las Casas y Valladolid', in *Estudios sobre política indigenista española en América*, Valladolid, pp. 9–27
Goody, Jack and Ian Watt. 1968. 'The consequences of literacy', in *Literacy and traditional societies*, ed. J. Goody, Cambridge, pp. 27–68
Granada, Luis de. 1588. *Introducción del símbolo de la fe*, Salamanca
Gregory the Great. 1884–5. 'Gregori episcopi turonensis vitae Patrum', in *Opera*, ed. W. Arndt and B. Krusch, Scriptores rerum Merovingicarum, Hanover 1891–9. *Registrum epistolarum*, ed. P. Ewald and L. M. Hartmann, Monumenta germaniae historica. *Epistolarum*, Berlin. 2 vols.
Guicciardini, Francesco. 1929. *Storia d'Italia* (1562) ed. C. Panigada, Bari. 5 vols.
Guthrie, W. K. C. 1957. *In the beginning. Some Greek views on the origins and the early state of man*, Ithaca, NY
Hale, Mathew. 1667. *The primitive origination of mankind considered and examined according to the light of nature*, London
Hamilton, B. 1963. *Political thought in sixteenth century Spain*, Oxford.
Hanke, L. U. 1938. 'The *requerimiento* and its interpreters', *Revista de historia de América*, 1, pp. 25–34
1959. *Aristotle and the American Indians*, Bloomington–London
1965. *The Spanish struggle for justice in the conquest of America*, Boston, Mass.
1968. *Estudios sobre Fray Bartolomé de Las Casas y la lucha por la justicia en la conquista española de América*, Caracas
1974. *All mankind is one*. De Kalb
Hardie, W. F. R. 1968. *Aristotle's ethical theory*, Oxford
Harris, Marvin. 1977. *Cannibals and kings*, New York
Harrisse, Henry. 1958. *Bibliotheca americana vetustissima*, ed. Carlos Sanz, Madrid
Hart, H. L. A. 1961. *The concept of law*, Oxford
Hartog, François. 1980. *Le miroir d'Hérodote. Essai sur la représentation de l'autre*, Paris
Heath, M. J. 1979. 'Renaissance scholars and the origins of the Turks', *Bibliothèque d'humanisme et renaissance*, 41, pp. 453–71
Heiberg, J. L. 1920. 'Théories antiques sur l'influence moral du climat', *Scientia*, 27, pp. 453–64
Helmont, Johannes Baptista van. 1648. *Ortus medicinae*, Amsterdam
Helmont, Mercurius von. 1667. *Kurtzer Entwurff des eigentlichen Natural-alphabets der heiligen Sprache*, Sulzbach
Hera, Alberto de la. 1956. 'El derecho de los indios a la libertad y la fe. La bula *Sublimis Deus* y los problemas indianos que la motivaron', *Anuario de historia del derecho español*, 26, pp. 119–39
Hinojosa, Ortiz de. 1963. 'Advertencias del doctor Ortiz de Hinojosa', in José A. Llaguno, *La personalidad jurídica del indio y el III Concilio Provincial mexicano (1585)*, Mexico
Hobbes, Thomas. 1968. *Leviathan* (1651), ed. C. B. Macpherson, Harmondsworth

243

Hodgen, Margaret. 1964. *Early anthropology in the sixteenth and seventeenth centuries*, Philadelphia

Hosius Stanislaus. 1559. *De origine haeresium nostri temporis*, Louvain

Hulme, Peter. 1978. 'Columbus and the cannibals. A study of the reports of anthropophagy in the journal of Christopher Columbus', *Ibero-amerikanisches Archiv*, Neue Folge, 4, pp. 115–39

Humboldt, Alexander von. 1836–9. *Examen critique de l'histoire de la géographie du nouveau continent et des progrès de l'astronomie nautique aux quinzième et seizième siècles*, Paris. 5 vols.

Huxley, G. L. 1980. 'Aristotle, Las Casas and the American Indians', *Proceedings of the Royal Irish Academy*, 80, pp. 57–68

Ibn Kahaldûn. 1958. *The Maquaddimah. An introduction to history*, trans. F. Rosenthal, New York

Jaeger, W. 1914. *Nemesios von Emesa*, Berlin

Janson, H. W. 1952. *Apes and ape-lore in the middle ages and the renaissance*, London

Jarcho, Saul. 1959. 'Origin of the American Indian as suggested by Fray Joseph de Acosta', *Isis*, 59, pp. 430–8

Jones, W. R. 1971. 'The image of the barbarian in medieval Europe', *Comparative studies in society and history*, 31, pp. 376–407

Jonkers, E. J. 1934. 'De l'influence du christianisme sur la législation relative à l'esclave dans l'antiquité', *Mnemosyne. Biblioteca classica batava*, 3rd series, 1, pp. 241–80

Jouanna, Arlette. 1979. *L'idée de race en France au XVIème siècle et au début du XVIIème siècle (1498–1614)*, Paris

Kahl, M. D. 1961. 'Bausteine zur Grundlegung einer missionsgeschichtlichen Phänomenologie des Hochmittelalters', in *Miscellanea historiae ecclesiasticae. Congrès de Stockholm août 1960*, Bibliothèque de la revue d'histoire ecclésiastique, 38, pp. 50–90

Kamen, Henry. 1971. 'El negro en Hispanoamérica 1500–1700', *Anuario de estudios americanos*, 28, pp. 121–37

Karsch-Haack, F. 1911. *Das gleichgeschlechtliche Leben der Naturvölke*, Munich

Kenny, Anthony, ed. 1964. St Thomas Aquinas, *Summa theologica*, London–New York. 22, *Dispositions for human acts* (Ia IIae q. 49–54)

Kerr, W. P. 1958. *The dark ages*, Edinburgh

Knowlson, James. 1975. *Universal language schemes in England and France, 1600–1800*, Toronto–Buffalo

Kottman, Karl A. 1975. 'Fray Luis de León and the universality of Hebrew. An aspect of sixteenth- and seventeenth-century language theory', *Journal of the history of philosophy*, 13, pp. 297–310

Kupperman, K. C. 1979. 'Nature's "rude garden". English and Indians as producers and consumers of food in early New England', *Comparative civilizations review*, 1, pp. 64–78

    1980. *Settling with the Indians. The meeting of the English and Indian cultures in America, 1580–1640*, Totowa, NJ

Labayes, Oleachea. 1958. 'Opinión de los teólogos españoles sobre dar estudios mayores a indios', *Anuario de estudios americanos*, 15, pp. 113–200

Lach, Donald. 1965. *Asia in the making of Europe*, Chicago. 1–

La Condamine, Charles M. de. 1745. *Relation abrégée d'un voyage fait dans l'intérieur de l'Amérique méridionale*, Paris

Lafaye Jacques. 1974. *Quetzalcoatl et Guadalupe. La formation de la conscience nationale au Mexique, 1531–1813* Paris

Lafitau, Joseph-François. 1724. *Moeurs des sauvages amériquains comparées aux moeurs des premiers temps*, Paris. 2 vols.

Lamalle, Edmundo. 1980. *Miscellanea Edmundo Lamalle nuncaptor* in Archivum historicum societatis Iesu 97

Landa, Diego de. 1975. *The Maya. Diego de Landa's 'Account of the Affairs of Yucatán'* trans. A. R. Pagden, Chicago

Landucci, Sergio. 1972. *I filosofi e i selvaggi 1580–1780*, Bari

La Primaudaye, Pierre de. 1580. *Academie Françoise, en laquelle il est traitté de l'institution des moeurs e de ce qui concerne le bien et heuresment vivre Edition troisieme, augumentée par l'autheur*, Paris

Larkin, Miriam Therese. 1971. *Language in the philosophy of Aristotle*, The Hague–Paris

Las Casas, Bartolomé de. 1552a. *Tratado comprobatorio del imperio soberano y principado universal que los Reyes de Castilla y León tienen sobre las Indias*, Seville

 1552b. *Aquí se contiene unos avisos y reglas para los confesores que oyeren confesiones de los españoles que son o han sido en cargo a los indios*, Seville

 1552c. *Aquí se contiene una disputa o controversía, entre el Obispo don fray Bartholomé de las Casas o Casaus y el doctor Ginés de Sepúlveda*, Seville

 1942. *Del único modo de atraer a todos los pueblos a la verdadera religión* [*De unico vocationis modo omnium gentium ad veram religionem*] (c. 1537), ed. A. Millares Carlo, Mexico

 1951. *Historia de las Indias* (1527– ), ed. Augustín Millares Carlo, Mexico. 3 vols.

 1958. *Los tesoros del Perú. De thesauris in Peru* (1566), ed. Angel Losada, Madrid

 1967. *Apologética historia sumaria* (1551– ), ed. Edmundo O'Gorman, Mexico. 2 vols.

 1975. *Argumentum apologiae adversus Genesium Sepulvedam theologum cordubensem* (1550), BNP, Fonds Latins, MS 12929, reproduced in facsimile in *Apologia*, ed. Angel Losada, Madrid

Ledesma, Martín de. 1560. *Secunda quartae*, Coimbra

Leibnitz, Gottfried Wilhelm von. 1718. *Otium hanoveranum sive miscellanea, Godfr. Guilielmi Leibnitii*, ed. Joachim Frederic Fell, Leipzig

Leite, Serafim. 1953. *Nóbrega e a fundação de São Paulo*, Lisbon

 1954. *Cartas dos primeiros jesuitas do Brasil*, São Paulo. 3 vols.

Lejeune, P. 1637. *Relations de ce qui s'est passé en la Nouvelle France en l'année 1636*, Paris

León, Luis de. (?1528–1591) 1892. *Mag. Luysii Legionensis augustiniani opera*, Salamanca. 7 vols.

León Pinelo, Antonio, de. 1943. *El paraíso en el nuevo mundo. Comentario apologético, historia natural y peregrina de las Indias occidentales, islas de Tierra Firme del Mar Océano* (1650), Lima

Le Roy, Louis. 1576. *De la vicissitude ou varieté des choses en l'univers*, Paris

Le Roy Ladurie, Emmanuel. 1966. *Les paysans de Languedoc*, Paris

Léry, Jean de. 1594. *Histoire d'un voyage fait en la terre du Brésil*, Geneva

Lescarbot, Marc. 1612. *Relation dernière de ce qui s'est passé au voyage du sieur de Poutrincourt en la Nouvelle France*, Paris

Lévi-Strauss, Claude. 1969. *The elementary structures of kinship*, trans. James Harle Bell *et al.*, London

Locke, John. 1975. *Essay concerning human understanding* (1690), ed. Peter H. Nidditch, Oxford

Lockhart, James. 1979. 'Capital and province, Spaniard and Indian. The example of late sixteenth-century Toluca', in *Provinces of early Mexico. Variants of Spanish American regional evolution*, ed. Ida Altman and James Lockhart, Los Angeles

Loeb, E. M. 1923. *The blood sacrifice complex*. Memoirs of the American Anthropological Association, 30, Wisconsin

Lohmann Villena, G. 1966. *Juan de Matienzo*, Seville

Lopeteguí, León. 1942. *El padre José de Acosta y las misiones*, Madrid

López, Gregorio. 1626. *Historia ecclesiástica y seglar de la Yndia oriental y occidental predicación del sancto Evangelio en ella por los Apóstoles*, Baeza

López, Gregorio. 1848. *Las siete partidas del rey Alfonso el Sabio glosadas por el Lic. Gregorio López (1555)*, Madrid

Losada, Angel. 1959. *Juan Ginés de Sepúlveda a través de su 'Epistolario' y nuevos documentos*, Madrid

Lovejoy, Arthur O., and George Boas. 1935. *Primitivism and related ideas in antiquity*, Baltimore

1948. *The Great Chain of Being. The history of an idea*, Cambridge, Mass.

McKee, E. W. 1980. 'From the land of Canaan to the land of Guinea. The strange odyssey of the sons of Ham', *American historical review*, 85, pp. 15–43

Maclean, Ian. 1980. *The renaissance notion of woman*, Cambridge

Maffei, Giovanni. 1589. *Historiarum indicarum libri XVI*, Cologne

Mahn-Lot, Marianne. 1973. 'Transculturation et évangélisation dans le Pérou du XVIᵉ siècle. Notes sur Domingo de Santo Tomás, disciple de Las Casas', in *Méthodologie de l'histoire et des sciences humaines. Mélanges en l'honneur de Fernand Braudel*, pp. 353–65, Paris

Mair, John (Johannes Major). 1519a. *In secundum librum sententiarum*, Paris

1519b. *In quartum sententiarum*, Paris

1519c. *In primum sententiarum*, Paris

1706. *Disputatio de potestate papae in rebus temporibus*, in *Joannis Gersoni opera omnia*, 2, Antwerp

1892. *A history of greater Britain*, ed. and trans. A. Constable, Edinburgh

Maldonado, Juan. 1549. *Ioannis Maldonatis opuscula quaedam docta simul et elegantia*, Burgos

Maluenda, Thomas. 1604. *De antichristi libri undecim*, Rome

Mandeville, John de (1322–56). 1919–23. *Mandeville's travels*, ed. P. Hamelin, London. 2 vols.

Maravall, J. A. 1966. *Antiguos y modernos*, Madrid

Marcos, Teodoro Andrés. 1947. *Los imperialismos de Juan Ginés de Sepúlveda en su Democrates alter*, Madrid

Markus, R. A. 1970. *Saeculum. History and society in the theology of St Augustine*, Cambridge

Martin of Braga, St (d. 579). 1950. *Martini episcopi bracarensis opera omnia*, ed. Claude W. Barlow, Papers and monographs of the American Academy in Rome, 12, New Haven

Martín del Río, Antonio. 1652. *Disquisitionem magicarum libri sex*, Venice

Martyr, Peter (Petrus Martyr Anglerius). 1530a. *Opus epistolarum*, Alcalá de Henares

1530b. *De orbe novo decades*, Alcalá de Henares

Matienzo, Juan de. 1967. *Gobierno del Perú (1567)*, ed. Guillermo Lohmann Villena, Paris–Lima

Maurer, A. A. 1974. 'The unity of science. St Thomas and the Nominalists', in

BIBLIOGRAPHY

*St Thomas Aquinas 1274–1974. Commemorative studies*, 2, pp. 269–91, Toronto

Mauss, Marcel. 1967. *The gift. Forms and functions of exchange in archaic societies* (translation of *Essai sur le don*), London

Maxwell, J. F. 1975. *Slavery and the Catholic Church*, London

Mechoulan, H. 1974. *L'antihumanisme de Juan Ginés de Sepúlveda. Etude critique du 'Democrates primus'*, Paris

Medina, José Toribio. 1956. *Historia del tribunal de la inquisición en Lima*, Santiago de Chile

*Mémoires de Trevoux. Mémoires pour l'historie des sciences et des beaux arts. De l'Imprimerie de S.A.S. á Trevoux.* 1724

Menéndez y Pelayo, M. 1949. *Estudios sobre el teatro de Lope de Vega*, Madrid

Mercado, Tomás de. 1571. *Summa de tratos y contratos*, Seville

Mersch, E. 1944. *La théologie du corps mystique*, Brussels

Mersenne, Marin. 1634. *Questions inoüyes*, Paris

Mesnard, Pierre. 1951. *L'essor de la philosophie politique au XVIᵉ siècle*, Paris

Miaja de la Muela, A. 1965. 'El derecho "totius orbis" en el pensamiento de Francisco de Vitoria', *Revista española de derecho internacional*, 18, pp. 341–64

Miller, H. W. 1955. 'Techne and discovery in *On ancient medecine*', *Transactions and proceedings of the American Philosophical Association*, 86, pp. 51–2

Miró Quesada, Aurelio. 1971. *El Inca Garcilaso y otros estudios*, Madrid

Mohtmann, C. 1952. 'Encore une fois: "Paganus"', *Virgiliae Christianae*, 6, pp. 109–21

Molina, Alonso de. 1571. *Vocabulario en lengua castellana y mexicana*, Mexico

Momigliano, A. 1977. *Essays in ancient and modern historiography*, Oxford

Monardes, N. 1574. *Diálogo del hierro y sus grandezas y excelencias*, bound with *Primera y segunda y tercera parte de la historia medicinal de las cosas que se traen de nuestras Indias occidentales que sirven en medicina*, Seville

Montaigne, Michel Eyquem de. 1962. *Essais de Montaigne* (1571–92), ed. Maurice Rat, Paris

Montesquieu, Charles de Secondat, baron de. 1758. *De l'esprit des lois*, Geneva

*Monumenta henricina*, 1960–74, Coimbra

Morelli, Cyriaco (Domingo Muriel, SJ). 1791. *Rudimenta iuris naturae et gentium libri duo*, Venice

Mörner, M. 1970. *La corona española y los foraneos en los pueblos de Indias en América*, Stockholm

Morse, Ruth. Forthcoming. 'Unfit for human consumption. Shakespeare's unnatural foods', in *Shakespeare Jahrbuch*

Motolinía (Fray Bernardino de Benavente). 1971. *Memoriales o libro de las cosas de la Nueva España y de los naturales de ella* (c. 1535–c. 1543), ed. Edmundo O'Gorman, Mexico

Muldoon, James. 1980. *Popes, lawyers and infidels. The Church and the non-Christian world, 1250–1550*, Liverpool

Needham, Joseph. 1959. *Science and civilisation in China*, Cambridge

Nóbrega, Manuel da. 1954. *Diálogo a conversão do gentio* (1559), ed. Serafim Leite, Lisbon

1955. *Cartas do Brasil e mais escritos*, ed. Serafim Leite, Coimbra

Noonan, John T. 1966. *Contraception. A history of its treatment by Catholic theologians*, Cambridge, Mass.

North, D. C. 1977. 'Markets and other allocation systems in history. The challenge of Karl Polyani', *The journal of economic history*, 6, pp. 703–16

Noue, François de la. 1967. *Discours politiques et militaires*, ed. F. E. Sutcliffe, Geneva

Oakley, F. 1962. 'On the road from Constance to 1688. The political thought of John Mair and George Buchanan', *Journal of British studies*, pp. 12–31

Olmi, G. 1976. *Ulisse Aldrovandi. Scienza e natura nel secondo Cinquecento*, in Quaderni di storia e filosofia della scienza, 4, Trent

Olschki, L. 1937. *Storia letteraria delle scoperte geografiche. Studi e richerche*, Florence

    1941a. 'Ponce de León's fountain of eternal youth. A history of a geographical myth', *Hispanic American historical review*, 21, pp. 362–85

    1941b. 'What Columbus saw on landing in the West Indies', *Proceedings of the American Philosophical Society*, 84, pp. 633–54

Otte, Enrique. 1975. 'Los jerónimos y el tráfico humano en el Caribe. Una rectificación', *Anuario de estudios atlánticos*, 32, pp. 187–204

Oviedo, Gonzalo Fernández de. 1535. *La historia general de las Indias, primera parte*, Seville

    1956. *Sumario de la natural historia de las Indias*, ed. Jose Miranda, Mexico, Buenos Aires

Pagden, Anthony. 1981. 'The "School of Salamanca" and the "Affairs of the Indies"', *History of universities*, 1, pp. 71–112

    1982. 'Cannibalismo e contagio', *Quaderni storici*, 50, pp. 147–64

Palafox y Mendoza, Juan de. 1650. *Virtudes del indio*, n.p.

Panofsky, E. 1945. *Albrecht Dürer*, Princeton

Paracelsus, Aureolus Theophrastus Bombast von Hohenheim. 1603. *Opera medico-chemicorum sive paradoxorum*, Frankfurt

Parker, Geoffrey. 1979. *The Dutch revolt*, Harmondsworth

Passmore, John. 1970. *The perfectibility of man*, London

Pauw, Cornelius de. 1770. *Recherches philosophiques sur les américains*, Berlin

Paz, Matías de. 1933. *De dominium regum Hispaniae super indos* (1512), ed. V. Beltrán de Heredia in *Archivium fratrum praedicatorum*, 3, pp. 133–81

Penrose, B. 1952. *Travel and discovery in the renaissance, 1420–1630*, Cambridge

Pereña, Luciano. 1956. *Misión de España en América*, Madrid

Pico della Mirandola, Giovanni. 1572–3. *Opera omnia*, Basle. 2 vols.

Plamenatz, John. 1963. *Man and society. A critical examination of some important social and political theories from Machiavelli to Marx*, London. 2 vols.

Plano Carpini, Ioannes de. 1929. *Istoria mongolorum*, in Sinica franciscana et relationes Fratrum Minorum saeculi XII et XLV, 1, Florence

Pocock, J. G. A. 1973. 'Verbalizing political acts. Towards a politics of speech', *Political theory*, 1, pp. 27–45

    1977. *Politics, language and time*, New York

Polyani, K. 1968. *Primitive, archaic and modern economies. Essays of Karl Polyani*, ed. G. Dalton, New York

Pontano, Giovanni (Joannes Jovianus Pontanus). 1518. *Opera omnia soluta oratione composita*, Venice. 4 vols.

Popkin, Richard H. 1976. 'The pre-Adamite theory in the renaissance', in *Philosophy and humanism. Renaissance essays in honour of Paul Oskar Kristeller*, ed. E. P. Mahoney, pp. 56–69, Leiden

*Primera crónica general* (1289). 1955, ed. R. Menéndez Pidal, Madrid. 2 vols.

Prosperi, Adriano. 1976. 'America e apocalisse. Note sulla "conquista spirituale" del novo mondo', *Critica storica*, 13, pp. 1–61

    1977–8. 'La religione, il potere, le élites. Incontro italospagnoli nell'età della contrariforma', *Annuario dell Instituto Storico Italiano per l'età moderna e contemporanea*, 29–30, pp. 499–529

Forthcoming. ' "Otras Indias", propaganda religiosa e azione missionaria della compagnia di Gesù nella seconda metá dell' 500'

Quine, W. V. 1966. *The ways of paradox and other essays*, New York

Quiroga, Pedro de. 1922. *Libro intitulado coloquios de la verdad* (c. 1555), ed. Julián Zarco Cuevas, Seville

Randles, W. G. L. 1959. *L'image du sud-est africain dans la littérature européenne au XVIᵉ siècle*, Lisbon

1968. *L'ancien royaume du Congo des origines à la fin du XIVᵉ siècle*, Paris

*Recopilación de leyes de los reynos de las Indias.* 1681. Madrid

Renaudet, A. 1953. *Préréforme et humanisme à Paris pendant les premières guerres d'Italie (1494–1517)*, Paris

Ricard, Robert. 1933. *La 'conquête spirituelle' du Méxique*, Paris

Ricci, Mateo (1552–1610). 1911–13. *Opere storiche*, ed. Pietro Tacchi Venturi, Macerta. 2 vols.

Rico, Francisco. 1978. ' "Laudes litterarum". Humanismo y dignidad del hombre en la España del renacimiento', in *Homenaje a Julio Caro Baroja*, pp. 895–914, Madrid

Rochefort, Charles. 1658. *Histoire naturelle et morale des Isles Antilles de l'Amérique*, Rotterdam

Romeo, Rosario. 1954. *Le scoperte americane nella coscienza italiana del Cinquecento*, Milan–Naples

Rossi, Paolo. 1971. *Philosophy, technology and the arts in the early modern era*, New York

Rowe, J. H. 1960. 'The origins of creator worship among the Incas', in *Essays in honour of Paul Radin*, ed. Stanley Diamond, pp. 408–29, New York

Russell, P. E. 1971. 'Fontes documentais castelhanas para a historia da expansão portuguesa na Guiné nos ultimos anos de D. Afonso', *Do tempo e da historia*, 4, pp. 5–33

1978. 'El descubrimiento de las Canarias y el debate medieval acerca de los derechos de los príncipes y pueblos paganos', *Revista de historia canaria*, 36, pp. 10–32

Ryle, Gilbert. 1963. *The concept of mind*, Harmondsworth

Sahagún, Bernardino de. 1956. *Historia general de las cosas de Nueva Espana* (1547–62), ed. Angel María Garibay, Mexico. 4 vols.

Santa Cruz, Alonso de. 1951. *Crónica de los Reyes Católicos* (1550–2), ed. Juan de Mata Carriazo, Seville

Santillán, Hernando de. 1968. *Relación del origen y gobierno de los incas* (1533), Biblioteca de autores españoles, 209, pp. 99–149, Madrid

Santo Tomás, Domingo de. 1560. *Grammática o arte de la lengua general de los indios de los reynos del Perú*, Valladolid

*Satan. Les études carmélitaines.* 1948. n.p.

Saunders, A. C. de C. M. 1982. *A social history of black slaves and freedmen in Portugal 1441–1555*, Cambridge

Schill, A. 1929. *Giovanni Pico della Mirandola und die Entdeckung Amerikas*, Berlin

Schlaifer, R. 1936. 'Greek theories of slavery from Homer to Aristotle', *Harvard studies in classical philology*, 47, pp. 165–204

Sepúlveda, Juan Ginés de. 1535. *J. Genesii Sepulvedae Cordubensis artium et theologiae doctoris, de conuentientia militaris disciplina cum christiana religione dialogus qui inscribitur Democrates*, Rome

1550. *Apologia Ioannis Genesii Sepulvedae pro libro De iustis belli causis*, Rome

1552. *Libri Aristotelis quos vulgo latini parvos naturales apellant*, Bologna

1780. *Joannis Genesii Sepulvedae cordubensis opera*, Madrid. 4 vols.

1879.'Proposiciones temerarias escandalosas y heréticas', in Antonio Marie Fabié, *Vida y escritos de don Fray Bartolomé de Las Casas*, 2, pp. 543–69, Madrid

1951. *Democrates segundo, o de las justas causas de la guerra contra los indios*, ed. Angel Losada, Madrid

Serrano y Sanz, Manuel. 1918. *Orígenes de la dominación española en América*, Madrid. 1 vol. (discontinued).

Silva, Juan de. 1621. *Advertencias importantes acerca del buen govierno y administracion de las Indias assi en lo espiritual como en lo temporal*, Madrid

Siméon, Rémi. 1885. *Dictionnaire de la langue nahuatl ou mexicaine*, Paris

Skelton, R. A. 1958. *Explorers' maps. Chapters in the cartographic record of geographical exploration*, London

Skinner, Quentin. 1970. 'Convention and the understanding of speech acts', *The philosophical quarterly*, 20, pp. 118–38

1972. 'Some problems in the analysis of political thought and action', *Political theory*, 2, pp. 277–303

1978. *The foundation of modern political thought*, Cambridge. 2 vols.

Solórzano Pereyra, Juan de. 1629–39. *Disputationem de Indiarum jure sive de justa Indiarum occidentalium inquisitione acquisitione et retentione*. Madrid. 2 vols.

1648. *Politica indiana sacada en lengua castellana de los dos tomos del derecho i govierno municipal de las Indias*, Madrid

Sorabji, R. 1974. 'Aristotle and the role of intellect in virtue', *Proceedings of the Aristotelian Society*, new series, 74, pp. 107–29

Soto, Domingo de. 1568. *De iustitia et iure*, Antwerp

1964. *Relectio 'De dominio'* (1534), ed. J. Brufau Prats, Granada

1965. *Deliberación en la causa de los pobres* (1545), Madrid

Standen, Hans. 1557. *Wahrhaftige Historie und Beschreibung eyner Landtschafft der Wilden, Nacketen, Grimmigen, Menschfresser Leuten, in der Newen Welt America gelegen*, Marburg

Stannard, J. 1966. 'Dioscorides and renaissance materia-medica', in *Materia Medica in the Sixteenth Century*, Analecta medico-historia, 1, ed. M. Florkin, pp. 1–21, Oxford

Stewart, Julian H., ed. 1930. *Handbook of South American Indians*, New York. 7 vols.

Suárez, Francisco. 1613. *Defensio fidei catholicae et apostolicae adversus anglicanae sectae errores*, Coimbra

1621. *Opus de triplici virtute theologica. Fide spe et charitate*, Paris

1954. *Disputatio XII. De bello* (1584), in Luciano Pereña, *Teoría de la guerra en Francisco Suárez*, Madrid

1971. *Tractatus de legibus ac Deo legislatore* (1612), ed. Luciano Pereña, Madrid. 12 vols.

Suárez de Peralta, Juan. 1949. *Tratado del descubrimiento de las Indias* (1589), Mexico

Sullivan, Robert E. 1953. 'The Carolingian missionary and the pagan', *Speculum*, 28, pp. 705–40

Tellechea Idígoras, José. 1959. 'Bartolomé de Las Casas y Bartolomé de Carranza, una página amistosa olvidada', *Scriptorium victoriense*, 6, pp. 7–34

1966. 'Perfil americanista de Fray Bartolomé Carranza OP', *XXXVI Congreso internacional de americanistas. España, 1964. Actas y memorias*, 4, pp. 691–9, Seville

Texeira da Mota, A. Forthcoming. 'A entrada de esclavos negros em Valencia de 1445–1482 e a mudança a vía trans-saariana para a vía atlántica', in *Mélanges Mauny*

Thevet, André. 1953. *Histoire de André Thevet angoumoisin cosmographe du Roy de deux voyages par lui faits aux Indes australes et occidentales*, in *Le Brésil et les brésiliens par André Thevet*, ed. S. Lussagnet, Paris

Tooley, M. J. 1953. 'Bodin and the mediaeval theory of climates', *Speculum*, 28, pp. 64–83

Torquemada, Juan de. 1723. *Las viente i un libros rituales i monarchia indiana*, Madrid. 3 vols.

Torraca, Luigi. 1949–50. 'A proposito di un recente episodio di antropofagia', *Atti della Accademia Pontaniana*, nuova serie, 3, pp. 113–25

Torres, Diego de. 1603. *Relatione breve del P. Diego de Torres della compagnia di Gesú circa il frutto che si racoglie con gli Indiana di quel Peru*, Rome

Tostado, Alonso de Madrigal, called 'El Tostado'. 1507. *Tostado sobre el Eusebio*, Salamanca

Tovar, Juan de. 1972. *Manuscrit Tovar (Relación del origen de los Yndios que havitan en esta Nueva España según sus historias)*, ed. Jacques Lafaye, Graz

Tuck, Richard. 1979. *Natural rights theories*, Cambridge

Tugnoli Pataro, S. 1979. 'La formazione scientifica e il "Discorso naturale" di Ulisse Aldrovandi', in *La scienza a corte. Collezionismo eclettico, natura e immagine a Mantova*, ed. D. A. Franchini *et al.*, Rome

Turnbull, Colin. 1972. *The mountain people*, New York

Tylor, Edward. 1871. *Primitive culture*, London

Ullmann, Walter. 1960. 'Some observations on the mediaeval evaluation of the "Homo naturalis" and the "Christianus"', in *L'homme et son destin d'après les penseurs du moyen âge. Actes du premier congrès international de philosophie médiévale*, pp. 145–51, Louvain–Paris

1977. *Mediaeval foundations of renaissance humanism*, London

Valadés, Diego de. 1579. *Rhetorica christiana*, Perugia

Vanegas, Alexio. 1583. *Primera parte de las differencias de los libros que ay en el universo*, Valladolid

Vázquez de Menchaca, Fernando. 1668. *Illustrium controversarium aliarumque usu frequentium*, Frankfurt

Vega, Garcilaso de la, 'el Inca'. 1943. *Comentarios reales de los incas (1616)*, ed. Angel Rosenblat, Buenos Aires. 3 vols.

Venturi, Pietro Tacchi. 1952. *La vita religiosa in Italia durante la primera etá della compagnia di Gesú*, Rome

Veracruz, Alonso de la. 1968. *The writings of Alonso de la Veracruz (c. 1507–84)* ed. E. J. Burrus, St Louis

Vespucci, Amerigo. 1966. *Mundus novus (1505)*, in *Colombo, Vespucci, Verazzano*, ed. L. Firpo, Turin

Vetancurt, Fr. Augustín de. 1673. *Arte de la lengua mexicana*, Mexico

1698. *Teatro mexicano. Descripción breve de los sucesos exemplares, históricos, políticos, militares y religiosos del nuevo mundo occidental de las Indias*, Mexico

Villoslada, Ricardo. 1938. *La universidad de Paris durante los estudios de Francisco e Vitoria, OP (1507–1522)*, Analecta gregoriana, 14, Rome

Vitoria, Francisco de. 1586. *Summa sacramentorum Ecclesiae*, Venice

  1932–52. *Comentarios de la Secunda Secundae de Santo Tomás* (1534–7), ed. V. Beltrán de Heredia, Salamanca. 6 vols.

  1934. *De iustitia*, ed. V. Beltrán de Heredia, Madrid. 2 vols.

  1952. *Comentarios al tratado de la ley (I–II, QQ, 90–108)* (1533–4), ed. V. Beltrán de Heredia, Madrid

  1960. *Obras de Francisco de Vitoria. Relecciones teológicas* (1527–41), ed. Téofilo Urdanoz, Madrid

  1967. *Relectio 'De indis'* (1539), ed. L. Pereña and J. M. Pérez Prendes, Madrid

Vivanti, Corrado. 1962. 'Alle origini dell' idea di civiltá. Le scoperte geografiche e gli scritti di Henrí de la Popelinière', *Rivista storica italiana*, 74, pp. 225–49

Vives, Juan Luis. 1785. *Opera omnia*, Valencia. 8 vols.

Voltaire, F. M. A. de. 1963. *Essai sur les moeurs et l'esprit des nations* (1754), ed. R. Pomeau, Paris

Walbank, F. W. 1957. *A historical commentary on Polybius*, Oxford. 3 vols.

Walker, D. P. 1972. *The ancient theology*, London

Warren, F. B. 1963. *Vasco de Quiroga and his pueblo-hospitals of Santa-Fé*, Washington

Weill, Edouard. 1954. 'De l'aspect éthique des origines grecques de la monnaie', *Revue historique*, 212, pp. 209–31

Weill, Raymond. 1960. *Aristote et l'histoire*, Paris

Wilks, M. 1964. *The problem of sovereignty in the late middle ages*, Cambridge

Winch, Peter. 1967. 'Understanding a primitive society', in *Religion and understanding*, ed. D. Z. Phillips, Oxford

Wokler, Robert. 1978. 'Perfectible apes in decadent cultures. Rousseau's anthropology revisited', *Daedalus*, 107, pp. 107–14

Wood, William. 1634. *New England's prospect. A true lively and experimental description of the part of America commonly called New England*, London

Ybot Léon, A. 1948. 'Juntas de teólogos asesoras del estado para Indias 1512–1550', *Anuario de estudios americanos*, 5, pp. 397–438

Zavala, Silvio. 1954. *De las islas del Mar Océano. Del dominio de los Reyes de España sobre los Indios*, Mexico

Zorita, Alonso de. 1909. *Historia de la Nueva España* (1585), ed. Manuel Serrano y Sanz, Madrid

  1963. *Breve y sumaria relación de los señores de la Nueva España* (c. 1570), ed. Joaquín Ramírez Cabañas, Mexico

Zurita, Fernando. 1586. *Theologicarum de indis quaestionum*, Madrid

# Index